Income and Wealth

Income and Wealth

Edward Ames

State University
of New York at
Stony Brook

HOLT, RINEHART AND WINSTON, INC.

New York Chicago San Francisco Atlanta
Dallas Montreal Toronto London Sydney

Library of Congress Catalog Card Number: 69–12579
SBN: 03—073620—X
Printed in the United States of America
1 2 3 4 5 6 7 8 9

Preface

This book, and its elementary companion, *An Introduction to Macroeconomic Theory* (Holt, Rinehart and Winston, Inc., 1968), present macroeconomics as a flexible method of theorizing which can be adapted to the study of a variety of economic questions. It encourages students to develop skill in answering questions of their own and others' devising using the system. In this respect it differs from most other books now on the market. These often summarize large segments of the *corpus* of professional literature and promote the authors' favorite economic policies at the expense, respectively, of students' active analytical and critical skills. In contrast, I have deliberately narrowed the subject matter and stressed problems of analysis rather than of political economy.

Undergraduate teachers point out that few of their students become professional economists, and assert that the objective of an undergraduate curriculum is primarily to train "citizens." These teachers are on solid ground when they argue that undergraduate economics must be simpler than graduate economics. Indeed, one of the real objections to undergraduate textbooks, which try to "cover" all topics of current research interest, is that a bewildering variety of literary and mathematical technique must be flashed before the students' eyes. The students learn to drop names, but not to understand the subject.

Teachers are wrong, it seems to me, when they argue that undergraduate economics must teach professional problems in a nonprofessional way. Students may not wish to become economists, but economics courses must still teach economics. Teachers are also wrong when they argue, as some seem to, that theory courses should teach students to jump to the conclusions laboriously reached by researchers, rather than to begin to master the reasoning process of professional economists. Theory courses, all too often, raise questions and answer them in such a way as to suggest that the subject is closed, and therefore dead.

Undergraduates are apt to consider economics courses as dull and trivial. Recognizing the complaint, their teachers may proceed in one of two directions. They may present emotional, controversial, political issues. Or they may admit fundamental analytical method into their courses. We see teachers moving in both directions. The future of the profession will be greatly affected by the response we make to current undergraduate criticism, for, after all, the undergraduate curriculum ultimately recruits the profession.

In introducing this book, I suggest that our trade should practice "economic science" rather than "political economy." I suggest that students will respond well to professional presentation of simple analytic questions. Economists in the past have learned more by reasoning than by emoting. In the future learning will be very much the same process it has always been. I urge that today's teachers, leaving politics to the politicians, should encourage interest in, and respect for, economic science in the student body. If they can do so, the future progress of the discipline is assured.

This point of view does not imply that policy issues are uninteresting or unimportant. It does suggest that we, as teachers, must view these issues as questions involving applications of theory. In fact, policy appears in theoretical questions in three main forms: (a) Does there exist a government policy which will change variable V in a direction desired by some politician? (b) Under what conditions will a particular policy change V in a direction desired by some politician? (c) Granted that a particular policy affects V as desired, does it have any side-effects on other variables not desired by that politician? These are legitimate questions. Under special conditions we can answer them. We should teach our students *how to answer questions like these*. This teaching problem is not the same as teaching our students *what the answers to these questions are*.

Economists do not have a very good record of anticipating economic conditions. In the 1920s nobody forecast the Great Depression. In the 1930s nobody forecast the wartime inflation. During the second World War, most economists forecast a return to mass unemployment after the war. The authors of the 1964 tax reduction did not foresee the war in Vietnam and the inflation which accompanied it. The architects of the U.S. foreign aid program anticipated a persistent dollar shortage, not a persistent dollar glut.

Since economists are capable of very large errors of this sort, they should be modest in their teaching. They can, with justice, claim that most of the time a good professional economist can reason better than a good amateur. They can teach their students how to reason about unfamiliar problems. The economic conditions these students will live through will be conditions unfamiliar to us. A study of today's problems will, in the main, be useless tomorrow. As economists and teachers, we hope that our students will reason intelligently about tomorrow's conditions; and we hope that one of them may propose a constructive solution to some problem which has not yet arisen. To prepare our man for this task, we can only teach him to think.

This book is a series of graduated exercises. I have presented several theories about national income, several theories about the national balance sheets, and several combinations of these. I have tried to present the main ideas which pervade contemporary thinking, and to show how these ideas are related to each other. But this attempt does not involve the simple replication of journal articles. The styles and technical contents of the professional literature are so varied that major simplifications must be made. I hope that I have managed to capture, in simple form, the main themes of contemporary writing.

Some readers have questioned one central theme in this book: the unification of income and balance sheet analysis. This theme appears in several forms. The discussion and application of social accounting stress identities such as "Investment is the change in earning assets," which connect income accounts to changes in balance sheet accounts. In Chapters 6–8 income and balance sheets are combined *in several ways* into a unified theory. The several ways correspond to fundamental theoretical views of the economic process expressed in more subtle form in professional literature.

Most of us were brought up to be either national income economists or monetary economists. We have had to spend a good deal of time worrying about the connection (or lack of it) between these two great branches of macroeconomics. There is no reason, however, for our students to experience the same difficulties, for the basis is now available to reduce the issues dividing the economic community into a few fundamental behavioral questions. I have, therefore, tried to present alternatives which take the general form: if consumer (business or bank) behavior is of one type, then the national income school will make correct predictions; if this behavior is of a different type, then the monetary school will make correct predictions. And, I assert, we do not know how economic units actually behave.

Some readers will exclaim, "But surely you have some opinion of your own about economic behavior!" To such readers I reply, "Naturally I can make guesses. But I don't like parading guesses as facts." Less crisply, I might ask what would happen if we locked, say, Brunner, Copeland, Friedman, Klein, Modigliani, Solow, and Tobin into a room until they reached a consensus about the consumption function or about the role of the interest rate in the behavior of consumers and investors. I would forecast a great loss to the profession due to death from starvation (or blows from blunt instruments).

During the very period this book was being written, the *American Economic Review* published papers, comments, replies, rejoinders, rebuttals, and barbed taunts—all about an empirical savings function which is presented as gospel in many current textbooks. The publication of the Brookings Model has evidently stimulated the output of megamodels by the profession, which would hardly have been the case if the Brookings results were generally accepted. I don't need to take sides in this debate among my learned colleagues. I need only tell my students that the controversy exists, and what the issues are. Hopefully, we shall one day discover where the truth of the matter lies.

Despite the bad temper often displayed in debates between the national income and the monetary theorists, great progress has been made in unifying these two great branches of macroeconomics. Empirically, we may cite the development of the flow of funds accounts. Theoretically, portfolio analysis and numerous studies of the demand for money have gradually made explicit the connection between balance sheets and national income. By over-simplifying for beginners, I have put everything into a rigid mold. I found the elements of the system under my hands, however, when I went to work. I do not apologize for speaking of income and monetary theory as if they were in a process of unification.

The greatest weakness of macroeconomics today lies in its treatment of prices. I hope not to offend those of my colleagues who have developed ingenious four-quadrant diagrams explaining price changes (among other things) in saying this. The available theories deal with "the price level," as if there were only one kind of goods, and the theories become very sticky indeed, if there are several kinds of goods in the system. It has seemed to me wise to point out in Chapter 9 the difficulties in macroeconomic price theory. (I dislike textbooks which talk as if all problems had been solved.)

I do not know when and how the macroeconomic theory of price will be cleaned up. I have suggested, in Chapter 10, that some adaptation of programming and input-output theory may take care of this issue. In doing so, I go beyond the subject matter normally treated in macroeconomics courses, and touch upon mathematical questions which are more advanced than those in the earlier part of the book. The discussion, however, is formulated in terms of a theory involving four prices and four quantities; it is as simple an example as I could devise. It would be presumptuous to describe it as a complete introduction to programming theory; but then, programming theory is not now a part of macroeconomics. Some day it may well be recognized as a part. If so, Chapter 10 would become the first part of a longer discussion.

At this date it seems unnecessary to justify the use of some mathematics in teaching economics. The profession uses mathematics; and we teach students some of what the profession knows. But the profession uses many kinds of mathematics; and we cannot expect undergraduates to know many kinds of mathematics. This book uses one kind of notation: vector-matrix notation. It uses one basic mathematical concept: the linear one-to-one mapping. It uses one form of calculation: the inversion of matrices. Within a linear framework I have tried to present and to apply a considerable variety of economic concepts. Mathematically speaking, this book is at about the level of difficulty of the freshman finite mathematics course. A linear algebra course is *not* required to use the book, for the concepts of basis, rank, range, null-space, and so on do not play a part in the presentation. A very limited use of the concept of inner product is used in the final chapters, but this use does not require prior knowledge of the subject. Chapter 2 presents all the mathematics needed. Other chapters deal with economics.[1]

The economics curriculum usually prescribes the calculus rather than finite mathematics. But the calculus is more difficult than finite mathematics.[2] A draft of this book was tried on students who had had a year of calculus but no finite or linear mathematics and no prior economics course.[3] The text was not impossibly difficult for this group of beginners, but I do not recommend it as a principles text. (Nor do I argue that linear mathematics should

[1] In contrast to the *Introduction to Macroeconomic Theory*, this book does include problems which force students to invert matrices. But the problems require no other mathematical skills.

[2] The appendix to Chapter 1 presents the connection between linear and nonlinear hypotheses more formally. This appendix is mainly for teachers who are used to the calculus.

[3] What did these students learn? About half of what I would have liked them to learn, and about twice as much as the usual principles course teaches.

displace the calculus for economics students generally. Indeed, in microeconomics it would be hard to avoid the calculus.)

The great virtue of linear methods, in the macroeconomic context, is that they are easy. Students can spend a minimal time on mathematics and a maximal time on economics. They acquire a method which can be applied to national income theory, to monetary theory, and to combinations of the two. Professional economists will recognize the limitations of linear methods. But they should also recognize the power of such methods to provide first approximations for the answers to interesting questions. One need only mention the way in which input-output and linear-programming techniques have contributed approximate solutions to otherwise unanswerable problems. Linear methods are not the last word in generality but they are simple and powerful. Indeed, when economists construct nonlinear macroeconomic theories, their comparative statics analysis is based on the proposition that in a sufficiently small neighborhood of equilibrium their theories behave as if they were linear. All a linear theory does is to assign constant values to the functions derived in the comparative statics results of nonlinear theories.

I have used no graphs in this book. Teachers are wrong in thinking that students find graphs easier than other techniques. Students do become intrigued with the artistic aspects of graphs, particularly the ingenious four-quadrant diagrams developed in a number of graduate programs. Unfortunately, students' art seems to overpower their economics. Linear methods are less arty; and I think it more crafty to use them in teaching students how to reason like an economist. Blackboards remain stubbornly two-dimensional. Linear methods liberate us from the tyranny of the plane.

I have certain practical recommendations to teachers using this book for the first time. It is important that students learn to work problems. Hence, it is important to see that they understand Chapter 2 so they can work the problems in later chapters. Liberal arts students are inclined to panic at mathematical notation, and one must be careful to make them do enough blackboard work in class to see that the use of vectors and matrices does not require superhuman abilities. Curiously enough, however, if too much time is spent on Chapter 2, students become persuaded that it is more difficult than it really is. The wise teacher will move on as soon as possible. Understanding will come as the problems in later chapters are solved. My own inclination is to omit the last section of Chapter 2 until this material is needed in Chapters 9–11.

Chapter 6 presents an interesting teaching problem. In this chapter the implications of several different behavioral assumptions are compared. Students, in many cases, are accustomed to the "right-answer" school of textbook writing; they seem appalled that one can, with a little ingenuity, construct theories which have different implications. I hope that teachers will not be as shocked as their students by the notion that there can be more than one explanation of the level of economic activity. For every monetary theory emerging from a midwestern university one can construct an ivy-league national income theory, and conversely.

Some problems involve results which are a familiar part of the literature. Other problems are designed to show that not all desirable objectives may be reached simultaneously. (For instance, reduction in demand for goods, in inflationary periods, may necessarily mean higher interest rates. One objective may be deemed desirable, the other undesirable.) Still other problems involve nontechnical comparison of the arguments of different chapters. I hope that these problems will be interesting—and that they will suggest other problems to those who reach this material.

If time is scarce, the following material is most easily omitted: Theory 2, Theory 5, Chapter 8, the section on "Reservation Prices and Capacity Limits" in Chapter 9, and Chapter 11. Some teachers will feel that Chapter 10, with its programming-type theory, introduces very large new questions, and can well be omitted; but if I were using this book I would try to retain it as a link between macroeconomics and microeconomics.

I owe a debt to a number of colleagues: to Keith Brown, James Shepherd, and Hugo Sommenschein who have taught from an early draft of the manuscript; and to Chiou-shuang Yan, who picked up a variety of errors in early drafts. Kenneth Avio, Juei-Ming Cheng, William Dawes, David P. Doane, Frank Maris, and Robert St. Louis who have been most helpful to me as teaching assistants, verifying my conjecture that one can learn and teach linear macroeconomics simultaneously. (I think we all had nervous moments.) For help in assembling the bibliography I must thank David P. Doane. I have borrowed, in the Appendix to Chapter 6, portions of a theory from the forthcoming doctoral thesis of Atif Kubursi; and I have a more generalized debt to Peter Stowe. All of these people, by their questioning, have contributed greatly to the clarification of my thinking. If opacity and error have remained in this book only I am to blame. Mrs. Doris Haught has had the difficult task of typing this manuscript for classroom use and for publication.

—EDWARD AMES

LAFAYETTE, INDIANA
FEBRUARY 1969

Contents

Income and Wealth

Introduction

Introductions to books tell readers what to expect. But if the book is designed to help readers learn something they didn't previously know, it is hard to tell them what to expect—except, perhaps, blood, sweat, and tears. Professional economists will understand the following description:

> This book is a collection of linear macroeconomic theories, arranged systematically in order of increasing scope. All theories are based on explicit social accounting schemes. Particular attention is paid to the integration of national-income and balance-sheet (particularly monetary) analysis. Behavioral hypotheses are all of a single, allocative type. Chapters 1 and 2 are methodological. Chapters 3 to 8 deal with macroeconomic theories in which prices (other than the interest rate) are not explicitly considered. Chapters 9 to 11 deal with theories in which prices appear explicitly. Static and comparative static analyses are given for all theories considered. A final chapter deals with the empirical confirmation of macroeconomic theories.

This paragraph will be pure gobbldygook for most readers, because it is full of technical terms. It provides a structure for the rest of the chapter, however. The following discussion aims at translating a number of terms into ordinary English and explaining the reasons for the appearance of the corresponding topics in this particular book. The terms in question are the following: *macroeconomics*; *theories* (especially linear theories); *systems of social accounts*; *allocative hypotheses*; *prices in macroeconomic theories*; *statics and comparative statics*; *empirical conformation of theories.*

MACROECONOMICS

Economics is the study of production and the exchange of goods and services. The problem is to explain what goods and how many goods are produced, what kinds of income, and how large incomes are earned, what kinds of wealth and how much wealth is available in a community. The problem is to explain why certain groups get "better off" over a period of time, either because they can buy more than formerly or because their position has improved relative to other groups. The subject is classified according to the size of the groups considered in particular problems. *Microeconomics* (from the Greek word *mikros*, meaning "small") is concerned with small groups and even individuals. *Macroeconomics* (from the Greek word *makros*, meaning "large") deals with large groups and, in some cases, entire countries. In this book, the point of view is resolutely macroeconomic.

Consider two examples of macroeconomic events. The output of consumer goods in the United States has shown a steady tendency to rise more rapidly than population. The standard of living, which is simply the ratio consumer goods/people, has therefore risen. In many other countries the standard of living has not risen. Why is it that in some countries the standard of living rises and in others it does not?

In the United States during the 1930s, at least one-fifth of the labor force was unemployed at any one time—something which has never happened before or since. There are practical reasons for studying this national disaster—another such period of mass unemployment would be most unpleasant for us all. So long as we do not know why that depression took place, we cannot be sure that another might not occur, or what might be done about it. Mass unemployment is a macroeconomic phenomenon.

The United States has never had something which economists call a hyperinflation. In Germany in 1923, prices rose to levels about one billion times as high as those in 1920. In mid-1946, prices in Hungary rose to levels 10^{56} times as high as at the end of 1944. The closest we have come to hyperinflation was during the Civil War, when prices in the Confederacy rose to levels which seemed at the time astronomical, although that rise has been "outdone" in many other countries. Hyperinflations are macroeconomic events.

What might be a macroeconomic event that college students might directly observe? One such event occurs every summer, when students are looking for part-time jobs. It is true that most such jobs are obtained after some sort of interview. The individual job-applicant knows that he is more likely to get a job if his appearance is neat and if his manners are good. His fate also depends on whether the personnel man he talks to is in a good mood and happens to like the applicant. But it is a fact that some summers even uncouth students can easily find jobs, and that other summers even the "most likely to succeed" types have trouble getting jobs. The difference is not ascribable to the personalities of students and personnel men as a group, or to chance, but rather to differences in something called "business conditions." These differences are quite tangible to job applicants, even if they may be difficult to describe precisely.

Most of us have acquaintances or relatives in business organizations. When we ask what they do, we are told that they spend their time talking to people, making telephone calls, writing letters, and so on. Some of the people involved are more able than others. We all have preferences as to the businesses we deal with—some stores have better goods and better manners than others. We know by reputation the names of some of the most successful business organizations, and we may actually have seen businesses close down in our neighborhoods. Individual businesses, like individual people, vary enormously, and some are much more successful than others.

Imagine, now, that at the end of the year we could interview all the businesses and ask them, "Did you sell more this year than last year? Did you earn more profit this year than last year?" and so forth. If the fate of the business depended solely on the personalities of the people who ran it, we should expect to find about as many increases as decreases in sales and about as many increases as decreases in profits.

As a matter of fact, the results of such surveys are quite different. Some years, most businesses increase their sales and their profits; other years, most businesses have reduced sales and profits. We cannot attribute this fact to personality—businessmen are probably as smart and as aggressive one year as the next.

An impressive list of such visible macroeconomic changes in conditions can be compiled. We know that some years almost all prices rise, and in other years almost all prices fall. We cannot explain this sort of change in terms of individual behavior, and economists therefore seek a systematic way of accounting for the various changes in economic conditions which regularly sweep over entire countries.

These changes must be changes in group behavior and not in individual behavior. When one tries to explain macroeconomic events in terms appropriate to individuals, he inevitably encounters the problem: granted that one individual decides to act differently this year, why isn't his decision offset by someone else who decides to make the opposite change?

The macroeconomist, in trying to account for the behavior of large groups of people or businesses, asks the question, "What would the world be like if people, as a group, followed certain rules of behavior?" The rules he tries out are arrived at in a variety of ways: intuition, opinion surveys, historical observation, and so on. They are usually very simple rules. The macroeconomist does not ordinarily assert that people never deviate from these rules, but he does try to determine what life would be like if the rules were consistently adhered to.

There are two reasons why it is difficult for beginners to relate the methods of macroeconomics to ordinary direct experience. First, we ordinarily come into direct contact only with individuals, and the notion of "group behavior" is an abstraction which is only partly satisfactory. Second, we are accustomed to so much variation in the behavior of people we know that it is difficult to realize the extent to which this variation is canceled out in large groups of people. These two concessions must be made, however, if one is to arrive at any understanding of the kinds of events which are the subject of our discussion.

Macroeconomic analysis, then, is a logical analysis of how the income and wealth of a community would change if people's behavior were of certain rigidly defined kinds. The macroeconomist is free to analyze any sort of hypothetical behavior he can imagine, but naturally he wants mainly to account for the way people in his own community behave. For this reason, his statements about behavior seek to be at least plausible. On the other hand, they are artificial, at least in the sense of being extremely clear-cut and abstract. We are all tempted to say, in looking at the formulation of an asserted pattern of behavior, "Gee whiz, people don't follow any rule *that* precisely." To this objection, the macroeconomist can only retort, "Gee whiz, yourself. If you want me to investigate what will happen if people act every which way, all I can say is that anything might happen. That is no way to understand what is going on in the world. As a matter of fact, people don't behave every which way, even if they are a bit erratic sometimes."

The objection just cited is partly based on the alleged tendency of individuals and groups to behave erratically. It is possible to make allowances for randomness in people's behavior. To do so, one need only say that "on the average" people's behavior follows a precise law, and that actual behavior in any short period of time is this average behavior plus some random element. A few courses in mathematical statistics, therefore, put the macroeconomist back in business with a theory which can handle erratic behavior of economic units.

But there is another more basic objection which is apt to be raised to macroeconomics. The economy, after all, is made up of a very large number of individual consumers and individual businesses. When one attempts to reason about a group, one is reasoning about the cumulative effects of individual actions. It is natural to wonder how the actions of the individual members of the group are related to the actions of the group. This issue will be stated somewhat more precisely as the discussion proceeds.

Economics is concerned with the twin phenomena of exchange and scarcity. These are probably the simplest of human relationships. Exchange—as the word implies—involves the participation of individuals in actions involving both giving something and receiving something. Each thing given must be useful to the recipient, for otherwise he would not accept it. Each individual participant will not give something without receiving something else, because things are "scarce." That is, they cannot be found, made, or otherwise acquired without effort of some kind.[1]

In speaking of "things," the preceding paragraph is too narrow. People exchange their work for paychecks, and work is hardly a "thing." People pay rent for the use of a house, and the use of a house is not the same thing as a house. But the economic similarity between goods (physical objects) and services is obvious on a moment's thought.

An economy is a set of persons and businesses who exchange goods and services. Each economic unit (person or business) may in principle exchange with each other economic unit. Thus if there are N economic units in an economy, the number of possible *pairs* of economic units carrying on exchange is $N(N-1)/2$.[2] In an economy with even 1,000,000 economic units (a small economy, by the way), there could thus be about 500,000,000,000 distinguishable kinds of acts of exchange between individual economic units. This is far too large a number to be manageable.

Macroeconomics puts individual economic units into groups and is basically concerned with exchange among the groups. Because the number of groups may be small, problems of exchange are reduced to manageable proportions. Macroeconomics is therefore almost a necessity for anyone trying to analyze an economy as a whole. With modern computing techniques it is possible to analyze numerically an economy broken up into a few hundred groups called *industries*. But this type of analysis, which is referred to as input-output,[3] as yet is applicable only to a rather narrow range of problems. When one wants to reduce an economy to a small enough collection of groups to be handled without a digital computer, one carries out macroeconomic analysis.

A very simple example will suffice to illustrate why statements that are true

---

[1] *Scarcity* is used in a technical sense. The people engaged in any act of exchange may be very, very rich. It is a rather bad pun to say, as some journalists do, that because the United States has a high standard of living (an "affluent society") scarcity in the technical sense does not exist. Go to a supermarket. How many goods did it give away?

[2] Each of the N units may exchange with $N-1$ other units. But if unit A exchanges with unit B, that is the same as unit B exchanging with unit A.

[3] An introductory treatment of this subject is found in C. S. Yan, *Input-Output Analysis* (New York: Holt, Rinehart and Winston, Inc., 1969). Chapter 10 of this book will present an application of this method of work to a very highly aggregated economy.

of individuals need not be true of groups. The example involves a very small group, and it is simple enough to be understandable.

Imagine a group with three members, A, B and C. Each member has a money income (Y), which he may spend on consumer goods (C) or save (S). That is,

$$Y_A = C_A + S_A \quad \text{for member A}$$

$$Y_B = C_B + S_B \quad \text{for member B}$$

$$Y_C = C_C + S_C \quad \text{for member C}$$

$$Y = C + S \quad \text{for the group, where}$$

$$Y = Y_A + Y_B + Y_C$$

$$C = C_A + C_B + C_C$$

$$S = S_A + S_B + S_C$$

It is very often assumed in macroeconomics that group consumption depends on group income. An example of this dependence is the function

$$C = aY + F$$

If this function is valid, when the combined income of the group increases by \$1, consumption rises by \$$a$.

Now suppose that for the individuals in the group, consumption depends on income in the following ways:

$$C_A = a_A Y_A + F_A$$

$$C_B = a_B Y_B + F_B$$

$$C_C = a_C Y_C + F_C$$

Thus each individual conforms to a behavior pattern like that ascribed to the group as a whole. If the consumption of the three individuals is summed, one obtains:

$$C = a_A Y_A + a_B Y_B + a_C Y_C + (F_A + F_B + F_C)$$

To make this statement compatible with the statement

$$C = aY + F$$

it must be the case that

$$aY = a_A Y_A + a_B Y_B + a_C Y_C$$

Thus, since $Y = Y_A + Y_B + Y_C$, it must be the case that

$$0 = (a - a_A) Y_A + (a - a_B) Y_B + (a - a_C) Y_C$$

so that one income, say that of C, is not independent of the incomes of other members of the group:

$$Y_C = \frac{a - a_A}{a_C - a} Y_A + \frac{a - a_B}{a_C - a} Y_B$$

The sticky point in this statement lies in the fact that the dependence among Y_A, Y_B and Y_C is formulated in terms of the *differences* between the coefficients a_A, a_B, and a_C and the coefficient a. To justify the use of the aggregate function, $C = aY + F$, one would have to explain why the incomes of the individuals in the group were always related by the equation:

$$0 = (a - a_A)Y_A + (a - a_B)Y_B + (a - a_C)Y_C$$

That is, one would need a theory of income distribution among individuals.

Most macroeconomists are only mildly disturbed by this sort of problem. They say, in effect, "If we can present a coherent macroeconomic theory and show that it explains important events in economic history, then it is up to others (not us) to provide a theory of individual behavior which is compatible with our results."

This argument passes the buck. It is very convenient to be able to pass the buck. Some economists do so with a clear conscience, others reluctantly. The author has a good excuse: this is a book of macroeconomics. Macroeconomics has interesting ideas which cannot at present be discussed on any other basis. It is unfortunate that economists have not yet succeeded in adequately tying together the theories of individual and of group behavior. It is not clear that they will soon be able to do so. Therefore it is best to recognize that economics is not yet well tied together and to consider the separate pieces on their own merits.

THEORIES

Macroeconomics deals with the *total* income and output of the community, the *total* amount of bank deposits, *total* government spending and tax collections, and other totals of this sort. At any moment each of these is a number, but over a period of time each of them may change. For this reason they will be called *variables*. Some variables are measured in numbers of dollars, some are quantities such as total number of jobs. A macroeconomic theory, therefore, explains what some collection of numbers will turn out to be, given stated conditions. This branch of economics is therefore inherently related to mathematics. It is impossible to discuss macroeconomics in a purely verbal way, because it tries to explain numbers. The numbers are measures of components of income and wealth, and therefore of the activities of households, businesses, government, and banks; understanding of changes in these numbers should imply understanding of the underlying economic activities.

A theory is an explanation of the values of certain *variables*. We might decide to make a theory about the interest rate on government bonds and the quantity of paper money in circulation, for example. At any moment, the interest rate is a number and the quantity of paper money in circulation is a number, but from one moment to the next these numbers may change. That is why we refer to them as *variables*. We shall denote the set of variables in a theory by $(V_1, V_2, \ldots, V_n)$, where the subscripts $1, 2, \ldots, n$ stand for the names of the variables. At any moment, each variable has a value, so that the set of variables is momentarily a set of numbers $(\bar{V}_1, \bar{V}_2, \ldots, \bar{V}_n)$.

A theory says that the variables take on particular numerical values because of the operation of some set of *factors*, which we denote by $(F_1, F_2, \ldots, F_m)$. The factors, like the variables, assume particular values at particular moments, and when they do, the factors become a set of numbers, say $(\bar{F}_1, \bar{F}_2, \ldots, \bar{F}_m)$.[4] If a theory has been made correctly, two things can be calculated:

(a) If a particular set of numbers $(\bar{F}_1 \cdots \bar{F}_m)$ is given (so that the factors in the theory assume particular values), then there is a single value which each of the variables may assume. That is

$$\text{the set } (\bar{F}_1 \cdots \bar{F}_m) \text{ implies a particular set } (\bar{V}_1 \cdots \bar{V}_n)$$

(b) Suppose that in some period, the values of the factors change from $(\bar{F}_1 \cdots \bar{F}_m)$ to $(\hat{F}_1 \cdots \hat{F}_m)$. There will then be a change of ΔF_1 in factor 1, ΔF_2 in factor 2, and so on. Therefore, there is a single set of *changes* which will take place in the variables. That is

$$\text{the set } (\Delta F_1 \cdots \Delta F_m) \textit{ implies a particular set } (\Delta V_1 \cdots \Delta V_n)$$

Another way of putting these statements is that a theory involves *a mapping* of sets $(\bar{F}_1 \cdots \bar{F}_m)$ into sets $(\bar{V}_1 \cdots \bar{F}_n)$ and *a mapping* of sets $(\Delta F_1 \cdots \Delta F_m)$ into sets $(\Delta V_1 \cdots \Delta V_n)$. These two mappings in general are not the same. There does exist a class of theory for which these two mappings are the same. Such theories are called *linear*. This book is concerned only with linear theories, because these theories are the simplest to analyze and are thus most suited for beginners.

In order to construct a theory, we assume that economic units (consumers, businesses, banks, and government) behave according to clearly defined rules, and we investigate the consequences of their behavior. We are free to assume any rules we like, but in this book the rules assumed are those which have seemed plausible to several considerable groups of economists. These

---

[4] Some readers (particularly teachers) may be familiar with a classification of variables into *endogenous* and *exogenous* sets. If such readers are puzzled by the usage of words in this chapter, they should consult the appendix to this chapter. Readers who have not encountered the other terminology will have no reason to use the appendix.

groups have reached quite different conclusions about how the economy works, and we are able to see why they differ by putting the theories side by side.

It will turn out that when we write down precisely what rules of behavior economic units follow, we obtain a set of statements which can be interpreted as a mapping. That is, when we assume that the behavior of economic units depends on variables $(V_1 \cdots V_n)$, and on factors $(F_1 \cdots F_m)$ in a specified way, we are able to say that when the variables take on the particular values $(\bar{V}_1 \cdots \bar{V}_n)$, then

the set $(\bar{V}_1 \cdots \bar{V}_n)$ *implies a particular set* $(\bar{F}_1 \cdots \bar{F}_m)$

and, moreover, if the variables change by amounts $(\Delta\bar{V}_1 \cdots \Delta\bar{V}_n)$

the set $(\Delta\bar{V}_1 \cdots \Delta\bar{V}_n)$ *implies a particular set* $(\Delta\bar{F}_1 \cdots \Delta\bar{F}_m)$

Of course these behavioral statements are also mappings, but they are "backwards." Instead of saying

$(\bar{F}_1 \cdots \bar{F}_m)$ *implies* $(\bar{V}_1 \cdots \bar{V}_n)$

the behavioral statements say

$(\bar{V}_1 \cdots \bar{V}_n)$ *implies* $(\bar{F}_1 \cdots \bar{F}_m)$

Consequently we must rewrite the behavioral statements so as to obtain other statements which are suitable for our needs. This rewriting is known as *inversion*. In the particular case where all theories are linear, inversion can be accomplished by following a well-defined (though rather boring) sequence of algebraic calculations.

The theories in this book are linear theories and are constructed according to standard rules.

(a) We select a set of variables, whose numerical values we seek to explain in terms of numerical values of some particular set of factors.

(b) We assume that the economic units figuring in our theory follow specified rules of behavior. We then verify that we have mapped the variables into the factors.

(c) We try to perform an algebraic operation called inversion on the statements in (b). If successful, we have constructed a mapping of the factors into the variables. If unsuccessful, we know that our theory is incomplete or internally inconsistent.

(d) By examining the inverse mapping, we are able to say how each of the factors affects each of the variables in the system.

By insisting that all theories be linear, this book makes it possible for beginners to investigate a wide variety of topics, for all topics are treated according to the same set of rules. This procedure, of course, is justified only as a first step in the direction of understanding economic problems. In research, and even in more advanced courses, the requirement that all theories be linear would be burdensome. That is why advanced work is more difficult than beginning work in economics—as in any field of study.[5]

One particular feature of linear theories is that they must involve "one-to-one mappings" if step (c) is to be undertaken. That is, for any set $(\bar{V}_1 \cdots \bar{V}_n)$ there exists exactly one set $(\bar{F}_1 \cdots \bar{F}_m)$ which can have "caused it," and for any set $(\bar{F}_1 \cdots \bar{F}_m)$ there exists exactly one set $(\bar{V}_1 \cdots \bar{V}_n)$.

Take a simple hypothetical theory in which it is alleged that the number of dollars spent by consumers (denoted by C) in a given year and the interest rate on U.S. government bonds (denoted by R) depend in a one-to-one way upon two factors: the number of inches of rainfall (denoted by I) and the number of games won by the New York Mets (denoted by G). In constructing the theory we have a one-to-one mapping

$$(\mathbf{I}, \mathbf{G}) \xleftrightarrow{\text{Theory}} (\mathbf{C}, \mathbf{R})$$

and in particular, suppose that in 1968 it is the case that

$$\mathbf{I} = \bar{\mathbf{I}}$$
$$\mathbf{G} = \bar{\mathbf{G}}$$
$$\mathbf{C} = \bar{\mathbf{C}}$$
$$\mathbf{R} = \bar{\mathbf{R}}$$

are all known. Now in 1969 rainfall increases from $\bar{R}$ to $(\bar{R} + \Delta R)$. Suppose the Mets win exactly as many games in 1969 as they did in 1968. Then in 1969 we would have

$$I = \bar{I} + \Delta I$$
$$G = \bar{G}$$
$$C = \bar{C} + \Delta C$$
$$R = \bar{R} + \Delta R$$

But we might ask: is there any number of games $\hat{G}$ which the Mets *might* have won, such that

[5] In more advanced work, where nonlinear theories are used, the calculus is necessary rather than simple algebra. In particular, step (c) is very much more difficult. If the calculus is used, however, steps (c) and (d) are replaced by the following: *Step* (c′). Show that, if the variables change by small enough amount, it is possible to construct a linear mapping of *changes* in variable into *changes* in factors. (This is called *differentiation.*) Use the rules of step (c) to perform an algebraic inversion which gives a linear mapping of changes in factors into changes in variables. *Step* (d′). Now go back from the mappings of changes to a system in which factors are mapped into variables. [This is called *integration* of the results of step (c′).]

$$I = \bar{I} + \Delta I$$
$$G = \hat{G}$$
$$C = \overline{C}$$
$$R = \overline{R}$$

If the theory is one-to-one, the answer to this question is "no." It might be that $C = \overline{C}$ *or* that $R = \overline{R}$ for some value $\hat{G}$, but *never both* $C = \overline{C}$ and $R = \overline{R}$ unless $\Delta I = 0$ and $G = \overline{G}$.

This example is not (in all likelihood) a good economic theory, but it does pave the way for a general remark. The United States economy has been characterized by alternate periods of unemployment and of price increases.[6] These have been considered by economists as due mainly (except in wartime) to changes in business spending (which we shall call *investment*) on new plant and equipment. One may ask whether it would be possible for a government to vary its spending in such a way as to exactly offset the effects of variations in business spending on the economy. To this question, theories of the kind presented here would necessarily answer "no." It might be that the government might exactly offset the effects of changes in business spending on some parts of the economy. There would necessarily be at least one sector of the economy which is affected differently by business and by government spending. Some economists would reject this particular conclusion; all economists can probably think of some conclusion they have reached which would be invalid if only one-to-one mappings had theoretical validity. Therefore, it is important to remember that the insistence on one-to-one mappings is a device used to make theories simpler for beginners.

This book is for use in a beginning course, and it therefore is constructed as simply as possible. The price of simplicity is a loss of variety in the forms of behavior which can be analyzed. To compensate for this loss of variety, there is an important offsetting gain: we may use a standard approach and a systematic method of analysis to deal with a considerable range of topics. The approach and method are, moreover, closely related to those which are used in more advanced work, so that readers who become used to this method of work will be able to adapt it readily to other methods.

A theory is inherently a simplification. It is an attempt to subject a complicated reality to a set of rules. If the theory does not match readily in important respects, it should be discarded—but it should not be discarded merely because it is simple. The great appeal of macroeconomics is that it suggests simple ways of looking at a few large "pieces" of the economy. The theories given here may be *too* simple; it is not easy, however, to understand

---

[6] Unemployment has never in the past hundred years been as severe as in the 1930s nor price rises as great as in the 1940s, of course.

the process of reasoning known as theorizing unless one learns it by first considering the simplest examples. In these examples, we consider parts of the economy taken separately, and we learn how to fit them together.

SYSTEMS OF SOCIAL ACCOUNTS

Once the decision has been made to aggregate the huge numbers of individual economic units into a few groups, it becomes necessary to decide the basis on which groups are to be chosen. In this book, economic units are grouped into the following classification: households, businesses, banks, government, and foreigners (foreigners, in the main are disregarded here). These are the classifications that are generally followed in twentieth-century macroeconomics.

Each individual economic unit is said to have an income, which is spent for specified purposes. Each unit is said to own a collection of things (assets), paid for either from borrowing or from current income in known ways. A group, likewise, has a collective income, used for specified purposes, and a collective set of assets, the means of purchase of which is known. The individual is assumed to have a set of accounts, consisting of an income statement and a balance sheet. These accounts are constructed in well-known ways by accountants; and the aggregation of individual accounts into the accounts of groups is studied and carried out by social accountants. It is possible to discuss social accounting in enormous detail and subtlety, but for the present it is sufficient to describe social accounting in a very schematic form, and this will be done in Chapter 1. Readers will be unable to prepare social accounts after reading that chapter, but they will have a basis for reading the accounts prepared by others. A macroeconomic theory is fundamentally a theory about variations in social accounts, since the variables in a macroeconomic theory are either components of these accounts or related in some direct way to these components.

The classification of economic units into households, businesses, banks, government, and foreigners exists for two reasons: (1) on logical grounds, this appears a natural way to classify them; (2) the classification accords well with our observations of economic life. There is nothing sacred about it, however, as we shall see.

The macroeconomics presented here is of twentieth-century origin. It owes its main development to the great depression of the 1930s. The enormous unemployment of this period was something which economists of the day simply could not explain at all. (As we shall see, it is still not possible to explain it well.) National income theory (Chapters 3 and 6 in particular) has been greatly influenced by dramatic happenings in the past fifty years, and historical notes have been inserted in several places to indicate where apparently abstract propositions originated as attempts to explain unexpected economic events. It is a mistake to think that theoretical economics is uninfluenced by current events.

In the modern world, economic life is dominated by large businesses, with "personalities" and accounts quite separate from those of people who depend on the business for their livelihood. Governments have become very large and are prominent in the daily affairs of individuals and businesses. Credit is used continuously by individuals and businesses. Credit comes mainly from banks; and for hundreds of years it has been clear that banking was a very special, and even mysterious, kind of business. The classification used in modern macroeconomics thus reflects the realities of modern life.

Modern macroeconomics, however, is not the only macroeconomics. For a century after 1776 there was an active group of macroeconomists. It is instructive to consider why their work came to an end: it ran into a set of logical and practical difficulties not unlike those facing modern macroeconomics.

The earlier macroeconomists are usually referred to as "the Classical School". Adam Smith, David Ricardo, and Karl Marx are the three most famous writers in this group; their macroeconomic work was mainly what we should call "national income analysis." Simultaneously, however, a group of monetary writers, notably Tooke and Overstone, were developing a "balance sheet analysis." The practical concerns of this group centered around the depressions of the late eighteenth and early nineteenth centuries and the inflation of the Napoleonic wars, just as the interests of the modern group have centered around more recent depressions and wartime inflations.

The social accounting of the earlier macroeconomists was based on a "class structure." Their main economic groupings were workers, farmers (tenant farmers, to be exact), landlords (who rented land to farmers), and capitalists (who owned factories and hired labor). They made no distinction between businesses and the owners of businesses, for businesses were mainly family affairs at the time. The four classes seemed natural, for in England during that period (as today) there were very clearly marked class demarcations for everyone to see. These classes seemed overwhelmingly important and obvious, and the behavior of the economy seemed to be overwhelmingly dominated by phenomena explainable by the existence of social classes.

It is always easier to see the mistakes of others than one's own. The problems of the older macroeconomics are now fairly obvious, and they are even remedied in part by modern macroeconomics.

Even if class distinctions are an important basis for classifying income earned, they are confusing when it comes to analyzing the spending of income. For the storekeeper cannot tell whether a particular dollar in his cash register came from wages, farm income, rent, or profit. Indeed, if some people earn income from more than one source, the consumer himself cannot tell how he earned any particular dollar of income.

Modern macroeconomics has made some advance over the older macroeconomics by making a distinction between personal and business income rather than distinctions based on the source of income. One important reason for the class distinctions was to explain the growth of the economy. Basically, the older macroeconomics thought of workers and landlords as consumers, and of farmers and capitalists as the sources of savings and investment and hence of economic development.[7] Savings (income not spent on consumption) and investment (additions to productive plant) are the main agencies of economic change in every macroeconomics.

In the simplest schemata of the old macroeconomics, workers did not save, and capitalists did not buy consumer goods. Thus the standard of living (consumption) could be determined by workers' incomes (wages) and the rate of development (investment) by capitalists' incomes (interest and profit).

In the simplest schemata of the new macroeconomics, businesses do not save and consumers do not invest.[8] It is the function of the banking system and "Wall Street" to move purchasing power from savers to investors.

Clearly there is something in common between the old macroeconomics and the new; but there has been a clarification and sharpening of the issues.

Modern macroeconomics makes a clear recognition of the difference between income accounts and balance sheet accounts.[9] This recognition is based on accounting practices, which have had to improve as businesses have grown in size and complexity.

Until very recently, there were two distinct kinds of macroeconomics: national product analysis, and monetary theory. The first is based on income accounting, the second on balance sheet accounting. Each tended to make claims about the other, but no formal connection could be made. Since 1945, enormous progress has been made in combining the two subjects. Once combination of the two has been tried, it becomes very natural. In this book, Chapters 3 and 4 deal with national product analysis, Chapter 5 with monetary analysis. Chapters 6 and 7 put the two together in what turns out to be a simple and straightforward way.

The distinctions between income and balance sheet analysis, and between national income and monetary theory now seem to be quite simple and clear. In a few years, the two branches of macroeconomics will probably be completely merged. Readers of modern economics will wonder what all the

---

[7] Karl Marx, of course, disliked capitalists. Nevertheless, in his economic reasoning, economic growth and development (as well as depression and poverty) were due to capitalists.

[8] This statement is not literally true. But to most macroeconomists, savings is mainly the result of household decisions and investment mainly the result of business decisions. Thus, retained business profits and new housing construction (the disregarded elements) appear as "complications" in modern macroeconomics.

[9] These are often called *flow* and *stock* accounts in the literature.

shouting has been about, just as they wonder today about an enormous literature in the 1930s about issues which can now be disposed of in a page or two. Hindsight is an immensely powerful weapon, with which each generation can dismiss the work of its predecessors. This book relies very heavily on recent research (for which the author can claim no credit) which has shown quite clearly how to put together the two great traditions of macroeconomics.

Because the fusion of the two macroeconomic traditions is so recent, there are still economists who are mainly national income theorists and others who are mainly monetary theorists. There is still a controversy about whether income elements or monetary elements can be thought of as "dominating" the economy. This controversy has a political as well as a professional element. National income theorists tend to look to government spending and taxation policies as means of curing our "macroeconomic ills"; monetary theorists look to policies affecting the banking system. Neither the economics nor the policies of this controversy have been fully worked out. Because the debate is still active, it is reflected in the text and especially in the problems of this book.

The new macroeconomics is still in the process of formation. It is not clear, therefore, who will turn out to have made the definitive contributions to it. Modern national income accounting derives from the work of Wesley Mitchell and the National Bureau of Economic Research, beginning in the 1920s. National income analysis started from the work of J. M. Keynes in the 1930s. Monetary analysis, as stated above, has a long and continuous history. From work by Knut Wicksell and Irving Fisher in the 1920s, it has continued to the present day, with Milton Friedman, George Horwich, Don Patinkin, and James Tobin as prominent contributors. The social accounting system which unifies national income and balance sheet accounting is the moneyflows accounting developed by Morris Copeland. The work of John Gurley and Edward Shaw was a pioneering attempt at the theoretical counterpart of Copeland's work. A very large literature exists in modern macroeconomics, and it is impossible to do justice to all the writers who have contributed to it.

THE ALLOCATIVE HYPOTHESIS

Theories are necessary because life is such a mess. Go to any source of macroeconomic data—the *Historical Statistics of the U.S.*, the *Survey of Current Business*, the *Federal Reserve Bulletin*—and you find page after page of numbers on the details of macroeconomic life. These statistics are themselves a distillation of the millions of economic interrelations among individual families and businesses and government agencies and banks. Theories try to bring order into mazes of numbers such as these.

A theory should be simpler than the data which it purports to explain. Otherwise one gets along just as well without it. Complicated explanations are sometimes necessary, but readers are rightly suspicious of them.

Where, however, does one find simplicity? In most of this book, theories are "allocative." An allocative principle may be applied to the income of a group in the economy, or it may be applied to the assets (the wealth, or things owned) of a group. An *allocative rule of behavior* says:

(a) Any economic group which has an income spends that income for various purposes. The amount of income spent for any purpose depends on the total amount of income available.

(b) Any economic group which has wealth (assets) decides on the forms in which that wealth is held. The amount of wealth held in any particular form depends on the total wealth available to the group.

These rules of behavior are too simple, as stated, to be applied literally to theories involving large numbers of variables. If, for instance, a theory involves both income and wealth accounts, it may be necessary to say:

(c) The spending of income for particular purposes depends on both the total income and the total wealth of the economic group in question.

(d) The amount of wealth held in any particular form by an economic group depends on both the total wealth and the total income of that group.

Most modern macroeconomics is based on one or more of these four hypotheses. Indeed, it is possible to present most of the current views about macroeconomic problems in terms of one or more of these hypotheses. Because this book is deliberately aimed at simplifying the subject for beginners, it uses allocated hypotheses wherever possible because they are so very simple.[10] Like every simplifying procedure, this practice entails some loss in "realism." Theories described here may turn out to be different in detail from those in the professional economic literature because they have been simplified according to a set of rules. The author hopes, however, that he has kept the spirit of the literature, even if he differs from it in detail.

PRICES IN MACROECONOMIC THEORY

Modern macroeconomics has made a considerable advance over the older macroeconomics. It has revised the basis on which it aggregates individual economic units into groups. It has clarified the social accounting system on which the analysis is based. In another respect, however, modern macroeconomics is open to a type of criticism which could be leveled at the older macroeconomics—and which, indeed, had a great deal to do with the decline

[10] In order, however, to keep the discussion reasonably close to professional writing, it is also necessary to discuss hypotheses in which behavior depends on one particular asset (money) rather than total assets. This special rule is not difficult for readers who are familiar with the use of the four allocative rules given here.

of macroeconomics in the period from about 1870 to about 1925. The criticism is this: macroeconomics lacks a good way to discuss price changes.

The money income of any consumer (or business) is arrived at by multiplying the number of units of services he performs by the number of dollars he receives per unit of services. (For example, the consumer may work 40 hours per week at $2.50 per hour to earn $100.00 per week.) Likewise, when the consumer spends his income, he buys a certain amount of goods, each unit of which costs a certain amount of money. (For example, five pounds of hamburger at $.59 per pound costs $2.95.) When his money income changes, and when his money spending changes, part of the changes represent changes in quantities of services sold (or quantities of goods bought), and part of the changes represent changes in price.

When macroeconomists aggregate individual economic units into groups, they form groups which earn many different kinds of income and spend income on many different kinds of goods. The notions of quantity and price, which are quite clear in the case of the individual, must be replaced by the notions of "quantity index" and "price index." There are important statistical problems in the construction of indexes; but it is necessary for macroeconomics to use them: when the income, or the expenditures, or the wealth of a group changes, part of the change is a change in the quantity of things involved, and part of the change is a change in prices. A proper theory will explain how much quantities change and how much prices change.

The older macroeconomics had a means of explaining the total incomes of the four social classes—workers, farmers, landlords, and capitalists. This theory, however, turned out to be unsatisfactory for the following reason. Suppose that there are two industries and two crops. Each industry has part of the workers and part of the capitalists; each crop has part of the farmers and part of the landlords. There may be, in principle, different prices for all four kinds of finished goods, and different incomes for members of any class in different industries (or producing different crops). The older macroeconomics had no good way of considering this problem. The *microeconomists*, who were concerned with the behavior of individual consumers, individual businesses, and individual industries made mincemeat of the macroeconomic arguments about price changes.

Modern macroeconomics has very much the same kind of difficulty. Macroeconomists can solve certain problems with efficiency and even elegance, but they have considerable difficulty with problems involving price. The theories in Chapters 3–8 may be thought of in two ways:

(1) They may be thought of as applying only to money values (prices *times* quantities); in this case they work out very nicely, but they do not give any results about price levels and quantity levels.

(2) They may be thought of as applying only to quantities (literally quantity indexes, which measure aggregations of quantities). In this case, it is necessary

to add to a "purely macroeconomic" theory a series of assumptions about price behavior. (This second part is usually based on microeconomic analysis.) When a "price part" is thus grafted onto a macroeconomic theory, the resulting theory is usually clumsy.

In one respect, the discussion in Chapters 3–8 involves the author in a particular piece of sleight-of-hand which is necessary, but not altogether nice. Most macroeconomists tend to start off from position (b). That is, they think of their theories as relating to quantities, and at some point supplement the "quantity part" with a "price part." The author, in contrast, thinks of his theories as relating to money values.

From a practical point of view, there is only one consequence. Most macroeconomists would include in Chapter 1 (on social accounting) a discussion of price and quantity indexes. They would then *specify* that the theories which follow relate to "real" national income, "real" consumption, and so on. (The word "real" means that changes in the variable in question are taken to be only changes in quantity, and price changes are specifically excluded.)[11] Then they would proceed to construct exactly the same sorts of theories as those presented by the author. The only difference would be in the economic interpretation of the symbols used.

The author (in private life) takes the variables in the theories to be money values rather than indexes of real quantities. He has tried to say nothing in Chapters 3–8 which is inconsistent with the other interpretation. In Chapter 10, he enters into his discussion of prices. Chapters 9 and 10 discuss the ways in which macroeconomists can graft a price theory onto a purely macroeconomic theory. In this portion of the discussion, he is again following the usual procedures.

Readers will find the author's reservations about the treatment of prices in modern macroeconomics in Chapters 9 and 10. These reservations are simple: (a) It is very difficult to set up theories in which the prices of different goods change in different ways, if one adheres to the general methods of macroeconomics; (b) if one persists, and does set up such a theory, that theory is very difficult to use. On the principle that a good theory is in some sense a simple theory, the author feels that macroeconomics has yet to develop a good way to take price changes into account.

Chapter 10 represents a suggestion as to how macroeconomics will get around this difficulty. Chapter 10 sets forth a theory which accounts for both price and quantity changes. This particular theory is based entirely on microeconomic methods—in particular it approaches macroeconomics from the point of view of the linear programming theory of the individual firm. Linear

---

[11] This procedure would cause trouble in Theory 7, where bond prices are shown to be related to interest rates, and where bond prices are allowed to vary. Later on, in Chapter 8 the same trouble would arise.

programming methods are not usually used in macroeconomics, but there is no reason why they should not be. If they can be adapted to this purpose as Chapter 10 suggests, they should provide a macroeconomic price theory which is an integral part of the system. The price theory of Chapter 10 is as natural a part of the system as the theory of "real" quantities.

But even if readers (or their teachers) disagree with the author's views on the relation between macroeconomics, as now discussed in the literature, and price theory, they should have no difficulty using his macroeconomic theories. With the one exception noted above, the reasoning in all the theories of Chapters 3–8 can be taken to apply either to "money variables" (values) or "real variables" (quantity indexes).

STATIC EQUILIBRIUM AND COMPARATIVE STATICS

If a theory is a one-to-one mapping of sets of factors $F = (F_1 \cdots F_m)$ into sets of variables $V = (V_1 \cdots V_n)$, then if F is known, V is also exactly known, and vice versa. This means that so long as F is unchanged, V will also be unchanged. Given a particular F, say $\bar{F}$, its image $\bar{V}$, under the mapping $\bar{V} = \bar{F}T$, is a *static equilibrium*. If $\bar{F}$ describes the environment, and T describes the reaction of economic groups to their environment, then $\bar{V}$ will describe the results of the economic processes.

Likewise, if there is a change in the set of factors, from F_1 to F_2, then the set of variables will change from $V_1 = F_1 T$ to $V_2 = F_2 T$. If (and only if) T is a linear mapping, changes in F (denoted by ΔF) will be related to changes in V (denoted by ΔV) by the mapping $\Delta V = \Delta F T$. That is, the relation T between ΔV and ΔF is exactly the same as that between V and F if, and only if, T is a linear mapping.

Comparative statistics is concerned with the relation between the set of factor changes ΔF and the set of variable changes ΔV. There are many theories in which comparative statics analysis is difficult. In the theories presented in this book, however, it is possible to determine the effect which a change in any factor has upon every variable. Indeed, a part of the technical discussion explains precisely how these effects are determined.

The analysis of a theory is not exhausted by a determination of the static equilibrium of the theory (the factor-into-variable mapping). Nor is it exhausted by the comparative statics analysis (the mapping of factor changes into variable changes). A complete analysis would also require a *dynamic analysis*.

A dynamic theory is a theory in which some or all of the variables vary in a prescribed way over time. For example, in many theories, *investment* is defined as a *change* in the plant and equipment in an economy over a period of time. The theory requires that if plant at time t is valued at K_t, and investment taking place between time t and time $(t + t')$ is I_t, then there will be plant $K_{t+t'} = K_t + I_t$ at time $(t + t')$. In order that this relation be valid, then, there is a particular pattern, say

$$K_t, K_{t+t'}, K_{t+2t'}, \ldots, K_{t+nt'}, \ldots$$

which will be observed in the amount of plant in the economy, given that investment follows the pattern

$$I_t, I_{t+t'}, I_{t+2t'}, \ldots, I_{t+nt'}, \ldots$$

over a period of time. In such a theory, equilibrium is thought of in terms of a "history" of the variables, beginning at time t, in response to some arbitrary "history" of the factors, beginning at time t.

Thus, in a dynamic theory, a "solution" takes the following form: the factors are a set $(F_1 \cdots F_m)$, but the individual factors are not numbers (as in static equilibrium). Rather, each factor is a function of time. Likewise the variables are a set $(V_1 \cdots V_n)$ of functions of time, and not a set of numbers.

Dynamic analysis is more difficult than statics and comparative statics. For this reason, it is much less thoroughly understood by economists. For the same reason, it is only briefly discussed in an appendix to Chapter 7. A number of theories with dynamic elements are presented, but these elements are not analyzed in depth.[12] Thus, readers will not have become totally learned by the time they have finished this book.

Readers will, however, have learned how to derive all the implications of a linear static theory. In practice, static theories are used by macroeconomists simply because dynamic theories are not generally understood. They should have a clear notion of the scope and limitations of an individual theory, and they will have seen how to enlarge a theory so as to make it more interesting and useful. These are the principal operations which theorists must perform.

EMPIRICAL CONFIRMATION

In this book, repeated reference will be made to a quarrel among macroeconomists. This quarrel goes back to the days when income and monetary analysis were quite distinct. Stated in a greatly oversimplified way, the participants tend to the following views:

(1) The national income buffs assert that changes in spending from current income are the decisive forces producing change in macroeconomic conditions.

---

[12] Jan Tinbergen and H. C. Bos, *Mathematical Models of Economic Growth* (New York: McGraw-Hill, Inc., 1962) is a collection of dynamic theories.

Money and other forms of wealth mirror conditions in the national income accounts. Therefore, manipulation of the wealth part of the economy will have no great effect upon the production of goods and services, which is the focal point of economic life.

(2) The money buffs assert that changes in wealth, and particularly money are the decisive forces in producing changes in macroeconomic conditions. The current production of goods and services mirrors attempts that holders of various forms of wealth have made to achieve their desires. Therefore, manipulation of the income part of the economy will have no great effect on the economy, since income is derived from attempts to alter the level and composition of wealth.

It is possible to state these two positions at much great length, and with a great deal more precision and passion than has been done here. Each position has eminent advocates in the economics profession. It is impossible to discuss macroeconomic questions without reference to a series of issues raised by the disputants.

It will be shown in later chapters that the issue in this quarrel depends largely on a small number of questions. One such question is the following: Do consumers decide how much to spend on consumer goods by looking at their current earnings, or do they decide by looking at the current balance in their bank accounts? Several issues of this sort are central to the dispute.

Everybody knows that there is no point in quarreling about matters of fact. Why don't the disputants simply find out what the facts are?

The answer to this question is easy. Both groups have tried to ascertain the facts, but the results are not yet conclusive. There is evidence to support all the contestants. Because economists cannot ordinarily make controlled laboratory experiments, they are limited to interpreting the historical record. Economists have had to devise statistical methods of great subtlety to approach the question of verification of theories, methods that have to be much more elaborate than those used in the formative periods of the physical sciences. These methods go back only to about 1950. It is now clear that economic statistical work done before that time cannot be trusted; and work done since has not been sufficient to settle the argument.

For this reason, this book takes the neutral, "We don't know," position. This position seems the only possible one for a non-combatant. Both sides can construct tenable theories, and in time we may find out which is right. Meanwhile, the reader can easily find out the issues involved. They are interesting ones.

Readers can now interpret the opening paragraph of this introduction. However, it would be more to the point for them to proceed to the first chapter, where real work begins. Chapters 1 and 2 are the usual dirty work which precedes the interesting part of any subject. Chapter 1 states why the social accounting system of macroeconomics is a coherent and closed set of data. Chapter 2 gives in some detail the logical and mathematical foundations for linear macroeconomic theories, and economics proper begins in Chapter 3. In some ways, the problems are more instructive than the text. The reader can start to use macroeconomic theory for constructive purposes when he is able to work problems such as these. He becomes a macroeconomist when he can propose problems himself.

Appendix to Introduction

FACTORS ARE EXOGENOUS VARIABLES AND PARAMETERS

Readers who have not heard of *endogenous* and *exogenous* variables are implored *not* to read this appendix, which will only confuse them. Readers who have heard the terms are implored to read it. They may have decided that (1) the word *variable* in this book may be associated with the word *endogenous variable* in other literature; and (2) the word *factor* may be associated with *exogenous variable*. The first conclusion would be permissible; the second would not be.

The usual terminology deals with a theory consisting of a vector **X** of endogenous variables; a vector **Y** of exogenous variables; and a mapping **H** of **Y** onto **X**. In this book we consider mappings which involve a vector **P** of parameters. The so-called *structural form* (which is here termed *behavioral*, a common alternative terminology) therefore is a mapping $\mathbf{X} = \mathbf{G}(\mathbf{X}, \mathbf{Y}, \mathbf{P})$. The so-called *reduced form* is an associated mapping $\mathbf{X} = \mathbf{H}(\mathbf{Y}, \mathbf{P})$. In nonlinear theories, one assumes the mapping **G** to be smooth, differentiable, and so on. Since **X** is a vector of functions (0-forms), one constructs the vector **dX** of 1-forms:

$$\mathbf{dX} = \mathbf{dXJ}_1 + \mathbf{dYJ}_2 + \mathbf{dPJ}_3$$

where the $\mathbf{J}_i$ are (Jacobian) matrices of partial derivatives. Then, denoting the unit matrix by **E**, we have

$$\mathbf{dX}(\mathbf{E} - \mathbf{J}_1) = \mathbf{dYJ}_2 + \mathbf{dPJ}_3$$
$$\mathbf{dX} = (\mathbf{dYJ}_2 + \mathbf{dPJ}_3)(\mathbf{E} - \mathbf{J}_1)^{-1}$$

and obtain the mapping **H** by integration.

In this book, the vector $(\mathbf{Y}, \mathbf{P})$ is called the *factor vector*. Theories are simplified in the following respects: The Jacobian $\mathbf{J}_1$ consists of constants, and the Jacobians $\mathbf{J}_2$ and $\mathbf{J}_3$ are unit matrices. Thus the behavioral form of the theory is written $\mathbf{X}(\mathbf{E} - \mathbf{G}) = (\mathbf{Y}, \mathbf{P})$. This is termed the *variable-into-factor mapping*. Since $(\mathbf{E} - \mathbf{G})$ is nonsingular, there exists a unique factor-into-variable mapping: $\mathbf{X} = (\mathbf{Y}, \mathbf{P})(\mathbf{E} - \mathbf{G})^{-1}$. If these theories were nonlinear, one would consider, for purposes of comparative statics, the locally linear mappings $\mathbf{dX}(\mathbf{E} - \mathbf{J}_1) = (\mathbf{dY}, \mathbf{dP})$ and its inverse $\mathbf{dX} = (\mathbf{dY}, \mathbf{dP})(\mathbf{E} - \mathbf{J}_1)^{-1}$.

The mapping $(\mathbf{E} - \mathbf{J}_1)$ may certainly be taken to be nonsingular, since the behavioral statements and accounting identities of the theory are independent of each other. But the reduction of $\mathbf{J}_2$ and $\mathbf{J}_3$ to unit matrices in this book does conceal something of economic interest. Suppose they were not unit matrices. Then a linear theory $\mathbf{X}(\mathbf{E} - \mathbf{G}) = (\mathbf{Y}, \mathbf{P})\mathbf{J}'$ would have a factor-into-variable mapping $\mathbf{X} = (\mathbf{Y}, \mathbf{P})\mathbf{J}'(\mathbf{E} - \mathbf{G})^{-1}$. There is no reason why the rank of $\mathbf{J}'$ should equal the rank of $(\mathbf{E} - \mathbf{G})$. There is no reason why the domain of $\mathbf{J}'(\mathbf{E} - \mathbf{G})^{-1}$ should have the same dimensionality as its range. Consequently this last mapping need not be one-to-one. This generalization would considerably alter the discussion of this book. In particular, it would require mathematical analysis going beyond finite mathematics into linear algebra.

However, it turns out that most of macroeconomics can be presented without using more difficult mathematics. (For an exception, see the discussion of Theory 9.) Indeed, it seems to be the case that the only reason for having $\mathbf{J}_2$ and $\mathbf{J}_3$ differ from unit matrices is to deal explicitly with microeconomic considerations. This book in general seeks to avoid the connection between macroeconomics and microeconomics, since this connection is in general difficult to make in any reasonably elementary way.

The introduction of parameters into the factor vector has been dictated by macroeconomic considerations. The parameter factors are, formally speaking, the "constant terms" in behavioral equations. As an example, one may cite the parameter F_C in the consumption function $C = aY + F_C$. These parameters are directly interpretable in terms of macroeconomic behavior. There are indeed cases (see again Theory 9) where such parametrization turns out to produce difficulties. Such cases seem to involve rather subtle points and to be unsuitable for discussions as simple as this one.

The essential reason for distinguishing between exogenous variables and parameters—and hence for the use of the term *factor*—is that exogenous variables are (in principle) observable, while parameters are not. Consider the consumption function of Theory 1: $C = aY + vL + F_C$, where Y is income, and L the quantity of money. Both L and F_C are factors in the system. However, the former is observable and the latter is not. One may make statistical inferences about the behavior of F_C over a period of time. Such an inference might be, "Over the period under consideration, F_C behaved like a series of observations of a normal random variable with mean m and variance v." As a result of statistical analysis, one might construct a series estimating F_C. This series would be the residuals of C about a regression function. Such a means of estimating F_C is, of course, fundamentally different from the procedure one uses in estimating the quantity of money at any given period.

In a closed theory of general macroeconomic equilibrium, all the factors would be parameters. Exogenous variables appear as parameters because a theory is not a closed system.

1

Social Accounts and Theoretical Definitions

This book deals with two subjects, income and wealth, and it explains the connection between them. The income and wealth discussed are those of a country as a whole. A country is an abstraction, and its income and wealth are abstractions. But a country is also a collection of people, to whom income and wealth may be quite tangible. We shall start by considering one part, a person, and move from him to the whole.

It is not obvious that there is a connection between the amount of the income and the amount of the wealth of any individual. If I have inherited $10,000,000 in cash and 10,000 acres of land, I might be considered wealthy. But if I sew my cash into my mattress, leave my land idle, and spend my days watching land and mattress, I may have no income at all. On the other hand, suppose I earn $1,000,000 a year at my job. If I spend all this income at racetracks and nightclubs, I may own nothing but the shirt on my back. Both of these forms of behavior might be foolish or unconventional, but both are quite possible. However, the larger a person's income is, the larger I would expect his wealth to be; and the greater his wealth, the larger I would expect his income to be. This statement asserts that out of a variety of possible ways of acting, people, on the average, choose one particular form of behavior. The logical connection (if any) between income and wealth, however, is not made clear simply by observing what most people do. It requires a special examination to make this connection clear.

The income and wealth of nations exhibit characteristics similar to those of individual people. The natural wealth of countries like Brazil and India exceeds that of countries like Japan and Britain, but is undeveloped. Consequently the income of the first pair is low and that of the second pair is high. But generally we expect wealthy countries (like the United States) to have high incomes and poor countries (like Portugal or Greece) to have low incomes.

Neither the income nor the wealth of a particular country stays the same, and the relative situations of countries change greatly over a period of time. Constantinople (now Istanbul) was the wealthiest city west of India in the Middle Ages. The Spaniards who conquered Mexico City found it wealthier than Rome or Constantinople. Marco Polo wondered at the wealth of China, and Vasco de Gama at the wealth of India. Yet Turkey, Mexico, China, and India are now poor countries—they are quite probably poorer than they were five hundred years ago.

Consequently, it is a natural question to ask why the wealth or the income of a country may change. Both of these would be measures of a country's well-being, if we knew what they were. To answer a question such as that just proposed, we go through three steps: (a) we define what we are talking about; (b) propose an answer; (c) see whether the answer is the right one. In this chapter, we shall define what we are talking about. The other chapters of this book propose answers to the question "Why do a country's income and wealth change?" By placing both income and wealth in a single question, we imply that the two "belong together" in some way as yet unspecified.

In scientific endeavor, part of the task is to learn what questions can be usefully answered. The general question in the preceding paragraph, "Why do a country's income and wealth change?", is too vague to be of much use. In any theory, one proposes smaller, sharper, more specific questions. Thus the theories in this book propose questions like, "What will happen to consumer spending if the quantity of money in the economy changes?" or "What will happen to the amount of government tax revenue if business investment changes?" The questions asked are answered within the framework of a theory. If the conditions assumed do not hold, the answer is not valid. Theorists are able to give several possible answers to a question, because they are able to construct several possible patterns of economic behavior.

Readers may wonder why one should advance several answers to a question—presumably only one of these is the right answer. But there is usually no single, right answer to this kind of question—only varying degrees of error. Economists, therefore, are usually in the position of trying to improve on an answer which has some good points and some bad points. Proposing answers, then, is a necessary and recognized part of economics. It is called theorizing, and a theory is a proposed answer to some question. It requires special training to be able even to propose an answer. It requires special training of a different sort to decide whether a proposal is acceptable. This is a "how-to-do-it" book. It tells you how to propose a serious answer to a serious question.

This book divides the community into four kinds of economic units: households, businesses (other than banks), banks, and government. It considers all units of any kind together, in a lump. This chapter tells how to "lump" economic units together. In order to explain this procedure, it first explains the things which must be combined.

The activities of an economic unit are described by the records it keeps. For present purposes, these records are called *accounts*. There are two basic sets of accounts. The first, called *balance sheet*, describes what the economic unit had at some moment, and how it got it. The second, called the *income statement*, describes what the business did in some period of time.

While businesses usually keep reasonably complete records, households do not. Nevertheless, it is convenient to talk as if all economic units kept good records. On this basis, the total wealth and the total income of a community consist of the sum of the wealth and of the income of all the economic units in the community. The process of adding up individual sets of accounts gives a set of *social accounts*. Some countries have reasonably complete and accurate statistics for many of their social accounts, and others do not. But it is convenient to talk about social accounts as if all the data required could actually be collected. If they could be, then proposed explanations of changes in income and wealth could be tested.

The explanations advanced here will be kept as simple as possible. That is, they will omit certain details on the grounds that they are unimportant. Sceptical readers—all readers should be sceptical—will ask themselves whether the omissions are really unimportant. To make this decision, they must determine whether the detail in question matters for the purpose at hand.

Let us consider an example. Mr. A buys a house from Mr. B for $20,000. A simple way of describing this transaction would be: Before the transaction Mr. A had $20,000 in cash, and Mr. B had a house. After the transaction Mr. B had $20,000, and Mr. A had a house. Actually, this description may omit a number of complicating details, because:

(1) Mr. B paid a commission to a real-estate agent for finding a buyer;

(2) Mr. A paid a lawyer to examine the title—if Mr. B did not have legal title to the house, he could not deliver it to Mr. A;

(3) If Mr. B sold the house for more than he paid for it, he may become liable to a capital gains tax to the Federal Government and perhaps a second tax to his state government;

(4) The bill of sale allocated property taxes currently due on the house between Mr. A and Mr. B;

(5) Mr. A registered his title to the house with an appropriate local government agency, so that his claim to ownership will be recognized; he paid a fee for this registration.

Do these various miscellaneous operations, undertaken in the course of transaction, matter enough to be itemized? The answer is, "That depends." For Mr. A and Mr. B they matter, because the various lawyers, real-estate agents, and tax officials will insist on being paid. If Mr. B has borrowed money (got a mortgage) on his house, he will have to show the lender that he has acquired the house with the money he borrowed; if Mr. A had borrowed money (got a mortgage) when he originally bought the house, he will have to pay off his debt from the proceeds of the sale. In analyzing the operations of the market for real estate, one would have to take into account all the various business and government interests which take part in the operation. But even so, if the side-payments made are relatively small compared to the basic $20,000, and if they do not have much effect on either Mr. A's or Mr. B's decisions about the transaction, we can retain the simple description given above: the sale of a standing house basically involves the transfer of $20,000 in cash from buyer to seller, and of a house from seller to buyer. The side-payments are "mere complications," even though they may be an important aspect of daily life to real-estate firms, lawyers, and tax-collecting agencies.

This example also brings out the difference between business accounting and social accounting. Mr. A gave up cash and received a house. Mr. B gave up a house and received cash. One event is described by four bookkeeping entries. Two of these are in Mr. A's books, and two are in Mr. B's books. Business or "double-entry" accounting takes into consideration the fact that there was an exchange of money for a house. Social accounting recognizes that more than one set of accounts is involved in any transaction, and social accounting may be thought of as "quadruple-entry" accounting. Business accountants will not be worried by the fact that both Mr. A and Mr. B have a record of the sale of the house. Social accountants must consider this fact. Suppose they forget it and then try to count how many houses changed hands during the year. Then they will count the house once when they look at Mr. A's records and a second time when they look at Mr. B's records. Thus social accounting involves problems which do not concern business accountants; but social accountants start from the same set of records as business accountants.

The next step is to describe the accounting data on which our later discussion rests. There follow short descriptions of balance sheets, income statements, the relation between balance sheets and income statements, and the "addition" process which combines the accounts of individual economic units into social accounts.

BALANCE SHEETS

The balance sheet of an economic unit lists the values of things owned by the unit and the way in which funds were acquired to buy these things. While any economic unit may be considered as having a balance sheet, it is simplest to discuss the balance sheets of businesses in detail, making some comparisons with other balance sheets as needed.

Things owned by a business are called *assets*, and the list of assets and their valuations makes up the *asset side* of the balance sheet. (A complete discussion of how values are placed on these assets is beyond the scope of this book.) Particular attention, however, will be paid to the following assets:

(1) *Cash* consists mainly of checking accounts in banks. Smaller amounts consist of paper money and coin.

(2) *Accounts receivable* are sums owed to the business by its customers.

(3) *Securities* consist of stocks and bonds issued by *other* economic units. (The securities issued by an economic unit are discused below.) These represent claims which the business has on other businesses (and government), and they are a source of income to the business.

(4) *Inventories* consist of raw materials, and partly finished and finished goods which are owned by the business.

(5) *Plant and equipment* consists of land, buildings, and machinery owned by the business.

Naturally, the composition of the assets of different kinds of economic units varies. Electric generating companies' assets consist mainly of plant. Financial institutions such as banks have almost no assets other than cash and securities. (To be exact, "loans" made directly to individual customers, securities bought in the mortgage and the corporate and government bond markets, and cash are the main assets.) For families, inventories are small, and houses make up most of the item corresponding to "plant and equipment." For companies in retail trade, accounts receivable are a large item, because consumer credit is an important aspect of doing business with the public. Some of these differences will be important considerations in our later work. For the moment, it is enough to note that they exist.

The balance sheet contains a second list, called the *liabilities side*, which divides assets according to the ways in which their purchase was financed: they were purchased either on credit, from contributions made by the owners of the business, or from profits of the business. These three categories cover all logical possibilities, so that the total of the liabilities side necessarily equals the total assets.

The fact that total assets equal total liabilities does not mean, of course, that one can necessarily identify how the purchase of individual assets of a business was financed. In some cases such association is possible. Suppose that the business (or family) bought land and buildings and obtained a *mortgage* loan to pay for them. Then the lender has a claim on that particular group of assets. Ordinarily, however, there is no such direct association between particular assets and particular items on the liabilities side of the balance sheet.

The debt of a business consists of *accounts payable*, which may be thought of as charge accounts owed by the business; of *loans* by banks and other financial institutions, made usually for periods of less than two years; and of *bonds*. Bonds are certificates ordinarily representing long-term debts (10 to 30 years). The company issuing the bonds guarantees repayment and interest to any legal owner. Consequently, bonds may be bought and sold and the composition of the creditors owning the bonds may change. (The creditor who makes a loan cannot sell the "IOU" to anyone else in any simple way.)[1]

The contribution of owners to the business is called *capital stock* and certificates are issued by the business to owners in proportion to their contribution. This capital stock is not a debt of the business. The owners of stock are not guaranteed any fixed return, but they have a claim on the earnings of the business.

Finally, if profits of the business are kept in the business, an *earned surplus* account appears on the liabilities side of the balance sheet.

Stocks and bonds, while they are both securities, are quite different from each other from a legal point of view. The income which owners of stock receive is called *dividends*, and it is different from the *interest* earned by bondholders. It usually varies with the profits earned by the business, while interest payments are fixed. There is more opportunity for gain, and also more risk of loss to stockholders.

In the interests of simplification, in this book we shall usually treat all securities as if they were bonds. This practice is followed in part to hold down the number of things which must be kept track of—and thereby to simplify the work. This combining of stocks and bonds under the heading "bonds" is also justified by the fact that securities are looked at mainly from the point of view of investors seeking a return in the form of income. Some investors buy stocks in order to obtain a share in the management of the business, which is one of the rights of stockholders. But in large corporations, most stockholders have no aspirations to a share in management, and are concerned only with a return on an investment. In this respect, they are not unlike bondholders.

Thus, the liabilities side of a balance sheet is composed of

(1) Accounts payable

---

[1] Most people think of bonds in terms of the savings bonds issued by the U.S. Government. These may not be bought and sold. However, they may be redeemed at fixed prices, whereas the price of "marketable" bonds varies from day to day with market conditions.

(2) Direct borrowings (loans)
(3) Securities issued
  (a) Bonds
  (b) Stocks
(4) Earned surplus

The relative importance of these accounts varies with different kinds of economic units. Electric power companies' liabilities accounts consist mainly of bonds, while stocks and earned surplus make up most of the liabilities side of other non-bank businesses. The deposits made by customers make up almost all of the liabilities side of bank balance sheets—because the bank owes these sums to its depositors and agrees to repay them at once (in the case of checking accounts) or in a month or two (in the case of savings accounts) if the depositors wish.

Nobody "owns" a family but its members, so that here the item "stocks" has no exact meaning. Also, families do not make profit, so that "earned surplus" has no exact meaning. But the term *net worth* is sometimes used to represent the difference between what a family owns and its debts. (This same term, net worth, also is used to denote the sum of capital stock and earned surplus in business accounts.)

It is common practice to designate balance sheets by what is called a T-diagram. For example, the T-diagram which has been described above would have the following format:

Assets	Liabilities
Cash	Accounts payable
Accounts receivable	Loans due
Securities	Bonds
Inventories	Stocks
Plant and equipment	Earned surplus

The balance sheets of firms and the balance sheets used in theories have numbers entered in the individual accounts. In formulating particular theories it will turn out to be useful to suppress even this amount of detail. In the next chapter, for instance, the following very simple balance sheet will appear:

Cash, M	Net worth, W
Plant and equipment, K	

Here most of the accounts have been suppressed, because a *very* simple theory is discussed. The symbols M, K, and W stand for variables. The purpose of the theory is to find out what numerical value each variable will have under certain conditions.

INCOME STATEMENTS

Income is received as a payment for goods produced or services rendered. Not all money received represents income. If I borrow from a bank, I receive money, but I do not receive income. If I sell an asset, such as a house or a car, I am also paid money, but this money is not income. Moreover, not all income is in the form of money. Thus farm labor (and college students) sometimes get paid room and board for their labor; businesses sell on credit and have income in the form of "accounts receivable," and so on.

To know whether an item represents income, we must have a definition of the activity of the economic unit in question. A builder who sells a house he has built receives income. If a family sells its house, it sells an asset and does not receive income. A statement of this sort depends on a way of recognizing house-builders and distinguishing between them and others. The example just given is fairly clear; other examples might be harder to sort out.

The *income statement* records the income of an economic unit and the uses to which it is put. We shall discuss the income statements of businesses in detail and then make some brief comparisons of such statements with the income statements of households.

The income statement accounts completely for the income received. Thus, by definition, for a business income equals cost plus profit. The total calculation runs as follows:

- *Income* equals the sum of
  - *Cost*, consisting of
    - variable cost
      - materials, supplies, and so on
      - labor
    - fixed cost
      - depreciation
      - rent
      - interest
      - taxes (other than profits taxes)
  - *Profit*, divided into
    - taxes on profit
    - dividends paid to stockholders
    - retained profits

The terms *variable cost* and *fixed cost* are based on the following principle: some costs depend on the level of a firm's output, while others do not. A firm can vary its labor costs by hiring workers or laying off workers; it can vary its materials costs by buying larger or smaller amounts from suppliers. But other costs do not vary with output. The interest payments of a business, for instance, depend on its borrowings, not on its output. Interest payments will be altered if the firm is able to borrow or to repay its debts, and if interest rates change. Thus the term "fixed" is defined only with reference to changes in output.

To some extent, the measurement of any of these quantities is artificial. A large firm buying from many suppliers and having large inventories of materials on hand may find it hard to tell exactly how much of its purchases was actually used in manufacturing finished goods and how much was put into storage.

Depreciation is the largest single element of uncertainty in the income statement. Depreciation measures the wearing out of plant and equipment owned by the firm. This wearing out is a cost to the business. If depreciation is not counted as a cost in the accounts, then the business will estimate its profits as being higher than if depreciation is considered. If these higher profits are then paid out as taxes or dividends, then when the plant and equipment are no longer usable, the business will have to raise outside funds to replace them (it may in fact be unable to do so because this practice is considered a sign of very bad management). Depreciation is an imputation: the business does not pay this cost to anyone. Instead, it charges a special account, which is akin to retained earnings in generating funds from inside the business. Accountants call the sum of profits and depreciation the *cash flow*, since both can be a source of funds which can be used to pay for expansion of the business.

In the discussion of balance sheets it was stated that for many investors interest and dividends were similar in principle, differing only in detail. From the point of view of management, dividends and interest both represent payments of income to outsiders; hence both reduce the amount of money which the firm can retain to help finance its growth. In this sense, "cash flow" terminology corresponds to the economic point of view used in the present discussion.

The income statement of households is different from that of businesses in several respects. "Costs" of a family represent its current spending on goods and services. The family has no owner, and therefore there are no "dividends," all "profit" being retained. But profit is simply that part of income which is not part of "cost." Thus if "cost," for a family, is associated with current spending, "profit" must be associated with savings.

The statement in the preceding paragraph is an attempt at reconciling business and family accounting methods. It is important to remember that this reconciliation can never be perfect because families, after all, are unlike businesses. Nevertheless, to the extent that there is some similarity between the two kinds of accounts, it is natural to emphasize it. This similarity encourages us to treat income of families and of businesses in a similar spirit, and it gives us a framework within which we can speak of a basic similarity of things which superficially are rather different.

THE RELATION BETWEEN BALANCE SHEETS AND INCOME STATEMENTS

So far, balance sheets and income statements have been treated as being quite distinct. Physically speaking, they are listed separately in the annual report of a business. However, there is a close relation between the two. This relation is described by saying that *changes in balance sheet accounts may be associated with elements in income statements.*

A very simple illustration of this principle is the case of depreciation. Depreciation is an item of cost. It measures the amount of wearing out of plant and equipment. If depreciation takes place, then the value of plant and equipment owned by the business decreases. So if a business does not buy any new plant, the *change* in the value of its plant during the course of a year should be the same as the cost item, depreciation.

Let us now consider a very condensed form of a balance sheet:

Assets	Liabilities
Cash (including accounts receivable)	Inside funds (earned surplus and accumulated depreciation)
Earning assets (all other assets)	Outside funds (debt plus capital stock)
Total	Total

This way of combining balance sheet accounts has the following rationale:

(1) Securities are owned by the firm because they yield a return. Plant, equipment, and inventory are all held because the business uses them to produce its output, and hence to make profits. In this sense they are different from cash and accounts receivables, which do not yield a return.

(2) Inside funds represent income earned and kept in the business. Outside funds are obtained by borrowing and from the owner's contribution to the business (capital stock).

This classification of the balance sheet also provides a tidy way of relating income accounts to changes in balance sheets.

(3) Saving consists of that part of a family's income which is not spent on goods and services. It consists of that part of a business's income which is not paid out to others in the form of costs, taxes, or dividends. That is, saving represents an increase in the net worth of an economic unit over some period of time. Net worth is thus the saving accumulated by the economic unit over the entire past. If net worth at the beginning of the year is W_0 and saving during the year is S, then net worth at the end of the year is $W_0 + S$.

(4) Investment consists of the purchase of income-earning assets by an economic unit during some period of time.

Saving may be used to pay off debt. If it is not so used, it may be kept in the form of increased cash balances, or it may be invested. Thus, for any individual some savings may be invested.

Investment may be paid for in a variety of ways. The economic unit may simply reduce its cash balance to pay for the investment, or it may borrow to pay for the investment, or it may pay for the investment out of savings.

No two concepts have caused macroeconomists more trouble than the concepts of saving and investment. This book refers only occasionally to saving. It is worth considering just why this is so, for it may annoy some readers. Saving is necessarily defined in a negative way:

1. Economic units save when they fail to spend part of their income.
2. Economic units save when they invest, providing that they fail to reduce their cash balances and also fail to increase their debts.

To measure saving, we proceed in one of two ways. We may define certain actions which we say constitute "spending one's income" and obtain saving by subtracting this spending from total income. Then we take the total increase in assets, subtract from it the increase in debts, and the remainder will be saving. For any individual, the two procedures yield the same results. But for the economy as a whole, the two methods use statistics which are generated in different ways, and there are important practical problems in reconciling the two methods of calculating.

In preparing theories such as those used in this book, we make suggestions as to how people behave. It is easier to say how people behave than how they fail to behave. Thus if economic behavior consists of buying consumer goods, buying plant, buying securities, holding cash and borrowing, we may have to assign a rule to people's behavior with regard to each activity. From these rules we may deduce a rule about their saving. It would be possible to assume rules about buying consumer goods, buying plant, buying securities, or holding cash and saving and from these deduce a rule about borrowing. But this alternative procedure seems to make for more difficult theories. As a matter of convenience the author finds it easier to leave saving as a variable which may (if the reader wishes) be derived from the rest of the system.

It is important for readers to remember that in a theory, concepts like investment, saving, and consumption are defined by the requirements of logic and consistency alone. When it comes to applying theories to the real world, economists must provide a clear reason for associating a theoretical term with some set of observable actions.

For example, consumption (in theory) consists of the purchase of goods and services. If a family buys a package of soft drinks and drinks them, it is consuming. If it stores them on the shelf, it is adding to inventory and hence investing. What if the family buys a refrigerator, a car, a house, or a suit of clothes? Our rule for deciding whether these purchases are consumption is: do they provide income? (If they provide income, they are earning assets and are hence investment.) But houses may be rented by their owners; many people need cars for business purposes; and even a suit of clothes may be bought to impress a customer. Consequently, in applying our rule, the social accountant will have to make great numbers of detailed decisions and guesses in order to provide information in a form which is relevant to the behavior rules proposed by a theory.

The detailed matching of accounting procedures to theoretical specifications is a subject in itself. It is treated in a superficial way in this book, which shows how to construct simple theories about income and wealth. The work of economists does not end when theories have been proposed, but it cannot properly be begun without such proposals.

The question of depreciation is one which usually causes trouble for beginners. Depreciation is a cost item in the income statement of a business. It is not, however, a cost paid to anyone outside the business. In this respect, it is an imputation. It is income which is not spent. It is, in this sense, saving and an addition to net worth.

But the depreciation account stands for the wearing out of plant in the production process. As the plant wears out, it is presumably worth less. Consequently, if the plant is valued each year, its valuation will fall each year. If the depreciation cost is correctly calculated, it will exactly equal the decline in the value of the plant. Therefore, the business may keep its books in one of two equivalent ways:

On a *gross* basis, the change in total assets due to investment is given by

Additions to plant = new plant purchased

which equals (if cash is held fixed)

Additions to the liabilities side of the balance sheet
= new borrowing *plus* depreciation charges

On a *net* basis, the change in total assets due to investment is given by

Additions to plant
= new plant purchased, *minus* wearing out of old plant (depreciation)

which equals (if cash is held fixed)

Additions to the liabilities side of the balance sheet
= new borrowings

Depreciation is an important practical source of funds for business. It represents income which is not paid out and (since most income is in cash) a large flow of cash into the business. On the other hand, it is not a very interesting item, because accounting practice is rather inflexible. Charges to depreciation accounts do not change much from year to year, and they do not add much of interest to the problems talked about later in this book. For this reason, most of the discussion will be on a "net basis." That is, the change in earning assets will be the same thing as investment, and the change in inside funds will be the same as retained profits, that is, saving.

The changes in balance sheets may involve quite a lot of bustle and noise, for the activities of certain kinds of business organizations are mainly concerned with these changes. When banks lend money, they change their assets and the debts of others. When individuals buy or sell in the stock market, they are changing the composition of their assets. When insurance companies invest the premiums they receive, their assets change. When families buy houses, their assets change. Certain kinds of businesses—banking, insurance companies, finance companies, and stockbrokers, for instance—are more involved in balance sheet transactions than in income transactions. These, taken collectively, form the "money market," sometimes also called the "capital market" or "financial markets." The operations of such companies are of very considerable interest, and dealing with them constitutes one important part of macroeconomics.

ADDING ECONOMIC UNITS TOGETHER

When social accounting records are compiled, the records of individual economic units must be *aggregated* so as to provide records pertaining to groups of economic units. In the extreme case, the aggregation pertains to entire economies. This *aggregation* must be performed in such a way as to maintain the natural connection between balance sheets and income statements that exists in the case of individual accounting records.

It is simplest to introduce the aggregation problem in terms of the relation between the family and its individual members. Imagine a family that has a member who is a college student. A part of the family income is used to pay for that education; some of the family debts may have been incurred to pay for tuition, dormitory fees, and so on. At regular intervals, tuition and dormitory bills must be paid. All of these transactions may be considered as being carried out by the family, and (if the family kept good records) would appear in its income statement and balance sheet accounts.

But the college education also enters into the financial dealings among the members of the family. The student may receive money from home. If he does, he may regard it as his own income, and he will spend it accordingly. (In fact, he may be the person who actually pays the tuition and dormitory fees.) The student may consider this sum to be a loan. In this case he spends the money, but he includes it in the statement of his debts. In still other cases, the money may represent sums he had earned the previous summer, which he had left with his parents, for safekeeping. In this case, the money the parents send him is a reduction in their debt to him. However the family may arrange its internal affairs, some things are "external" (somebody must pay the tuition fee) and some are "internal" (such as the terms on which the parents provide funds to the student). From the accounting point of view, so long as the family is considered as an economic unit, its internal arrangements do not matter in the preparation of income and balance sheet accounts. But the members of the family may also have dealings with each other, and these dealings may be quite important to the individuals involved. So each member of the family, in principle, might have his own income and balance sheet as well. Providing that we are quite clear about whether we are talking about the family or about its individual members, we should be able to relate the various transactions and accounts.

If the family is *disaggregated*, the balance sheets of the members of the family include debts owed by and owed to other members of the family; payments made to other members of the family are counted as expenditures; payments received from other members of the family are counted as income. If the family is aggregated into a single unit, the debts among its members disappear from the balance sheets, and payments among them are treated merely as *transfer payments* (as one may transfer money from one pocket to another without earning or spending income).

These general rules apply to the aggregation of economic units in general. But the application of these rules leads to results that are apt to be surprising at first sight. For this reason, it is necessary to consider them in a little more detail.

In *aggregating balance sheets*, the objectives are (1) to obtain a complete listing of the assets, debts, and net worth of the group, and (2) to eliminate, therefore, from this listing, obligations among members of the group. If these objectives are accomplished, the usual definitions of investment and savings can be applied to transactions of the group.

As an example of balance sheet aggregation, let us consider a hypothetical group consisting of Firm A, Firm B, and Bank C. These three units have the following balance sheets:

Firm A

Cash,	C_A	Debt,	L_A
Plant,	K_A	Net worth,	W_A

Firm B

Cash,	C_B	Debt,	L_B
Plant,	K_B	Net worth,	W_B

Bank C

Loans,	$L_B + L_O$	Deposits,	$C_A + C_O$

(Here L_O stands for loans to "others" and C_O the deposits of "others.") Thus firm A keeps its cash on deposit with Bank C and has borrowed from someone else; Firm B has borrowed from Bank C, but keeps its cash on deposit elsewhere.

If the three balance sheets are simply added up, the following balance sheet would hold:

Cash,	$C_A + C_B$	Debt,	$L_A + L_B$
Plant,	$K_A + K_B$	Deposits,	$C_A + C_O$
Loans,	$L_B + L_O$	Net worth,	$W_A + W_B + W_C$

However, Bank C owes Firm A the amount of Firm A's account with it; and Firm B owes Bank C the amount of its debt. Thus the two entries C_A and L_B appear on both sides of this balance sheet, which indicates that they must be thought of as internal accounts. To obtain the *consolidated* balance sheet of the group, it is necessary to eliminate these internal accounts. The balance sheet for the group is therefore

Consolidated Balance Sheet

Cash,	C_B	Debt,	L_A
Plant,	$K_A + K_B$	Deposits,	C_O
Loans,	L_O	Net worth,	$W_A + W_B + W_C$

If Bank C is considered as an isolated economic unit, an increase in its lending to Firm B would be an investment, since the loan bears interest. This interest would be income to Bank C. If the three economic units are considered as a group, however, an increase in lending to Firm B by Bank C would not be an investment of the group, since the total assets on the consolidated balance sheet are unaffected. An increase in L_O, loans to others, would still be an investment. Interest paid by Firm B to Bank C would be considered as merely a transfer within the group, and would not be a part of the consolidated income of the group.

This particular example was chosen because the group was a bit miscellaneous. Usually one thinks of forming groups of "similar" types of economic units. The rules used, however, are capable of general application.

The consequences of these rules are apt to startle readers who come across them for the first time. Let us suppose that the economy consists of households, businesses, and banks. The balance sheets of these three groups have already been consolidated, and have the following form:

Households

Cash,	C_H	Debt,	L_H
Houses,	K_H	Net worth,	W_H
Securities,	B_H		

Businesses

Cash,	C_B	Debt,	L_B
Plant,	K_B	Securities,	$B_H + B_B$
Securities,	B_B	Net worth,	W_B

Banks

Loans,	$L_H + L_B$	Deposits,	$C_H + C_B$
		Net worth,	W_F

Now, before making the consolidation, let us consider several features of these balance sheets:

(1) The business balance sheet has not been properly consolidated. Because it lists business holdings of securities as an asset and as a liability, one must conclude that improper accounting has taken place. This objection may be made, even if one recognizes that businesses do, in fact, hold stocks and bonds issued by other businesses.

(2) The business balance sheet lists both securities and net worth. Actually, corporate accounting would list the receipts from sales of capital stock as a net worth account. What is designated here as *net worth* is merely total retained profits (accumulated business savings).

These two questionable features of the balance sheets of the three sectors turn out not to matter. For when the three sectors are consolidated, the terms C_H, C_B, B_H, B_B, L_H, and L_B must all be eliminated from the balance sheet, since they appear on both sides of it. Thus the consolidated balance sheet for the economy is

Consolidated Balance Sheet

Houses,	K_H	Net worth,	$W_H + W_B + W_F$
Plant,	K_B		

Thus in a consolidated national balance sheet, securities, money, and debt are all viewed as things that the economy owes itself. To most people, an even more shocking proposition appears when government is taken into account. For if the national debt is a government liability, and if government bonds are among the assets of households, businesses, and banks, then these particular items all cancel out when a national, consolidated balance sheet is prepared.

On the other hand, if households or businesses or banks or government have either borrowed from foreigners, or made loans to foreigners, these borrowings and lendings appear on the national balance sheet.

Now examine the simplified consolidated national balance sheet given above. It has two kinds of assets: housing, which is among the earning assets of households, and plant, which is among the earning assets of business. Increases in either of these two assets therefore constitute investment for the economy as a whole.[2] Consequently we can associate *investment for an economy* with the construction of housing and of new plant. (In practice, theorists associate investment mainly with the construction of new plant, because they are interested in business investment decisions and their effect on the economy. It tends to confuse discussion if household decisions to build houses are mixed up with business decisions, for the two seem to involve different problems.)

On the other hand, the liabilities side of the consolidated balance sheet consists of the net worth (accumulated saving) of households, businesses, and banks. A change in net worth, of course, is called saving; (or current saving, if there is danger of confusion with accumulated saving). In this balance sheet, then, saving equals investment, and this is one of the important elementary equalities of national income analysis as well.

To make such a statement as this, and to construct a consolidated balance sheet such as that shown above is *not* to assert that securities are "of no consequence in the economy." Indeed, the central contention of monetary theory is that all forms of credit are of consequence to the economy. The consolidated balance sheet does not deny that individuals and businesses may invest by buying stocks and bonds—indeed the only way to prepare the consolidated balance sheet was to use balance sheets in which stocks and bonds *do* appear and "consolidate them out"

But in order to analyze the behavior of an economy (such as that of the United States), in which the securities markets do play a role, it is necessary to use a social accounting system that is sufficiently disaggregated for securities to appear in it. Thus if it were important to take these markets into account, in the problem under consideration, one would list separately the balance sheets of households, businesses and banks, so as to keep the variables in the problem in open view.

Historical Remark. Before the invention of national income analysis, monetary theory discussed investment in terms of securities markets. We shall see in Chapter 5 that there is a close connection between such markets and the monetary system. After the depression of 1929, however, monetary economists were mainly preoccupied with debt and monetary problems. National

---

[2] Additions to business inventory are properly a part of business investment. They are not listed in this balance sheet in order to simplify the text. Indeed, throughout this book, "investment" is taken to be, for practical purposes, the construction of new plant and equipment. Some monetary and business cycle theories (notably those of R. G. Hawtrey and of Wesley C. Mitchell) place particular emphasis on changes in investment in inventories. These theories, then, will not properly be discussed in this book.

income theory, which came into being at that time, formulated the problem of the great depression in a new way: Why was the production of plant and equipment so low that large numbers of people were unemployed? The early national income theorists tended to feel that securities were "only paper," and that "real" economic problems involved the production of goods and securities. In their view, investment should be considered only in terms of the rate of production of new plant and equipment. A generation of students was taught to *forget* the obvious fact that individual households and individual businesses frequently (if not usually) invest in securities to some extent at least. Since about 1950, an improved understanding of the relation between social balance sheets and social income statements has clarified the connection between securities markets and the production of new plant and equipment. There are still economists, however, who think of investments as being "only" securities, or as being "only" construction.

The aggregation problem in income accounting is called the *value added problem*. It exists because businesses (and households) buy from each other. Consequently, when groups of businesses are formed by aggregation, some of their sales must be treated as transfers within the group.

Consider the following example. Coal is used to make steel, and steel is used to make automobiles. The income accounts of coal producers list wages, taxes, interest, and profits as offsets to the income obtained from the sale of coal. The accounts of the steel producers list coal, wages, taxes interest, and profits as offsets to the income obtained from the sale of steel. The accounts of automobile producers list steel, wages, taxes, interest, and profits as offsets to the income obtained from the sale of automobiles. The combined payments of wages, taxes, interest, rent, and profits of these industries as a group should be the same as their total income (assuming away other raw materials, for convenience). But if the total sales of the three industries are simply added together, they will exceed the total uses to which these sales are put. This is because the sales of the coal mines figure as a cost to the steel industry, and the sales of the steel mills figure as a cost to the automobile industry.

The *value added* principle amounts to this: if A and B are two firms, with sales S_A and S_B, then the group consisting of these two firms has sales equal to

$$S_G = S_A + S_B - (S_{AB} + S_{BA})$$

where S_{AB} and S_{BA} represent, respectively, the sales by A to B, and the sales by B to A. If A and B are themselves aggregations of firms, the same formula can be applied.

Likewise, if one household purchases services from other households, these purchases constitute transfer payments (as S_{AB} and S_{BA} did) and do not appear in the aggregated income and expenditures of households.

This aggregation rule is necessary to the construction of social accounts. It has some curious consequences. If (for instance) banks are aggregated into the business sector (as they are in statistical practice of the United States), then interest payments by business to individuals are considered as income to individuals; interest payments by businesses to other businesses and to banks are considered as transfer payments. The economic theory of the firm does not distinguish among these various kinds of interest payments. Thus the data on interest payments in the national income accounts are not those which economists would use if they are interested in (for example) business responses to changes in interest rates.

These peculiarities of social accounting procedures are not grounds for criticism. If the accounts are carefully put together, the economist can "unscramble" them and put them together differently if the problem he is working on so requires. They do mean that economists must consider carefully the connection between the statistics, as ordinarily published, and the statistics that he needs in order to work on the problem of interest to him.

The national *income*, then, consists of income earned by all businesses, by households, and by government, providing that no particular item is counted more than once. Businesses receive income from other businesses, from households, and from government. That is, they receive a part of the total spending by other businesses, by households, and by government. As a whole, income is earned if and only if goods and services are produced, so that the national income and the national product are the same thing. The national product, of course, consists of goods and services consumed by households and government. It also includes goods and services purchased by business. These business purchases consist of acquisition of plant, equipment, and inventories by businesses. Since these purchases add to the earning assets of business, they constitute investment. Thus:

Y (the total national product)
equals C (consumption by households)
plus I (investment by businesses)
plus G (government spending)

Two Remarks

1. We disregard foreign trade in this book. Transactions with foreign countries represent a source of income and also a use of purchasing power. In analyzing countries which depend heavily on foreign trade—such as the European countries—this omission would be an important source of error.

2. The classifications given here are based on the needs of this book. As a matter of fact, in part of this book, we disregard government and pretend, therefore, that $Y = C + I$, with $G = 0$. It would be sensible for many purposes to break up the aggregates listed here. For instance, in the United

States, consumer spending on "nondurables" (food, clothing, gasoline, fuel, and rent) is relatively stable, while expenditures on "durables" (furniture, household appliances, and automobiles) is subject to fluctuations of a much greater amplitude and complexity. A detailed analysis of the economy might well require breaking C into parts.

Although the national product is equal to the combined income of households, business and government, it is difficult to compute the separate components in detail. Strictly speaking, the calculation to be made is:

Y	(the total national income)
equals Y_C	disposable personal income (household income after taxes)
plus Y_B	disposable business income (that is, retained business profits)
plus Y_G	tax revenue

Accountants are reluctant to treat retained business profits as "disposable business income," because this treatment would imply that dividends are a cost of production, which is not really so. But it is not right to include dividends both as business income and also as household income. And tax revenue such as sales taxes goes directly to government without ever passing through the income accounts of businesses.

Data on total household income is collected according to the legal form of that income (that is, wages, interest, rent, dividends, and so on). We know how much income households earn, and we know what total personal income taxes are, but we have no way of knowing how much of any given *kind* of personal income is paid out in taxes. The reason is that the federal income tax laws are based on total income from all sources and are not computed separately on each kind of income.

The usual national income statistics are calculated according to the rule:

Y	(total national income)
equals H	personal income *before* taxes[3]
plus B	business income (total profits *minus* dividends; or retained profits *plus* profits tax)
plus T	indirect business taxes (that is, tax revenue on sales and excise taxes)[4]

[3] This is the sum of wages, interest, rent, and dividends paid to households.

[4] Some economists maintain that these indirect business taxes do not represent a part of the value of output because government collects these taxes without having contributed to making goods and services. If indirect taxes are subtracted from the gross income and the gross product, a valuation "at factor cost" rather than "at market prices" is obtained.

Historical Remark. Economists in the eighteenth and early nineteenth centuries were much interested in the shares of the national income received by labor, landowners, and money-lenders. Entire theories of economics were developed on the assumption that certain types of service were "productive" and others were not. The eighteenth-century French "Physiocratic," and the nineteenth-century American "Single Tax" writers held that only land was productive. English economists from Adam Smith to Ricardo held that only labor was productive, and this view is still held by Marxists. These theories are too complicated and too imprecise to be discussed here. But it is easy to see that the classification of income into wages, rent, interest, and dividends would be the same as the determination of the income of "economic classes," providing that each household obtains all its income from a single source. Modern economics concentrates on the utilization of income $(C + I + G)$ rather than on the sources of income.

The first known attempt at computing the national income was made in England around 1600 by Gregory King. Not until the middle of the nineteenth century was the attempt repeated. During the 1920s and early 1930s a number of current estimates of national income were made for various countries. These estimates were considered at the time to be mere curiosities, albeit of interest to economic historians. In the late 1930s, however, it was realized that such information, if made available promptly, was of great usefulness to government and business in interpreting economic conditions. The change in attitude occurred because theories about shortrun changes in the national income were developed. Since 1946 the U.S. Department of Commerce has made quarterly estimates of the national income and product, and has made a steady effort to improve its reporting. This system of accounts owes its present state to the pioneering statistical work of the National Bureau of Economic Research and to the theoretical work of J. M. Keynes.

The portion of the analysis which deals with balance sheets derives from a much older branch of economics—monetary economics. Much of it goes back to the time of the Napoleonic Wars, when British wartime inflation and postwar recession brought about a major development of economic analysis. In the United States, the development of current banking statistics dates from the establishment of the Federal Reserve System in 1913. Analytical discussion of the banking system has thus been going on for a long time. The formal attempt to combine income statement and balance sheet analysis stems, in recent years, from empirical work by Morris Copeland, the initiator of the "moneyflows" system of accounts, and from the theoretical work on "financial intermediaries" by Gurley and Shaw.

The statistical work done so far is more complete in its calculations of changes in assets and liabilities than in its reporting of total levels of these accounts. There are great practical difficulties arising in the consolidation of balance sheets maintained on differing accounting principles by different businesses and by the absence of balance sheet data for households. Even in the banking system, where statistics are much more detailed and complete than in other sectors of the economy, it has only recently become possible to separate business and household bank balances.

One subject which has attracted considerable interest in recent years is the connection between changes in price and changes in quantity. The next four chapters explain in fairly simple ways the connection between incomes and balance sheets. The connection between price and quantity changes in either income or balance sheet accounts remains much more troublesome. Theories which separate these two effects are, in the main, much more difficult than the kind presented here.

One feature of any discipline seems to be, however, that problems turn out to be simpler than was originally thought. The theory presented here as Tiny Model 1 was the subject of very learned discussion in the 1930s. It did not reach the undergraduate program in any satisfactory form until the first edition of Samuelson's *Economics*, in 1946. It now appears very simple—in this book it is disposed of in a page or two.[5] But it continues to be a building block in more comprehensive theories.

Definitive books are those that deal with subjects which are dead because nothing further needs to be known about them. The subjects discussed here are very much alive. To put it differently, a lot remains to be learned. The theories presented here are partial theories. None claims to deal with the entire economy. But the careful reader can get exercise in putting together pieces of the economy. In time he will become able to do more realistic, and hence more difficult work.

---

[5] See also Paul A. Samuelson, *Economics*, 7th ed. (New York: McGraw-Hill, Inc., 1967).

2

Simple Theories

This chapter sets down ground-rules for formulating theories of a particularly simple and convenient sort. Beginners might wonder why theories in general are discussed, rather than particular theories to deal with particular problems. The reason is that all the theories presented in later chapters follow a single set of rules. Progress from one theory to a better one is easy, providing a satisfactory standard working procedure exists.

All the accounting systems in Chapter 1 generate numbers. Consumption, plant, cash balances, and so on, are all represented by numbers (or the sums of numbers) taken from business records. Consequently, from one point of view, theories about income and wealth are explanations of why the numbers in the social accounts are what they are. Since mathematics deals with numbers and sets of numbers, theories of income and wealth must necessarily deal with mathematical questions. But mathematics alone cannot tell us how to construct a theory of income or wealth. Such a theory must describe how people, businesses, and governments behave. Not all mathematical theories are suitable for economics, but only theories which represent (in abstract form, of course) some important aspect of people's behavior. Thus part of a theory must come from outside mathematics. This chapter tells how to use certain forms of mathematical thinking. Later chapters demonstrate that these forms are useful, by applying them to economic questions.

The theories presented here consist of:

(1) A set of *variables* which the theory is to explain (such as the national product, consumption, prices, the amount of plant and equipment in the economy, the level of employment).

(2) A set of *factors* which, taken collectively, determine the values of all of the variables in the system.

(3) A *relation* between variables and factors which can be shown to explain how the factors determine the values of all the variables in the system.

A FIRST EXAMPLE

Tiny Model 1

Our first example of a theory will be called Tiny Model 1. It is the simplest imaginable theory of the national income, and for this reason it is always taught to beginners. This theory assumes two things to be true:

(1) The national product accounts are as follows:

$$Y = C + I$$

where $Y =$ national product, $C =$ consumption, and $I =$ investment.

This statement is derived from the definition of the national product in Chapter 1, simplified by disregarding government spending.

(2) Consumer spending depends on income, in the following way:

$$C = aY + F_C$$

a and F_C are constants.

This statement says that whenever the national income (the national product) increases by \$1, consumption will increase by \$$a$. This conclusion is valid, because

$$C' = a(Y + 1) + F_C$$
$$C = aY + F_C$$

Subtracting gives the change in consumption ($C' - C$) resulting from the \$1 increase in income.

$$C' - C = a$$

The symbol a is called the "marginal propensity to consume" for historical reasons which need not concern us.

If people consume more when their incomes rise, $a > 0$. But they do not consume all of their income—they save some, also. Saving has been defined in Chapter 1 as an increase in net worth. The way people increase their net worth is by spending less than they earn. Thus saving is defined for the present purpose as

$$S = Y - C = Y - aY - F_C$$
$$= (1 - a)Y - F_C$$

If income rises by \$1, saving will change by \$(1 − a)

$$S' = (1 - a)(Y + 1) - F_C$$
$$S = (1 - a)\,Y \qquad - F_C$$
$$S' - S = (1 - a)$$

If people save more when their income rises, $(1 - a) > 0$. This will be our assumption. Therefore, a is greater than zero and less than one.

Tiny Model 1 says that if investment (I), the marginal propensity to consume (a), and autonomous[1] consumption (F_C) are given, consumption and the national product are uniquely determined. To show that this is indeed so, write

$$Y = C + I$$
$$C = a\,Y + F_C$$

Substitute the second equation in the first.

$$Y = aY + F_C + I$$
$$(1 - a)Y = F_C + I$$
$$Y = \frac{1}{1-a} F_C + \frac{1}{1-a} I$$

So Y is determined by a, F_C and I. Now substitute for Y in the second equation:

$$C = a\left(\frac{1}{1-a} F_C + \frac{1}{1-a} I\right) + F_C$$
$$= \left(1 + \frac{a}{1-a}\right) F_C + \frac{a}{1-a} I$$
$$= \frac{1}{1-a} F_C + \frac{a}{1-a} I$$

---

[1] Consumption is thought of as being in two parts. One part (aY) depends on the national income. It may be called *induced* consumption. The other part (F_C) is called *autonomous* because it does not depend on anything in the system.

So C is determined by a, F_C and I. This shows that if F_C and I are known, we may calculate what C and Y will be. But it does not prove that there is only one possible value of C and one possible value of Y for any given values of I and F_C.

Imagine that $I = \underline{I}$ and $F_C = \underline{F}_C$ represent fixed levels of investment and autonomous spending. Suppose that there are two amounts of consumption C_1 and C_2 and two levels of national product Y_1 and Y_2 which are compatible with $\underline{I}$ and $\underline{F}_C$. Then

$$\frac{a}{1-a}\underline{I} + \frac{1}{1-a}\underline{F}_C = C_1$$

and

$$\frac{a}{1-a}\underline{I} + \frac{1}{1-a}\underline{F}_C = C_2$$

Subtract the second from the first

$$0 = C_1 - C_2 \text{ or } C_1 = C_2$$

Similarly it can be shown that

$$0 = Y_1 - Y_2 \quad \text{or} \quad Y_1 = Y_2$$

Thus there is exactly one solution; that is, one value of C and one value of Y for any given values of I and F_C.

Thus Tiny Model 1 states that if the pair (I, F_C) are known, the pair (Y, C) are uniquely determined. It also says that if the pair (Y, C) are known, the pair (I, F_C) are uniquely determined. Therefore, the theory actually may be thought of in two ways. The first is represented by the pair of equations

$$\begin{aligned} \frac{a}{1-a}I + \frac{1}{1-a}F_C &= C \\ \frac{1}{1-a}I + \frac{1}{1-a}F_C &= Y \end{aligned} \tag{2.1}$$

The second is represented by the pair of equations we started with

$$\begin{aligned} Y - C &= I \\ -aY + C &= F_C \end{aligned} \tag{2.2}$$

There is a reason for considering both ways of writing this theory. One of them is closer to ordinary experience; the other enables us to answer two questions about the economy. The statement $C = aY + F_C$ has an intuitive meaning about how consumers act, and it is natural to formulate a statement about consumers in a form such as this. But suppose we wish to find out the consequence on the economy of an increase of one dollar in investment or autonomous consumption. In the first case,

$$\frac{a}{1-a}(I+1) + \frac{1}{1-a}F_C = C_1$$

$$\frac{a}{1-a}I \qquad + \frac{1}{1-a}F_C = C$$

Subtracting, $$\frac{a}{1-a} = (C_1 - C)$$

In the second case,

$$\frac{1}{1-a}(I+1) + \frac{1}{1-a}F_C = Y_1$$

$$\frac{1}{1-a}I \qquad + \frac{1}{1-a}F_C = Y$$

Subtracting, $$\frac{1}{1-a} \qquad = (Y_1 - Y)$$

since $1 > a > 0$, $1/(1-a) > 1$, and $a/(1-a) > 0$. Thus, if investment increases by one dollar, consumption increases, and national product increases by more than one dollar.

In this Tiny Model, three features are presented which will characterize all the theories presented in this book:

(1) The model includes a definition of the part of the social accounts under discussion (here, $Y = C + I$), and a description of the behavior assumed to hold for the economic units in question (here, $C = aY + F_C$). This set of statements can be written in matrix-vector form, as a mapping of the variables [here the vector (Y, C)] into the factors [here the vector (I, F_C)].

(2) Corresponding to this mapping, there is derived an inverse mapping, which carries the factors into the variables. In fact, the mapping associated with the theory is one-to-one. For every factor vector there is exactly one variable vector, and for every variable vector there is exactly one factor vector.

(3) All the statements in the theory are linear equations in the factors and variables.

By restricting ourselves to linear theories, we are able to use simple mathematical methods for analyzing economic relations. We have reason to suppose that economic relations are nonlinear. (For example, many economists feel that the larger Y is, the smaller a should be in this theory.) In this case, the analysis of the implications of the theory requires the use of the calculus. Theories which use the calculus have the interesting feature that when they are examined locally, they are linear. That is, if we choose some particular pair of initial values (Y_0, C_0) for the variables Y, C, and ask about the consequences of *small* changes in I and F_C, given that starting point, the analysis will be exactly like that of a linear theory.

STATEMENTS IN A THEORY

A theory consists of a number of statements. Each statement involves some variables and some factors. We shall first consider the forms that individual statements take, and then show how to put the statements together to make a theory. Both the individual statements and the theory as a whole will be, in mathematical terms, *linear*. The precise meaning of this term will be explained below.

Three kinds of statements are used in these theories:

(1) Some statements are *accounting definitions*. Tiny Model 1 defined national product as the sum of consumption and investment: $Y = C + I$. Some other theory might specify, for example, that total assets (A) consist of money (M) and of plant and equipment (K). This statement may be written in several mathematically equivalent forms:

$$A = M + K$$

$$0 = A - M - K$$

$$M = A - K$$

The way this statement is written depends on the role which the three symbols have in the theory. For example, if the theory specifies that the amounts of money and plant are all determined by various other factors, then A, M, and K are all *variables* in our particular theory, and the second formulation is used. If the theory states that plant and total assets are variables, while the amount of money is a *factor* determined from outside, then the third statement is more convenient because it places all the factors on one side of the equation and all the variables on the other.

(2) Some statements involve *initial conditions*. Suppose one element of the theory states that investment (I) is the same as the change in plant and equipment (ΔK). Then the amount of plant today (K) is equal to the amount of plant yesterday (K_0) plus today's investment (I). This statement may be written in several forms:

$$K = K_0 + I$$

$$K_0 = K - I$$

It is natural to regard K_0 as an independent factor. The values of the variables in the economy today may be influenced by the stock of plant available to start with. As we consider the economy today, nothing can be done to influence K_0, which is one of the outcomes of yesterday's economic activity. By writing this statement in the second form, we separate factors on the left side and variables on the right side of the equation. (Tiny Model 1 did not happen to include a statement of initial conditions.)

(3) Some statements are *behavioral*, and describe how economic units are assumed to behave. Such behavior is usually conditional: it is influenced by economic variables of one sort or another. On the other hand, such behavior is partly autonomous. Consider two common statements:

(1) Consumer spending is influenced by the size of their income, and by their cash balances.

(2) Investment is influenced by the interest rate.

The first of these statements would be written[2]

$$C = aY + vM + F_C$$

The second would be written

$$I = cR + F_I$$

Ordinarily, statements of this sort will be written, respectively, in the form:

$$F_C = C - aY - vM$$
$$F_I = I - cR$$

In statements written this way, it is assumed that C, Y, M, I, and R are variables, while F_C and F_I are factors. Written in this way, the factors appear on one side and the variables on the other side of the equation.

In *behavioral* statements, coefficients (such as a, v, and c in these two illustrations) are often assumed to be of known sign but of unknown magnitude. Thus in connection with the statement about consumer spending just given, it might be stated that $a > 0$, $v > 0$, because the larger people's incomes are, the more spending we expect them to carry on; and the larger are the balances in peoples' bank accounts, the more we expect them to spend. In the statement about investment given above, we might say $c < 0$ because the more it costs to borrow (as a means of financing investment), the less borrowing (and investing) we expect to take place.

Terms like F_C and F_I appear in behavioral statements because the sort of proposition given in the last paragraph does not exhaust the possibilities. That is, changes in consumption or investment take place partly because of changes in attitudes, and not merely because of changes in the environment. We may regard the quantity of consumption as being partly "induced" by the level of income and cash balances; but it is only partly induced. In part,

[2] Tiny Model 1 had a simpler form of this statement: $C = aY + F_C$.

consumers decide "autonomously" how much they will spend. They may change their minds about how much to spend *at a given income and at a given level of bank balances*, and this, in our statement, involves a change in the factor F_C.

All three kinds of statements are *linear*. Linear statements are used because they are mathematically simple and because linear theories turn out to be very much like the nonlinear theories which are in most common use. The reason for using the term "linear" is illustrated by the following observations about the statement

$$C = aY + vM + F_C$$

(1) If Y and F_C are constant, the relation between C and M,

$$C = vM + (aY + F_C)$$

will be a straight line when plotted on a graph with axes measuring C and M;

(2) If M and F_C are constant, the relation between C and Y,

$$C = aY + (vM + F_C)$$

will be a straight line when plotted on a graph with axes measuring C and Y;

(3) If Y and M are constant, the relation between C and F_C,

$$C = F_C + (aY + vM)$$

will be a straight line when plotted on a graph with axes measuring C and F_C.

All statements made in the simple theories in this book will be linear. A theory, in fact, is considered to be a system of linear equations. Although linear relations are extremely simple, and therefore rigid, they provide a very convenient place to start. One of their great virtues is illustrated in the following way. Suppose consumption behaves as stated, and that it is observed in two consecutive periods. In period 1,

$$C_1 = aY_1 + vM_1 + F_{C1}$$

while in period 2,

$$C_2 = aY_2 + vM_2 + F_{C2}$$

If for some variable x, Δx means "the change in x," we may obtain the change in consumption ($\Delta C = C_2 - C_1$) by subtraction:

$$\Delta C = a\Delta Y + v\Delta M + \Delta F_C$$

the statement about the quantity purchased (C) has exactly the same form as the statement about change in quantity purchased (ΔC). In nonlinear theories (that is, theories involving nonlinear relations), statements about the amount of consumption are different in form from statements about change in the amount of consumption.[3] There are therefore two steps, rather than one, to be taken in nonlinear analysis: to show the dependence of the variables on the factors in the theory; and to show how variables change when factors change. In linear theories, the two steps turn out to be the same.[4]

A THEORY IS A MAPPING

In discussing statements, it was said several times that a statement is basically an equation; and it was also stated that terms involving factors "belong" on one side of the equation and terms involving variables belong on the other side.[5] In order to achieve this result, it is necessary to decide what is variable and what is factor *in a particular theory*. It is not necessary to say "once a factor, always a factor." Some theories in this book, for instance, treat the quantity of money as a factor given from outside; others treat the quantity of money as a variable determined by other factors. One aspect of the discussion, in fact, concerns the way in which economists can gradually expand the scope of their theories, increasing thereby the number of variables whose values are explained by the theory.

Suppose, now, that a set of statements exists, and that collections of factors and variables have been made. This set is to be considered as a theory, if certain things are true of it. To specify the properties of a theory, we look at what the theory is supposed to do.

Formally speaking a theory says that given some vector of factors

$$\mathbf{F} = (\mathbf{F}_1 \cdots \mathbf{F}_m) \tag{2.3}$$

the economy determines some vector of variables

$$\mathbf{V} = (\mathbf{V}_1 \cdots \mathbf{V}_n) \tag{2.4}$$

---

[3] *Technical remark:* Imagine a particular nonlinear relation involving the same variables as (2): $C = aY^2 + bYM + cM^2 + F_C$. It would be inconvenient to formulate an expression for ΔC. By means of the calculus one might write the change in consumption as

$$\begin{aligned} dC &= 2aYdY + b[YdM + MdY] + 2cMdM + dF_C \\ &= [2aY + bM]dY + [2cM + bY]dM + dF_C \end{aligned}$$

but the form of this statement is quite different from the form of the original one. Nonlinear systems usually involve the use of calculus, while linear systems can be studied by more elementary means.

[4] Linear equations are not an unmixed blessing. In the statement $\Delta C = a\Delta Y + V\Delta M + \Delta F_C$, the quantity a, for example, is a given number. Many economists think that the higher the level of the national product, the *more* people will save (the *less* they will spend) as their income rises. If this is true, a gets smaller as Y gets larger. This possibility is ignored here. In this sense, linear equations may be unable to take into account a phenomenon that might be important.

[5] One advantage of linear theories is that it is always possible to write a statement in this way. If consumption, for instance, followed the rule $C = Y^{\alpha}(M + F_C)^{v}$, then it would not be possible to express this relation in a way that put Y, C, M on one side of the equation and F_C on the other.

in a specified way. Since the theory is linear (as will be shown) this means that given a vector of *changes* in the factors,

$$\mathbf{\Delta F} = (\mathbf{\Delta F}_1, \mathbf{\Delta F}_2, \ldots, \mathbf{\Delta F}_m)$$

we can determine the changes in the variables

$$\mathbf{\Delta V} = (\mathbf{\Delta V}_1, \mathbf{\Delta V}_2, \ldots, \mathbf{\Delta V}_m)$$

in exactly the same way. The theory is thus a *mapping*. We do not yet have an explicit way of taking a particular vector **F**, and constructing its image, $\mathbf{FT} = \mathbf{V}$, for any particular theory. The next section will tell how to carry out such mappings.

In a *linear mapping*, if $\mathbf{F}_1$ and $\mathbf{F}_2$ are vectors, and *a* and *b* are numbers, then $(a\mathbf{F}_1 + b\mathbf{F}_2)\mathbf{T} = (a\mathbf{F}_1)\mathbf{T} + (b\mathbf{F}_2)\mathbf{T}$. In particular, if $a = 1$, $b = -1$, $(\mathbf{F}_1 - \mathbf{F}_2)\mathbf{T} = \mathbf{F}_1\mathbf{T} - \mathbf{F}_2\mathbf{T}$. Thus $\Delta\mathbf{F} = \mathbf{F}_1 - \mathbf{F}_2$ and $\Delta\mathbf{V} = \mathbf{V}_1 - \mathbf{V}_2$ are related by the equation $\Delta\mathbf{V} = \Delta\mathbf{FT}$. Thus **T** maps **F** into **V** and also $\Delta\mathbf{F}$ into $\Delta\mathbf{V}$. This particularly useful fact makes linear mappings simple to use.

If a linear mapping **T** is *one-to-one*, any vector **V** is the image of exactly one vector **F**. If $\mathbf{V} = \mathbf{F}_1\mathbf{T}$ and $\mathbf{V} = \mathbf{F}_2\mathbf{T}$, then $\mathbf{F}_1$ is the same vector as $\mathbf{F}_2$. Thus, $\theta = \mathbf{V} - \mathbf{V} = (\mathbf{F}_1 - \mathbf{F}_2)\mathbf{T}$ if and only if the vector $\mathbf{F}_1 - \mathbf{F}_2$ is the null vector θ.

If **T** is a known, linear one-to-one mapping and **V** a given vector, we may wish to find a vector **F** such that $\mathbf{FT} = \mathbf{W}$. That is, we ask what is the vector whose image is **V**. To answer this question, we construct a mapping $\mathbf{T}^{-1}$ (read *T-inverse*) which has the following properties:

Whatever vector **F** we may start with, its image under **T** is **FT**. So when we apply $\mathbf{T}^{-1}$ to **FT**, we want to end up with **F** again. That is

$$(\mathbf{FT})\mathbf{T}^{-1} = \mathbf{VT}^{-1} = \mathbf{F}$$

Whatever vector **V** we start with, we apply $\mathbf{T}^{-1}$ to it to obtain a vector $\mathbf{VT}^{-1}$. So when we apply **T** to $\mathbf{VT}^{-1}$ we want to end up with **V**. That is

$$(\mathbf{VT}^{-1})\mathbf{T} = \mathbf{FT} = \mathbf{V}$$

Thus taking any vector **W**, whether we apply first **T** and second $\mathbf{T}^{-1}$, or whether we apply first $\mathbf{T}^{-1}$ and then **T**, we should end up with **W**. This means that $\mathbf{T}^{-1}$ must be the inverse of **T**, **T** must be the inverse of $\mathbf{T}^{-1}$, and thus $(\mathbf{T}^{-1})^{-1} = \mathbf{T}$.

If **T** has an inverse, it has exactly one inverse. Suppose the contrary, that **T** had two inverses, $\mathbf{T}_1^{-1}$ and $\mathbf{T}_2^{-1}$. From the vector $\mathbf{V} = \mathbf{FT}$ it would be possible to infer that $\mathbf{VT}_1^{-1} = \mathbf{F}_1$ and $\mathbf{VT}_2^{-1} = \mathbf{F}_2$. Either $\mathbf{F}_1$ is the same vector as $\mathbf{F}_2$ or it is not. If $\mathbf{F}_1 = \mathbf{F}_2$, then $\mathbf{T}_1^{-1}$ and $\mathbf{T}_2^{-1}$ always have the same images (remember **V** is an arbitrary vector) and, hence, are the same mapping. If $\mathbf{F}_1$ and $\mathbf{F}_2$ are different, then we would have $\mathbf{F}_1\mathbf{T} = \mathbf{F}_2\mathbf{T} = \mathbf{V}$, which means that **V** is the image of two vectors. In this case **T** would not be a one-to-one mapping.

We can therefore write any *given* theory either as a mapping $\mathbf{V} = \mathbf{FT}$ or as a mapping $\mathbf{F} = \mathbf{VS}$. $\mathbf{S}$ will be the inverse of $\mathbf{T}$ and $\mathbf{T}$ will be the inverse of $\mathbf{S}$. Mathematically the two forms are interchangeable. Economists usually find it convenient to start with the mapping $\mathbf{F} = \mathbf{VS}$ and to calculate the inverse mapping from this. The variable-into-factor mapping usually has a direct interpretation in terms of the economic behavior of the households, businesses, banks, and government units that figure in the theory. The inverse, or factor-into-variable mapping, is then derived to give a complete statement of the implications of the theory. The next section starts from a mapping, $\mathbf{F} = \mathbf{V}\,\mathbf{T}$, and shows how to construct the mapping explicitly from the behavioral statements of the theory.

It is useful to repeat that the use of linear one-to-one mappings in this book is designed to ensure simplicity. It is possible to derive most of the basic results of macroeconomics from such mappings. But other linear mappings, and nonlinear mappings, are also studied by economists. They are avoided here only because they involve the use of more difficult mathematics than the theories given here; and in the author's opinion, they do not yield notably better results.

THE MATRIX OF A THEORY

A theory may be represented as a system of equations. In this book, all theories are linear, so all equations are linear equations. Every system of linear equations may be expressed as a transformation of a vector. That is, if $\mathbf{V}$ stands for a vector of variables $(\mathbf{V}_1 \cdots \mathbf{V}_\mathbf{n})$, and if F stands for a vector of factors $(\mathbf{F}_1 \cdots \mathbf{F}_\mathbf{n})$, then a transformation $\mathbf{T}$ such that $\mathbf{F} = \mathbf{VT}$ may be written as a *matrix*. A matrix is an array of numbers, arranged in rows and columns. If $\mathbf{F} = \mathbf{VT}$, then the array has the form

$$\mathbf{F} = (\mathbf{F}_1 \cdots \mathbf{F}_\mathbf{m}) = (\mathbf{V}_1 \cdots \mathbf{V}_\mathbf{n}) \begin{pmatrix} t_{11} & t_{12} & \cdots & t_{1m} \\ t_{21} & t_{22} & \cdots & t_{2m} \\ & & \cdots & \\ t_{n1} & t_{n2} & \cdots & t_{nm} \end{pmatrix} = \mathbf{VT}$$

t_{ij} = the element in row i column j of the matrix $\mathbf{T}$.

This equation is another way of writing the equations

$$\begin{aligned} \mathbf{F}_1 &= \mathbf{V}_1 t_{11} + \mathbf{V}_2 t_{21} + \cdots + \mathbf{V}_n t_{n1} && \text{(all the } t\text{'s are in column 1)} \\ \mathbf{F}_2 &= \mathbf{V}_1 t_{12} + \mathbf{V}_2 t_{22} + \cdots + \mathbf{V}_n t_{n2} && \text{(all the } t\text{'s are in column 2)} \\ &\overline{\qquad\qquad\qquad\qquad\qquad\qquad} \\ \mathbf{F}_m &= \mathbf{V}_1 t_{1\mathbf{m}} + \mathbf{V}_2 t_{2\mathbf{m}} + \cdots + \mathbf{V}_n t_{nm} && \text{(all the } t\text{'s are in column } m\text{)} \end{aligned}$$

Conversely, this set of equations may always be rewritten in the vector matrix form above.

Example Tiny Model 1 consisted of two statements

$$I = Y - C$$
$$F_C = -aY + C$$

In vector-matrix form, this model is:

$$\mathbf{F} = (\mathbf{I}, \mathbf{F_C}) = (\mathbf{Y} - \mathbf{C}, -\mathbf{aY} + \mathbf{C}) = (\mathbf{Y}, \mathbf{C})\begin{pmatrix} 1 & -a \\ -1 & 1 \end{pmatrix} = \mathbf{VT}$$

The inverse form of this matrix consisted of the equations

$$Y = \frac{1}{1-a} I + \frac{1}{1-a} F_C$$

$$C = \frac{a}{1-a} I + \frac{1}{1-a} F_C$$

In vector-matrix notation, this becomes

$$\mathbf{V} = (\mathbf{Y}, \mathbf{C}) = \left(\frac{1}{1-a}\mathbf{I} + \frac{1}{1-a}\mathbf{F_C}, \frac{a}{1-a}\mathbf{I} + \frac{1}{1-a}\mathbf{F_C}\right)$$
$$= (\mathbf{I}, \mathbf{F_C})\begin{pmatrix} \frac{1}{1-a} & \frac{a}{1-a} \\ \frac{1}{1-a} & \frac{1}{1-a} \end{pmatrix} = \mathbf{FT}^{-1}$$

A theory, then, involves specification of a vector of factors **F**, a vector of variables **V**, and a matrix **T**. If two different theories are "about the same things," then they have the same vectors **F** and **V**, but the matrices of the two theories are different. The differences exist because different behavior is assumed. If two theories are about the same variables, but involve different sets of factors, then both the factor vectors and the matrices will be different:

$$\mathbf{F} = \mathbf{VT}$$
$$\mathbf{F}' = \mathbf{VT}'$$

Thus, any set of linear equations may be written in matrix-vector notation. For example,

$$u = Ax + By + Cz$$
$$v = Dx + Ey + Fz$$
$$w = Gx + Hy + Iz$$

may be written

$$(\mathbf{u}, \mathbf{v}, \mathbf{w}) = (\mathbf{x}, \mathbf{y}, \mathbf{z})\begin{pmatrix} A & D & G \\ B & E & H \\ C & F & I \end{pmatrix} \tag{2.5}$$

The elements of column one of the matrix are the coefficients of the first equation; the elements of column two of the matrix are the coefficients of the second equation; the elements of column three are the coefficients of the third equation. And if this system of equations is a complete linear economic theory involving a one-to-one relation between vectors of variables and vectors of factors, there would be an *inverse matrix* which would enable us to write

$$(\mathbf{x}, \mathbf{y}, \mathbf{z}) = (\mathbf{u}, \mathbf{v}, \mathbf{w}) \begin{pmatrix} \underline{A} & \underline{D} & \underline{G} \\ \underline{B} & \underline{E} & \underline{H} \\ \underline{C} & \underline{F} & \underline{I} \end{pmatrix} \tag{2.6}$$

The matrix of Tiny Model 1 had two rows and two columns (as did its inverse). The matrix of equation 2.5 and its inverse in equation 2.6 have three rows and three columns. Matrices with n rows and n columns are called *square*; n is the *order* of the matrix.

However, not all matrices are square. The equation

$$(\mathbf{u}, \mathbf{v}) = (\mathbf{x}, \mathbf{y}, \mathbf{z}) \begin{pmatrix} A & D \\ B & E \\ C & F \end{pmatrix}$$

corresponds to the pair of equations

$$u = Ax + By + Cz$$
$$v = Dx + Ey + Fz$$

Here the matrix has three rows and two columns, and it would be called *rectangular*.

Rectangular matrices *never* have inverses. *Some* square matrices do not have inverses. But in this book a theory always has a matrix with an inverse. If it does not have an inverse, it is not possible to explain how changes in each factor affect each variable. To show that some set of equations is a theory, one simply writes the matrix of the theory and shows that it has an inverse.

Readers may ask the following question: If a theory may be written either as a system of linear equations or as a vector-matrix equation, why use the less familiar vector-matrix notation? There are several advantages to the use of matrices:

(1) The purpose of the inversion operation stands out clearly when inversion is thought of as changing a variable-into-factor mapping into the associated factor-into-variable mapping.

(2) To find out how a change in any factor affects the individual variables in the theory, it is necessary to find the solution to the equations. In finding this solution, one is forced to find everything that appears in the inverse

matrix. It is frequently easier to work directly with matrices, because computational techniques can be easily developed for matrices.

(3) Comparison of two theories is simplified if one puts their matrices side by side. The differences in their underlying assumptions become quite clear.

(4) It is often convenient to break a complicated problem into parts, study the parts separately, and then combine them. It is easier to carry out this combination with matrix methods than with systems of equations, for the work done on the partial theories becomes a portion of the necessary calculations on the unified theory. Chapters 3–8 will repeatedly illustrate this proposition.

SUMMATION NOTATION

In what follows, it is sometimes necessary to add up a list of symbols. The sum of the n indexed symbols $(V_1, V_2, \ldots, V_n)$ may be written as

$$V_1 + V_2 + V_3 + \cdots + V_n$$

A more compact way of writing this sum is by using the summation sign $\sum$:

$$\sum_{i=1}^{n} V_i$$

This is read as "the sum of the V_i, i ranging from 1 to n." That is, allow i to be all the whole numbers from a lower limit of 1 (written at the lower end of the summation sign $\sum$) to an upper limit of n (written at the upper end of $\sum$). Where there will be no confusion about which terms are included in the sum, we may write simply $\sum V_i$.

The $\sum$ notation simply represents repeated addition. It is also used for sums of products:

$$\sum_{i=1}^{n} V_i W_i = (V_1 W_1) + (V_2 W_2) + (V_3 W_3) + \cdots, + (V_n W_n)$$

Finally it may be that *double* sums appear. Set

$$W_i = \sum_{j=1}^{m} a_{ij} y_j \qquad (i = 1, \ldots, n)$$

This means that each of the n variables $W_1, W_2, \ldots, W_n$ is a linear function of the variables $y_1, y_2, \ldots, y_m$. Consequently, a_{ij} is the coefficient of y_j in the ith equation (that is, the equation identifying W_i). We may substitute for w_i in the sum

$$\sum_{i=1}^{n} V_i W_i = \sum_{i=1}^{n} V_i \left(\sum_{j=1}^{m} a_{ij} y_j \right)$$

It is permissible to move the second summation sign:

$$\sum_{i=1}^{n} V_i W_i = \sum_{i=1}^{n} \sum_{j=1}^{m} V_i a_{ij} y_j = \sum_{j=1}^{m} \sum_{i=1}^{n} V_i a_{ij} y_j$$

and since $V_i a_{ij} y_j = a_{ij} V_i y_j = V_i y_j a_{ij}$, we may switch these symbols about behind the two summation signs. That is:

$$\sum_{j=1}^{m} \sum_{i=1}^{n} V_i a_{ij} y_j = \sum_{i=1}^{n} \sum_{j=1}^{m} a_{ij} V_i y_j$$

The transformation of a vector by a matrix is written, in summation notation, as follows:

$$(\mathbf{V}_1, \mathbf{V}_2, \ldots, \mathbf{V}_n) \begin{pmatrix} a_{11} & a_{12} & \cdots & a_{1n} \\ a_{21} & a_{22} & \cdots & a_{2n} \\ a_{n1} & a_{n2} & \cdots & a_{nn} \end{pmatrix} = (\sum a_{\mathbf{i1}} \mathbf{V_i}, \sum a_{\mathbf{i2}} \mathbf{V_i}, \ldots, \sum a_{\mathbf{in}} \mathbf{V_i})$$

TWO MORE TINY MODELS

Tiny Model 2

Tiny Model 2 does for the balance sheet accounts what Tiny Model 1 did for national income. It is the simplest theory about its subject known to man. We start off by asserting that there are two kinds of assets: cash, and plant and equipment, and that there is no debt. Thus the balance sheet is

Cash,	M	Net worth, W
Plant and equipment,	K	

This balance sheet states that

$$W = M + K$$

Now suppose that the community's demand for plant and equipment depends partly on total assets, so that

$$K = bW + F_K$$

This second statement is about plant and equipment. It says that two things affect the amount of plant that people wish to own. One of these is their total wealth, the other is "business tastes." These two things are "additive": bW is the holding of plant which is induced by wealth. We suspect that the coefficient b is between 0 and 1. It is positive because we suspect that if people have larger amounts of assets, they will want more plant. It is less than 1 because we suspect that if people have larger amounts of assets, they will also want more cash. The demand for money is

$$
\begin{aligned}
M &= W - K \\
&= W - bW - F_K \\
&= (1 - b)W - F_K
\end{aligned}
$$

Therefore, if businesses hold more plant as their assets grow, $b > 0$; if they also hold more cash as their assets grow, $(1 - b) > 0$, so that $1 > b > 0$.

F_K is an indicator of the amount of "autonomous" plant holdings. We shall think of changes in business habits as taking place in F_K rather than in b.

Now let us express Tiny Model 2 in vector-matrix form. There are two factors, M and F_K; two variables, K and W; the two forms of the theory are

$$(\mathbf{M}, \mathbf{F_K}) = (\mathbf{W}, \mathbf{K})\begin{pmatrix} 1 & -b \\ -1 & 1 \end{pmatrix}$$

$$(\mathbf{W}, \mathbf{K}) = (\mathbf{M}, \mathbf{F_K})\begin{pmatrix} \dfrac{1}{1-b} & \dfrac{b}{1-b} \\[2ex] \dfrac{1}{1-b} & \dfrac{1}{1-b} \end{pmatrix}$$

The reader with a good memory will have noticed that this present section, "Two More Tiny Models," of this chapter is almost verbatim the same as the "A First Example" section at the beginning of the chapter, except that

M has replaced I

F_K has replaced F_C

W has replaced Y

K has replaced C

b has replaced a

In other words, these theories have similar structure, even though they are about different sectors of the economy. The similarity of structure is emphasized by the similarity of the two matrices; the difference in subject is shown by comparing the names of the variables and factors.

Clearly it is a great advantage to have a uniform way of looking at different parts of the economy, if it makes sense. We shall naturally try to use a uniform approach, although we shall not always be able to stick to it.

Tiny Model 3

A large part of microeconomics is concerned with the "theory of price formation." Although microeconomics does not, strictly speaking, concern us, it is useful to present Tiny Model 3, which is a theory of what the price and quantity traded will be in the case of a single, arbitrarily selected commodity. The case selected for examination is that of the "isolated market"; what goes on in such a market is completely independent of what goes on in other markets.

For present purposes, the basic hypotheses are

(1) The amount that buyers are willing to buy depends on the price they must pay: the higher the price, the *less* buyers will want. Specifically:

$$q_D = ep_D + F_D \qquad (e < 0)$$

The subscript D stands for demand. The factor F_D is called the "level of demand" and stands for everything (income, taste, fashion, whim) other than price which affects consumer willingness to buy.

(2) The amount that sellers are willing to sell depends on the price that they receive when they sell: The higher the price, the *more* sellers will want to sell. Specifically:

$$q_S = fp_S + F_S \qquad (f > 0)$$

The subscript S stands for supply. The factor F_S is called the "level of supply" and stands for everything other than price which affects the willingness of sellers to sell.

(3) The price buyers pay is equal to the price sellers receive. That is, we ignore taxes, dealers' commissions, delivery costs, and so on. That is, $p_D = p_S = p$.

(4) The market is functioning satisfactorily only if everyone who wants to buy can find a willing seller and everyone who wants to sell can find a willing buyer. If this condition is met[6], $q_D = q_S = q$.

Given these four conditions,

$$F_D = q - ep$$
$$F_S = q - fp$$

This means that p, called the *equilibrium price*, and q, the *equilibrium quantity*, are given by inverting the relation:

$$(\mathbf{F_D}, \mathbf{F_S}) = (\mathbf{q}, \mathbf{p})\begin{pmatrix} 1 & 1 \\ -e & -f \end{pmatrix}$$

that is, by

$$(\mathbf{F_D}, \mathbf{F_S})\begin{pmatrix} \dfrac{-f}{e-f} & \dfrac{-1}{e-f} \\[2ex] \dfrac{e}{e-f} & \dfrac{1}{e-f} \end{pmatrix} = (\mathbf{q}, \mathbf{p})$$

[6] Observe that the converse is not necessarily true. Even if $q_D = q_S$, it may be that communications in the market are such that some buyers do not have access to all sellers, or some sellers do not have access to all buyers. In this case, the market may not work satisfactorily because willing buyers and sellers cannot find each other.

That is, there is a single price and a single quantity which can exist in a market in which conditions (1) to (4) hold, and in which the levels of demand and supply (F_D and F_S) are given.

THE ECONOMIC MEANING OF THE INVERSE MATRIX

Addition and Subtraction of Vectors

Suppose that Tiny Model 3 is true, and we look at this particular market at two different dates. The demand equation will be

$$F_{D1} = q_1 - ep_1$$

at time 1, and

$$F_{D2} = q_2 - ep_2$$

at time 2. The difference between these two observations is

$$\Delta F_D = \Delta q - e\Delta p$$

where Δ means "the change in," so that

$$\Delta F_D = F_{D2} - F_{D1}$$
$$\Delta q = q_2 - q_1$$
$$\Delta p = p_2 - p_1$$

Similarly, the supply equation, at the two dates, will be

$$F_{S1} = q_1 - fp_1$$
$$F_{S2} = q_2 - fp_2$$

so that

$$\Delta F_S = \Delta q - f\Delta p$$

If these two expressions are written in vector matrix form

$$(\Delta \mathbf{F_D}, \Delta \mathbf{F_S}) = (\Delta \mathbf{q}, \Delta \mathbf{p})\begin{pmatrix} 1 & 1 \\ -e & -f \end{pmatrix}$$

Notice that the structure of this equation is exactly the same as the structure of the original form of the theory. That is, the matrix is exactly the same as before. Likewise, the inverse equation relating *changes* in factors to *changes* in variables.

$$(\Delta \mathbf{q}, \Delta \mathbf{p}) = (\Delta \mathbf{F_D}, \Delta \mathbf{F_S})\begin{pmatrix} \dfrac{-f}{e-f} & \dfrac{-1}{e-f} \\[2ex] \dfrac{e}{e-f} & \dfrac{1}{e-f} \end{pmatrix}$$

is of exactly the same structure as the corresponding relation between factors and variables.

This result is true of vectors of any order. If $\mathbf{F}_1 = (\mathbf{f}_1, \mathbf{f}_2, \ldots, \mathbf{f}_n)$ and $\mathbf{F}_2 = (\mathbf{f}'_1, \mathbf{f}'_2, \ldots, \mathbf{f}'_n)$ are vectors of the same order, then $\Delta\mathbf{F}$ is defined as the vector $(\mathbf{f}'_1 - \mathbf{f}_1, \mathbf{f}'_2 - \mathbf{f}_2, \ldots, \mathbf{f}'_n - \mathbf{f}_n) = \Delta\mathbf{F}_2, \ldots, \Delta\mathbf{F}_n)$. If $\mathbf{M}$ is a matrix, such that $\mathbf{F} = \mathbf{VM}$, then $\mathbf{F}_1 = \mathbf{V}_1\mathbf{M}$ and $\mathbf{F}_2 = \mathbf{V}_2\mathbf{M}$ mean that $\Delta\mathbf{F} = \Delta\mathbf{VM}$; moreover $\Delta\mathbf{V} = \Delta\mathbf{FM}^{-1}$ where $\mathbf{M}^{-1}$ is the inverse of $\mathbf{M}$.

The theories used in this book are all *linear*. Theories that are linear (and only such theories) have the notable feature that a single structure is common to the relation between factors and variables, and the relation between *changes* in factors and *changes* in variables. Thus linear theories are particularly easy to use, and particularly suitable for beginners.

Our operations on vectors and matrices of every order are simply applications of the following three rules:

(1) If $\mathbf{a}$ is a number and $\mathbf{V} = (\mathbf{V}_1 \ldots \mathbf{V}_n)$ a vector, the $\mathbf{aV}$ is the vector $(\mathbf{aV}_1, \mathbf{aV}_2, \ldots, \mathbf{aV}_n)$.

(2) If $\mathbf{V} = (\mathbf{V}_1, \mathbf{V}_2, \ldots, \mathbf{V}_n)$ and $\mathbf{W} = (\mathbf{W}_1, \mathbf{W}_2, \ldots, \mathbf{W}_n)$ are vectors of the same order, then $\mathbf{V} + \mathbf{W}$ is the vector $(\mathbf{V}_1 + \mathbf{W}_1, \mathbf{V}_2 + \mathbf{W}_2, \ldots, \mathbf{V}_n + \mathbf{W}_n)$.

(3) If $\mathbf{V}$, $\mathbf{W}$ are vectors and M is a matrix, then

$$\mathbf{VM} + \mathbf{WM} = (\mathbf{V} + \mathbf{W})\mathbf{M}$$

The Economic Interpretation of the Inverse Matrix

Theories consist of pairs of matrix equations

$$\mathbf{F} = \mathbf{VM}$$
$$\mathbf{V} = \mathbf{FM}^{-1}$$

Here $\mathbf{F}$ is a vector of factors which are taken to be given, and which collectively determine $\mathbf{V}$, a vector of economic variables. From such a pair, as we have just seen, we can derive the pair

$$\Delta\mathbf{F} = \Delta\mathbf{VM}$$
$$\Delta\mathbf{V} = \Delta\mathbf{FM}^{-1}$$

Any vector

$$\Delta\mathbf{F} = (\Delta\mathbf{f}_1, \Delta\mathbf{f}_2, \ldots, \Delta\mathbf{f}_n)$$

may be thought of as the sum of the vectors

$$\Delta\mathbf{F}_1 = (\Delta\mathbf{f}_1, 0, 0, \ldots, 0)$$
$$\Delta\mathbf{F}_2 = (0, \Delta\mathbf{f}_2, 0, \ldots, 0)$$
$$\Delta\mathbf{F}_3 = (0, 0, \Delta\mathbf{f}_3, \ldots, 0)$$
$$\ldots$$
$$\Delta\mathbf{F}_n = (0, 0, 0, \ldots, \Delta\mathbf{f}_n)$$

Each of these vectors is associated with the following economic event: *one factor, and only one factor changes.* Consequently if

$$\Delta\mathbf{V} = \Delta\mathbf{F}\mathbf{M}^{-1}$$

we may write this as the sum of the effects of the isolated changes:

$$\begin{aligned}\Delta\mathbf{V} &= \Delta\mathbf{V}_1 + \Delta\mathbf{V}_2 + \cdots + \Delta\mathbf{V}_n = \Delta\mathbf{F}_1\mathbf{M}^{-1} + \Delta\mathbf{F}_2\mathbf{M}^{-1} + \cdots \Delta\mathbf{F}_n\mathbf{M}^{-1}\\ &= (\Delta\mathbf{F}_1 + \Delta\mathbf{F}_2 + \cdots + \Delta\mathbf{F}_n)\mathbf{M}^{-1} = \Delta\mathbf{F}\mathbf{M}^{-1}\end{aligned}$$

This is true because

$$\begin{aligned}\Delta\mathbf{V}_1 &= \Delta\mathbf{F}_1\mathbf{M}^{-1}\\ \Delta\mathbf{V}_2 &= \Delta\mathbf{F}_2\mathbf{M}^{-1}\\ &\cdots\\ \Delta\mathbf{V}_n &= \Delta\mathbf{F}_n\mathbf{M}^{-1}\end{aligned}$$

When we calculate $\Delta\mathbf{F}_i\mathbf{M}^{-1}$ (i is any one of the numbers $1 \cdots n$), so as to obtain $\Delta\mathbf{V}_i$, we are calculating the effects which a change in $\mathbf{F}_i$ has upon each of the variables in the theory.

We write out $\Delta\mathbf{F}_i\mathbf{M}^{-1} = \Delta\mathbf{V}_i$ in full

$$(\mathbf{0}, \ldots, \mathbf{0}, \Delta\mathbf{f}_i, \mathbf{0}, \ldots, \mathbf{0})\begin{pmatrix} m_{11} & m_{12} & \cdots & m_{1n}\\ m_{21} & m_{22} & \cdots & m_{2n}\\ & \cdots & & \\ m_{i1} & m_{i2} & \cdots & m_{in}\\ & \cdots & & \\ m_{n1} & m_{n2} & \cdots & m_{nn}\end{pmatrix} = (m_{i1}\,\Delta f_i, M_{i2}\,\Delta f_i, \ldots, M_{in}\,\Delta f_i)$$

$$= (\Delta\mathbf{V}_1^{(i)}, \Delta\mathbf{V}_2^{(i)}, \ldots, \Delta\mathbf{V}_n^{(i)})$$

(here m_{ij} is the element in row i, column j of M^{-1}. Therefore,

$$\begin{aligned}\Delta V_1^{(i)} &= m_{i1}\Delta f_i\\ \Delta V_2^{(i)} &= M_{i2}\Delta f_i\\ &\cdots\\ \Delta V_n^{(i)} &= m_{in}\Delta f_i\end{aligned}$$

If f_i changes by one unit, we have $\Delta f_i = 1$; then these equations become

$$\begin{aligned}\Delta V_1^{(i)} &= m_{i1} = \text{the effect on } V_1 \text{ of a unit change in } f_i\\ \Delta V_2^{(i)} &= m_{i2} = \text{the effect on } V_2 \text{ of a unit change in } f_i\\ &\cdots\\ \Delta V_n^{(i)}) &= m_{in} = \text{the effect on } V_n \text{ of a unit change in } f_i\end{aligned}$$

The problems presented in the discussion of Tiny Models 1–3 involved special cases of this proposition.

We are interested in the inverse matrix of a theory because the elements this inverse matrix measure the effects of unit changes in the factors upon the variables of the theory. This interpretation makes the matrix into a set of propositions implied by the theorem.

In the future, when a theory has been written both ways (that is, both as a variable-into-factor mapping and as an "inverse," or factor-into-variable mapping), a table of *implications* will be given. For Tiny Model 3, for instance, the table would appear as shown in Table 2.1.

TABLE 2.1

THE IMPLICATIONS OF TINY MODEL 3

THE EFFECT OF A UNIT CHANGE IN	THE EFFECT OF A UNIT CHANGE UPON Quantity (q)	Price (p)
The level of demand (ΔF_D)	$\frac{-f}{e-f}$	$\frac{-1}{e-f}$
The level of supply (ΔF_S)	$\frac{e}{e-f}$	$\frac{1}{e-f}$

HOW TO TEST AN INVERSE MATRIX

To *compute* the inverse of a given matrix, it is necessary to use methods such as those given in the next section of this chapter. Readers who wish to be able to develop theories of their own should go through that discussion with care. But some readers will be satisfied with learning about the theories discussed here. They will not wish to compute inverses on their own. However, they may still wish to be able to verify that some matrix **N** is actually the inverse of another matrix **M**. This section tells how to make such a test.

First, it is easy to see that there is a matrix which is like the number 1 in the following sense: if n is *any* number, $n \times 1 = n$. There is a matrix $\mathbf{E_m}$ of every order m, which is like 1, in the sense that $\mathbf{VE}_m = \mathbf{V}$ for every vector with m components. Let $m = 4$. Then

$$\mathbf{E}_4 = \begin{pmatrix} 1 & 0 & 0 & 0 \\ 0 & 1 & 0 & 0 \\ 0 & 0 & 1 & 0 \\ 0 & 0 & 0 & 1 \end{pmatrix}$$

The matrix $\mathbf{E}_m$ is called "the unit matrix of order m." Usually "of order m" will be dropped in this book, for it will be clear from the context what the order of the matrix is.

Second, suppose we start with a theory that says $\mathbf{F} = \mathbf{VM}$, where **F** and **V** are vectors and **M** is a matrix. Then the inverse of **M** is a matrix such that

$\mathbf{V} = \mathbf{F}\mathbf{M}^{-1}$. Therefore $\mathbf{FM}^{-1} = (\mathbf{VM})\mathbf{M}^{-1} = \mathbf{V}(\mathbf{MM}^{-1})$. If **F**, **V**, and **M** were numbers, $\mathbf{M}^{-1}$ would be the reciprocal of **M**: $\mathbf{M}^{-1} = 1/\mathbf{M}$, and $(\mathbf{MM}^{-1}) = 1$. Since **M** is a matrix, $\mathbf{MM}^{-1}$ is not a number, but rather a unit matrix. Testing some matrix **B** to see whether it is the inverse of another matrix **A** involves *multiplying* two matrices together to see whether their *product* is a unit matrix.

Matrix multiplication in general is discussed in the next section of this chapter. Here we illustrate a particular case, where one matrix **B** is the inverse of another matrix **A**. **B** is the inverse of **A**, then

$$\begin{pmatrix} a_{11} & a_{12} & \cdots & a_{1n} \\ a_{21} & a_{22} & \cdots & a_{2n} \\ & \cdots & & \\ a_{n1} & a_{n2} & \cdots & a_{nn} \end{pmatrix} \begin{pmatrix} b_{11} & b_{12} & \cdots & b_{1n} \\ b_{21} & b_{22} & \cdots & b_{2n} \\ & & \cdots & \\ b_{n1} & b_{n2} & \cdots & b_{nn} \end{pmatrix} = \begin{pmatrix} 1 & 0 & \cdots & 0 \\ 0 & 1 & \cdots & 0 \\ & & \cdots & \\ 0 & 0 & \cdots & 1 \end{pmatrix}$$

The ith row of **A** is the set of numbers:

$$a_{i1}, a_{i2}, \ldots, a_{in}$$

The jth column of **B** is the set of numbers

$$b_{1j}, b_{2j}, \ldots, b_{nj}$$

In the unit matrix, the *diagonal* elements equal 1; these are the elements in positions 11, 22, 33, ... nn. The *off diagonal* elements equal zero. These are elements in positions such that the row index is different from the column index.

Rule: If **B** is the inverse of **A**, then the sum

$$\sum_{k=1}^{n} a_{ik} b_{kj} = a_{i1}b_{1j} + a_{i2}b_{2j} + \cdots + a_{in}b_{nj}$$

is equal to 1 if $i = j$. If $i \neq j$, the sum is equal to zero.

Here are some easy examples of inverses, which readers should check for themselves:

$$\begin{pmatrix} a & 0 & 0 & 0 \\ 0 & b & 0 & 0 \\ 0 & 0 & c & 0 \\ 0 & 0 & 0 & d \end{pmatrix} \begin{pmatrix} 1/a & 0 & 0 & 0 \\ 0 & 1/b & 0 & 0 \\ 0 & 0 & 1/c & 0 \\ 0 & 0 & 0 & 1/d \end{pmatrix} = \begin{pmatrix} 1 & 0 & 0 & 0 \\ 0 & 1 & 0 & 0 \\ 0 & 0 & 1 & 0 \\ 0 & 0 & 0 & 1 \end{pmatrix}$$

$$\begin{pmatrix} 1 & a & b \\ 0 & 1 & 0 \\ 0 & 0 & 1 \end{pmatrix} \begin{pmatrix} 1 & -a & -b \\ 0 & 1 & 0 \\ 0 & 0 & 1 \end{pmatrix} = \begin{pmatrix} 1 & 0 & 0 \\ 0 & 1 & 0 \\ 0 & 0 & 1 \end{pmatrix}$$

$$\begin{pmatrix} 1 & -a \\ -1 & 1 \end{pmatrix} \begin{pmatrix} \dfrac{1}{1-a} & \dfrac{a}{1-a} \\ \dfrac{1}{1-a} & \dfrac{a}{1-a} \end{pmatrix} = \begin{pmatrix} 1 & 0 \\ 0 & 1 \end{pmatrix}$$

(Note: If $a = 1$, the second left matrix is not defined, because numbers may not be divided by zero. Therefore, if $a = 1$, the first left matrix has no inverse.)

$$\begin{pmatrix} a & b \\ c & d \end{pmatrix} \begin{pmatrix} \dfrac{d}{ad - bc} & \dfrac{-b}{ad - bc} \\ \dfrac{-c}{ad - bc} & \dfrac{a}{ad - bc} \end{pmatrix} = \begin{pmatrix} 1 & 0 \\ 0 & 1 \end{pmatrix}$$

This is the general formula for inverses of matrices of order 2, *except when* $ad = bc$. If the equality holds, the first left matrix has no inverse.

$$\begin{pmatrix} 1 & -a & 0 & 0 \\ -1 & 1 & 0 & 0 \\ -1 & 0 & 1 & 0 \\ 0 & -b & -d & 1 \end{pmatrix} \begin{pmatrix} \dfrac{1}{1-a} & \dfrac{a}{1-a} & 0 & 0 \\ \dfrac{1}{1-a} & \dfrac{1}{1-a} & 0 & 0 \\ \dfrac{1}{1-a} & \dfrac{a}{1-a} & 1 & 0 \\ \dfrac{b+d}{1-a} & \dfrac{b+ad}{1-a} & d & 1 \end{pmatrix} = \begin{pmatrix} 1 & 0 & 0 & 0 \\ 0 & 1 & 0 & 0 \\ 0 & 0 & 1 & 0 \\ 0 & 0 & 0 & 1 \end{pmatrix}$$

Footnote for students of calculus: If consumption were a *nonlinear* function of income, Tiny Model 1 would become

$$Y = C + I$$
$$C = f(Y, \theta)$$

Here θ is a parameter of f. Then if I and θ are given,

$$Y = f(Y, \theta) + I$$

or

$$0 = g(Y, \theta, I)$$

If this is true, Y is implicitly a function of θ and I. In the neighborhood of a solution of this system,

$$dY = dC + dI$$
$$dC = \frac{\delta C}{\delta Y} dY + \frac{\delta C}{\delta \theta} d\theta$$

Here $\dfrac{\delta C}{\delta \theta}$ may be set equal to 1 by suitably scaling θ. Rearranging these terms

$$dI = dY - dC$$
$$d\theta = -\frac{\delta C}{\delta Y} dY + dC$$

In matrix-vector notation

$$(\mathbf{dI}, \mathbf{d\theta}) = (\mathbf{dY}, \mathbf{dC})\begin{pmatrix} 1 & -1 \\ -\dfrac{\delta C}{\delta Y} & 1 \end{pmatrix}$$

In particular, when C is a linear function of Y, $\dfrac{\delta C}{\delta Y}$ is a constant, which is denoted by a in this book.

In other words, the coefficients that appear in a matrix may be thought of as the partial derivatives of functions. By limiting the discussion to linear functions, we keep the theories in this book particularly simple. Properties that otherwise would be true only in the neighborhood of a point hold true everywhere, because the functions used have no bends in them.

In the nonlinear case, the inverse mapping

$$(\mathbf{dI}, \mathbf{d\theta})\begin{pmatrix} \dfrac{1}{1-\delta C/\delta Y} & \dfrac{\delta C/\delta Y}{1-\delta C/\delta Y} \\ \dfrac{1}{1-\delta C/\delta Y} & \dfrac{1}{1-\delta C/\delta Y} \end{pmatrix} = (\mathbf{dY}, \mathbf{dC})$$

would be used to express Y and C explicitly as functions of I and θ:

$$Y = \int dY = \int\left(\frac{1}{1-\delta C/\delta Y}\right)dI + \int\left(\frac{1}{1-\delta C/\delta Y}\right)d\theta + Constant$$

$$C = \int dC = \int\left(\frac{\delta C/\delta Y}{1-\delta C/\delta Y}\right)dI + \int\left(\frac{1}{1-\delta C/\delta Y}\right)d\theta + Constant$$

But it is not necessary to go into these more difficult mathematical problems where linear functions are involved.

MATRICES AS LINEAR MAPPINGS

This section is a more detailed discussion of vectors and matrices. Anyone who intends to make calculations involving matrices is well advised to go through it, even though it is strictly necessary only to the analysis of Chapters 9–11.

Vector Spaces

The notion of vector has already been introduced in the following way: A vector is an ordered set of numbers, such as $\mathbf{V} = (\mathbf{V}_1, \mathbf{V}_2, \ldots, \mathbf{V}_n)$. If each *component* of $\mathbf{V}$(each of the numbers $V_1, V_2, \ldots, V_n$) is in some set, then all vectors V, such that $V_1 \in S_1$, $V_2 \in S_2, \ldots, V_n \in S_n$, form a set. This set will be a *vector space* V, if the following properties hold.

(1) If $\mathbf{V}$ is in V, then $\mathbf{aV}$ is in V, for any number a, Multiply $\mathbf{V}$ by a in the following fashion:

$$\mathbf{aV} = a(\mathbf{V}_1, \mathbf{V}_2, \ldots, \mathbf{V}_n) = (\mathbf{aV}_1, \mathbf{aV}_2, \ldots, \mathbf{aV}_n)$$

That is, when $\mathbf{V}$ is multiplied by a, each component of $\mathbf{V}$ is multiplied by a.

(2) If $\mathbf{V}_1$ and $\mathbf{V}_2$ are in V, then $\mathbf{V}_1 + \mathbf{V}_2$ is in V. Add the vectors $\mathbf{V}_1$ and $\mathbf{V}_2$ as follows:

$$\mathbf{V}_1 = (\mathbf{V}_1, \mathbf{V}_2, \ldots, \mathbf{V}_n)$$
$$\mathbf{V}_2 = (\mathbf{V}_1', \mathbf{V}_2', \ldots, \mathbf{V}_n')$$
$$\mathbf{V}_1 + \mathbf{V}_2 = ([\mathbf{V}_1 + \mathbf{V}_1'], [\mathbf{V}_2 + \mathbf{V}_2'], \ldots, [\mathbf{V}_n + \mathbf{V}_n'])$$

That is, addition of two vectors means adding their corresponding components. Thus, addition is defined *only* for vectors having the same numbers of components.

(3) There is a vector $\boldsymbol{\theta}$ in V (called the *null vector* or the *zero vector*), such that $\mathbf{V} + \boldsymbol{\theta} = \mathbf{V}$ for every $\mathbf{V}$ in V. Construct $\boldsymbol{\theta}$ as follows:

$$\boldsymbol{\theta} = (\mathbf{0}, \mathbf{0}, \ldots, \mathbf{0})$$

(4) For every vector $\mathbf{V}$ in V, there exists a vector $-\mathbf{V}$ in V, such that $\mathbf{V} + (-\mathbf{V}) = \boldsymbol{\theta}$. Construct $-\mathbf{V}$ as follows:

$$\text{If } \mathbf{V} = (\mathbf{V}_1, \mathbf{V}_2, \ldots, \mathbf{V}_n)$$
$$-\mathbf{V} = (-\mathbf{V}_1, -\mathbf{V}_2, \ldots, -\mathbf{V}_n)$$

Economists will notice that it makes no sense to add some vectors, even if they have the same numbers of components. For instance, the vectors

$$(\mathbf{Y}, \mathbf{C}, \mathbf{I})$$

and

$$(\mathbf{W}, \mathbf{p}, \mathbf{r})$$

both contain three symbols. But if

Y = national product
C = consumption
I = investment
W = wage level
p = price level
r = rate of interest

it makes no economic sense to add the two together to make, say

$(\mathbf{Y} + \mathbf{W},\ \mathbf{C} + \mathbf{p},\ \mathbf{I} + \mathbf{r})$. It might make sense in some contexts to combine them as a single vector:

$$(\mathbf{Y}, \mathbf{C}, \mathbf{I}, \mathbf{w}, \mathbf{p}, \mathbf{r})$$

If one did so, he would be combining two three-dimensional spaces to form a six-dimensional space. In later chapters, theories are sometimes combined so as to account for a larger number of variables. These combinations are not the same as the vector additions just described.

Linear One-to-One Mappings

Suppose a vector of factors:

$$\mathbf{F} = (\mathbf{F}_1, \mathbf{F}_2, \ldots, \mathbf{F}_m)$$

which is to be related in a one-to-one way with a vector of macroeconomic variables:

$$\mathbf{V} = (\mathbf{V}_1, \mathbf{V}_2, \ldots, \mathbf{V}_n)$$

Then any theory T that states that the variables depend on the factors

$$\mathbf{FT} = \mathbf{V}$$

can be "inverted." That is, the theory may be "inverted" without any additional economic information. The "inverse" theory $\mathbf{T}^{-1}$ states that the factors depend on the variables.[7]

A theory $\mathbf{T}$ is said to be linear in the following case: Let $\mathbf{F}_1$ and $\mathbf{F}_2$ be arbitrary vectors; let a and b be arbitrary numbers. Then $(a\mathbf{F}_1 + b\mathbf{F}_2)$ is a vector, according to our rules for operations on a vector. A theory (mapping) $\mathbf{T}$ is linear if

$$(a\mathbf{F}_1 + b\mathbf{F}_2)\mathbf{T} = a\mathbf{F}_1\mathbf{T} + b\mathbf{F}_2\mathbf{T}$$

That is, the image of a linear combination $(a\mathbf{F}_1 + b\mathbf{F}_2)$ under $\mathbf{T}$ is the same vector as that linear combination $(a\mathbf{F}_1\mathbf{T} + b\mathbf{F}_2\mathbf{T})$ of the images of the vectors $\mathbf{F}_1$ and $\mathbf{F}_2$ taken separately.

There has so far been no instruction given as to how to *construct* a linear mapping, let alone a one-to-one mapping. We shall therefore define something called a *matrix*, and show that a matrix is a linear mapping.

A *matrix* is an array of numbers, arranged in rows and columns. There follow several examples of matrices.

---

[7] The relations denoted by T and T^{-1} are related in a purely algebraic way. (That is, they are connected by the same sort of rule that says that two pounds of hamburger at \$.59 a pound cost \$1.18.) By computing T^{-1} we derive implications of T which are not immediately apparent from the statement of the original mapping T.

$$\begin{pmatrix} 1 & 2 \\ 3 & 4 \end{pmatrix} \begin{pmatrix} 1 & 0 & 0 \\ 0 & 10 & 0 \\ 0 & 0 & 34 \end{pmatrix} \begin{pmatrix} b_{11} & b_{12} \\ b_{21} & b_{22} \\ b_{31} & b_{32} \end{pmatrix} \begin{pmatrix} c_{11} & c_{12} & c_{13} \\ c_{21} & c_{22} & c_{23} \end{pmatrix}$$

In a *square* matrix, the number of rows is equal to the number of columns; in a *rectangular* matrix these two numbers are unequal. A matrix may have any number of rows and any number of columns. A matrix may be designated as a single letter **M**; an individual *element* of a matrix has two subscripts denoting the row and column in which the element is located. Thus the matrix **M** is sometimes written (m_{ij}). If **M** has r rows and s columns, $i = 1 \cdots r$ and $s = 1 \cdots s$, so that m_{23} is the element in row 2 and column 3.[8] The *order* of a square matrix is the number of its rows (columns)

A matrix is associated with a mapping. Suppose a vector $\mathbf{V} = (\mathbf{V}_1, \mathbf{V}_2, \ldots, \mathbf{V}_n)$ and a square matrix of order n:

$$\mathbf{M} = \begin{pmatrix} m_{11} & m_{12} & \cdots & m_{1n} \\ m_{21} & m_{22} & \cdots & m_{2n} \\ & & \cdots & \\ m_{n1} & m_{n2} & \cdots & m_{nn} \end{pmatrix}$$

Then the image of **V** under the mapping **M** is defined by

$$\mathbf{VM} = (\mathbf{V}_1, \mathbf{V}_2, \ldots, \mathbf{V}_n) \begin{pmatrix} m_{11} & m_{12} & \cdots & m_{1n} \\ m_{21} & m_{22} & \cdots & m_{2n} \\ & & \cdots & \\ m_{n1} & m_{n2} & \cdots & m_{nn} \end{pmatrix}$$

$$= \left(\sum_{i=1}^{n} \mathbf{V}_i m_{i1}, \sum_{i=1}^{n} \mathbf{V}_i m_{i2}, \ldots, \sum_{i=1}^{n} \mathbf{V}_i m_{in} \right)$$

Thus **VM** is a vector; and the jth component ($j = 1, \ldots, n$) of the vector **VM** is given by

$$\mathbf{V}_1 m_{ij} + \mathbf{V}_2 m_{2j} + \mathbf{V}_3 m_{3j} + \cdots + \mathbf{V}_n m_{nj}$$

These rules imply that a matrix is a linear mapping. Let

$$\mathbf{F}_1 = (\mathbf{X}_1, \mathbf{X}_2, \ldots, \mathbf{X}_n)$$

$$\mathbf{F}_2 = (\mathbf{Y}_1, \mathbf{Y}_2, \ldots, \mathbf{Y}_n)$$

$$\mathbf{M} = \begin{pmatrix} m_{11} \cdots m_{1n} \\ \cdots \\ m_{n1} \cdots m_{nn} \end{pmatrix}$$

---

[8] Sometimes the *first* subscript is used to designate the column and the second the row. It is usually made clear in context when this is the case.

Then

$$aF_1 + bF_2 = (aX_1 + bY_1, aX_2 + bY_2, \ldots, aX_n + bY_n)$$

$$(aF_1 + bF_2)M = (aX_1 + bY_1, aY_2 + bY_2, \ldots, aX_n + bY_n)\begin{pmatrix} m_{11} & \cdots & m_{1n} \\ & \cdots & \\ m_{n1} & \cdots & m_{nn} \end{pmatrix}$$

$$= (\sum(aX_j + bY_j)m_{j1}, \sum(aX_j + bY_j)m_{j2}, \ldots, \sum(aX_j + bY_j)m_{jn})$$

$$= a(\sum X_j m_{j1}, \sum X_j m_{j2}, \ldots, \sum X_j m_{jn})$$

$$+ b(\sum Y_{j1}, \sum Y_j m_{j2}, \ldots, \sum Y_j m_{jn})$$

$$= a(X_1, X_2, \ldots, X_n)\begin{pmatrix} m_{11} & \cdots & m_{1n} \\ & \cdots & \\ m_n & \cdots & m_{nn} \end{pmatrix}$$

$$+ b(Y_1 \cdots Y_n)\begin{pmatrix} m_{11} & \cdots & m_{1n} \\ & \cdots & \\ m_{n1} & \cdots & m_{nn} \end{pmatrix}$$

$$= aF_1M + bF_2M$$

Matrices have some characteristics that make them like numbers.

(1) There is exactly one number m having the property that whatever number f is considered, $fm = m$. This is the number $m = 0$. The vector image **FM** is a vector; if whatever vector **F** considered, **FM** is the null-vector **0**, then **M** is the matrix consisting entirely of zeros. This matrix is called the *zero matrix* and is written **0**. There is one such matrix of each order.

(2) There is exactly one number m having the property that whatever f is, $fm = f$. This is the number $m = 1$. There is one matrix of each order having the property that $\mathbf{FM} = \mathbf{MF} = \mathbf{F}$ for every vector **F**. This matrix will be designated **E**, and is called the *unit matrix*. The unit matrix of order 4 is written:

$$\mathbf{E} = \begin{pmatrix} 1 & 0 & 0 & 0 \\ 0 & 1 & 0 & 0 \\ 0 & 0 & 1 & 0 \\ 0 & 0 & 0 & 1 \end{pmatrix}$$

(*Note:* The elements of this matrix containing 1s are called diagonal elements. The set of all diagonal elements of any matrix is called the *diagonal* of the matrix.)

Matrices may be added and multiplied. We do not have much occasion to use matrix addition, but it is convenient to define it. A matrix **C** is the *sum* of two matrices **A** and **B** if for every vector **V**, $\mathbf{VC} = \mathbf{V}(\mathbf{A} + \mathbf{B})$ $= \mathbf{VA} + \mathbf{VB}$. This condition is satisfied if any element of **C**, say c_{ij} is the sum of the corresponding elements of **A** and **B**:

$$c_{ij} = a_{ij} + b_{ij}$$

($i, j = 1, \ldots, n$, n is the order of matrix).

A matrix **C** is the *product* of matrices **A** and **B** for every vector **V**

$$\mathbf{VC} = \mathbf{V}(\mathbf{AB}) = (\mathbf{VA})\mathbf{B}$$

In other words, the image of **V** under **C** is the image of **VA** under **B**, for every vector **V**. To construct a way of achieving this condition, we proceed as follows:

The vector **VC** is written as

$$(\mathbf{V}_1\mathbf{V}_2 \cdots \mathbf{V}_n)\begin{pmatrix} c_{11} & c_{12} & \cdots & c_{1n} \\ c_{21} & c_{22} & \cdots & c_{2n} \\ & & \cdots & \\ c_{n1} & c_{n2} & \cdots & c_{nn} \end{pmatrix} = \left(\sum \mathbf{V}_i c_{i1}, \sum \mathbf{V}_i c_{i2}, \ldots, \sum \mathbf{V}_i c_{in}\right)$$

The vector **VAB** is written as:

$$(\mathbf{V}_1\mathbf{V}_2 \cdots \mathbf{V}_n)\begin{pmatrix} a_{11} & a_{12} & \cdots & a_{1n} \\ a_{21} & a_{22} & \cdots & a_{2n} \\ & & \cdots & \\ a_{n1} & a_{n2} & \cdots & a_{nn} \end{pmatrix}\begin{pmatrix} b_{11} & b_{12} & \cdots & b_{1n} \\ b_{21} & b_{22} & \cdots & b_{2n} \\ & & \cdots & \\ b_{n1} & b_{n2} & \cdots & b_{nn} \end{pmatrix}$$

$$= \left(\sum \mathbf{V}_i a_{i1}, \sum \mathbf{V}_i a_{i2}, \ldots, \sum \mathbf{V}_i a_{in}\right)\begin{pmatrix} b_{11} & b_{12} & \cdots & b_{1n} \\ b_{21} & b_{22} & \cdots & b_{1n} \\ & & \cdots & \\ b_{n1} & b_{n2} & \cdots & b_{nn} \end{pmatrix}$$

$$= \left(\sum_i \mathbf{V}_i \sum_j a_{ij} b_{j1}, \sum_i \mathbf{V}_i \sum_j a_{ij} b_{j2}, \ldots, \sum \mathbf{V}_i \sum a_{ij} b_{j2}\right)$$

Consequently, whatever **V** may be, $\mathbf{VC} = \mathbf{VAB}$ if

$$\begin{pmatrix} c_{11} & c_{12} & \cdots & c_{1n} \\ c_{21} & c_{22} & \cdots & c_{2n} \\ & & \cdots & \\ c_{n1} & c_{n2} & \cdots & c_{nn} \end{pmatrix} = \begin{pmatrix} \sum_j a_{1j} b_{j1} & \sum_j a_{1j} b_{j2} & \cdots & \sum_j a_{1j} b_{jn} \\ \sum_j a_{2j} b_{j1} & \sum_j a_{2j} b_{j2} & \cdots & \sum_j a_{2j} b_{jn} \\ & & \cdots & \\ \sum_j a_{nj} b_{j1} & \sum_j a_{nj} b_{j2} & \cdots & \sum_j a_{nj} b_{jn} \end{pmatrix}$$

This rather frightening way of multiplying matrices may be thought of as follows: to calculate element c_{ki} in row k column i of **C**, we multiply the elements in *row k* of **A** by the corresponding elements in *column i* of **B**, and add the products:

$$c_{ki} = \sum_{j=1}^{n} a_{kj} b_{ji} = a_{k1} b_{1i} + a_{k2} b_{2i} + \cdots + a_{kn} b_{ni}$$

An important difference between multiplying numbers and multiplying matrices is that in multiplying matrices, the order of multiplication matters. In multiplying numbers, order does not matter: $2 \times 3 = 3 \times 2 = 6$. However, this simple example of matrix multiplication,

$$\begin{pmatrix} 1 & a \\ 0 & 1 \end{pmatrix} \begin{pmatrix} 1 & 0 \\ b & 1 \end{pmatrix} = \begin{pmatrix} (1+ab) & a \\ b & 1 \end{pmatrix}$$

$$\begin{pmatrix} 1 & 0 \\ b & 1 \end{pmatrix} \begin{pmatrix} 1 & a \\ 0 & 1 \end{pmatrix} = \begin{pmatrix} 1 & a \\ b & (1+ab) \end{pmatrix}$$

shows that the product **AB** is not necessarily the same as the product **BA**.

Matrix Inversion

The inverse of a matrix **T** is written $\mathbf{T}^{-1}$. It enables us to perform the following operation. Suppose **X** and **Y** are vectors such that $\mathbf{X} = \mathbf{YT}$. Then

$$\mathbf{XT}^{-1} = (\mathbf{YT})\mathbf{T}^{-1} = \mathbf{Y}(\mathbf{TT}^{-1}) = \mathbf{Y}$$

The relation $\mathbf{Y}(\mathbf{TT}^{-1}) = \mathbf{Y}$ must hold for every **Y**. Consequently, the product of the matrices **T** and $\mathbf{T}^{-1}$ must be a matrix that leaves every vector unchanged Such matrices are of the form

$$\begin{pmatrix} 1 & 0 \\ 0 & 1 \end{pmatrix} \begin{pmatrix} 1 & 0 & 0 \\ 0 & 1 & 0 \\ 0 & 0 & 1 \end{pmatrix} \begin{pmatrix} 1 & 0 & 0 & 0 \\ 0 & 1 & 0 & 0 \\ 0 & 0 & 1 & 0 \\ 0 & 0 & 0 & 1 \end{pmatrix}$$

They are the *unit matrices* of orders 2, 3, 4, and so on.

Thus, to invert a matrix **T**, we seek another matrix $\mathbf{T}^{-1}$ such that $\mathbf{TT}^{-1}$ will be a unit matrix.

If **T** is a 1×1 matrix (t), then $\mathbf{T}^{-1}$ will be the 1×1 matrix $(1/t)$. Matrices of larger order take more work to invert, except in simple cases. In this book, most of the theories have (or are based on) matrices that are easy to invert.

Inverting Matrices of Order 2. The Tiny Models presented in this chapter are for the smallest matrices that are not numbers—matrices of order 2. It happened that these matrices were the same since, for practical purposes, the numbers in each were the same. It is easy to give a general formula for inverting matrices of order 2:

$$\begin{pmatrix} a & b \\ c & d \end{pmatrix} \begin{pmatrix} \dfrac{d}{ad-bc} & \dfrac{-b}{ad-bc} \\ \dfrac{-c}{ad-bc} & \dfrac{a}{ad-bc} \end{pmatrix} = \begin{pmatrix} 1 & 0 \\ 0 & 1 \end{pmatrix}$$

except in the case where $ad - bc = 0$. In this case it is not possible to invert the matrix.[9] Where a theory involves a matrix that cannot be inverted, the theory does not involve a one-to-one mapping of factors into variables, and such a theory is unacceptable in terms of the analysis we are engaged in.

Block Notation and the Inversion of Matrices of Larger Order. Matrices have been considered as arrays of numbers. Suppose, however, that we can construct two theories, both mapping vectors of factors into vectors of variables in one-to-one fashion. Then for each theory there will be an invertible matrix, say,

$$M_2 = \begin{pmatrix} a_{11} & a_{12} & \cdots & a_{1n} \\ a_{21} & a_{22} & \cdots & a_{2n} \\ & \cdots & & \\ a_{n1} & a_{n2} & \cdots & a_{nn} \end{pmatrix} \quad M_2 = \begin{pmatrix} b_{11} & b_{12} & \cdots & b_{1n} \\ b_{21} & b_{22} & \cdots & b_{2n} \\ & \cdots & & \\ b_{n1} & b_{n2} & \cdots & b_{nn} \end{pmatrix}$$

It may be that these theories have some parts in common. These parts might consist of certain statements common to both. This similarity would be reflected by the fact that certain columns of M_1 would have the same elements as the corresponding columns of M_2. Alternatively, certain *blocks* of elements reappear in several theories, including theories involving matrices of different orders.

For example, in Chapter 3, we considered matrices of the form

$$\begin{pmatrix} M_{11} & M_{12} \\ M_{21} & M_{22} \end{pmatrix}$$

in which the symbol M_{ij} stands for a square or rectangular block of numbers. For instance M_{11} may be the matrix

$$\begin{pmatrix} 1 & -a \\ -1 & 1 \end{pmatrix}$$

---

[9] The quantity $ad - bc$ is called the *determinant* of the matrix. Similar formulas exist for calculating determinants of matrices of higher order. These general determinants are tedious to compute, and for purposes of this book they are unnecessary. We propose an iterative approach to computing inverses of matrices by looking at inverses of pieces of them.

of Tiny Model 1 and M_{22} may be the matrix

$$\begin{pmatrix} 1 & -b \\ -1 & 1 \end{pmatrix}$$

of Tiny Model 2. Written as a mapping, the theory takes the form

$$(\mathbf{F}_1, \mathbf{F}_2)\begin{pmatrix} M_{11} & M_{12} \\ M_{21} & M_{22} \end{pmatrix} = (\mathbf{V}_1, \mathbf{V}_2) \tag{2.7}$$

However, $\mathbf{F}_1$, $\mathbf{F}_2$, $\mathbf{V}_1$, $\mathbf{V}_2$ do not stand for single numbers but rather for sets of numbers. A special case of theory 2.7 is the theory

$$(F_1, F_2)\begin{pmatrix} M_{11} & 0 \\ 0 & M_{22} \end{pmatrix} = (\mathbf{V}_1, \mathbf{V}_2) \tag{2.8}$$

(Here the symbols "0" stand for blocks of zeros. The theory represented by equation 2.8 may be written in the form

$$\begin{aligned} \mathbf{F}_1\mathbf{M}_{11} &= \mathbf{V}_1 \\ \mathbf{F}_2\mathbf{M}_{22} &= \mathbf{V}_2 \end{aligned} \tag{2.9}$$

This statement (equation 2.9) says that $\mathbf{V}_1$ depends only on the factors listed in $\mathbf{F}_1$; $\mathbf{V}_2$ depends only on the factors listed in $\mathbf{F}_2$. In contrast, the theory 2.7 states that:

$$\begin{aligned} \mathbf{F}_1\mathbf{M}_{11} + \mathbf{F}_2\mathbf{M}_{21} &= \mathbf{V}_1 \\ \mathbf{F}_1\mathbf{M}_{12} + \mathbf{F}_2\mathbf{M}_{22} &= \mathbf{V}_2 \end{aligned}$$

That is, the factors listed in $\mathbf{F}_2$ affect $\mathbf{V}_1$, and the factors listed in $\mathbf{F}_1$ affect $\mathbf{V}_2$. Even so, the more complicated first theory (2.7) may have certain blocks in common with the simpler theory (2.8).

The nondiagonal blocks M_{12} and M_{21} basically consist of linkages between "little" theories pertaining only to some of the variables and some of the factors in the system.

A matrix written in *block form* always has square diagonal blocks. (These are the blocks M_{11}, M_{22}.) Nondiagonal blocks (the blocks M_{12} and M_{21}) may be rectangular. For example, a block matrix may have the following structure:

$$\begin{array}{cccc} & \text{2 columns} & \text{3 columns} & \\ \mathbf{M} = & \Big(M_{11} & M_{12} \Big) & \text{2 rows} \\ & \Big(M_{21} & M_{22} \Big) & \text{3 rows} \end{array}$$

In this case, the blocks making up the vectors must be defined so that multiplication is possible: in $\mathbf{F} = (\mathbf{F}_1, \mathbf{F}_2)$, $\mathbf{F}_1$ must have two components, and $\mathbf{F}_2$ must have three components if the vector $\mathbf{FM}$ is to be calculated according to the rules set forth above.

There are two reasons for using block notation in matrices. The first is economic: Where successive theories contain elements in common, the matrices associated with the theories have blocks in common. This notation emphasizes the similarity. The second reason is computational: It is much easier to calculate the inverse of a large matrix if smaller parts of it have already been inverted. It is convenient to start with a small block and to invert the matrix in steps.

The block matrix

$$\begin{pmatrix} M_{11} & 0 \\ 0 & M_{22} \end{pmatrix}$$

is called *block-diagonal.* This is because the nondiagonal blocks M_{12} and M_{21} are zeros. The inverse of a block-diagonal matrix is calculated by inverting the blocks separately:

$$\begin{pmatrix} M_{11} & 0 \\ 0 & M_{22} \end{pmatrix} \begin{pmatrix} M_{11}^{-1} & 0 \\ 0 & M_{22}^{-1} \end{pmatrix} = \begin{pmatrix} E & 0 \\ 0 & E \end{pmatrix}$$

The two block matrices

$$\begin{pmatrix} M_{11} & M_{12} \\ 0 & M_{22} \end{pmatrix} \quad \text{and} \quad \begin{pmatrix} M_{11} & 0 \\ M_{21} & M_{22} \end{pmatrix}$$

are called *block-triangular*. Readers may verify that

$$\begin{pmatrix} M_{11} & M_{12} \\ 0 & M_{22} \end{pmatrix} \begin{pmatrix} M_{11}^{-1} & -M_{11}^{-1} M_{12} M_{22}^{-1} \\ 0 & M_{22}^{-1} \end{pmatrix} = E$$

and

$$\begin{pmatrix} M_{11} & 0 \\ M_{21} & M_{22} \end{pmatrix} \begin{pmatrix} M_{11}^{-1} & 0 \\ -M_{22}^{-1} M_{21} M_{11}^{-1} & M_{22}^{-1} \end{pmatrix} = E$$

In both cases, where a matrix has blocks of zeros, its inverse also has blocks of zeros. (This does not mean that if some *element* of M_{11} or M_{12} is zero, the corresponding element in the inverse will necessarily be zero.)

Sometimes a matrix can be inverted by a succession of steps involving only block-triangular matrices. Thus the matrix

$$\begin{pmatrix} a & 0 & d & 0 \\ b & c & e & 0 \\ 0 & 0 & f & 0 \\ g & h & i & j \end{pmatrix}$$

can be inverted by stages, following the sequence

$$\begin{pmatrix} a & 0 \\ b & c \end{pmatrix} \begin{pmatrix} a & 0 & d \\ b & c & e \\ 0 & 0 & f \end{pmatrix}, \begin{pmatrix} a & 0 & d & 0 \\ b & c & e & 0 \\ 0 & 0 & f & 0 \\ g & h & i & j \end{pmatrix}$$

At each stage in this inversion, a block-triangular matrix is inverted.

Sometimes, a theory is written in a form that does not seem to be block-triangular, but which can be made block-triangular. Thus the matrix

$$(\mathbf{F}_1, \mathbf{F}_2, \mathbf{F}_3, \mathbf{F}_4) \begin{pmatrix} I & 0 & 0 & J \\ G & F & E & H \\ C & B & A & D \\ K & 0 & 0 & L \end{pmatrix} = (\mathbf{V}_1, \mathbf{V}_2, \mathbf{V}_3, \mathbf{V}_4) \tag{2.12}$$

looks as if it were not block-triangular. However, if the variables are rearranged so that the vector variable becomes $(\mathbf{V}_2, \mathbf{V}_3, \mathbf{V}_1, \mathbf{V}_4)$ the columns of the matrix must also be rearranged:

$$(\mathbf{F}_1, \mathbf{F}_2, \mathbf{F}_3, \mathbf{F}_4) \begin{pmatrix} 0 & 0 & I & J \\ F & E & G & H \\ B & A & C & D \\ 0 & 0 & K & L \end{pmatrix} = (\mathbf{V}_2, \mathbf{V}_3, \mathbf{V}_1, \mathbf{V}_4)$$

Now rearrange the order of the factors, so that the factor vector becomes $(\mathbf{F}_2, \mathbf{F}_3, \mathbf{F}_1, \mathbf{F}_4)$. Then the rows of the matrix must also be rearranged:

$$(\mathbf{F}_2, \mathbf{F}_3, \mathbf{F}_1, \mathbf{F}_4) \begin{pmatrix} F & E & G & H \\ B & A & C & D \\ 0 & 0 & I & J \\ 0 & 0 & K & L \end{pmatrix} = (\mathbf{V}_2, \mathbf{V}_3, \mathbf{V}_1, \mathbf{V}_4) \tag{2.13}$$

The matrix is now in block-triangular form. It is much easier to invert (2.13) than to invert 2.12, even though the two say the same thing.

It will often save the reader time if, before inverting a matrix, he rearranges the variables and factors so as to reveal the block-triangular structure of a theory.

If M_{11} and M_{22} are both invertible, all block-diagonal and block-triangular matrices containing them will also be invertible. But in general, invertibility of M_{11} and of M_{12} does not imply that M is invertible. For instance, let

$$M \equiv \begin{pmatrix} M_{11} & M_{12} \\ M_{21} & M_{22} \end{pmatrix} \equiv \begin{pmatrix} M_{11} & M_{12} \\ M_{11} & M_{12} \end{pmatrix}$$

Then even if M_{11} and M_{22} are both invertible, the matrix as a whole is not.

The general rule for inverting block matrices is

$$\begin{pmatrix} A & B \\ C & D \end{pmatrix} \begin{pmatrix} (A - BD^{-1}C)^{-1} & -(A - BD^{-1}C)^{-1}BD^{-1} \\ -(D - CA^{-1}B)^{-1}CA^{-1} & (D - CA^{-1}B)^{-1} \end{pmatrix} = \begin{pmatrix} E & 0 \\ 0 & E \end{pmatrix}$$

as may be verified. Naturally this inversion is more tedious than the inversion of block-diagonal and block-triangular matrices. In beginning work, it is natural to consider block-triangular theories first before taking on the more difficult cases. In Chapter 6, for instance, we shall look at theories of the form

$$\begin{pmatrix} A & 0 \\ C & D \end{pmatrix}$$

and

$$\begin{pmatrix} A & B \\ 0 & D \end{pmatrix}$$

in detail and omit the rather messy

$$\begin{pmatrix} A & B \\ C & D \end{pmatrix}$$

simply because this procedure makes computation much easier.

Our work proceeds by a process of gradual escalation. Consequently, theories involving matrices such as

$$\begin{pmatrix} M_{11} & M_{12} & M_{13} \\ M_{21} & M_{22} & M_{23} \\ M_{31} & M_{32} & M_{33} \end{pmatrix}$$

will usually turn out to be expressible as

$$\begin{pmatrix} \overline{M}_{11} & \overline{M}_{12} \\ \overline{M}_{21} & \overline{M}_{22} \end{pmatrix}$$

where

$$\overline{M}_{11} = \begin{pmatrix} M_{11} & M_{12} \\ M_{21} & M_{22} \end{pmatrix}$$

$$\overline{M}_{12} = \begin{pmatrix} M_{13} \\ M_{23} \end{pmatrix}$$

$$\overline{M}_{21} = (M_{31} \quad M_{32})$$

$$\overline{M}_{22} = (M_{33})$$

some parts of which have already been studied. Thus the results of one chapter may turn out to be usable in later chapters.

The general mathematical formulas for inverting matrices become very complicated indeed. The matrices presented here are usually rather simple to invert, because

(1) In a general mathematical formula for inverting large matrices, each element of a matrix is treated as an arbitrary number. A theory usually specifies

that many elements of the matrix are zero or one, and thus simplifies the task of inversion.

(2) The whole purpose of a theory is to present a simple way of looking at a complicated problem. The simpler a theory is, the smaller the number of connections asserted to exist between pairs of variables; and hence the larger the number of zero elements in the matrix expressing the theory.

(3) A book of *simple* economic theory will present theories involving a relatively small number of variables; and each theory will involve a relatively small number of connections among the variables. That is, simple theories mean large numbers of ones and zeros in the matrix expressing the theory. The larger the number of ones and zeros, the easier it is to invert a matrix.

(4) Even simple theories can be useful in understanding the economy, if they make good use of the basic concepts of social accounting, and if they express in some elementary form the principal ideas that economists have developed over the years.

Appendix to Chapter 2

In the text, primary attention is paid to the consequences of a change in one or more of the *factors* in a theory upon each of the *variables* in that theory. But it is also possible to estimate what happens to each of the variables in the theory, supposing that the factors are all unchanged, and that one of the *coefficients* of the matrix changes. This appendix explains how to compute this effect.

Suppose that $\mathbf{M}$ is an invertible matrix. Its inverse is $\mathbf{M}^{-1}$. If m_{ij} is the element in row i, column j of $\mathbf{M}$, we will write $\overline{m}_{ij}$ for the corresponding element of $\mathbf{M}^{-1}$. Suppose now that we consider a matrix $(\mathbf{M} + \Delta\mathbf{M})$. $\Delta\mathbf{M}$ is a square matrix. In this problem, we suppose that $\Delta\mathbf{M}$ has only one non-zero element. What is the relation between $\mathbf{M}^{-1}$ and $(\mathbf{M} + \Delta\mathbf{M})^{-1}$? The problem is to evaluate $\mathbf{\Psi}$, where $\mathbf{\Psi} = (\mathbf{M} + \Delta\mathbf{M})^{-1} - \mathbf{M}^{-1}$.

$$\mathbf{M}\mathbf{M}^{-1} = \mathbf{E}$$

$$(\mathbf{M} + \Delta\mathbf{M})(\mathbf{M}^{-1} + \mathbf{\Psi}) = \mathbf{E}$$

$$\mathbf{M}\mathbf{M}^{-1} + \Delta\mathbf{M}\mathbf{M}^{-1} + \mathbf{M}\mathbf{\Psi} + \Delta\mathbf{M}\mathbf{\Psi} = \mathbf{E}$$

$$\Delta\mathbf{M}\mathbf{M}^{-1} + (\mathbf{M} + \Delta\mathbf{M})\mathbf{\Psi} = \mathbf{0}$$

Multiply both sides by $\mathbf{M}^{-1}$. Then

$$\mathbf{M}^{-1}\Delta\mathbf{M}\mathbf{M}^{-1} + \mathbf{M}^{-1}(\mathbf{M} + \Delta\mathbf{M})\mathbf{\Psi} = 0$$

$$(\mathbf{E} + \mathbf{M}^{-1}\Delta\mathbf{M})\mathbf{\Psi} = -\mathbf{M}^{-1}\Delta\mathbf{M}\mathbf{M}^{-1}$$

Since $\Delta\mathbf{M}$, by assumption, has only one nonzero element, it is a matrix of the form

$$\mathbf{\Delta M} = \begin{pmatrix} 0 & \cdots & 0 & \cdots & 0 \\ & & \cdots & & \\ 0 & \cdots & \Delta m_{ij} & \cdots & 0 \\ & & \cdots & & \\ 0 & \cdots & 0 & \cdots & 0 \end{pmatrix}$$

Therefore $\mathbf{M}^{-1}\mathbf{\Delta M}$ is some matrix of the form

$$\mathbf{M}^{-1}\,\mathbf{\Delta M} = \begin{pmatrix} \overline{m}_{11} & \cdots & \overline{m}_{1j} & \cdots & \overline{m}_{in} \\ & & \cdots & & \\ \overline{m}_{i1} & \cdots & \overline{m}_{ij} & \cdots & \overline{m}_{in} \\ & & \cdots & & \\ \overline{m}_{ni} & \cdots & \overline{m}_{nj} & \cdots & \overline{m}_{nn} \end{pmatrix} \begin{pmatrix} 0 & \cdots & 0 & \cdots & 0 \\ & & \cdots & & \\ 0 & \cdots & \Delta m_{ij} & \cdots & 0 \\ & & \cdots & & \\ 0 & \cdots & 0 & \cdots & 0 \end{pmatrix}$$

$$= \begin{pmatrix} 0 & \cdots & \overline{m}_{1j}\,\Delta m_{ij} & \cdots & 0 \\ & & \cdots & & \\ 0 & \cdots & \overline{m}_{ij}\,\Delta m_{ij} & \cdots & 0 \\ & & \cdots & & \\ 0 & \cdots & \overline{m}_{nj}\,\Delta m_{ij} & \cdots & 0 \end{pmatrix}$$

That is, $\mathbf{M}^{-1}\mathbf{\Delta M}$ consists of zeros except in column j. The elements of column j have elements equal to those of $\mathbf{M}^{-1}$, each multiplied by Δm_{ij}, the change in the element in row i, column j of $\mathbf{M}$.

From the equation $(\mathbf{E} + \mathbf{M}^{-1}\mathbf{\Delta M})\mathbf{\Psi} = -\mathbf{M}^{-1}\mathbf{\Delta M}\mathbf{M}^{-1}$, one obtains the equation $\Psi = -(\mathbf{E} + \mathbf{M}^{-1}\mathbf{\Delta M})^{-1}\mathbf{M}^{-1}\mathbf{\Delta M}\mathbf{M}^{-1}$. The right hand side seems to be messy, but it can be computed by brute force.

(1) $\mathbf{M}^{-1}\mathbf{\Delta M}\mathbf{M}^{-1}$ is computed by multiplying $\mathbf{M}^{-1}\mathbf{\Delta M}$ on the right by $\mathbf{M}^{-1}$.

$$\mathbf{M}^{-1}\,\mathbf{\Delta M}\mathbf{M}^{-1} = \begin{pmatrix} 0 & \cdots & \overline{m}_{1j}\,\Delta m_{ij} & \cdots & 0 \\ & & \cdots & & \\ 0 & \cdots & \overline{m}_{ij}\,\Delta m_{ij} & \cdots & 0 \\ & & \cdots & & \\ 0 & \cdots & \overline{m}_{nj}\,\Delta m_{ij} & \cdots & 0 \end{pmatrix} \begin{pmatrix} \overline{m}_{11} & \cdots & \overline{m}_{1i} & \cdots & \overline{m}_{1n} \\ & & \cdots & & \\ \overline{m}_{j1} & \cdots & \overline{m}_{ji} & \cdots & \overline{m}_{jn} \\ & & \cdots & & \\ \overline{m}_{n1} & \cdots & \overline{m}_{ni} & \cdots & \overline{m}_{nn} \end{pmatrix}$$

$$= \begin{pmatrix} \overline{m}_{1j}\,\Delta m_{ij}\,\overline{m}_{j1} & \cdots & \overline{m}_{1j}\,\Delta m_{ij}\,\overline{m}_{ji} & \cdots & \overline{m}_{1j}\,\Delta m_{ij}\,\overline{m}_{jn} \\ & & \cdots & & \\ \overline{m}_{ij}\,\Delta m_{ij}\,\overline{m}_{j1} & \cdots & \overline{m}_{ij}\,\Delta m_{ij}\,\overline{m}_{ji} & \cdots & \overline{m}_{ij}\,\Delta m_{ij}\,\overline{m}_{jn} \\ & & \cdots & & \\ \overline{m}_{nj}\,\Delta m_{ij}\,\overline{m}_{j1} & \cdots & \overline{m}_{nj}\,\Delta m_{ij}\,\overline{m}_{ji} & \cdots & \overline{m}_{nj}\,\Delta m_{ij}\,\overline{m}_{jn} \end{pmatrix}$$

The element in row r, column s of $\mathbf{M}^{-1}\mathbf{\Delta M}\mathbf{M}^{-1}$ is thus given by the formula $\Delta m_{ij}(\overline{m}_{rj}\overline{m}_{js})$.

(2) The matrix $(\mathbf{E} + \mathbf{M}^{-1}\Delta\mathbf{M})$ is of the form

$$\begin{pmatrix} 1 & 0 & \cdots & K_1 & \cdots & 0 \\ 0 & 1 & \cdots & K_2 & \cdots & 0 \\ & & & \cdots & & \\ 0 & 0 & \cdots & (1 + K_j) & \cdots & 0 \\ & & & \cdots & & \\ 0 & 0 & \cdots & K_n & \cdots & 1 \end{pmatrix}$$

The terms $K_1 \cdots K_n$ are in this case equal to $\overline{m}_{ij}\Delta m_{ij}$, $\overline{m}_{2j}\Delta m_{ij} \cdots \overline{m}_{nj} m_{ij}$. The inverse of this type of matrix has the form

$$\begin{pmatrix} 1 & 0 & \cdots & -\dfrac{K_1}{1 + K_j} & \cdots & 0 \\ 0 & 1 & \cdots & -\dfrac{K_2}{1 + K_j} & \cdots & 0 \\ & & & \cdots & & \\ 0 & 0 & \cdots & \dfrac{1}{1 + K_j} & \cdots & 0 \\ 0 & 0 & \cdots & -\dfrac{K_n}{1 + K_j} & \cdots & 1 \end{pmatrix}$$

That is to say that

$$(\mathbf{E} + \mathbf{M}^{-1}\,\Delta\mathbf{M})^{-1} = \begin{pmatrix} 1 & 0 & \cdots & -\dfrac{\overline{m}_{1j}\,\Delta m_{ij}}{1 + \overline{m}_{jj}\,\Delta m_{ij}} & \cdots & 0 \\ 0 & 1 & \cdots & -\dfrac{\overline{m}_{2j}\,\Delta m_{ij}}{1 + \overline{m}_{jj}\,\Delta m_{ij}} & \cdots & 0 \\ & & & \cdots & & \\ 0 & 0 & \cdots & \dfrac{1}{1 + \overline{m}_{jj}\,\Delta m_{ij}} & \cdots & 0 \\ & & & \cdots & & \\ 0 & 0 & \cdots & = \dfrac{\overline{m}_{nj}\,\Delta m_{ij}}{1 + m_{ij}\,\Delta m_{ij}} & \cdots & 1 \end{pmatrix}$$

(3) Consequently, $\Psi = -(\mathbf{E} + \mathbf{M}^{-1}\Delta\mathbf{M})^{-1}(\mathbf{M}^{-1}\Delta\mathbf{M}\mathbf{M}^{-1})$ is computed as follows:

$$= -\begin{pmatrix} 1 & 0 & \cdots & -\dfrac{\overline{m}_{1j}\,\Delta m_{ij}}{1+\overline{m}_{jj}\,\Delta m_{ij}} & \cdots & 0 \\ 0 & 1 & \cdots & -\dfrac{m_{2j}\,\Delta m_{ij}}{1+\overline{m}_{jj}\,\Delta m_{ij}} & \cdots & 0 \\ & & & \cdots & & \\ 0 & 0 & \cdots & \dfrac{1}{1+\overline{m}_{jj}\,\Delta m_{ij}} & \cdots & 0 \\ & & & \cdots & & \\ 0 & 0 & \cdots & -\dfrac{\overline{m}_{2j}\,\Delta m_{ij}}{1+\overline{m}_{jj}\,\Delta m_{ij}} & \cdots & 1 \end{pmatrix} \begin{pmatrix} \Delta m_{ij}\,\overline{m}_{1j}\,\overline{m}_{j1} & \cdots & \Delta m_{ij}\,\overline{m}_{1j}\,\overline{m}_{jn} \\ & \cdots & \\ \Delta m_{ij}\,\overline{m}_{nj}\,\overline{m}_{j1} & \cdots & \Delta m_{ij}\,\overline{m}_{nj}\,\overline{m}_{jn} \end{pmatrix}$$

$$= -\begin{pmatrix} \left(\Delta m_{ij}\,\overline{m}_{1j}\,\overline{m}_{j1} - \dfrac{\Delta^2 m_{ij}\,\overline{m}_{1j}\,\overline{m}_{ij}\,\overline{m}_{j1}}{1+\overline{m}_{jj}\,\Delta m_{ij}}\right) & \cdots & \left(\Delta m_{ij}\,m_{1j}\,m_{jn} - \dfrac{\Delta^2 m_{ij}\,\overline{m}_{1j}\,\overline{m}_{ij}\,\overline{m}_{jn}}{1+\overline{m}_{jj}\,\Delta m_{ij}}\right) \\ & \cdots & \\ \left(\Delta m_{ij}\,\overline{m}_{nj}\,\overline{m}_{j1} - \dfrac{\Delta^2 m_{ij}\,\overline{m}_{nj}\,\overline{m}_{ij}\,\overline{m}_{j1}}{1+\overline{m}_{jj}\,\Delta m_{ij}}\right) & \cdots & \left(\Delta m_{ij}\,m_{nj}\,m_{jn} - \dfrac{\Delta^2 m_{ij}\,\overline{m}_{nj}\,\overline{m}_{ij}\,\overline{m}_{jn}}{1+\overline{m}_{jj}\,\Delta m_{ij}}\right) \end{pmatrix}$$

The element in row u in column v of $\boldsymbol{\Psi}$ is therefore

$$\Psi_{uv} = -\left(\Delta m_{ij}\,m_{uj}\,m_{jv} - \frac{\Delta^2 m_{ij}\,\overline{m}_{uj}\,\overline{m}_{ij}\,\overline{m}_{jv}}{1+\overline{m}_{jj}\,\Delta m_{ij}}\right)$$

If Δm_{ij} is small, then its square is even smaller. (For example $.01 \times .01 = .0001$.) By a well-known approximation procedure, we may say that for *small* changes in m_{ij}, the change in the inverse matrix is approximately

$$(\Psi_{uv}) = -\Delta m_{ij}\begin{pmatrix} \overline{m}_{1j}\overline{m}_{j1} & \cdots & \overline{m}_{1j}\overline{m}_{jn} \\ & \cdots & \\ \overline{m}_{nj}\overline{m}_{jn} & \cdots & \overline{m}_{nj}\overline{m}_{jn} \end{pmatrix}$$

Consequently, if

$$\mathbf{V}_1 = \mathbf{F}\mathbf{M}^{-1}$$

$$\mathbf{V}_2 = \mathbf{F}(\mathbf{M}^{-1} + \Psi)$$

Then, approximately,[10]

$$\Delta \mathbf{V} = (\mathbf{V}_1 - \mathbf{V}_2) = \mathbf{F}(\mathbf{M}^{-1} - \mathbf{M}^{-1} - \Psi) = -\mathbf{F}\Psi$$

For example, if a changes in Tiny Model 1,

$$\begin{pmatrix} 1 & -a + \Delta a \\ -1 & 1 \end{pmatrix}^{-1}$$

is approximately

$$\begin{pmatrix} \dfrac{1}{1-a} & \dfrac{a}{1-a} \\ \dfrac{1}{1-a} & \dfrac{1}{1-a} \end{pmatrix} - \Delta a \begin{pmatrix} \dfrac{a}{(1-a)^2} & \dfrac{a}{(1-a)^2} \\ \dfrac{1}{(1-a)^2} & \dfrac{1}{(1-a)^2} \end{pmatrix}$$

So a small change in the coefficient a of this matrix is associated with the following changes.

$$\Delta \mathbf{V} = -\mathbf{F}\Psi$$

$$(\Delta \mathbf{Y}, \Delta \mathbf{C}) = \Delta \mathbf{a}(\mathbf{I}, \mathbf{F_C}) \begin{pmatrix} \dfrac{a}{(1-a)^2} & \dfrac{a}{(1-a)^2} \\ \dfrac{1}{(1-a)^2} & \dfrac{1}{(1-a)^2} \end{pmatrix}$$

This can be verbally expressed in the following way:

If the marginal propensity to consume changes by a *small* amount, Δa, then,

(1) The change in national product is given by

$$\Delta a \left[\frac{a}{(1-a)^2} I + \frac{1}{(1-a)^2} F_C \right]$$

which is greater than zero.

(2) The change in consumption is given by

$$\Delta a \left[\frac{a}{(1-a)^2} I + \frac{1}{(1-a)^2} F_C \right]$$

which is greater than zero.

(3) The change in national product is equal to the change in consumption; that is, investment is fixed.

---

[10] Readers who have taken a course in the calculus will recognize that this procedure, in the limit, amounts to taking the derivatives of the elements of $\mathbf{M}^{-1}$ with respect to changes in elements of $\mathbf{M}$.

The formula given in this appendix may be used to estimate the effect of changes in any *single* coefficient in any matrix of any theory in this book. Economists find it useful to be able to make this sort of calculation, but find it rather a bore to do it often. The main use of this formula is for the following situation. Suppose we have a theory with matrix $\mathbf{M}$, and that we have calculated $\mathbf{M}^{-1}$. We want to alter one of the behavioral statements by adding one more term to it. Then we add one more nonzero element to the matrix. What happens to the inverse may then be determined by using this formula.

If two or more elements of $\mathbf{M}$ are assumed to change simultaneously, different formulas must be used. These, generally speaking, are much more difficult to use. The reason, formally, is that the product $\mathbf{M}^{-1}\Delta\mathbf{M}$ is a matrix with more than one nonzero column. Therefore, every term in the product $\mathbf{M}^{-1}\Delta\mathbf{M}\mathbf{M}^{-1}$ is a sum of several terms. There are times when it is necessary to deal with such situations, but these are not happy ones.

3

The Level of the National Product

THE ORGANIZATION OF THE REST OF THE BOOK

Two subjects have been discussed: What is a social accounting system? And what is a theory? The social accounts were shown to consist of two interrelated sets of records: the national income and the national balance sheet. In discussing theories, three extremely simple Tiny Models were presented: one dealt with the national product, the second with the national balance sheet, and the third with prices in a single market.

The national income and national balance sheet will form the major unifying themes of this book. Their relative roles in determining what people own and what they do is a major source of argument among macroeconomists. It is not clear that both sets of records are of the same intrinsic interest and importance. One group of economists considers the national income accounts as the main item of interest—the changes in the balance sheets are merely consequences of income changes. The second group considers the balance sheet accounts as the main item of interest—the changes in the income accounts are merely consequences of balance sheet changes.

In a small way, the controversy is illustrated by Tiny Models 1 and 2. These reflect two basic positions held by economists. In one case, investment is held to be the main "factor" influencing the behavior of the economy. In the second, the quantity of money is held to be the main factor influencing the economy. While these two theories are almost childishly simplified, they express this one central issue as to "what makes the economy tick." In more subtle and indirect forms, the two Tiny Models reappear in the most advanced and difficult macroeconomic theories.

Even though the Tiny Models were stated as if they were quite unrelated, they are really interconnected. For changes in the quantity of money in Tiny Model 2 bring about changes in the quantity of plant desired. Changes in plant are changes in earning assets, and hence investment, by the reasoning of Chapter 1. Thus, investment is not really a factor (say the proponents of Tiny Model 2). It is a variable explainable by the quantity of money!

Or change the reasoning, just to show a proper impartiality. Tiny Model 2 has no debt account, so all increases in assets are increases in net worth. Chapter 1 associated increases in net worth with savings, Tiny Model 1 shows that if investment increases, savings will also increase; an increase in investment will therefore increase total assets, and hence should affect the quantity of money. Thus the quantity of money is not really a factor (say the proponents of Tiny Model 1). It is a variable explainable by the level of investment!

The views attributed in the last two paragraphs to the contestants are certainly not expressed as carefully or as precisely as they would be in an article written for professional economists. But like good caricatures, they are recognizable (if a bit unflattering) likenesses of two widely held opinions. If professional economists differ, beginners can hardly expect to be satisfied with any pat answer given them, but they should expect to be told clearly what the issue is.

The remainder of this book is concerned with assembling reasonably precise introductions to income economics and to balance sheet economics, and with explaining the relation between them. Fortunately, it is possible to set forth simple theories that explain the workings of pieces of the economy in the manner approved by one or more of the contestants, and readers will not find it hard to get some practice in analyzing the two views. When it comes to reconciling the two, it is not hard to state the issue and to explain why the conflict is still unresolved.

We turn first to economic theories about the national income, then to theories about the national balance sheets. And finally, the relations between these two parts of the economy will be explored. It will first be useful to spell out just why Tiny Models 1 and 2 are unsatisfactory.

Tiny Model 1 says that the level of the national product depends on the level of consumer demand (F_C) and on investment (I). There is no explanation at all of how businesses decide how much to invest; they just do. Model 2 says that the wealth (total assets) of the community depends on business demand for plant and equipment (F_K) and on the quantity of money M. There is no reason for the amount of money to be one number rather than another, and there is no explanation of how money "enters the economy."

It is no criticism of either theory to say that some factors remain unexplained. Every theory leaves something unexplained. Only if we cease being men and become gods will we overcome this difficulty.

Neither is it a criticism of either theory to say that some behavior implied by the theory is noneconomic. Thus, in saying that consumption depends in part on income, $C = aY + F_C$, we imply that part of consumption, in particular F_C, is determined by something outside the economy. (The economy consists of Y, C, I, and nothing else, and F_C does not depend on any of these.) All economic theories must recognize that *part* of human actions are not explained within the context of economic phenomena.

But one can reasonably object to the treatment of investment (I) as a factor. Tiny Model 1 says that businessmen decide on investment without even looking at what is going on around them. We might perfectly well grant that businesses invest partly because they think something *will* happen (and what *will happen* is not necessarily the same as what *is happening*.) But one might guess that businesses would not last very long if their managers did not look to see what was happening around them.

Tiny Model 2 does not explain how money enters the economy. It does not relate money to income in any way. It suggests that "someone" (if so, who?) can simply change at will the amount of money.

Finally, one can object that the two models are completely independent of each other. Unless they are put together, economists are saying that: (1) There is no connection between the amount of plant and equipment and the gross national output. If there were, the variable K would have to appear in Tiny Model 1. (2) There is no connection between investment and the demand for plant, since I appears in Tiny Model 1, and K in Tiny Model 2. This is odd, because Chapter 1 pointed out that if an economy has K_0 plant today and if today's investment is I, then the economy will have $(K_0 + I)$ plant tomorrow.

THEORY 1: MONEY, INTEREST, AND THE NATIONAL PRODUCT

In economic literature,[1] Theory 1 was the successor to first Tiny Model 1. It treats investment as something to be explained, not as an independent factor.

---

[1] A nonlinear version of this theory is given in P. A. Samuelson, *Foundations of Economic Analysis* (Cambridge, Mass., 1948), p. 276. Samuelson says that this theory is essentially that of J. M. Keynes's, *General Theory of Employment, Interest and Money* (London, 1935). We cannot be sure of this assertion, because Keynes's book is in many places very obscure.

It does so at the cost of making the amount of money an independent factor, as Tiny Model 2 did.

A new variable appears in Theory 1—the *rate of interest*. This variable is generally considered to be of fundamental importance in the operations of the economy.

The rate of interest is a price—the price we pay when we borrow money, and the price we are paid when we lend money. Businesses borrow money in order to buy plant and equipment. In this respect, borrowing is associated with investing.[2] The rate of interest should influence investment decisions. This influence is rather simply explained.

Suppose a business is deciding whether or not to build a new factory. The decision is based on a calculation that shows whether or not the proposed factory can be operated profitably. This calculation is like an income statement, but the figures in it are estimates about the future, not reports about the past. One of the costs to be estimated is the cost of borrowing enough to pay for the factory.

If the business had enough retained profits, it could pay for a new factory building without borrowing. But if the operation of the new factory would not cover interest charges, the business would do better to lend its retained profits to someone else rather than to "lend them to itself" and build the factory.

The annual interest cost is the cost of the new factory times the interest rate. The higher the interest rate at the time the calculation is made, the less profitable the operation of the factory will seem.

Imagine businesses as having collectively a long list of investment projects. At any moment, the going rate of interest rules out part of the list. The higher the rate of interest, the more projects will be ruled out. Theory 1 assumes that the demand for investment (the list of acceptable projects) is related to the interest rate (R):

$$I = dR + F_I$$

here R is the rate of interest, and $d < 0$. The factor F_I reminds us that the rate of interest is not the only thing affecting the demand for investment.

The rate of interest, from the lender's point of view, is a source of income that is earned by transferring cash to a borrower for a period of time. Lenders incur a cost when they hold cash, the cost of the income they have given up. The demand for money, then, is assumed to have the form[3]

$$L = eR + F_L$$

[2] Of course, consumers also borrow whenever they buy on credit. This book does not consider consumer credit at all. (Business and government are assumed to be the only borrowers.)

[3] The original version of this theory, by Keynes, assumes that there is a "transactions demand" for money. That is, desired cash balances depend on current rates of spending (and hence on Y). This version is simpler. See Appendix to this Chapter.

where e is negative. The symbol L stands for *liquidity*. Economic units are said to be liquid when they have enough cash for their needs. Obviously this is a fuzzy notion.[4] By selecting this particular relation to define liquidity, we give one precise interpretation to the concept.

The amount of money is assumed to be determined from outside the system by "the government". We write:

$$L = F_M$$

to indicate that F_M, the supply of money, is a factor. In this way, we imply that the economy adjusts itself to the amount of money which the government decides to supply. One part of this adjustment mechanism is shown if we substitute F_M for L in the liquidity statement. For then

$$F_M = eR + F_L$$

$$R = \frac{F_M - F_L}{e}$$

which shows that the interest rate adjusts itself according to the values assumed by F_L and F_M.

In Theory 1, households do not simply decide between consuming and saving. They consume, they hold cash, and they lend. Their behavior with respect to cash holdings (liquidity) has already been described. Their consumption is assumed to follow the rule:

$$C = aY + vL + fR + F_C$$

Here, consumption depends in part on income, as in Tiny Model 1. It also depends on L, the amount of money consumers have: The more cash they have on hand, the more we expect them to spend, so v is positive. However, the higher the rate of interest, the less consumers will spend, for the return is greater from making loans. Thus f is negative.

It is not necessary to introduce a separate statement about the supply of saving to businesses by households. If this supply were denoted by S, then,

$$S = Y - C - L$$
$$= (1 - a)Y - (f + e)R - vL - (F_C + F_L)$$

That is, $Y - C - L = S$ can be derived without difficulty from the other two statements.[5]

---

[4] Do not confuse cash with profit. A business selling on credit may have large profits but be extremely short of cash because its assets consist mainly of accounts receivable. A business may be operating at a loss but have large amounts of cash on hand.

[5] This particular formulation of consumer behavior is used because there are economists who maintain that consumer spending is more influenced by the size of consumer cash balances than by the size of the national income. These theorists, in effect, set $a = 0$.

The coefficient a in the consumption statement is a "pure number." That is, it relates spending on consumption to income, both of which are designated in the same units. Thus a is "dimension-free," and may be thought of as a pure number. (See the interpretation of a in Tiny Model 1).

In contrast, coefficients such as f are not dimension-free. The coefficient f, for instance, relates changes in C (measured in current or fixed dollar prices) to changes in R (measured in percent per year). Since R is a number of order .05, and C a number of order 6×10^{11}, f must be a very large number. Similarly the coefficient e relates numbers of dollars in bank deposits to a rate of interest.

Students of scientific method tend to raise a general question about the appearance of dimensional coefficients in a theory. They suggest that theories in which coefficients are pure numbers have easier and more natural interpretations than theories in which there are many dimensional coefficients. In this theory, for example, it is much easier to suggest a value for a than to suggest values for f and e. Most economists would expect a to be between .75 and 1 rather than between 0 and .25. This suggestion is simple because the economic content of a has an intuitive meaning. The intuitive content of dimensional coefficients is frequently obscure.

Theory 1 denotes the rate of interest by the symbol R. Later on, in Theory 7 and Theory 9, we will see that there is a way of analyzing the interest rate that does not involve introducing R as an explicit variable, and which therefore eliminates the need for one set of dimensional coefficients.

Theory 1 says that "the Government" is able to control the quantity of money. Thus L, the demand for money, must be equal to F_M, the amount of money provided by the authorities. F_M, then, is a factor.

The theory now contains five statements:

(1) The national product

$$Y = C + I$$

(2) A consumption function

$$C = aY + fR + vL + F_C$$

(3) A demand for investment

$$I = dR + F_I$$

(4) A demand for money

$$L = eR + F_L$$

(5) A supply of money F_M, which must equal demand

$$L = F_M$$

The demand for money (4) and the supply of money are here somewhat arbitrarily grafted on the tail of Tiny Model 1. This feature of Theory 1 reflects the fact that in 1935 the entire concept of reasoning on the basis of systematic national accounts was new. It has taken a number of years of discussion to clarify the structure of social accounts. Today, we would either include an entire balance sheet or omit balance sheet accounts from the theory altogether.

As in Tiny Model 1, the *marginal propensity to save*, $(1 - a)$, is assumed greater than zero, so that part of every additional unit of income is saved.[6] The coefficient v is greater than zero: the more money there is, the more people spend and hence (other things being equal), the less they save. The rate of interest is an incentive to save, so $(b + e)$ must be negative. Holding cash means not lending money. Therefore, holding cash means giving up income. An increase in the interest rate therefore reduces the amount of cash people want to hold. Thus, e is negative; and it is natural to suppose that consumption will also be reduced by increases in the interest rate, so b is also negative.

This system of equations may be written in vector-matrix notation as follows:

$$(\mathbf{0},\ \mathbf{F_C}, \mathbf{F_I}, \mathbf{F_L}, \mathbf{F_M}) = (\mathbf{Y}, \mathbf{C}, \mathbf{I}, \mathbf{R}, \mathbf{L}) \begin{pmatrix} 1 & -a & 0 & 0 & 0 \\ -1 & 1 & 0 & 0 & 0 \\ -1 & 0 & 1 & 0 & 0 \\ 0 & -f & -d & -e & 0 \\ 0 & -v & 0 & 1 & 1 \end{pmatrix}$$

This system is block-triangular, and it contains Tiny Model 1 in the upper left. The inverse system may be shown to be:

$$(\mathbf{0}, \mathbf{F_C}, \mathbf{F_I}, \mathbf{F_L}, \mathbf{F_M}) \begin{pmatrix} \dfrac{1}{1-a} & \dfrac{a}{1-a} & 0 & 0 & 0 \\ \dfrac{1}{1-a} & \dfrac{1}{1-a} & 0 & 0 & 0 \\ \dfrac{1}{1-a} & \dfrac{a}{1-a} & 1 & 0 & 0 \\ \dfrac{-f-d}{e(1-a)} & \dfrac{-f-da}{e(1-a)} & -\dfrac{d}{e} & -\dfrac{1}{e} & 0 \\ \dfrac{f+ev+d}{e(1-a)} & \dfrac{f+ev+da}{e(1-a)} & \dfrac{d}{e} & \dfrac{1}{e} & 1 \end{pmatrix} = (\mathbf{Y}, \mathbf{C}, \mathbf{I}, \mathbf{R}$$

Table 1 interprets the elements of the inverse matrix. It will be seen that the arrangement of the table follows the structure of the matrix.[7]

---

[6] In this context "savings" means "lending to business," because that part of income held as cash is accounted for by L.

[7] Readers will note that the first component of the factor vector is a zero. This component will change if and only if the national product is redefined so that output no longer is the sum of consumption and investment. Such a change would alter the structure of the theory and is ruled out by hypothesis.

TABLE 3.1

THE IMPLICATIONS OF THEORY 1

THE EFFECT OF A UNIT CHANGE IN	THE EFFECT UPON			
	National product	Consumption	Investment	Interest rate
The level of consumer demand (F_C)	$\frac{1}{1-a}$	$\frac{1}{1-a}$	0	0
Autonomous investment (F_I)	$\frac{1}{1-a}$	$\frac{a}{1-a}$	1	0
The level of liquidity demand (F_L)	$\frac{-f-d}{e(1-a)}$	$\frac{-f-da}{e(1-a)}$	$-\frac{d}{e}$	$-\frac{1}{e}$
The quantity of money (F_M)	$\frac{f+ev+d}{e(1-a)}$	$\frac{f+ev+da}{e(1-a)}$	$\frac{d}{e}$	$\frac{1}{e}$

Problem 3.1 If $1 > a > 0$, $v > 0$, $b < 0$, $d < 0$, $e < 0$, is it possible to determine the signs of all these expressions?

Problem 3.2 Suppose an increase of $1 in antonomous investment (F_I). The government wishes to stabilize the interest rate by changing the quantity of money (F_M). What must it do?

Problem 3.3 Suppose a decrease of $1 in antonomous investment (F_I). The government wishes to stabilize total investment (I) by altering the quantity of money (F_M). What change in the quantity of money will stabilize total investment? What will be the combined effect of the changes in F_I and F_M on the national product?

Problem 3.4 Suppose consumers decide they wish to hold larger amounts of cash (F_L increases by $1). What will be the effect on the actual amount of money in the economy if nothing is done by the government? What will the government have to do to the supply of money (F_M) in order to stabilize (1) the national product; (2) the interest rate; (3) the national product *and* the interest rate?

Problem 3.5 Suppose that all the factors in the system are given. What is the direction effect on the values of the variables if there is an increase in a? In v? In b? In d? In e?

In this theory, there are several elements that have been the object of debate both among professional economists and the public.

What use is money? The usual answer is that money is useful because it can be used to buy goods. If so, then the demand for money is different from the demand for other things. If I buy a steak, I buy it because I like steak.

However, it seems that if I hold money, it is not because I like money. I like the things I can get with it. Why don't I get them instead of holding money? Well, I do not want them now.

One of the statements of Theory 1 says that people want to "buy" money. One consequence of this statement is that changes in the level of liquidity demand (F_L) and in the quantity of money (F_M) both affect the national product and its components.

Today this view seems harmless enough. In the 1930s it was revolutionary. The usual explanation of depression ran in terms of prices. Look at Tiny Model 3. If prices are *above* equilibrium levels, then the quantity demanded (q_D) will be less than the quantity supplied (q_S) so that there are unsalable goods. If the "goods" in question is labor, then there will be unemployment. The way to reduce unemployment is to cut wages, for then ($q_S - q_D$), which represents unemployment, will drop to zero.

The view in Theory 1 says something quite different: In a depression, there is unemployment because the demand for goods is so small that few people need be employed to make the goods. Instead of buying goods, people hoard money (that is, F_L is very large). An increase in F_L automatically reduces both consumption and investment. But it can be offset if there is a sufficient *increase* in the quantity of money.

The older theory prescribed a *decrease* in the money supply. This prescription followed from what is called the "quantity theory of money," which related the price level to the quantity of money. The theory used the formula $MV = PQ$, where M is the quantity of money, V is a constant called "velocity," P the price level, and Q the level of output.[8] If the trouble in a depression is that there are unsold goods, and if there are unsold goods because prices are too high, then a decrease in the money supply (on this formula) would *lower* prices and therefore eliminate unemployment.[9]

Comment on Theory 1

This theory is included in this book because it has an important place in the development of macroeconomics. It marks the first attempt at relating monetary analysis to national product analysis. Moreover, something very close to Theory 1 is still taught in sophomore economics courses all over the United States. Out of respect to tradition, one must include this theory.

Unfortunately, there are grave difficulties to the use of this theory. These are seen most clearly in terms of the principle of social accounting that associates entries in income statements with *changes* in balance sheets. In

---

[8] This theory is mentioned again in the first part of Chapter 5.

[9] This desperately brief summary does not do justice to the formula or to the views of its modern adherents (who are still numerous). But it is not an unreasonable view of one side of the debate in the 1930s. The formula in this paragraph will appear in Chapter 5.

Theory 1, households have a choice of buying consumer goods, *hoarding*, and *saving*. In this context, *hoarding* must mean a change in cash balances, and *saving* must mean an increase in earning assets (stocks, bonds, savings deposits, and so on). But the term *hoarding* is used loosely to denote total holdings of cash. Saving is used properly to denote an increase in net worth, and also (more loosely) to denote the total net worth and even total earning assets.

When one reads Keynes's main works, his *Tract on Monetary Reform* (1924), his *Treatise on Money* (1931), and his *General Theory of Employment, Interest and Money* (1935), one underlying theme is that people who hold idle cash are not using their resources for productive purposes. (In periods of inflation this behavior may be socially desirable, but in depressions it is not.) In an income theory this means that people keep part of their income as idle cash. But such behavior means hoarding some *increase* in the money supply. Statement (4) should therefore be written $\Delta L = eR + F_1$, and in Statement (5) F_M must be interpreted as the amount by which the government *increases* the money supply. But to be consistent with monetary economics generally, we should wish to have consumption depend on L and not on ΔL in Statement (2), and also in the saving function:

$$S = (1 - a)Y + (f + e)R - vL - (F_C + F_L)$$

Thus statements about L and about ΔL are mingled in a confusing way in Theory 1.

Thus if one applies social accounting definitions consistently, the usual formulation of Theory 1 turns out to be unsatisfactory. The difference between the usual formulation and that in the previous paragraph is subtle, and many economists do not, in fact, make it in their thinking. The author is a little uneasy at presenting "for the record" a theory which has an important place in the development of economics, but which has a subtle inconsistency. He therefore warns the reader that he will have to get used to combining income and balance sheet notions in an orderly way. Theories 2, 5, and especially 8 are designed to show how this combination may be carried out.

Problem 3.6 A somewhat simpler theory than Theory 1 states that

$$Y = C + I$$
$$C = aY + bR + F_C$$
$$I = dR + F_I$$

In this theory the rate of interest (R) appears as a factor. Suppose that R can be controlled by "the government," Is it possible that whatever may be the decrease in autonomous investment (F_I), "the government" can prevent the national income from falling by forcing down the interest rate?

Problem 3.7 Discuss the connection between the views given in Theory 1 and the views implicit in the preceding problem.

Problem 3.8 It sometimes clarifies the basis of our theorizing to reason by analogy. Tiny Model 2 is an analogy to Tiny Model 1. It has the same mathematical structure as Tiny Model 1, but the variables have different names. Construct an analog to Theory 1 by renaming variables. For Y use W (total assets), for C use K (plant and equipment), for I use M (cash), for L use Y (total output), and retain R, the rate of interest. Then the factors F_C, F_I, F_L, and F_M will be replaced by F_K, F_M, F_Y, and $\bar{Y}$, respectively. Consider the meanings of the statements of the variable-into-factor mapping and the implications of the theory that you obtain by relabeling Table 1. How much of this analog makes sense? How much of it seems strange? Do you find any new objections to the way Theory I was put together?

THEORY 2: COMBINING THE INCOME AND BALANCE SHEET ACCOUNTS

Theory 1 obviously is a step forward from Tiny Model 1. Investment is one of the variables explained by the theory, and not something originating "outside" the system. Two new variables appear, the rate of interest (R) and the quantity of money (M). It was assumed that a demand for money and a supply of money existed as well as demand for consumer goods and for investment.

But Theory 1 is messy. Money is an asset. Investment is a change in another asset. If *part* of the balance sheet is involved in a theory, all of the balance sheet should be listed. But Theory 1 does not give any balance sheet.

The theory says that consumers spend some of their income for consumption; they keep some in the form of cash; and they lend some to business. But is cash that accumulated in this way the entire money supply? Some cash must be carried forward from one day (month, year) to the next. Where is it?

Theory 2 makes use of Tiny Models 1 and 2. That is, it has both a balance sheet and an income account. It is therefore more complete than Theory 1, which is quite unclear about the balance sheet accounts.

Theory 2, like Theory 1, explains the level of investment. Unlike Theory 1, Theory 2 does *not* introduce the rate of interest. In a sense, this may seem unfortunate, because there is every reason to believe that interest is an important economic variable. But as a general rule, one would prefer to have simple theories. Why introduce more variables than necessary?[10]

---

[10] Theory 7 and the appendix to Chapter 6 provide a method of introducing the interest rate into theories of this kind. But it is simpler to postpone this until later.

The effect of combining Tiny Models 1 and 2 is to give a simultaneous treatment of income and wealth, which is closely related to the topics already considered. Theory 2 explains both consumption (C) and investment (I). In this sense it is an improvement over Tiny Model 1, which leaves investment a factor. The theory also explains total wealth (W) and the amount of plant and equipment in the economy (K). Money (M), the other asset of the community, is still a factor; it must continue to be until there is an explanation of how it can be increased or decreased. Such an explanation requires the specification of a special "banking sector" of the economy, and we are not yet ready for that.

Two elements of Theory 2 are familiar. The national product consists of consumption and investment:

$$Y = C + I$$

The national wealth (there is no debt) consists of money and plant:

$$W = M + K$$

If plant was K_0 at the beginning of the period, and if investment during the period is I, then the amount of plant at the end of the period is K.

$$K = K_0 + I$$

Because of this connection, the total demand for plant simultaneously determines the demand for investment (that is, for new plant).

Consumer behavior is described by

$$C = aY + vM + F_C$$

This statement includes a term (vM) which was not present in the corresponding statement in Tiny Model 1. The term (aY) implies, for $a > 0$, that the larger people's income is, the more they will spend. The new terms vM says, for $v > 0$, that the more money people have, the more they will spend.[11] The objection might be raised that when people have spent their money they will not have it any more. This objection is not valid, however, because whenever A spends *money* to buy *things*, B sells *things* to acquire *money*. As a result of the transaction, money changes hands, but it does not disappear.

The demand for plant is the same as in Tiny Model 2, that is:

$$K = bW + F_K$$

Finally, the amount of money is fixed from outside:

$$M = F_M$$

---

[11] Readers must wait for a fuller explanation of our motives in including this new term. The explanation will be given below, after the whole system has been set forth.

It is now possible to write these statements as mapping variables into factors:

$$\begin{aligned}
0 &= Y - C - I \\
F_C &= -aY + C \qquad\qquad\qquad\qquad -vM \\
0 &= \qquad\qquad\qquad W - K - \;\; M \\
F_K &= \qquad\qquad -bW + K \\
K_0 &= \qquad -I \qquad\quad +K \\
F_M &= \qquad\qquad\qquad\qquad\qquad\quad M
\end{aligned}$$

In vector-matrix notation, then:

$$(\mathbf{0}, \mathbf{F_C}, \mathbf{0}, \mathbf{F_K}, \mathbf{K_0}, \mathbf{F}_M) = (\mathbf{Y}, \mathbf{C}, \mathbf{W}, \mathbf{K}, \mathbf{I}, \mathbf{M}) \begin{pmatrix} 1 & -a & 0 & 0 & 0 & 0 \\ -1 & 1 & 0 & 0 & 0 & 0 \\ 0 & 0 & 1 & -b & 0 & 0 \\ 0 & 0 & -1 & 1 & 1 & 0 \\ -1 & 0 & 0 & 0 & -1 & 0 \\ 0 & -v & -1 & 0 & 0 & 1 \end{pmatrix}$$

This matrix contains two blocks which are recognizable:

$$\mathbf{M}_{11} = \begin{pmatrix} 1 & -a \\ -1 & 1 \end{pmatrix} \text{ is the matrix of Tiny Model 1}$$

$$\mathbf{M}_{22} = \begin{pmatrix} 1 & -b \\ -1 & 1 \end{pmatrix} \text{ is the matrix of Tiny Model 2}$$

In block form, then, the matrix is

$$\begin{pmatrix} M_{11} & 0 & 0 \\ 0 & M_{22} & M_{23} \\ M_{31} & M_{31} & M_{33} \end{pmatrix}$$

The trouble with this way of writing it is that there is a block

$$\begin{pmatrix} M_{22} & M_{23} \\ M_{32} & M_{33} \end{pmatrix}$$

that is *not* block-triangular. Inversion of this matrix will be messy. However, it is possible to arrange the matrix into blocks in a different way, so that inversion can be undertaken as a series of inversions on block-triangular matrices:

$$\left(\begin{array}{cc|ccc|c} 1 & -a & 0 & 0 & 0 & 0 \\ -1 & 1 & 0 & 0 & 0 & 0 \\ \hline 0 & 0 & 1 & -b & 0 & 0 \\ 0 & 0 & -1 & 1 & 1 & 0 \\ \hline -1 & 0 & 0 & 0 & -1 & 0 \\ \hline 0 & -v & -1 & 0 & 0 & +1 \end{array}\right) = \begin{pmatrix} M_{11} & 0 & & 0 \\ M_{21} & M'_{22} & M''_{22} & 0 \\ & 0 & M'''_{22} & \\ M_{31} & M_{32} & & M_{33} \end{pmatrix}$$

The inversion involves three steps:

Step A We write

$$\left(\begin{array}{cc|c} 1 & -b & 0 \\ -1 & 1 & 1 \\ \hline 0 & 0 & -1 \end{array}\right)$$

and invert, using the rule for block-triangular matrices:

$$\begin{pmatrix} 1 & -b \\ -1 & 1 \end{pmatrix}^{-1} = \begin{pmatrix} \frac{1}{1-b} & \frac{b}{1-b} \\ \frac{1}{1-b} & \frac{1}{1-b} \end{pmatrix}$$

$$(-1)^{-1} = (-1)$$

$$-\begin{pmatrix} 1 & -b \\ -1 & 1 \end{pmatrix}^{-1} \begin{pmatrix} 0 \\ 1 \end{pmatrix} (-1)^{-1} = -\begin{pmatrix} \frac{1}{1-b} & \frac{b}{1-b} \\ \frac{1}{1-b} & \frac{1}{1-b} \end{pmatrix} \begin{pmatrix} 0 \\ 1 \end{pmatrix} (-1)$$

$$= -\begin{pmatrix} \frac{b}{1-b} \\ \frac{1}{1-b} \end{pmatrix} -(1) = \begin{pmatrix} \frac{b}{1-b} \\ \frac{1}{1-b} \end{pmatrix}$$

Combining these three operations:

$$\begin{pmatrix} 1 & -b & 0 \\ -1 & 1 & 1 \\ 0 & 0 & -1 \end{pmatrix}^{-1} = \begin{pmatrix} \frac{1}{1-b} & \frac{b}{1-b} & \frac{b}{1-b} \\ \frac{1}{1-b} & \frac{1}{1-b} & \frac{1}{1-b} \\ 0 & 0 & -1 \end{pmatrix}$$

Step B We write

$$\mathbf{M_B} = \left(\begin{array}{cc|ccc} 1 & -a & 0 & 0 & 0 \\ -1 & 1 & 0 & 0 & 0 \\ \hline 0 & 0 & 1 & -b & 0 \\ 0 & 0 & -1 & 1 & 1 \\ -1 & 0 & 0 & 0 & -1 \end{array}\right)$$

and invert it, using the rule for block-triangular matrices:

$$\begin{pmatrix} 1 & -a \\ -1 & 1 \end{pmatrix}^{-1} = \begin{pmatrix} \dfrac{1}{1-a} & \dfrac{a}{1-a} \\[2ex] \dfrac{1}{1-a} & \dfrac{1}{1-a} \end{pmatrix}$$

$$- \begin{pmatrix} 1 & -b & 0 \\ -1 & 1 & 1 \\ 0 & 0 & -1 \end{pmatrix}^{-1} \begin{pmatrix} 0 & 0 \\ 0 & 0 \\ -1 & 0 \end{pmatrix} \begin{pmatrix} 1 & -a \\ -1 & 1 \end{pmatrix}^{-1}$$

$$= - \begin{pmatrix} \dfrac{1}{1-b} & \dfrac{b}{1-b} & \dfrac{b}{1-b} \\[2ex] \dfrac{1}{1-b} & \dfrac{1}{1-b} & \dfrac{1}{1-b} \\[2ex] 0 & 0 & 1 \end{pmatrix} \begin{pmatrix} 0 & 0 \\ 0 & 0 \\ -1 & 0 \end{pmatrix} \begin{pmatrix} \dfrac{1}{1-a} & \dfrac{a}{1-a} \\[2ex] \dfrac{1}{1-a} & \dfrac{1}{1-a} \end{pmatrix}$$

$$= \begin{pmatrix} \dfrac{b}{1-b} & 0 \\[2ex] \dfrac{1}{1-b} & 0 \\[2ex] -1 & 0 \end{pmatrix} \begin{pmatrix} \dfrac{1}{1-a} & \dfrac{a}{1-a} \\[2ex] \dfrac{1}{1-a} & \dfrac{1}{1-a} \end{pmatrix} = \begin{pmatrix} \dfrac{b}{(1-b)(1-a)} & \dfrac{ab}{(1-b)(1-a)} \\[2ex] \dfrac{1}{(1-b)(1-a)} & \dfrac{a}{(1-b)(1-a)} \\[2ex] -\dfrac{1}{1-a} & -\dfrac{a}{1-a} \end{pmatrix}$$

therefore, M_B^{-1} may be put together as

$$\begin{pmatrix} \dfrac{1}{1-a} & \dfrac{a}{1-a} & 0 & 0 & 0 \\[2ex] \dfrac{1}{1-a} & \dfrac{1}{1-a} & 0 & 0 & 0 \\[2ex] \dfrac{b}{(1-b)(1-a)} & \dfrac{ab}{(1-b)(1-a)} & \dfrac{1}{1-b} & \dfrac{b}{1-b} & \dfrac{b}{1-b} \\[2ex] \dfrac{1}{(1-b)(1-a)} & \dfrac{a}{(1-b)(1-a)} & \dfrac{1}{1-b} & \dfrac{1}{1-b} & \dfrac{1}{1-b} \\[2ex] -\dfrac{1}{1-a} & -\dfrac{a}{1-a} & 0 & 0 & -1 \end{pmatrix}$$

Step C Finally, the matrix as a whole,

$$\left(\begin{array}{ccccc|c} 1 & -a & 0 & 0 & 0 & 0 \\ -1 & 1 & 0 & 0 & 0 & 0 \\ 0 & 0 & 1 & -b & 0 & 0 \\ 0 & 0 & -1 & 1 & 1 & 0 \\ -1 & 0 & 0 & 0 & -1 & 0 \\ \hline 0 & -v & -1 & 0 & 0 & -1 \end{array}\right)^{-1}$$

written in block-triangular is inverted by the same procedure. It will be good exercise for the reader to make this inversion himself.

$$\mathbf{M}^{-1} = \begin{pmatrix} \frac{1}{1-a} & \frac{a}{1-a} & 0 & 0 & 0 & 0 \\ \frac{1}{1-a} & \frac{1}{1-a} & 0 & 0 & 0 & 0 \\ \frac{b}{(1-a)(1-b)} & \frac{ab}{(1-a)(1-b)} & \frac{1}{1-b} & \frac{b}{1-b} & \frac{b}{1-b} & 0 \\ \frac{1}{(1-a)(1-b)} & \frac{a}{(1-a)(1-b)} & \frac{1}{1-b} & \frac{1}{1-b} & \frac{1}{1-b} & 0 \\ \frac{-1}{1-a} & \frac{-a}{1-a} & 0 & 0 & -1 & 0 \\ \frac{v(1-b)+b}{(1-a)(1-b)} & \frac{v(1-b)+ab}{(1-a)(1-b)} & \frac{1}{1-b} & \frac{b}{1-b} & \frac{b}{1-b} & 1 \end{pmatrix}$$

The matrix **M** of the mapping $\mathbf{F} = \mathbf{VM}$ consists entirely of ones and zeros except for the three symbols a, v, b. Consequently, the elements of the inverse mapping $\mathbf{M}^{-1}$ consists of functions of these symbols. All the behavioral characteristics of the economy are summed up in these symbols. There is a controversy among economists over the numerical value of these three symbols.

If a is zero, consumer spending does not change when consumer income changes. Some economists hold this view.

If a is not zero, consumers will spend a, and save $(1 - a)$ out of every dollar of additional income. Most economists would maintain that a is greater than zero and less than 1, for this would mean some spending and some saving from every additional dollar earned.

If v is zero, consumer spending does not change when consumers have "more money in the bank." Most economists would deny that v is zero, but few normally include nonzero v in their hypotheses about consumer spending. (This is more a matter of laziness than of conviction.)

If v is not zero, we would expect it to be positive; if people have more cash their spending will rise.

Finally, people who maintain that income alone is an important problem and that balance sheet analysis does not really matter will be inclined to set $b = 0$.

If b is not zero, then it measures how much more plant and equipment the community will want if its total assets rise by one dollar. The number $(1 - b)$ measures the additional amount of money the community will want to hold if its total assets rise by one dollar. Most economists would expect b to be between zero and one—as total assets rise, the community will wish both larger cash balances and more plant and equipment.

Problem 3.9 Suppose that the factors in Theory 2 are all fixed. What is the effect on the variables of the system of increases in a? In b? In v?

Problem 3.10 What would a change in component 1 of the factor vector mean? What would a change in component 3 of the factor vector mean?

Problem 3.11 The factor K_0 measures the stock of plant and equipment at the beginning of the period. Computationally, all the variables in the system change if K_0 changes. What economic meaning may be attached to the vector $(\Delta Y/\Delta K_0, \Delta C/\Delta K_0, \Delta W/\Delta K_0, \Delta K/\Delta K_0, \Delta I/\Delta K_0, \Delta M/\Delta K_0)$?

Problem 3.12 Interpret the assertions $a = 0$, $b = 0$, $v = 0$ in terms of what they say about economic behavior.

Problem 3.13 If $b = 0$ and $v = 0$, Theory 2 reduces to something discussed earlier in this book. What?

Problem 3.14 If $a = 0$ and $v = 0$, Theory 2 reduces to something discussed earlier in this book. What?

Historical Note. The use of the demand hypothesis,

$$C = aY + vM + F_C$$

is designed to bring into a single system both the income theorists, who say

$$C = aY + F_C$$

and the "older school," of the 1920s who said

$$Y = vM$$

Interestingly enough, Keynes is an example of both schools of thought. In his *Tract on Monetary Reform* (1925) he used the second idea: income and money are related by a term called "income velocity." In his *General Theory of Employment, Interest and Money* (1935) he used the first: income and consumption were related by a term called "the marginal propensity to consume." Theory 2 does not violate the spirit of either theory by combining them in this way. In the 1920s, the first kind of theory was a natural one, for the big policy question had to do with finding the right amount of money (a balance sheet concept); in the 1930s, the second kind of theory was a natural one, for the big policy question had to do with finding the right level of the national income.

Does it matter which of these theories is right? To answer this question, the values of the coefficients in $\mathbf{M}^{-1}$ must be given special numerical values. Table 2 shows how to do this, by comparing the general answer already given with three special cases:

(1) Consumer spending depends on the size of cash balances but not on the level of income. In this case, set $a = 0$ in every element of $\mathbf{M}^{-1}$ where a appears.

(2) Consumers' spending depends on the level of income, but not on the size of their cash balances. In this case set $v = 0$ in every element of $\mathbf{M}^{-1}$ where v appears.

(3) The demand for plant (and hence the demand for investment) does not depend on total assets. In this case, set $b = 0$ in every element of $\mathbf{M}^{-1}$ when b appears.

Table 3.2 gives a complete comparison, and it is necessary to note only a few interesting points. For instance, if $a = 0$, an increase in the demand for plant adjusts the economy without altering the level of consumption. Otherwise, consumption is affected by this change. The national product increases *more* in response to given changes in investment demand if $a > 0$ than if $a = 0$; and more if $b > 0$ than if $b = 0$. The magnitude of consumer response to increases in cash balances, v, affects the response of the national product and consumption to changes in the quantity of money; but it plays no other role in the system.

In the most general terms, one can see that the three terms, a, b, and v, have the effect of making the various variables in the economy *more* responsive to changes in any of the various factors. If all of them are zero, the responses become either 1 or 0.

Perhaps from the beginner's standpoint, this particular theory may be regarded as a generalization of the multiplier principle. In the 1930s, economists were very much excited by the discovery of the relation $1/(1 - a)$ between changes in investment and changes in national product. The principle is that a relatively small cause may have a relatively large effect. This principle is important, and it continues to underlie a great deal of modern thinking on government policy. The government is a relatively small part of the economy, but many economists hope that small changes in government spending or taxation will have large effects on the economy.

In the general case, a unit increase in consumer demand causes an increase of $1/(1 - a)$ in national product, whereas an equal increase in the demand for plant and equipment causes a larger increase, namely $1/(1 - a)(1 - b)$. This property of the theory is consistent with the opinion of most economists

TABLE 3.2

THE IMPLICATIONS OF THEORY 2

THE EFFECT OF A UNIT INCREASE OF	THE EFFECT OF THE UNIT INCREASE UPON National product	Consumption	Invest-ment	Wealth	Plant and equip-ment	Money
	General Case					
F_C Consumption Demand	$\frac{1}{1-a}$	$\frac{1}{1-a}$	0	0	0	0
F_K Demand for Plant and Equipment	$\frac{1}{(1-a)(1-b)}$	$\frac{a}{(1-a)(1-b)}$	$\frac{1}{1-b}$	$\frac{1}{1-b}$	$\frac{1}{1-b}$	0
F_M Supply of Money	$\frac{v(1-b)+b}{(1-a)(1-b)}$	$\frac{v(1-b)+ab}{(1-a)(1-b)}$	$\frac{1}{1-b}$	$\frac{b}{1-b}$	$\frac{b}{1-b}$	1
	Special Case $a=0$					
F_C Consumption Demand	1	1	0	0	0	0
F_K Demand for Plant and Equipment	1	0	$\frac{1}{1-b}$	$\frac{1}{1-b}$	$\frac{1}{1-b}$	0
F_M Supply of Money	$\frac{v(1-b)+b}{1-b}$	$\frac{v(1-b)}{1-b}$	$\frac{1}{1-b}$	$\frac{b}{1-b}$	$\frac{b}{1-b}$	1
	Special Case $v=0$					
F_C Consumption Demand	$\frac{1}{1-a}$	$\frac{1}{1-a}$	0	0	0	0
F_K Demand for Plant and Equipment	$\frac{1}{(1-a)(1-b)}$	$\frac{a}{(1-a)(1-b)}$	$\frac{1}{1-b}$	$\frac{1}{1-b}$	$\frac{1}{1-b}$	0
F_M Supply of Money	$\frac{b}{(1-a)(1-b)}$	$\frac{ab}{(1-a)(1-b)}$	$\frac{1}{1-b}$	$\frac{b}{1-b}$	$\frac{b}{1-b}$	1
	Special Case $b=0$					
F_C Consumption Demand	$\frac{1}{1-a}$	$\frac{1}{1-a}$	0	0	0	0
F_K Demand for Plant and Equipment	$\frac{1}{1-a}$	$\frac{a}{1-a}$	1	1	1	0
F_M Supply of Money	$\frac{v}{1-a}$	$\frac{v}{1-a}$	1	0	0	1

hat changes in investment are more significant than changes in consumer astes. Business investment seems subject to more violent changes (in per- :entage terms) than consumer spending, and the economy usually seems to espond more closely to changes in investment than to changes in consumer spending.

Response to an Objection. The reader may ask why we bother with setting out three special cases. At most, one of them is right, so that at least two are unnecessary. There are two answers. First, it requires a very subtle statistical analysis to determine which values of a, b, and v are correct in any particular historical period; and economists are not satisfied with existing studies on the subject. Indeed, there is an active debate on these matters in he professional literature. Second, even if there were a way of assigning values to these quantities for some one period in the past (say the last ten years), there is no assurance that consumers and businesses cannot, or will not change their habits, and thus alter the numerical values of their coefficients in the future. The way of expressing the system that has been used here explains the logic of the theory and is thus more useful to an understanding of the economy than the selection of questionable and temporary numerical values would be.

The argument about the numerical values of a, b, and v is part of a general argument. Do disturbances in business conditions result mainly from factors associated with the income accounts or from factors associated with the balance sheet accounts? Is the remedy for such disturbances to be found in he monetary sector, or is it in spending policies of business and government? This issue runs through all of this book—and indeed through all macro- economics.

Problem 3.15 The government, says Theory 2, can influence the national income and consumption by altering the supply of money, except in one special case. What is this case?

Problem 3.16 The government, says Theory 2, can influence the total productive capacity of the country (plant and equipment) by changing the supply of money, except in one special case. What is this case?

Problem 3.17 Suppose autonomous demand for plant (F_K) declines by $1. How can the supply of money be altered so as to stabilize (1) total investment, (2) the national product, (3) both total investment and the national product in the general case?

COMPARISON OF THEORIES 1 AND 2

Theories 1 and 2 have three variables in common: the national product, consumption, and investment. The supply of money in both is a factor given from outside. This supply, in equilibrium, is always equal to the demand for money. The interest rate appears only in Theory 1; total wealth and plant and equipment appear only in Theory 2. Thus the two theories are only partly comparable, because they explain different (although overlapping) sets of variables. The comments that follow are based on a comparison of Tables 1 and 2.

An increase in the level of consumption demand (F_C) or in the level of investment demand (F_I in Theory 1 and F_K in Theory 2) turn out to have the same effects on the national product, consumption, and investment in both theories, *providing that* in Theory 2, $b = 0$. If $b = 0$, then the demand for plant is unaffected by the total wealth of the community. If, however, an increase in total wealth means an increase in the amount of plant and equipment desired, then a factor $(1 - b)$ appears in the denominators of the fractions in Table 2, causing them to differ from those in Table 1.

A change in the supply of money (F_M) has rather different effects in the two theories. In Theory 2 it affects investment because of its impact on the amount of plant desired. In Theory 1 it affects investment through the interest rate; an increase in the money supply means that the interest rate falls, and therefore the amount of investment desired rises; this impact is measured by d/e, containing the two coefficients associated with these effects.

Changes in the supply of money have more complicated effects on the national product and on consumption. If $b = 0$ in Theory 2, and if $b = d = 0$ and $e = -1$ in Theory 1, then the two formulas turn out to be the same: $v/(1 - a)$. That is, the effects turn out to depend on the ratio of v (the effect on consumption of a change in cash holdings) to the marginal propensity to save $(1 - a)$. This result is complicated, in general, by the "side-effects" associated with the demand for money (in Theory 1) and for plant and equipment (in Theory 2).

This comparison illustrates the way in which a pair of theories may differ. Even if Tiny Model 1 is taken as a starting point, there are various ways of expanding it. Once the differences between the theories have been clarified, as here, it may be possible to find a single theory to include both (just as Theory 2 was developed out of Tiny Models 1 and 2). It is also possible to make statistical studies to see whether the facts bear out one theory rather than the others.

Problem 3.18 Make tables that show for Theories 1 and 2 the effect (positive or negative) that increase in each of the behavioral coefficients of the theories would have upon the variables in the system. Interpret your results.

Problem 3.19 The theories in this book do not, in the main, deal with the allocation of income between wage-earners and property-owners. But here is a rudimentary collection of theories dealing with these matters. Wage income is W, property income is P. Then,

$$Y = C + I$$
$$Y = W + P$$

Assume that investment depends upon property income:

$$I = bP + F_I$$

and that wage-earners and property-owners spend different amounts out of any increment of income:

$$C = a_1 W + a_2 P + F_C$$

Finally, consider several possible statements:

(1) Property income is fixed by law: $P = F_P$

(2) Collective bargaining fixes the ratio of wages to property income: $P = KW$

(3) Collective bargaining fixes total wage payments: $W = F_W$

Determine, for cases (1), (2), and (3) how changes in factors affect the variables in the system.

Appendix to Chapter 3

IS-LM CURVES

Theory 1 is very close to a topic called *IS-LM curves* in the literature. Theory 1 actually yields the same results as the *IS-LM* curve analysis, but it may be helpful to readers of other books to see the connection spelled out. The *IS-LM* curve analysis is two things. First, it is a way to solve a system of equations in steps. Instead of taking a matrix and inverting it, one divides the system of equations into two parts, simplifies each part, and combines the two at the end, getting the same results as Theory 1. Second, however, the *IS-LM* analysis treats the economy as consisting of "goods" and "money." One group of equations deals with "goods," the other with "money."

$$Y = C + I \tag{A3.1}$$

$$C = aY + bR + vL + F_C \tag{A3.2}$$

$$I = \quad dR \quad + F_I \tag{A3.3}$$

$$L = gY + eR \quad + F_L \tag{A3.4}$$

$$L = F_M \tag{A3.5}$$

In this version of Theory 1, we have introduced the coefficient g—the demand for money depends on income as well as the interest rate. This change is made so that the theory will resemble more exactly the other literature on the subject.

First, the so-called *IS* curve is derived. Equations A3.2, A3.3, and A3.4 are substituted into Equation A3.1:

$$\begin{aligned} Y &= C + I \\ &= [aY + bR + vL + F_C] + [dR + F_I] \\ &= [aY + bR + F_C + V(gY + eR + F_L)] + dR + F_I \end{aligned}$$

Terms involving Y are now collected on the left:

$$Y[1 - a - vg] = R[b + ve + d] + [F_C + vF_L + F_I]$$

so that

$$Y = \frac{b + ve + d}{1 - a - vg} R + \frac{F_C + vF_L + F_I}{1 - a - vg} \qquad \text{(A3.6)}$$

Thus, income is a linear function of the interest rate.

Second, the so-called *LM* curve is derived by substituting Equation A3.5 into Equation A3.4:

$$\begin{aligned} F_M &= gY + eR + F_L \\ Y &= -\frac{e}{g} R - \frac{F_L - F_M}{g} \end{aligned} \qquad \text{(A3.7)}$$

Thus, there is a second linear function relating income and the interest rate. Equations A3.6 and A3.7 are of the form

$$\begin{aligned} Y - \beta_1 R &= K_1 \qquad [\, IS \text{ curve} = \text{(A3.6)}] \\ Y + \beta_2 R &= K_2 \qquad [LM \text{ curve} = \text{(A3.7)}] \end{aligned}$$

and it is possible, therefore, to solve for Y and R in terms of K_1 and K_2. Naturally, the solution is the same as that which would have been obtained for Theory 1 *if* the coefficient g had been included in the matrix.

The *IS-LM* curve analysis is very convenient for blackboard demonstrations. It is used as a teaching device where students cannot use algebraic methods. Despite its rather forbidding name, however, it is basically a means of solving theories like Theory 1 in parts, rather than as a whole.

Indeed, readers who wonder what difference it makes that the coefficient g was introduced into A3.4 are urged to solve A3.6 and A3.7 for Y and R. (That is easy.) Then they will be readily able to compute the effects of changes in all the factors upon Y and R, and then to obtain the rest of the inverse matrix by substituting into the other equations of the system. In this way they will have an exercise in working with *IS-LM* analysis as well as in investigating the consequences of a change in the behavioral assumptions of a theory.

The usual interpretation given to A3.6 is that the demand for goods equals the supply of goods. The usual interpretation given to A3.7 is that the demand for money equals the supply of money. Thus, the *IS-LM* system is taken to describe the interaction of the goods section and the monetary section of the economy.

4 Government and the Economy

The theories presented so far have ignored the fact that countries have governments. The national products were defined as $Y = C + I$, meaning, of course, that output consisted of the purchases of households and businesses. In this chapter, a small step is made in the direction of reality, and government is admitted in a certain, special way. The procedure will parallel that used so far in the two-sector theories. Theory 3 will explain the connection between government income and spending on the one hand and the national income and product on the other. This theory is basically like Tiny Model 1, but more complicated in detail. Theory 4 will be presented as a precise formulation of a political controversy about the role of government in the economy. Finally, Theory 5 will combine national product and wealth accounts, much in the spirit of Theory 2.[1]

[1] Theory 1 was a first attempt at a theory involving prices. This problem will be discussed again in Chapter 5, but it would be messy to introduce it here.

THEORY 3: GOVERNMENT AND THE NATIONAL PRODUCT

The government has all sorts of complicated effects on the economy. Business cannot be carried on without laws and courts (one of the roles of which is to interpret and enforce contracts). In some economies (as in the United States), government has encouraged businesses to compete with each other; in other cases (as in most of Europe) governments have encouraged businesses not to compete, but to divide markets by agreement, to fix prices, and so on. There is no simple way even to list all the ways in which legal and political arrangements affect the economy, and this book will not even try to do so. It will discuss a few matters in detail.

In this book the government has two functions: It buys goods and it collects taxes. As a buyer of goods, it enters into the national product, the definition of which now becomes

$$Y = C + I + G$$

Consumption (C) and investment (I) are thus joined by government spending (G). The government raises income from taxes (T), and it has a surplus or deficit given by ($G - T$). It is natural to ask how the government can pay for the goods it buys if it does not have enough tax revenue. The present theory does not answer this question, but two informal suggestions can be made. First, the government can print paper money; second, it can sell bonds. Both money and bonds are part of the assets (wealth) of the community, and therefore they do not enter explicitly into the income accounts. The reader must wait for Theory 8, which imbeds the income theory given here into a more comprehensive system.

Tax revenue is assumed to be described by the relation:

$$T = tY + F_T$$

This statement says that when the national product increases, tax revenue increases also, and t is taken to be positive. It will also be assumed that t is less than 1. That is, when income increases, not all of the increase goes to the government.

The reasoning behind this statement is simple. The two main sources of government revenue in all civilized countries are called income taxes and excise taxes. An income tax is collected from people (or businesses) on the basis of their incomes: The more each person earns, the more tax he pays, and the more income the community earns, the more taxes it pays.[2] Excise taxes are taxes levied on the sale of particular products such as gasoline, tobacco, and liquor—many governments depend heavily on such taxes. These tax collections presumably depend on income, because when consumers have more income, they buy more of the taxed goods and hence pay more taxes. The relation between excise taxes and income is obviously much trickier than that given here, but this particular formulation probably contains an important part of the connection.

Not all taxes are related to income. State and local governments in the United States have traditionally depended on taxes on property (land and buildings, in particular). This sort of tax does not vary automatically with income. For this reason a term F_T enters into the statement about taxes.

Tiny Model 1 had the following to say about consumption:

$$C = aY + F_C$$

This means that consumption depends on total income. But if consumers are liable to an income tax, their spending must depend on income *after* tax, rather than total income. In the present theory, the simplest way of taking this important fact into account is to say that:

$$C = a(Y - T) + F_C$$

For the moment, assume that investment and government spending are independent of the rest of the system. That is, they are factors rather than variables:

$$I = F_I$$
$$G = F_G$$

Now for the mechanics of obtaining the factor-into-variable mapping. The discussion thus far gives us the variable-into-factor mapping:

$$(\mathbf{0}, \mathbf{F_C}, \mathbf{F_T}, \mathbf{F_G}, \mathbf{F_I}) = (\mathbf{Y}, \mathbf{C}, \mathbf{T}, \mathbf{G}, \mathbf{I})\begin{pmatrix} 1 & -a & -t & 0 & 0 \\ -1 & 1 & 0 & 0 & 0 \\ 0 & a & 1 & 0 & 0 \\ -1 & 0 & 0 & 1 & 0 \\ -1 & 0 & 0 & 0 & 1 \end{pmatrix}$$

---

[2] This statement is a typical macroeconomic exaggeration. Imagine that high-income groups are subject to a high tax and low-income groups to a low tax. It is then arithmetically possible in some year for low income groups to get increased incomes, and high income groups to get reduced incomes, in such a way that total income rises and tax payments fall. The reader can easily construct an example of this sort. Since this book aims at simplicity, it does not have occasion to go into this sort of complication.

This matrix contains Tiny Model 1 in its upper left corner:

$$\begin{pmatrix} 1 & -a \\ -1 & 1 \end{pmatrix}$$

and it is block-triangular, since there is a 3 × 2 block of zeros in the upper right. The inverse of the matrix may be shown to be

$$\begin{pmatrix} 1 & -a & -t & 0 & 0 \\ -1 & 1 & 0 & 0 & 0 \\ 0 & a & 1 & 0 & 0 \\ -1 & 0 & 0 & 1 & 0 \\ -1 & 0 & 0 & 0 & 1 \end{pmatrix}^{-1} = \begin{pmatrix} \frac{1}{1-a(1-t)} & \frac{a(1-t)}{1-a(1-t)} & \frac{t}{1-a(1-t)} & 0 \\ \frac{1}{1-a(1-t)} & \frac{1}{1-a(1-t)} & \frac{t}{1-a(1-t)} & 0 \\ \frac{-a}{1-a(1-t)} & \frac{-a}{1-a(1-t)} & \frac{1-a}{1-a(1-t)} & 0 \\ \frac{1}{1-a(1-t)} & \frac{a(1-t)}{1-a(1-t)} & \frac{t}{1-a(1-t)} & 1 \\ \frac{1}{1-a(1-t)} & \frac{a(1-t)}{1-a(1-t)} & \frac{t}{1-a(1-t)} & 0 \end{pmatrix}$$

TABLE 4.1

THE IMPLICATIONS OF THEORY 3:
GOVERNMENT AND THE NATIONAL PRODUCT

THE EFFECT OF A UNIT CHANGE IN	THE EFFECT OF A UNIT CHANGE UPON		
	National product	Consumption	Tax revenue
F_C (Consumer demand)	$\frac{1}{1-a(1-t)}$	$\frac{1}{1-a(1-t)}$	$\frac{t}{1-a(1-t)}$
F_T (Property taxes)	$\frac{-a}{1-a(1-t)}$	$\frac{-a}{-1\,a(1-t)}$	$\frac{1-a}{1-a(1-t)}$
F_G (Government spending)	$\frac{1}{1-a(1-t)}$	$\frac{a(1-t)}{1-a(1-t)}$	$\frac{t}{1-a(1-t)}$
F_I (Investment)	$\frac{1}{1-a(1-t)}$	$\frac{a(1-t)}{1-a(1-t)}$	$\frac{t}{1-a(1-t)}$

The present Theory 3 has an intimate connection with Tiny Model 1. The *investment multiplier* in the latter was $1/(1-a)$, in this case it is $1/[1-a(1-t)]$. In the first case, it was said that if consumers received an additional dollar of income, they consumed an additional a, so that they *saved* $(1 - a)$, which appears in the denominator.

In Theory 3, when consumers receive an addition dollar of income, they pay t in additional taxes. Therefore they have $(1 - t)$ left, and of this they spend $a(1 - t)$. Consequently, for every additional dollar of income *before* taxes, savings increase by $[1 - a(1 - t)]$, that is, by exactly the denominator of the investment multiplier. In other words, the two theories are very much the same.

Historical Remark. The last two lines of Table 1 are the same. That is, in this theory, a dollar's change in investment has the same effect throughout the economy as a dollar's change in government spending. This theory is known in the popular press as "Keynesian," even though economists will be far more inclined to consider Theory 1 in Chapter 3 as Keynesian.

Theory 3 represents a rationalization of a major political discovery, which had a profound effect on American life for thirty years. In 1929, the United States entered a period of massive depression. By 1932, over one quarter of the labor force was unemployed, and business conditions were in all respects worse than they ever have been (before *or* since). In those days, everyone believed that government deficits were in general undesirable, although no theory of any consequence existed which could be stated as precisely as, for example, Table 4.1. Consequently, in the elections of 1932, both Republicans and Democrats advocated reduced government spending—which, if Table 4.1 is valid, means that they both advocated policies which would make the depression worse.

The Democrats won the election, because the electorate blamed President Hoover either for causing the depression or for massive indifference to its consequences. We would now consider this verdict unfair. No convincing explanation has ever been given for the violence of this depression, but it affected the entire world, and no country was able to combat it successfully for a long time except by using Nazi or Communist methods.

When Roosevelt came into office, there were so many unemployed that mass starvation seemed to threaten. Disregarding the professional advice of economists (and following that of politicians and social workers), Roosevelt began providing relief to the unemployed. Everyone expected business conditions to become worse because of the increased government deficit. However, it turned out that if the government gave money to the unemployed, they promptly spent it. When they spent it, business earned income; and when business received more income, it hired more people, and unemployment fell. To the surprise of economists, business conditions improved considerably in 1933–1934.

The entire development of macroeconomics has been profoundly influenced by these shocking events. At the time, they dumbfounded the experts.

Theory 3 gives the easy explanation of what happened. We should *not* conclude that Theory 3 is the *true* explanation of this period. It would require considerable historical analysis to determine that matter. But it is a fact that Theory 3 was developed in order to explain the depression of 1929–1932 and the partial recovery of 1933–1934.

For thirty years after 1932, Democratic presidential candidates devoted a great deal of effort to campaigning against poor President Hoover. They had very considerable success. The Republicans felt, evidently, that in order to be true to themselves, they could not possibly admit the existence of any reasoning so simple as that of Theory 3. They have also tended to lose elections. Democrats, on the other hand, have felt that a policy that worked in 1933 would always work, and they are inclined, as a matter of principle, to try to solve all problems by increasing government spending. Not all problems can be solved in this way, and so the Republicans, who often talk foolishly about depressions, often talk sensibly about other economic matters. The Democrats, who often talk sensibly about depressions, often talk foolishly about other economic matters.

It is difficult for students in the late 1960s to appreciate the enormous emotional content that Theory 3 has for economists of their parents' age. In purely professional terms, they will say that this theory was the first explanation offered for the depression of the 1930s and the principal remedy for it that seemed to be available at the time. The depression itself was as important a topic of popular concern in the 1930s as Outer Space, pot, the Hydrogen Bomb, and Communist China are in the late 1960s.

Theory 4 formulates a real problem concerning the effect of government on the economy. If the answer to this problem were known, then an issue that can now only be debated about could be resolved. It is a precise statement (in a very simple form) of an economic issue that divides political liberals from political conservatives, and, as such, is of interest outside the narrow circle of professional economists.

Problem 4.1 Suppose property taxes (F_T) are increased by \$1. What is the effect on the budget surplus or deficit?

Problem 4.2 Suppose the government has a deficit equal to D. If spending (F_G) increases by \$1, by how much will property taxes (F_T) have to be increased in order that the deficit be held constant?

Problem 4.3 Suppose that the government increases its spending (F_T) by \$1 and alters property taxes (F_T) in such a way as to keep the deficit constant. What is the effect of this fiscal policy upon the national product and upon consumption?

Problem 4.4 Suppose a decline of \$1 in antonomous consumer demand (F_C). Can the government exactly offset the resulting changes on *both* the national product *and* on consumption (1) by changing government spending; (2) by changing property taxes; (3) by some combination of the two?

Problem 4.5 Suppose that tax laws are given, and that government spending varies in such a way that the budget is always balanced. Incorporate this condition into Theory 3, and show how the economy changes in response to the remaining independent factors.

Problem 4.6 Suppose that the government has decided that it must offset the effects of changes in investment, so that $F_G = G + I$ is some constant. What is the effect on the economy of changes in investment, assuming

(1) A given tax law:

$$T = tY + F_T$$

(2) A requirement that in addition to this tax law,

$$T = G$$

(Solve this problem under the conditions assumed for Theories 3 and 4.)

Problem 4.7 The United States Government has a number of spending programs that "automatically" increase as the national product declines. For instance, when the national product declines, employment also declines and unemployment compensation payments rise. When the national product falls, the cost of agricultural price support programs rises. Suppose that $G = xY + F_G$, where $x < 0$. Under the conditions of Theories 3 and 4, is there a value of X that will guarantee that declines in investment will have no effect on the national product?

Problem 4.8 At the time the Federal Income tax was reduced in 1964, some proponents of the tax argued that a reduction in tax rates would increase the national income so much that total Federal tax collections would actually rise. In Theories 3 and 4, consider the two tax systems

$$T = t_1 Y + F_{T1}$$
$$T = t_2 Y + F_{T2}$$

where $t_1 > t_2$, $F_{T1} > F_{T2}$, and determine whether this conclusion would be tenable, given constant levels for the other factors of the system.

THEORY 4: GOVERNMENT AND INVESTMENT

Most undergraduates who take economics courses do not intend to become professional economists, but all will become voters. Most teachers of undergraduate economics courses feel, therefore, that a part of their role is to help their students become intelligent voters. Some of these teachers feel that if their students are to be intelligent voters, they must adopt the political views of their professors. But the more responsible teachers recognize that economists themselves have quite varied political opinions; and therefore most political parties (and factions within political parties) will be able to find some supporters among professional economists. Whatever political group one considers, its views on economic questions can certainly be formulated in an illiterate fashion; and in most cases, its views can also be formulated in a literate fashion. Professional economists, as partisans, can keep their political friends from saying stupid things and sometimes even (if these friends are in power) dissuade them from doing stupid things.

Political questions arise, in part, because different political groups want different things. In such cases, any economist can, in principle, be employed by any political group. One can imagine (in the extreme) an economist, in wartime, acting as consultant on tax policy to both warring powers. It is unlikely that any economist would be trusted by both parties; if he were, it is unlikely that he would be so indifferent to the outcome of the war that he would be willing to work for both sides. But, on a strictly professional level, he could do so.

Political questions also arise, in part, because there is a variety of opinion on the truth of some matter, and no scientific answer is yet possible. In cases like this, political disagreement is associated with professional disagreement. One would hope that if professional economists were to resolve the issue conclusively, the political factions would be able to recognize that an answer exists, so that controversy is unnecessary.

One example of a problem that has been resolved has to do with "bimetalism." In the nineteenth century and before, money consisted largely of metal coin. Some countries used gold coin, others used silver coin. A few, including the United States, had both kinds. Countries that wished to use both sorts of coin had to decide whether or not to keep the prices of the two kinds stable relative to each other. This decision involved a dilemma: If the relative prices of the two kinds of money were fixed, then people tended to hoard one kind and only the other would remain in general use; if prices were not fixed, both remained in use; but grave uncertainty arose in the conduct of business, for it was in principle necessary in each contract to specify what kind of money was to be used. In the late 1800s there was important political agitation on the question of maintaining both kinds of coin; it reached its peak in the presidential election of 1896, when McKinley beat Bryan in a campaign largely concerned with monetary issues.

It is mostly unlikely that this issue could be taken seriously today. Professional economists would now say that Bryan's sound argument was that the quantity of money should be increased as a means of increasing incomes (particularly for farmers), a proposition defensible in terms of the theories given here; but that increases in the quantity of money can be more readily achieved through the formation and utilization of a central bank (see Chapter 5) than by making silver coins. We should now say that McKinley's sound argument was that unless care is taken to avoid undue increase in the amount of money, prices will tend to rise, but that there may be better ways of stabilizing the amount of money than by insisting on the use of gold coins. Professional economists today would urge both McKinley and Bryan to concentrate on the central question—how large should the money supply be if it is to stabilize income and prices—rather than on the issue of gold and silver coinage. Political leaders of all persuasions now get better advice than formerly, so that certain controversies have simply disappeared. The general issue of the connection between money and economic activity is still full of unsolved issues.

The greatest political issue that was resolved in principle in the 1930s was whether increases in government spending might affect the level of the national product. That issue is solved in Theory 3. If one theory can be constructed to show how *some* effect is produced by changes in government spending, others can presumably be constructed to show how other effects might come about. The intelligent citizen, whatever his political beliefs, has no reason to doubt the *logical* consistency of Theory 3; but the world may or may not behave in the way depicted by this theory.

It is useful to replace Theory 3 by a theory that differs from it in the following respect: Investment will be taken to depend partly on other variables in the system, instead of being completely "outside" the system. This theory, then, has something in common with Theory 1, in which the interest rate was introduced as a variable affecting investment. However, this time no new variables will be introduced. We shall reduce the number of nonzero elements in the matrix of Theory 3 by replacing the relation $I = F_I$, by the relation

$$I = cC + gT + hG + F_I$$

connecting investment with consumption, taxes, and government spending. Consequently Theory 3, written out in full, is

$$(\mathbf{0}, \mathbf{F_C}, \mathbf{F_T}, \mathbf{F_G}, \mathbf{F_I}) = (\mathbf{Y}, \mathbf{C}, \mathbf{T}, \mathbf{G}, \mathbf{I}) \begin{pmatrix} 1 & -a & -t & 0 & 0 \\ -1 & 1 & 0 & 0 & -c \\ 0 & a & 1 & 0 & -g \\ -1 & 0 & 0 & 1 & -h \\ -1 & 0 & 0 & 0 & 1 \end{pmatrix}$$

The first four columns of the matrix of Theories 3 and 4 are the same; only the last column is changed.

Why write such a theory? The point is that with this theory one can comment usefully on a political controversy over government spending. This controversy is one step higher than the controversy over Theory 3. It recognizes that government spending affects the national income; and in fact Theory 3 emerges as a special case of Theory 4 (set $c = g = h = 0$). When Theory 3 is thus generalized, an interesting problem is obtained.

Investment, in a private-enterprise economy, takes place whenever business *expects* to make a profit from operating the proposed facility. Expectations pertain to the future, not to the present. One obtains an expectation about the future partly by looking at the present, partly by looking at the past, and partly by completely extraneous means.[3]

The present theory says that consumption affects investment and, in particular, that $c \geq 0$. The mechanism posited is the following: The more consumption there is today, the more business expects there to be tomorrow. The larger the size of its expected market, the more plant and equipment business will decide it needs, so the more investment there will be.[4]

The present theory says that taxes affect investment and, in particular, that $g \leq 0$. An increase in tax payments reduces investment. The justification of this view would be just like the explanation of why increases in the interest rate reduce investment. That is, the firm estimates the capacity and hence the sales to be obtained from the new facility, and the cost of operating the facility. If taxes rise, the expected cost of the new facility rises, and expected profits fall. Any increase in taxes might therefore be expected to reduce investment.[5]

Finally, the present theory states that government spending affects investment. But there are two widely different views about the nature of the effect. Both views can be documented for individual industries.

(1) Political conservatives say that $h < 0$, for two reasons. The first is that government spending may compete with business. *Example:* if the government builds a hydroelectric dam on the Wabash River, this project will cause private public utilities *not* to build such plants on the Wabash. More generally, if business sees that government spending is rising, it infers that ultimately the business sector of the economy will be forced to contract. Thus, even if the dam did not directly replace a private project, it would cause reductions in investment in general.

(2) Political liberals say that $h > 0$ for two reasons. First, government spending leads directly to business investment. *Example:* if the government builds a hydroelectric dam on the Wabash River, the project will cause nearby businesses to expand. The workers on the building project must be

---

[3] Economists call factors unrelated to the economy "psychological," and they mean by this "irrational." No slur on psychologists is intended.

[4] Some economists make investment depend on the *change* in consumption, not the amount of consumption, as here. This assumption would follow, if in this theory balance sheet items were present, and if the demand for *plant* depended on the *amount* of consumption. Then investment (the change in plant) would depend on the change in consumption. This hypothesis is called the *accelerator* hypothesis. It is interesting, but more difficult than anything we use here.

[5] To the extent that business can "pass taxes on" and make its customers or stockholders pay them, this argument is weakened. At this point we are not saying whether g is close to zero, or whether investment is greatly affected by taxes. The point is that it is implausible that increased taxes should *increase* investment.

fed, clothed, lodged, and entertained. Later, the dam will attract power-using firms into the area, and so on. More generally, if business sees that government spending is rising, it infers that it will receive increased orders, both from the government and from government employees; to meet this increase in orders, business therefore invests more.

Both of these views are plausible. One need only read what businessmen say about government in the annual reports of corporations or in the financial newspapers to be aware that many of them seem to be very suspicious of government. If they do not lie about their true sentiments, something like the "conservative investment function" ($h < 0$) is defensible. On the other hand, one need only look at cities like Oak Ridge, Tennessee, Groton, Connecticut, San Diego, California, or Seattle, Washington to see cases where government spending (on atomic energy, submarines, and the "aerospace" industries) have had indirect effects on housing construction and all sorts of business investments. If this evidence is not completely misleading, something like the "liberal investment function" ($h > 0$) is defensible.

As a matter of fact, if both hypotheses are plausible, and if there is evidence in favor of both, the only question would be, "Which is the more important"? In this problem, the symbol h would be regarded as a sum of two influences: $h = h_C + h_L$, and one would seek to evaluate relative magnitudes. We will not have to worry about this problem here. The point is, simply, that the answer to the problem is one in applied economics (is h a positive or a negative number in the conditions of country A in year Y?) and not merely one for speech-makers to emote about.

Part of investment does not depend on the other variables in the system. Denoted by F_I, it is called "autonomous" investment in traditional terminology. The rest of investment, $I - F_I$, is called "induced," because it depends on the other variables in the system. F_I is of course a factor.

In the present state of our knowledge, the political contestants try to resolve the argument by standing nose-to-nose and shouting "$h > 0$!" or "$h < 0$!" at each other. This may seem silly to some bystanders, because a question of fact is involved. Why do not these people find out where the truth lies? Two answers to this question can be given: (1) Some efforts have been made; but (as we shall see in our last chapter), it is not easy, at best, to answer such questions. (2) Although the question is important, people with strong political views do not want to try too hard for an answer; they are afraid they might be wrong. Here is a case where the interested reader may be invited to devise a way of finding the truth about this argument. The argument itself is getting nowhere.

Why should it matter whether h is greater than, or less than zero? To answer this question, we must invert the matrix, so as to obtain the factor-into-variable mapping. The inverse of the matrix to Theory 4 is

$$
\begin{pmatrix}
1 & -a & -t & 0 & 0 \\
-1 & 1 & 0 & 0 & -c \\
0 & a & 1 & 0 & -g \\
-1 & 0 & 0 & 1 & -h \\
-1 & 0 & 0 & 0 & 1
\end{pmatrix}^{-1}
=
\begin{pmatrix}
\dfrac{1}{D} & \dfrac{a(1-t)}{D} & \dfrac{t}{D} & 0 & \dfrac{ca(1-t)+gt}{D} \\[2ex]
\dfrac{1+c}{D} & \dfrac{1-gt}{D} & \dfrac{t(1+c)}{D} & 0 & \dfrac{c+gt}{D} \\[2ex]
\dfrac{g-a(1+c)}{D} & \dfrac{-a(1-g)}{D} & \dfrac{1-a(1+c)}{D} & 0 & \dfrac{-ca(1-g)+g(1-a)(1+c)}{D} \\[2ex]
\dfrac{1+h}{D} & \dfrac{a(1-t)(1+h)}{D} & \dfrac{t(1+h)}{D} & 1 & \dfrac{a(h-c)(1-t)-h-gt}{D} \\[2ex]
\dfrac{1}{D} & \dfrac{a(1-t)}{D} & \dfrac{t}{D} & 0 & \dfrac{1-a(1-t)}{D}
\end{pmatrix}
$$

where $D = (1 - gt) - a(1 - t)(1 + c)$.

Table 4.2 is the interpretation given to the elements of the inverse matrix just calculated. Let us note that $1/D$ measures the effect of increased autonomous investment on the national product, and is thus the investment multiplier. In Tiny Model 1, the corresponding multiplier was $1/1 - a$. The quantity D may be interpreted as follows:

The quantity a represents the amount spent from a unit increase in income after taxes; t is the tax rate. Hence $a(1 - t)$ represents the change in consumption from a unit increase in income *before* taxes; $a(1 - t)(1 + c)$ adjusts this change for the increase in investment associated with the change in consumption just mentioned. That is, the final term of D represents a change in consumption. $(1 - gt)$ measures the net increase in income after taxes.

TABLE 4.2

THE IMPLICATIONS OF THEORY 4

EFFECT OF A T CHANGE IN	THE EFFECT OF A UNIT CHANGE UPON			
	National product	Consumption	Taxes	Investment
he level of onsumption	$\frac{1+c}{D}$	$\frac{1-gt}{D}$	$\frac{t(1+c)}{D}$	$\frac{c+gt}{D}$
roperty taxes)	$\frac{g-a(1+c)}{D}$	$\frac{-a(1-g)}{D}$	$\frac{1-a(1+c)}{D}$	$\frac{-ca(1-g)+g[1-a(1+c)]}{D}$
overnment ending)	$\frac{1+h}{D}$	$\frac{a(1-t)(1+h)}{D}$	$\frac{t(1+h)}{D}$	$\frac{a(h-c)(1-t)-h-gt}{D}$
utonomous vestment)	$\frac{1}{D}$	$\frac{a(1-t)}{D}$	$\frac{t}{D}$	$\frac{1-a(1-t)}{D}$

Thus D represents the amount of saving per unit of additional income; it is one dollar income minus taxes on one dollar additional income minus spending generated by one dollar additional income. This multiplier is more involved than the earlier multipliers, because Theory 4 involves more internal connections than the earlier theories.

Note that in this theory, if investment increases by one dollar, the national product goes *up* by $1/D$. We say "up" because we suppose that at a higher level of income, the community saves more ($d > 0$).[6] However, an increase in government spending increases the national product by $(1 + h)/D$.

Conclusion: If the political conservatives are right, and h is between 0 and -1, if the government wished to compensate for a decline of \$1 in autonomous business investment, it would have to increase spending by more than \$1.

If an extreme conservative view is right, and $h < -1$, an increase of \$1 in government spending decreases investment by more than \$1. In this case, $(1 + h)/D$ is negative. To offset a decline in autonomous investment, then, the government should *reduce* spending, so as to stimulate investment and hence increase the national product. But in wartime, when resources are scarce, and the government wishes to reduce civilian purchasing power, it should (in this view) *increase* its spending so as to contract the civilian sector.

If the political liberals are right, h is positive, and an increase of \$1 in government spending would more than offset a decline of \$1 in autonomous investment. However, in wartime, this argument, a reduction in government spending (presumably non-military) would be more effective in restricting civilian purchasing power than an equal restriction in business investment.

No convincing answers have been given by economists to the question "What is the numerical value of h?" Obviously, if such answers could be given, there would be one less controversy. Let us observe, in passing, that even if one knew for sure that in some particular year, h had some particular numerical value, there would be no certainty that the next year h would remain unchanged. For h, like all the other symbols used in these theories, is a way of summarizing people's behavior. There is a great deal we do not know about people, including how changeable they are.

Problems 4.9 to 4.16 Answer problems 4.1 to 4.8 under the conditions assumed in Theory 4. Compare these new answers with those given for the first set of problems. Discuss, in connection with each, how the answer is affected by the conservative and the liberal political hypotheses.

THEORY 5: GOVERNMENT, INCOME, AND WEALTH

This theory will do what Theory 2 did. It will set up income accounts and a balance sheet for an economy having a government as well as household and business sectors.

---

[6] Note that $D = 1 - a(1 + c) + t(a + ac - g)$. If $g < 0$ (taxes reduce investment), the last term is positive. Indeed, the smaller g is (the *more* taxes reduce investment), the greater D is. That is, the less $1/D$ is, the less investment increases the national product.

When government was included in the national-product accounts, the number of variables grew by two (government spending and government income) as compared to Tiny Model 1, which is comparable to it. When we expand the theory to include balance sheet items, we will also have to expand the number of variables.

In other words, this theory will end up as a system involving eleven variables and eleven factors (some of them identities).

In looking at this theory, readers should not merely look at the statements included in the theory, at the mechanics of matrix inverting, and at the individual results derived from this theory. It will turn out that the particular theory used here is easy to use, in the sense that it is closely related to our earlier work, and also easy to invert. In this sense, it is a very natural theory for a person who has read this book to use.

But when the theory has been set up, so that everyone knows what the theory says, and everyone can see that it really is a theory, it will turn out that the theory continues to be unsatisfactory in some ways, which we shall describe. Space does not permit (and the technical skill of beginners does not justify) an attempt to correct the technical difficulties of this particular theory.

A very important part of learning anything (including economics) consists in knowing how to evaluate what has been done. A beginners' discussion of macroeconomic theories should include both "results" (that is, how to use what is known to find out something that is not known) and "strategy" (that is, how to decide what to do next). Theory 5 is a long step forward from Tiny Models 1 and 2, but it is not the last word in economics. Beginners should be pleased at having got so far, and also aware that they do not know everything yet.

In studying Theory 5, readers might ponder the following curious fact. The theory being set forth is really very simple—one can be sure that the real world is more complicated that this theory says it is. The theory is being kept simple so that the reasoning process can be kept clear and in front of every reader. "Practical" people are fond of saying that theorists do not take enough variables (or factors) into account. This would suggest that the practical man will spend his time on "large" systems of this sort, and the theorist on small ones; and this is not the case. What the "practical" people usually mean is that they can jump to the conclusions implied by some theory such as this one without doing the work either of setting the theory down explicitly or of inverting the matrix associated with the theory. Readers of this book should know enough by now not to believe them.

The first step will be to specify the economy under discussion. The income accounts are the same as in Theories 3 and 4:

$$Y = C + I + G \tag{4.1}$$

When the balance sheet is taken into account, the variables in Theory 2 are retained, and new ones are introduced. That is, the national assets certainly include money (M) and plant and equipment (K). However, it is also necessary to take into account the financing of the government deficit.

Is it possible or not for government spending to differ from tax revenue? If it is, then a theory should say how it is done. Theory 5 says that the government finances its deficits partly by borrowing and partly by printing paper money. When it borrows, it sells bonds.[7] These bonds are held by someone, and the total national debt (B) is therefore one of the assets of the non-governmental sectors of the economy. That is, the balance sheet of the economy[8] is written

$$W = M + B + K \tag{4.2}$$

Moreover, the financing of the government deficit is expressed by:

$$G = T + \Delta M + \Delta B \tag{4.3}$$

That is, the only paper money printed and the only bonds issued are used to finance government deficits. It may turn out that there is a surplus ($G < T$); and in this case the amount of money may fall ($\Delta M < 0$) and/or part of the national debt may be retired ($\Delta B < 0$).

Statement 4.3 is the first explanation of "where the money comes from." In Theories 1 and 2, the quantity of money appeared as a factor, not a variable. Actually, in the American economy (as in most others), the government *may* print paper money to finance a deficit (the Civil War was mainly financed this way), but selling bonds is more common today. Moreover, the amount of paper money in use may rise even if there is no government deficit. Readers need not believe this statement now, but it will be shown to be true in a later chapter. And most money is in bank accounts anyhow.

---

[7] Anyone who has worked out Theory 1 will realize that the interest rate is a cost to the government; and that the government (like business) may take this price into account in making decisions to borrow. It is perfectly possible to introduce the interest rate as a variable in this system, but things are getting complicated enough without it.

[8] Strictly speaking, the private sector. Readers are reminded that in Chapter 2 we said we would disregard the government's balance sheet. There, of course, the national debt appears as a liability. If the private and government balance sheets were combined, the national debt would appear both as asset and as liability and would cancel out.

Historical Remark. Before the invention of paper money, metal coin was the only form of currency. In this situation, government deficits were covered (apart from borrowing) in two ways. The government might have a Treasure (literally stacks of gold or silver bars), which could be made into coins, or else coins collected in earlier periods. Alternatively, the government might melt down the coins that came in as tax revenue and remake them, either into smaller coin, or coin of standard size containing larger amounts than formerly of "base metals" (such as copper). Thus a given weight of gold or silver would be made into a larger amount of money in order that the amount of currency be increased.

Consequently, besides the identity

$$K = K_0 + I \tag{4.4}$$

which links total plant and equipment to investment in Theory 2 (remember that I is the same thing as ΔK), we use the identities

$$M = M_0 + \Delta M \tag{4.5}$$

$$B = B_0 + \Delta B \tag{4.6}$$

which link the values of the variables in the preceding period (denoted by subscript 0) with their values in the current period.

Three of the symbols so far may be treated as factors (K_0, M_0, B_0); they represent "yesterday's values" of variables, and as of today they are given numbers. The remaining eleven (Y, C, I, T, G, W, M, B, K, ΔM, ΔB) are to be determined by the theory. Five statements have been made so far; six more will be required before a theory has been completed. These statements will presumably say what is thought to determine the demand for the three components of the national product (C, I, G) and for the three kinds of assets in the community (M, B, K).

In one case, (G), the matter is simple enough. We take government spending to be determined by "noneconomic factors," so that

$$G = F_G \tag{4.7}$$

Investment is the same thing as the change in plant. Consequently, if the demand for total plant is specified, and if the plant at the beginning of the period is given, the demand for investment is given by subtraction. Conversely, if the plant at the beginning of the period is given, and the demand for new plant is known, then the demand for total plant is obtained by addition. In other words, the demand for investment goods and the demand for plant cannot be independent of each other, since one is derivable from the other.

Likewise, it is impossible to make independent statements about the total demand for government bonds, which is a balance sheet item, and the demand for new bonds, which is one use to which consumers can put their incomes. Finally, a similar restriction holds about money.

The current income (after taxes) of individuals is used to buy consumer goods, to buy bonds, and to hold in the form of cash. But if there is a given income (after taxes), then any two choices imply the third. (If my income is \$10,000 after taxes, and I decide to keep \$500 in cash and to buy \$500 in government bonds, I do not have to decide how much to spend, because \$10,000 – \$500 – \$500 = \$9,000, and my decision is already made for me.)

These restrictions have to be made in order to avoid inconsistencies in the statements that make up the theory. As a practical matter, we should also like to keep the theory simple. In this case, a simple theory would have (if possible) a block-triangular matrix, because the mathematics of such matrices are much more convenient. Moreover, as a practical matter, it would be nice if the theory were as similar as possible to something that had already been discussed, since the reader will then be on relatively familiar ground.

If an economist's objective is to be *right*, as distinct from being simple, the fact that a matrix is not block-triangular will not deter him. This criterion is used because the theories considered here are purposely kept simple for beginners. And if the economist were dissatisfied with earlier work in the profession, he would have no great reason to include pieces of it in his theories. But in this case, an author may be pardoned if, in the last part of his Chapter 4, he uses material from the first part of Chapter 4.

Therefore, Theory 4 will be used as a statement of the national accounts. This theory consisted of five statements, one of which has been repeated in the discussion above. The other four included a consumption function:[9]

$$C = a(Y - T) + F_C \tag{4.8}$$

a statement about tax revenue:

$$T = tY + F_T \tag{4.9}$$

and a statement about investment:

$$I = cC + gT + hG + F_I \tag{4.10}$$

[9] It would be nice to discuss once again the possibility that consumption depends on cash balances rather than on income. But it will turn out that such a theory is more difficult, computationally, than this one.

Therefore, it turns out that, given a careful specification of the national accounting system, plus Theory 4, there is *almost* enough to make a theory. Only one more statement is needed. This statement *must be* either about money or bonds; it *may be* either about total demand (in the balance sheet) or about the allocation of current income to the purchase of this type of asset.

Two statements appear particularly natural, given the type of reasoning found in Theory 2:[10]

$$M = mW + \mathbf{F}_M \tag{4.11a}$$

$$B = nW + F_B \tag{4.11b}$$

These two statements are "portfolio" type statements, which assert that asset-owners try to keep the composition (in percentage terms) of their assets stable. The percentage composition would be completely stable if $F_M + F_B = 0$; actually the statements given here do and not provide for stable proportions, since the factors F_M and F_B are in principle capable of variation.

The consequence of adopting either of these statements is to strengthen the relations existing among the various assets in the community. In contrast, a statement that said

$$M = vY + F_L \tag{4.11c}$$

would strengthen the links between income accounts and balance sheet accounts. If this way of theorizing were correct, asset-holders would not have an explicit policy dictating the composition of their assets. Rather, their thinking would have the following rationale: look at cash balances, and from this decide aggregate spending; from levels of spending at any moment, determine what assets to acquire, and hence the composition of the balance sheet. In contrast, the other theories allow preferences as to the composition of the balance sheet to influence current output.

Each of the three statements, (11a), (11b), and (11c) has a certain plausibility. To illustrate the workings of government in the economy, the entire system will be elaborated using (11a). The variable-into-factor mapping turns out to be block-triangular, providing that the elements of Theory 4 are collected. It also turns out that one can invert more readily by presenting the individual statements of the theory in a slightly different order from that given in the foregoing discussion.

---

[10] The use of the symbol F_M, in preference to F_L was explained in connection with Theory 2.

$$
\begin{gathered}
(\mathbf{0}, \mathbf{F_C}, \mathbf{F_T}, \mathbf{F_G}, \mathbf{F_I}, \mathbf{F_M}, \mathbf{0}, \mathbf{M_0}, \mathbf{B_0}, \mathbf{K_0}, \mathbf{0}) \\
= (\mathbf{Y}, \mathbf{C}, \mathbf{T}, \mathbf{G}, \mathbf{I}, \mathbf{W}, \mathbf{M}, \mathbf{B}, \mathbf{K}, \Delta\mathbf{M}, \Delta\mathbf{B})
\begin{pmatrix}
1 & -a & -t & 0 & 0 & 0 & 0 & 0 & 0 & 0 & 0 \\
-1 & 1 & 0 & 0 & -c & 0 & 0 & 0 & 0 & 0 & 0 \\
0 & a & 1 & 1 & -g & 0 & 0 & 0 & 0 & 0 & -1 \\
-1 & 0 & 0 & 0 & -h & 0 & 0 & 0 & 0 & 0 & 1 \\
-1 & 0 & 0 & 0 & 1 & 0 & 0 & 0 & 0 & -1 & 0 \\
0 & 0 & 0 & 0 & 0 & -m & 1 & 0 & 0 & 0 & 0 \\
0 & 0 & 0 & 0 & 0 & 1 & -1 & 1 & 0 & 0 & 0 \\
0 & 0 & 0 & 0 & 0 & 0 & -1 & 0 & 1 & 0 & 0 \\
0 & 0 & 0 & 0 & 0 & 0 & -1 & 0 & 0 & 1 & 0 \\
0 & 0 & 0 & 0 & 0 & 0 & 0 & -1 & 0 & 0 & -1 \\
0 & 0 & 0 & 0 & 0 & 0 & 0 & 0 & -1 & 0 & -1
\end{pmatrix}
\end{gathered}
$$

In this matrix, Theory 4 appears in the upper left. If this theory had tried to repeat the analysis of Theory 2, and consider the possibility that consumer spending depends on cash balances rather than on current income after taxes, these would have been the symbol $-v$ in row 7 column 2 of the matrix. This single nonzero term would have meant that the matrix was not block-triangular, and would greatly have complicated the task of inverting it.

Problem 4.17 What would the matrix be if statement 4.11b were substituted for 4.11a?

Problem 4.18 What would the matrix be if statement (11c) were substituted for 4.11a?

Problem 4.19 Suppose it were desired to compare the consequences of (11a) with those of (11c). Why is it easier (from a computational point of view) to start with the theory containing 4.11a than with the theory containing 4.11c?

Problem 4.20 Compute exact formulas for the X's, Y's and Z's in Table 4.3. (This is like doing pushups—very good exercise and not much fun.) Interpret the results.

The mechanics of inverting are simplified by the fact that we can make use of Theory 4. That is, the upper left 5×5 block has already been inverted. Next, the lower right 6×6 block may be inverted. Divide this block, namely

$$
\begin{pmatrix}
-m & 1 & 0 & 0 & 0 & 0 \\
1 & -1 & 1 & 0 & 0 & 0 \\
0 & -1 & 0 & 1 & 0 & 0 \\
0 & -1 & 0 & 0 & 1 & 0 \\
0 & 0 & -1 & 0 & 0 & -1 \\
0 & 0 & 0 & -1 & 0 & -1
\end{pmatrix}
$$

into four 3 × 3 parts . The two diagonal parts invert readily:

$$\begin{pmatrix} -m & 1 & 0 \\ 1 & -1 & 1 \\ 0 & 1 & 0 \end{pmatrix}^{-1} = \begin{pmatrix} -\frac{1}{m} & 0 & -\frac{1}{m} \\ 0 & 0 & -1 \\ \frac{1}{m} & 1 & \frac{1-m}{m} \end{pmatrix}$$

$$\begin{pmatrix} 0 & 1 & 0 \\ 0 & 0 & 1 \\ -1 & 0 & -1 \end{pmatrix}^{-1} = \begin{pmatrix} 0 & 1 & -1 \\ 1 & 0 & 0 \\ 0 & -1 & 0 \end{pmatrix}$$

The inverse of the entire 6 × 6 block follows the rule for block matrices.

$$\begin{pmatrix} 0 & 1 & -1 & 0 & 1 & -1 \\ 1 & m & -m & 0 & m & -m \\ 1 & m & (1-m) & 0 & -(1-m) & (1-m) \\ 1 & m & (1-m) & 0 & m & -m \\ 1 & m & -m & 1 & m & -m \\ -1 & -m & -(1-m) & 0 & -m & -(1-m) \end{pmatrix}$$

The formula for block-triangular matrices given in Chapter 3 was

$$\begin{pmatrix} M_{11} & M_{12} \\ 0 & M_{22} \end{pmatrix}^{-1} = \begin{pmatrix} M_{11}^{-1} & -M_{11}^{-1}M_{12}M_{22}^{-1} \\ 0 & M_{22}^{-1} \end{pmatrix}$$

The only problem remaining is to compute the upper right block of the inverse.

$$\mathbf{M}_{12}\mathbf{M}_{22}^{-1} = \begin{pmatrix} 0 & 0 & 0 & 0 & 0 & 0 \\ 0 & 0 & 0 & 0 & 0 & 0 \\ 0 & 0 & 0 & 0 & 0 & -1 \\ 0 & 0 & 0 & 0 & 0 & 1 \\ 0 & 0 & 0 & 0 & -1 & 0 \end{pmatrix} \begin{pmatrix} 0 & 1 & -1 & 0 & 1 & -1 \\ 1 & m & -m & 0 & m & -m \\ 1 & m & (1-m) & 0 & -(1-m) & (1-m) \\ 1 & m & (1-m) & 0 & m & -m \\ 1 & m & -m & 1 & m & -m \\ -1 & -m & -(1-m) & 0 & -m & -(1-m) \end{pmatrix}$$

$$= \begin{pmatrix} 0 & 0 & 0 & 0 & 0 & 0 \\ 0 & 0 & 0 & 0 & 0 & 0 \\ 1 & m & (1-m) & 0 & m & (1-m) \\ -1 & -m & -(1-m) & 0 & -m & -(1-m) \\ -1 & -m & m & -1 & -m & m \end{pmatrix}$$

$$
\mathbf{M}_{11}^{-1}\mathbf{M}_{12}\mathbf{M}_{22}^{-1} = \begin{pmatrix}
\frac{1}{D} & \frac{a(1-t)}{D} & \frac{t}{D} & 0 & \frac{ca(1-t)+gt}{D} \\
\frac{1+c}{D} & \frac{1-gt}{D} & \frac{t(1+c)}{D} & 0 & \frac{c+gt}{D} \\
\frac{g-a(1+c)}{D} & \frac{-a(1-t)}{D} & \frac{1-a(1+c)}{D} & 0 & \frac{-ca(1-g)+g[1-a(1+c)]}{D} \\
\frac{1+h}{D} & \frac{a(1-t)(1+h)}{D} & \frac{t(1+h)}{D} & 1 & \frac{c(1+h)(1-t)+gt(1+h)+h}{D} \\
\frac{1}{D} & \frac{a(1-t)}{D} & \frac{t}{D} & 0 & \frac{1-a(1-t)}{D}
\end{pmatrix}
$$

$$
\begin{pmatrix}
0 & 0 & 0 & 0 & 0 & 0 \\
0 & 0 & 0 & 0 & 0 & 0 \\
1 & m & (1-m) & 0 & m & (1-m) \\
-1 & -m & -(1-m) & 0 & -m & -(1-m) \\
-1 & -m & m & -1 & -m & m
\end{pmatrix}
$$

[where $D = 1 - gt - a(1-t)(1+c)$]

Here D is the same as in Theory 4. Notice now that in the second matrix of this last expression,

(1) the elements of column 2 are multiples of the corresponding elements of column 1.

(2) the elements of column 5 are the same as the corresponding elements of column 2.

(3) the elements of column 6 are the same as the corresponding elements of column 3.

(4) the elements of column 4 will turn out to be the same as the corresponding elements of $\mathbf{M}_{11}^{-1}$. (Hint: Carry out the multiplication so as to find the elements of column 4 of the product.)

The individual elements this product matrix are messy fractions involving a, c, g, h, t, and D. Granted that it may be interesting to know exactly what some of them may be later on, let us first simply denote the matrix $\mathbf{M}_{11}^{-1}M_{12}\mathbf{M}_{22}^{-1}$ as follows:

$$
\mathbf{M}_{11}^{-1}\mathbf{M}_{12}\mathbf{M}_{22}^{-1} = \begin{pmatrix}
X_1 & mX_1 & Y_1 & Z_1 & mX_1 & Y_1 \\
X_2 & mX_2 & Y_2 & Z_2 & mX_2 & Y_2 \\
X_3 & mX_3 & Y_3 & Z_3 & mX_3 & Y_3 \\
X_4 & mX_4 & Y_4 & Z_4 & mX_4 & Y_4 \\
X_5 & mX_5 & Y_5 & Z_5 & mX_5 & Y_5
\end{pmatrix}
$$

This form is a lot less painful for both reader and typesetter than the explicit product of the two matrices.

The elements of the inverse matrix give us the factor-into-variable mapping:

$$
(\mathbf{Y, C, T, G, I, W, M, B, K, \Delta M, \Delta B})
= (\mathbf{0, F_C, F_T, F_G, F_I, F_M, 0, M_O, B_O, K_0, 0})
$$

$$
\begin{pmatrix}
\frac{1}{D} & \frac{a(1-t)}{D} & \frac{t}{D} & 0 & \frac{ca(1-t)+gt}{D} & X_1 & mX_1 & Y_1 & Z_1 & mX_1 & Y_1 \\
\frac{1+c}{D} & \frac{1-gt}{D} & \frac{t(1+c)}{D} & 0 & \frac{c+gt}{D} & X_2 & mX_2 & Y_2 & Z_2 & mX_2 & Y_2 \\
\frac{g-a(1+c)}{D} & \frac{-a(1-t)}{D} & \frac{1-a(1+c)}{D} & 0 & \frac{g-a(c+g)}{D} & X_3 & mX_3 & Y_3 & Z_3 & mX_3 & Y_3 \\
\frac{1+h}{D} & \frac{a(1-t)(1+h)}{D} & \frac{t(1+h)}{D} & 1 & \frac{c(1+h)(1-t)+gt(1+h)+h}{D} & X_4 & mX_4 & Y_4 & Z_4 & mX_4 & Y_4 \\
\frac{1}{D} & \frac{a(1-t)}{D} & \frac{t}{D} & 0 & \frac{1-a(1-t)}{D} & X_5 & mX_5 & Y_5 & Z_5 & mX_5 & Y_5 \\
0 & 0 & 0 & 0 & 0 & 0 & 1 & -1 & 0 & 1 & -1 \\
0 & 0 & 0 & 0 & 0 & 1 & m & -m & 0 & m & -m \\
0 & 0 & 0 & 0 & 0 & 1 & m & (1-m) & 0 & -(1-m) & (1-m) \\
0 & 0 & 0 & 0 & 0 & 1 & m & (1-m) & 0 & m & -m \\
0 & 0 & 0 & 0 & 0 & 1 & m & -m & 1 & m & -m \\
0 & 0 & 0 & 0 & 0 & -1 & -m & -(1-m) & 0 & -m & -(1-m)
\end{pmatrix}
$$

Theory 5 contains eleven variables, but only five factors: F_C (the level of consumer demand), F_T (property taxes), F_G (government spending), F_I (autonomous investment), and F_L (the level of the demand for money). That was because of the eleven statements making up the theory, three were "identities" defining the national product, the balance sheet, and the government income and expenditures accounts, respectively), and three listed initial conditions (for money, government bonds, and plant and equipment, it was necessary to relate *totals* to *changes* in totals). Consequently, the tabulation of effects of changes in factors upon variables is not as complicated as one might have expected from a system as large as this (Table 4.3).

Theory 5 is a theory that includes income accounts and balance sheet accounts. The variables and factors may therefore be grouped according to the set of accounts to which they relate. That is, the variable-into-factor mapping may be written in block-form:

$$(\mathbf{V_Y}, \mathbf{V_W})\begin{pmatrix} M_{YY} & M_{YW} \\ 0 & M_{WW} \end{pmatrix} = (\mathbf{F_Y}, \mathbf{F_W})$$

Here **V** and **F** stand for vectors of numbers, the subscripts **Y** and **W** stand for "income" and "wealth" (the subsets into which all variables and factors are partitioned), and the **M**'s stand for the blocks into which the matrix of the theory is partitioned. Then, when the factor-into-variable mapping was constructed, it turned out that

$$(\mathbf{V_Y}, \mathbf{V_W}) = (\mathbf{F_Y}, \mathbf{F_W})\begin{pmatrix} M_{YY}^{-1} & -M_{YY}^{-1} M_{YW} M_{WW}^{-1} \\ 0 & M_{WW}^{-1} \end{pmatrix}$$

and from this version, when there are changes in factors,

$$(\Delta\mathbf{V_Y}, \Delta\mathbf{V_W}) = (\Delta\mathbf{F_Y}, \Delta\mathbf{F_W})\begin{pmatrix} M_{YY}^{-1} & -M_{YY}^{-1} M_{YW} M_{WW}^{-1} \\ 0 & M_{WW}^{-1} \end{pmatrix}$$

Now consider two cases:

(1) Only factors associated with *income* change, so that $\Delta\mathbf{F_W} = \mathbf{0}$. Then, multiplying through:

$$(\Delta\mathbf{V_Y}, \Delta\mathbf{V_W}) = (\Delta\mathbf{F_Y}\mathbf{M_{YY}^{-1}}, -\Delta\mathbf{F_Y}\mathbf{M_{YY}^{-1}}\mathbf{M_{YW}}\mathbf{M_{WW}^{-1}})$$

(2) Only factors associated with *wealth* change, so that $\Delta\mathbf{F_Y} = \mathbf{0}$. Then, multiplying through:

$$(\Delta\mathbf{V_Y}, \Delta\mathbf{V_W}) = (\mathbf{0}, \Delta\mathbf{F_W}\mathbf{M_{WW}^{-1}})$$

Thus, changes in factors associated with income affect variables associated with wealth. However, changes in factors associated with wealth *do not* affect variables associated with income.

TABLE 4.3

THE IMPLICATIONS OF THEORY 5: GOVERNMENT, NATIONAL PRODUCT AND WEALTH

THE EFFECT OF A UNIT CHANGE UPON	THE EFFECT OF A UNIT CHANGE IN F_C: (Consumer Demand)	F_T: (Property taxes)	F_G: (Government spending)	F_I: (Autonomous investment)	F_L: (Demand for money)
Y (National Product)	$\frac{1+c}{D}$	$\frac{g-a(1+c)}{D}$	$\frac{1+h}{D}$	$\frac{1}{D}$	0
C (Consumption)	$\frac{1-gt}{D}$	$\frac{-a(1-t)}{D}$	$\frac{a(1-t)(1+h)}{D}$	$\frac{a(1-t)}{D}$	0
T (Tax Payments)	$\frac{t(1+c)}{D}$	$\frac{1-a(1+c)}{D}$	$\frac{t(1+h)}{D}$	$\frac{t}{D}$	0
I (Investment)	$\frac{c+gt}{D}$	$\frac{g-a(c+g)}{D}$	$\frac{c(1+h)(1-t)+gt(1+h)+h}{D}$	$\frac{1-a(1-t)}{D}$	0
M (Quantity of Money)	mX_2	mX_3	mX_4	mX_5	1
B (Government Debt)	Y_2	Y_3	Y_4	Y_5	-1
K (Plant and Equipment)	Z_2	Z_3	Z_4	Z_5	0
ΔM (Paper Money Printed)	mX_2	mX_3	mX_4	mX_5	1
ΔB (New Bond Sales)	Y_2	Y_3	Y_4	Y_5	-1

An example of this principle is found in the last column of Table 4.3. The first four entries of this column are zeros. The demand for money is a demand for a wealth variable, so that changes in F_L have no effect on the national income accounts.

The *mathematical virtue* of block-triangular matrices is that such matrices are much easier to invert than the more general kind. It is natural, then, to begin with such matrices, as was done in this case. But the use of such theories has *economic content*, also.

For example: Imagine a system with a larger number of asset variables. In particular, suppose that part of the assets of the community consist of bonds, and some of stocks. If we were to construct a block-triangular theory like Theory 5 to describe this system, it would turn out that the stock market was affected by changes in the national income, but that changes in the stock market itself had no effect on the national product.

Such a theory might well be true, but it is not obvious that it is. An obvious case of difficulty is that of the 1929–1932 depression. This depression was the most severe in American history. Current discussion of it agrees that the first sign of it was a violent decline in stock market prices beginning in October 1929. The obvious way to begin an analysis of this event is to try to explain why an event occurring in the wealth accounts might have an impact on the income accounts. Theory 5 explicitly says such an impact is impossible. Obviously, then, it would be inconsistent with the view that people held in the early 1930s.

More generally, a considerable body of evidence exists to show that usually stock market prices begin to fall *before* declines in income, investment, and consumption begin. If we take the view that an effect cannot precede its cause, we would have to say that any block-triangular theory of income and wealth such as Theory 5 would be inconsistent with this piece of evidence.

A *remedy* for this defect would be to construct a theory which was not block-triangular. Theory 2 was a theory of this sort. To make inversion of the matrix of that theory easier, the ordering of variables and factors was made different from that of Theory 5. If the elements of Theory 2 are rearranged, so as to match those of Theory 5 as closely as possible, it turns out that:

The thing that keeps Theory 2 from being block-triangular is its consumption function:

$$C = aY + vM + F_C$$

The corresponding statement for Theory 5 would be

$$C = a(Y - T) + vM + F_C$$

We shall now show the strategic importance of introducing a statement of this sort in Theory 5.

The general formula for inverting matrices by blocks is:

$$\begin{pmatrix} A & B \\ C & D \end{pmatrix}^{-1} = \begin{pmatrix} (A - BD^{-1}C)^{-1} & -(A - BD^{-1}C)^{-1}BD^{-1} \\ -(D - CA^{-1}B)^{-1}CA^{-1} & (D - CA^{-1}B)^{-1} \end{pmatrix}$$

We shunned this form in Theory 5, because it is a greater chore to invert $(A - BD^{-1}C)$ than to invert A, and to invert $(D - CA^{-1}B)$ than to invert D. There is no particular reason to make all these calculations now. We may look at A^{-1}, and also at D^{-1}, and observe that these do not have zero elements in only one column. It is reasonable to suppose, considering the way matrix multiplication works, that $(A - BD^{-1}C)^{-1}$ and $(D - CA^{-1}B)^{-1}$ will have fewer zero elements than A^{-1} and D^{-1}. But suppose they do not. Then we may write

$${}^{-1} = \begin{pmatrix} 0 & 0 & 0 & 0 & 0 \\ 0 & -v & 0 & 0 & 0 \\ 0 & 0 & 0 & 0 & 0 \\ 0 & 0 & 0 & 0 & 0 \\ 0 & 0 & 0 & 0 & 0 \\ 0 & 0 & 0 & 0 & 0 \end{pmatrix}$$

$$\begin{pmatrix} \dfrac{1}{D} & \dfrac{a(1-t)}{D} & \dfrac{t}{D} & 0 & \dfrac{ca(1-t)+gt}{D} \\ \dfrac{1+c}{D} & \dfrac{1-gt}{D} & \dfrac{t(1+c)}{D} & 0 & \dfrac{c+gt}{D} \\ \dfrac{g-a(1+c)}{D} & \dfrac{-a(1-t)}{D} & \dfrac{1-a(1-c)}{D} & 0 & \dfrac{g-a(c+g)}{D} \\ \dfrac{1+c}{D} & \dfrac{a(1-t)(1+h)}{D} & \dfrac{t(1+h)}{D} & 1 & \dfrac{c(1+h)(1-t)+gt(1+h)+h}{D} \\ \dfrac{1}{D} & \dfrac{a(1-t)}{D} & \dfrac{t}{D} & 0 & \dfrac{1-a(1-t)}{D} \end{pmatrix}$$

$$= \begin{pmatrix} 0 & 0 & 0 & 0 & 0 \\ \dfrac{-v(1+c)}{D} & \dfrac{-(1-gt)v}{D} & \dfrac{-t(1+c)v}{D} & 0 & \dfrac{-(c+gt)v}{D} \\ 0 & 0 & 0 & 0 & 0 \\ 0 & 0 & 0 & 0 & 0 \\ 0 & 0 & 0 & 0 & 0 \\ 0 & 0 & 0 & 0 & 0 \end{pmatrix}$$

Consequently, if we denote the elements of $-(D - CA^{-1}B)^{-1}$ by (d_{ij}), we will have (assuming zeros and ones in column 4)

$$
-(\mathbf{D} - \mathbf{CA}^{-1}\mathbf{B})^{-1}\mathbf{CA}^{-1} = \begin{pmatrix} d_{11} & d_{12} & d_{13} & 0 & d_{15} & d_{16} \\ d_{21} & d_{22} & d_{23} & 0 & d_{25} & d_{26} \\ d_{31} & d_{32} & d_{33} & 0 & d_{35} & d_{36} \\ d_{41} & d_{42} & d_{43} & 0 & d_{45} & d_{46} \\ d_{51} & d_{52} & d_{53} & 0 & d_{55} & d_{56} \\ d_{61} & d_{62} & d_{63} & 0 & d_{65} & d_{66} \end{pmatrix} \times
$$

$$
\begin{pmatrix} 0 & 0 & 0 & 0 & 0 \\ \dfrac{-v(1+c)}{D} & \dfrac{-(1-gt)v}{D} & \dfrac{-t(1+c)v}{D} & 0 & \dfrac{-(c+gt)v}{D} \\ 0 & 0 & 0 & 0 & 0 \\ 0 & 0 & 0 & 0 & 0 \\ 0 & 0 & 0 & 0 & 0 \\ 0 & 0 & 0 & 0 & 0 \end{pmatrix}
$$

$$
\begin{pmatrix} \dfrac{-v(1+c)d_{12}}{D} & \dfrac{-v(1-gt)d_{12}}{D} & \cdots & 0 & \dfrac{-v(c+gt)d}{D} \\ \dfrac{-v(1+c)d_{22}}{D} & \dfrac{-v(1-gt)d_{22}}{D} & \cdots & 0 & \dfrac{-v(c+gt)d}{D} \\ & & \cdots & & \\ \dfrac{-v(1+c)d_{62}}{D} & \dfrac{-v(1-gt)d_{62}}{D} & \cdots & 0 & \dfrac{-v(c+gt)d}{D} \end{pmatrix}
$$

The point of this demonstration is simple: If any single element of the block **C** is different from zero, then *most* of the elements of the corresponding block of the inverse will be different from zero.[11]

Hence, if consumption is influenced at all by the size of people's bank accounts (or in this theory, by the size of the bankroll in their pockets), then income accounts will be affected by changes in the wealth accounts.

In particular, therefore, the last column of Table 4.3 would not contain zeros. That is, if people's demand for money changed, the consumption, investment tax payment, and the national product would all be affected.

The way chosen here to make this point is not the only possible way. Suppose, for example, that there were a tax on total assets. Then it would

[11] This statement says, "If any income variables are affected by any asset variables, then Theory 5, as given here, will be misleading. For it will turn out that changes in existing assets—M_0, B_0, K_0—or in factors involving demand for assets—F_I, F_M—will affect the national income and its components."

be the case that

$$T = tY + wW + F_T$$

and the number $-w$ would replace a zero in the lower left block of the matrix.

Again, suppose that investment depends partly on how much plant is already in existence. (The reason might be that if a firm has a large plant already, then when it looks at a given market it will see less reason to expand than if it only has a small plant.) Then:

$$I = cC + gT + hG + kK + F_I$$

and the number $-k$ would replace a zero in the lower left block of the matrix.

To say that all of these statements are plausible does not mean that they are true. They are made to point out again that Theory 5 was given in that form so that the calculation of the inverse matrix would be simple. This is not a sound economic reason, although it is a good reason for beginners. It is easier to make things complicated than to make them clear.

Moreover, to say that some element of an inverse matrix is nonzero does not say enough to satisfy serious students. Each particular element of the inverse has the economic interpretation:

$$\bar{m}_{ij} = \frac{\Delta V_j}{\Delta F_i}$$

and economists want to know whether it is positive or negative, "large" or "small." As we have seen in Table 4.3, some of these terms have (at best) complicated interpretations. Thus in the table

$$\frac{\Delta I}{\Delta F_G} = \frac{c(1+h)(1-t) + gt(1+h) + h}{D}$$

$$= \frac{h[1 + gt + c(1-t)] + gt + c(1-t)}{D}$$

there is no great problem in saying that gt is less than zero and that $c(1-t)$ is greater than zero. But what their sum is, and what the entire numerator of this fraction may be is certainly not obvious to the naked eye. It is partly for this reason that plausible arguments exist on both sides of the policy issue "What effect has an increase in government spending on the economy?" To admit that consumption, government revenue, or investment, may be affected by balance sheet items is to admit that terms like $\Delta I/\Delta F_C$ are more complicated to interpret than this formula indicates.

Historical Remark. Economists in the late 1930s were strongly tempted by theories like Theory 3, which is a particularly simple form of Theory 4. When the United States became involved in arming for World War II in 1940 and in fighting it in 1942, government spending increased enormously, and unemployment vanished. On the basis of something like Theory 3, most economists predicted that at the end of the war, when government spending fell again, the economy would fall back into the depressed conditions of the 1930s. Of course, nothing of the sort took place. There was no return to the state of depression of the 1930s. Theory 3 or Theory 4 would have to explain this fact by saying that F_C or F_I changed in consequence of the war. There is no obvious reason why this change should have occurred.

Suppose, however, that one of the suggested modifications were made in Theory 4, so that the matrix was not block-triangular. We might then ask the following question: Suppose an economy in which all factors are constant except one—the government debt increases. It increases (we suppose) at an even rate, since government deficits are held constant. Does this increase in debt affect the economy?

The answer to this question is "yes." We can compute, from the inverse of a "modified Theory 4" matrix, the elements

$$\Delta Y/\Delta B_0,\ \Delta C/\Delta B_0,\ \Delta I/\Delta B_0$$

and so forth. These are simply elements of row 10 of this inverse.

They answer the question, "What is the difference between things as they are, and things as they would be if the government debt were $1 larger than it actually is?"

Anyone who tries to answer the question, "Why didn't the Great Depression return after World War II?" would be involved in problems of this sort.

A piece of unfinished business is, "What do we do about money?" The theories presented so far have been rather cagey about money. Some theories have omitted it completely (Tiny Model 1, Theories 3 and 4). That is not good, because money is obviously one important part of economic life. Some theories have treated it as if it fell from the heavens like rain (Theories 1 and 2). This is unsatisfactory, because it would be nice to know how money enters the economy, and these theories did not say. They merely said it got there somehow.

Theory 5 says how money enters the economy: The government prints it to pay for some of its purchases. This statement is a step forward, and is even partly true. In all wars, governments run deficits, and in all recent wars, these deficits have been partly covered by printing money. But in any developed economy, most money is not paper money, but balances in bank accounts, and most payments are made by check, and not by handing over paper money.

None of the theories so far has included banks. A consideration of banks was promised the reader at the beginning of this book. It is time to consider them explicitly; that way we can suggest better ways of coping with that stuff called money. Our next chapter will therefore try to explain about banks.

Problem 4.21 It is sometimes held that increases in the government debt have undesirable consequences. Table 3 provides certain conclusions (under rather special conditions) about this question. The change in the government debt is a variable in this theory, so that it changes in response to factor changes. Are there any factor changes in Theory 3 that produce (1) an increase in the government debt and (2) at the same time decreases in consumption? In investment?

Problem 4.22 Continuing in the same vein, are there any factor changes in Theory 3 that increase new bond sales (the government deficit) and are associated with decreases in consumption? In investment?

Problem 4.23 Suppose there were no government bonds, and government deficits were financed by printing paper money. Consider whether government deficits would be "good" or "bad" for the economy, defining "good" and "bad."

Problem 4.24 Compare what Theories 1 and 5 say about the effects of changes in the demand for money.

Problem 4.25 Go to Theory 3 and make the following changes: (1) replace "G" by "X" (for exports); (2) replace "T" by "F" (for imports). Then show that Theory 3 can be reinterpreted as a simple theory about the effects of foreign trade upon the national product.

Problem 4.26 Make a similar reinterpretation of Theory 4 as a theory about the effects of foreign trade.

Problem 4.27 Extend Theory 3 so as to make a four-sector theory (households, business, government, foreigners) about the national product.

5

Money and the Economy

MONEY AS A BALANCE SHEET ITEM

Money has been discussed in Theories 1, 2, and 5, but we have never carefully defined and examined it. In this chapter, attention will be given to considering the origins and functions of money. Money is one of the earliest and most remarkable of human inventions. Despite its great antiquity (it seems to be as old as wheels or written language), a great deal remains to be learned about it.

In theoretical work, money is treated as an abstract entity. In any particular country, at any particular time, there are "things used as money" which satisfy only imperfectly the abstract definitions that may be convenient to the theorist. Consequently, there is always some problem in deciding what "kinds of things" should be considered as money in a particular real problem.

For the purposes of this book, money has two basic attributes. First, money is something used to make payments for goods and services. Second, money is an asset of its owner. Unlike "productive assets" such as plant and equipment, securities, and so on, money does not yield any income to its owner. Therefore, an increase in money assets is not an investment.[1]

A very simple view of money can be seen in the simplest social accounts scheme. The national product schema says that $Y = C + I$: output consists of consumer goods and investment goods. The national income schema says that $Y = C + S$: income is either consumed or saved. Therefore, by subtraction,

$$0 = Y - Y = (C + I) - (C + S) = I - S$$

and savings equal investment. If the national balance sheet has the form

Assets		Liabilities	
Money,	M	Debt,	D
Plant,	K	Net worth,	W

then changes in the balance sheet satisfy the identity

$$\Delta M + \Delta K = \Delta D + \Delta W$$

Investment is the change in plant, and savings the increase in net worth. Thus,

$$\Delta M + \Delta K = \Delta M + I = \Delta D + \Delta W = \Delta D + S = \Delta D + I$$

Subtracting $I = \Delta K$ from both sides of the equation,

$$\Delta M = \Delta D$$

The change in the quantity of money in the economy is therefore equal to the change in debts of the economy. The quantity of money changes if and only if there is an equal change in the debts of the community.

This view of money is appealingly simple. It even is partly true; it will be shown that there is a very close connection between bank lending and the money supply. But there is one trouble with the balance sheet on which this demonstration rests. It seems to say that there can be an increase in debt for the economy as a whole with no increase in assets held in the form of IOUs. Bonds, notes, and accounts receivable are assets to their owners, as well as debts of other people. In this balance sheet, it seems that nobody owns bonds. Something has been left off: a creditor's balance sheet. In other words, the

---

[1] Textbooks on money define money as a unit of account (prices of goods and services are quoted in units of money); as a medium of exchange (goods and services are exchanged for money, not bartered); as a store of value (money may be kept without any loss in the number of money units held by the owner); and as a medium for deferred payments (contractual payments to be made in the future may be defined in money terms).

balance sheet given above cannot be a national balance sheet.[2] It must be the balance sheet of a part of the economy. A true "national balance sheet" would supplement the balance sheet given above with the balance sheet of a creditor sector.

In the modern economy, the banks act as a creditor sector. Money, moreover, is a liability of the banks. That is, people deposit money in banks, and banks lend money to people. Thus the balance sheets of the bank and nonbank sectors are (in very simplified form) these:

Nonbanks

Money,	M	Debt,	D
Plant,	K	Net worth,	W_N

Banks

Loans,	D	Deposits,	M
		Net worth,	W_B

The nonbank balance sheet is exactly that given in the preceding example, but there is a slightly different calculation:

For the nonbanks

$$\Delta M + \Delta K = \Delta D + \Delta W_N$$

For the banks

$$\Delta D = \Delta M + \Delta W_B$$

Savings in the economy is the increase in net worth of banks and nonbanks. That is,

$$\Delta W_N + \Delta W_B = \Delta M + \Delta K - \Delta D + \Delta D - \Delta M = \Delta K$$

Since ΔK is investment, savings equal additions to plant, as before. But the increase in debt is not equal to the increase in money, since

$$\Delta M = \Delta D - \Delta W_B$$

In most economies ΔW_B is small compared to ΔD, so one can say ΔM is "close to" ΔD. The close relation between increases in money and increases in debt are clear.

Readers are presumably familiar with the idea that banks "create money." This creation process will be analyzed in more detail later on. For the present,

---

[2] An apparent exception: if all the debt shown is owed to foreigners. But this situation requires a good deal of further explanation, for each country has its own kind of money. Foreigners can lend us foreign money. Foreign money does not help us buy things at home, where we need our own money. There may be situations where this fact does not matter. If all money consists of silver or gold coin, things are simple. Borrow foreign coin, melt the coin, make domestic coin, and all is well. (Only a few countries make use of silver or gold coin, and these forbid its export. This example is therefore not relevant to the modern world.) But generally, different countries use different kinds of money, and money as such is thus not imported and exported.

it is more important to return to the statement in the third paragraph of this chapter, which said, "For the purposes of this book, money has two basic attributes." This statement said "money *has*," and not "money *is*," and readers may wonder why no real definition of money was given. As a matter of fact, most theoretical economists avoid this question; in dealing with the subject, they say such things as, "For present purposes, the United States money supply consists of coin plus paper currency outside banks plus demand deposits (checking accounts)." They are therefore very careful not to say that this sum really represents the money supply, but to say only that this is a working rule for measurement purposes.

The prevailing caution about saying exactly what is and what is not money is apt to be confusing and annoying to readers who do not understand the reason for caution. It would be useful to consider just why economists take this attitude and to consider an example in somewhat greater detail.

WHAT IS MONEY?—EXAMPLES

Consider an economy with no banks, which has two sectors, a private and a government sector. Assume that the private sector lends to the government (by buying bonds). The government has cash assets, which may be supposed to be a heap of money in a vault. This "money" may be anything that pleases the reader: coins, gold bars, strings of wampum, packages of cigarettes. The main point is this: We make an inventory of money at the beginning of our story, and we have no way to change the total stock. The balance sheets of the two sectors, then, have the following form:

Private Sector

Money, M_p Bonds, B Plant, K	Net worth, W_p

Government

Money, M_G	Bonds, B Net worth, W_G

Savings is a change in net worth. Since there are two sectors, there are two kinds of savings:

Private Savings:

$$\Delta W_p = \Delta M_p + \Delta B + \Delta K$$

Government Savings:

$$\Delta W_G = \Delta M_G - \Delta B$$

There is a fixed total of money in the system. Some is in the government vault, some in the safes of the private sector. Money held by the private sector can increase only if there is an equal decrease in the amount of money held by the government:

$$\Delta M_p = -\Delta M_G$$

For the entire economy, savings equals investment:

$$\begin{aligned} S &= \Delta W_p + \Delta W_G \\ &= \Delta M_p + \Delta B + \Delta K + \Delta M_G - \Delta B \\ &= -\Delta M_G + \Delta B + \Delta K + \Delta M_G - \Delta B \\ &= \Delta K \end{aligned}$$

and this change in plant is the same as I, investment, in the national product accounts.

Therefore, the expression in the last paragraph may be written

$$S = \Delta W_p + \Delta W_G = I$$

Subtract $S = I = \Delta K$ from each member of this equation:

$$\begin{aligned} 0 &= \Delta W_p + \Delta W_G - \Delta K \\ &= \Delta M_p + \Delta B + \Delta W_G \end{aligned}$$

But savings of any sector is the difference between that sector's current income and current spending. For the government, in particular, savings are the difference between tax collections (T) and spending (G) in the national product accounts:

$$0 = \Delta M_p + \Delta B + T - G$$

Therefore, the change in private holdings of money are

$$\Delta M_p = G - T - \Delta B$$

The interesting feature of money, from the historical point of view, is that nobody is sure what constitutes money. Consider this last example. Suppose the government has a deficit but cannot sell bonds, because bonds have not been invented, or because nobody trusts the government. Then,

$$\Delta M_p = G - T$$

The private money supply rises by the amount of the government deficit, or falls by the amount of the government surplus. The increase in privately held money "takes the place of" an increase in government borrowing.

If the government budget is in balance (so that $G = T$), the money held by the private sector will fall if the government sells bonds and rise if the government pays off its bonded debt. In this sense, money and bonds are substitutes for each other in the stock of assets held by the private sector of the economy.

Imagine now a somewhat fanciful case. Suppose the government wants to acquire as much money as possible to store in its vaults.[3] It can do this by reducing expenses or (more probably) by raising taxes and (most probably) by borrowing.

Suppose that the government, by borrowing, has acquired almost all the money in the community, and stored it in the vault. The situation, then, will be that when people try to sell goods to each other, they will have a hard time finding a buyer with money. On the other hand, people do have assets, in particular government bonds. Economists would predict that some people will start making payments for goods with these bonds rather than with money. If the use of bonds becomes widespread enough, it will even be possible to say that people use bonds *as if* bonds were money. At that point, there will be two groups of observers: (1) Some will say, "Bonds are not really money; the real money is mainly in the government vault." (2) Others will say, "Since the stuff in the vault is not, in fact, used as money, and since the bonds are in fact used as money, then bonds are money and the stuff in the vault is demonetized."

Most economists would probably belong to the second group. The two groups, however, might find it unnecessary and foolish to argue about this matter. They would agree that bonds were used to make payments, having replaced the earlier "money" for most practical purposes. Indeed, if the stuff in the vault were used as a means of paying for wartime purchases, then they might agree to the following proposition: In peacetime, "money" consists of bonds; in wartime, it consists also of stuff from the government vault, and also bonds.

It is certainly very inconvenient for theorists when something that was formerly very much like money stops being used as money; and when something that was not formerly used as money (indeed, that may never have existed) starts to be used as money. Such changes in the list of things that are more or less money do occur. These changes are a part of the subject matter studied by monetary economists. They involve more subtle and difficult problems than can be studied in this book.

The following historical example will illustrate these problems. In the period from 1000 to 1500, the English kings had tax-collectors in major towns who were supposed to deliver tax payments (literally heaps of silver coins), on stated dates, to the king in London. The king, however, had to pay his suppliers. If he lacked coins, he would pay his bills in the following way: A piece of wood called a tally, of specified size, would be carefully notched, the notches indicating the size of the payment to be made. The tally was then split, and half given to the king's supplier. The supplier then went

[3] Historically, governments have often wanted to do this because they expected war and wanted to build up a fund in peacetime to pay for the cost of the war.

to a tax-collector, who regarded the tally as a sort of check, and therefore paid the supplier. The tax-collector would then return the tally to the king when he settled his accounts, so as to show what happened to the tax money he had collected. The king's officers would match the half of the tally returned by the tax collector, to make sure that it fitted the half they had retained, and that no "forged checks" were being given the king.

If the king were at war, or otherwise extravagant, he would issue tallies in excess of his tax collections, and some of his suppliers would be unable to obtain coin for their tallies. The tallies thus had some of the properties of the "government bonds" in the hypothetical example. On the other hand, tallies could be used to pay tax obligations, and suppliers could therefore sell their tallies for coin to taxpayers—perhaps at a discount—if they were short of coin. Indeed, tallies were used for a number of wholesale business transactions (they were usually "made out" for sums too large for the "man in the street" to use in retail trade). And the king was often not deceitful: he issued tallies to suppliers who knew they would not be paid for some time, and who therefore included interest charges in their bills.

For much of the Middle Ages, the English kings were engaged in wars on the continent of Europe. These wars were quite expensive to wage. (Sometimes, when successful, they were profitable, for there would be plunder, payments of tribute, and ransom from defeated enemies.) The main expenses of the army were for food, men, and horses. These had to be met in coin. So while a war was in progress, the king evidently took coin out of England to pay his troops. Also, he had a deficit, so that the number of tallies in the hands of his suppliers would rise.

Suppose one asks, "What is the effect of a war on the medieval English money supply?" If by *money* we mean coin in the hands of the private sector, we get one answer: it decreases. If by *money* we mean coin plus tallies, we may get quite a different answer: it may well increase. Moreover, if coins and tallies are not quite interchangeable, we cannot say that economic conditions are independent of the relative numbers of coins and tallies in the hands of the public.

Nobody much cares about what went on in the Middle Ages. Since we do not care, we can afford to be objective. That is one reason why it is useful to use this particular example. Examples from today's economy are closer to us and are therefore more difficult to analyze. But consider several examples of contemporary "things" that are more or less money in the United States economy of the 1960s.

1. *Savings deposits* can ordinarily be converted into currency whenever the depositor wishes. But the bank may, if it wishes, force depositors to wait 30 to 60 days before allowing withdrawal of the deposit.

2. *Treasury bills.* The United States Treasury borrows large sums for periods of 90 days to a year. Lenders receive a saleable document called a

Treasury bill. This bill can be sold at any time, since there is an active market in these bills. The holder of a Treasury bill, then, does not hold "money," in the same way he would if he held currency or a checking account, but he can get currency or a checking account in 24 hours by selling his bill.

3. *Certificates of deposit.* Instead of opening a savings deposit, it is possible to buy a certificate of deposit. Such a certificate of deposit resembles a check on a bank, but it cannot be cashed at the bank for a stated period—usually six months. (When it is cashed, the bank pays interest on the deposit.) During the intervening period, the certificate may be sold by one holder to another holder. In this respect, it is almost like a Treasury bill, which is almost the same as a balance in a checking account.

4. *Federal funds.* Most private banks are required to keep a "reserve," or deposit in a Federal Reserve Bank. Part of this deposit may be converted into currency, but the balance must be at least a certain percentage of the bank's own checking accounts at all times. When one bank finds its reserves are too low, it may borrow "federal funds" for a few days from another bank. These "federal funds" are transferred by check from one account to another of the Federal Reserve Banks. In this respect they are like checking accounts, and these, after all, are used as money. But only banks have accounts in Federal Reserve Banks, so no bank can pay Federal funds to anybody who is not a bank.

5. *Eurodollar deposits.* In the 1960s a new kind of "money" came into widespread use in Europe. Large European banks would lend, and accept deposits in an "imaginary money" called the Eurodollar. A borrower can repay a debt either by a check on a Eurodollar account or by a check on a United States bank account. A depositor may write checks on his account or get his bank to give him a check on a United States bank where the European bank has an account. Most Eurodollar transactions have nothing to do with United States banks, however, and all Eurodollar transactions take place outside the United States. No United States bank need accept a check made out in Eurodollars, and no country in the world has a monetary unit called the Eurodollar. A great deal of business is evidently carried on in Eurodollars—nobody, at the time of this writing, knows exactly how much. Many non-American businesses, and some American businesses, treat Eurodollars as if they were checking accounts in United States banks, which they certainly are not.

In what follows, it is necessary to restrict our attention to two kinds of "money"—checking accounts and currency. Unless such a restriction is made, the theories become very complicated indeed. In fact, it is quite difficult to make theories involving many kinds of money, even though such theories are ultimately needed to discuss many practical problems. But even with this limitation, it is possible to explore some interesting relations between money and economic activity in general.

THE CREATION OF MONEY BY BANKS

Tiny Model 4

It is probably a familiar proposition to readers that banks "create" money. The first section of this chapter gave a simple demonstration of the equality between increases in bank deposits and bank loans. It is worth emphasizing that this demonstration did not explain how increases in either total deposits or total loans could take place. (It might be that neither could increase.) The following very simple example will describe quite credible, everyday transactions that have the effect of increasing the loans and deposits of an ordinary banking system.

Suppose the economy consists of two banks, with balance sheets as given in Figure 5.1.

BANK 1

Currency,*	50	Deposits,	90
Loans,	50	Net worth,	10

BANK 2

Currency,	50	Deposits,	90
Loans,	50	Net worth,	10

TOTAL

Currency,	100	Deposits,	180
Loans,	100	Net worth,	20

* Currency is coin and paper money

FIG. 5.1

Consider now the following set of transactions:

1. Mr. A borrows 10 from Bank 1. He gives the bank his IOU (a note), and receives 10 in currency.
2. Mr. A buys something from Mr. B, paying 10 for it in currency.
3. Mr. B deposits his 10 in currency in his bank account with Bank 2. Now the balance sheets of the banks is as shown in Figure 5.2:

BANK 1

Currency,	40	Deposits,	90
Loans		Net worth,	10
old,	50		
Mr. A,	10		

BANK 2

Currency,	60	Deposits,	
		old,	90
Loans,	50	Mr. B,	10
		Net worth,	10

TOTAL

Currency,	100	Deposits,	190
Loans,	110	Net worth,	20

FIG. 5.2

A comparison of Figure 5.2 with Figure 5.1 shows that the amount of bank credit has increased by 10, and the amount of bank deposits has increased by 10. The increase in lending is associated with the increase in the amount of bank deposits. Bank deposits are the principal kind of assets that people in modern economies consider to be "cash," and for this reason, we associate the increase in bank deposits with an increase in the quantity of the abstraction called *money*.

Let us now become more specific. We assume that all bank accounts are checking accounts (more technically, these are called *demand deposits*). We ignore savings accounts and therefore savings banks. Banks with demand deposits are called *commercial banks*. Money in the hands of households and businesses is either in the form of demand deposits or currency. (We shall disregard coin and treat all currency as paper money.)

In the example just given, the assets of commercial banks were stated to consist of currency and loans. Actually, currency is a very small part of the total assets of banks. Commercial banks' cash assets are called *reserves*. They are mostly kept in special deposits (called *reserve accounts*) with the Federal Reserve Banks.[4] The Federal Reserve System prescribes the minimum reserves that member banks must keep. These *required reserves* are stated as percentages of banks' deposits. Thus, given a total amount of deposits, each bank must keep a certain amount of reserves. It may, if it wishes, have *excess reserves*. Normally, banks do not want excess reserves. Banks, after all, try to make profits. They earn income by lending money, and any cash they hold is cash that could earn income if only it could be loaned to someone.

Because banks have an incentive to lend as much as possible, subject to their reserve requirement, it is possible to treat the quantity of bank deposits (money) analytically. The simplest way of doing so is to construct Tiny Model 4, which is a special interpretation of Tiny Model 2. If we disregard the net worth of banks,[5] the balance sheet of the banking system may be described as

$$M = R + L$$

That is, deposits (M) make up the liabilities side of the balance sheet, while reserves (R) and loans (L) make up the assets.

Left to themselves, banks tend to keep too little cash. (Cash holdings earn no income for banks; income comes from loans.) Thus, if depositors suddenly want to convert deposits into currency, they may be unable to do so.

---

[4] Some small banks do not belong to the Federal Reserve System. These *nonmember banks* actually keep their reserves in deposits with the larger *member banks* belonging to the Federal Reserve System. For simplicity, our theories treat all banks as if they were member banks.

[5] Net worth of banks is only a few percent of their balance sheet totals. The net worth accounts of banks tends to be stable, and only in rather specialized problems does this account play any role. Therefore the accounts, for present purposes, are omitted from the theory.

In this case some (or all) banks become bankrupt, for they cannot pay their creditors (the depositors). The Federal Reserve System therefore requires that reserves (cash) be at least equal to r percent of deposits. (The System varies r from time to time.) Banks may have *excess* reserves (that is, reserves in excess of requirements), which may be denoted F_R. Thus,

$$R = rM + F_R$$

divides total reserves into *required* reserves (rM) and excess reserves (F_R). It follows that loans depend on excess reserves and the reserve ratio r:

$$L = M - R = (1 - r)M - F_R$$

Consequently,

$$(\mathbf{R}, \mathbf{F_R}) = (\mathbf{M}, \mathbf{L})\begin{pmatrix} 1 & (1-r) \\ -1 & -1 \end{pmatrix}$$

That is,

$$(\mathbf{M}, \mathbf{L}) = (\mathbf{R}, \mathbf{F_R})\begin{pmatrix} \frac{1}{r} & \frac{1-r}{r} \\ -\frac{1}{r} & -\frac{1}{r} \end{pmatrix}$$

Thus, the quantity of money (M) and of bank loans (L) can be explained by the level of bank reserves (R) and by the excess reserves (F_R) desired by the banks; and of course by the reserve ratio (r) set by Federal Reserve. Obviously F_R is something that the banks (collectively) decide upon. Bank reserves are beyond their control.

The implications of Tiny Model 4, then, are given in Table 5.1.

TABLE 5.1

THE IMPLICATIONS OF TINY MODEL 4

THE EFFECT OF A UNIT INCREASE IN	THE EFFECT UPON	
	Demand deposits (M)	Bank loans (L)
Total bank reserves, (ΔR)	$1/r$	$(1 - r)/r$
Excess reserves, (ΔF_R)	$-1/r$	$-1/r$

Since r is less than one, an increase of \$1 in excess reserves decreases the quantity of money and of bank loans by more than \$1. An increase of \$1 in bank reserves will increase the quantity of money by more than \$1. It will ncrease the quantity of bank loans, providing that $r < 1$; it will increase bank oans by more than \$1, providing $r < .5$.

In Tiny Model 4, there is no explanation of what determines the total level of bank reserves. This subject will be explained in the next section.

THEORY 6. A PURE BANKING THEORY

The Federal Reserve System is a collection of banks. Their deposits consist of the reserves (cash assets) of the private banks. It is natural to consider a very simple theory of the relation between the Federal Reserve System and the private banks. Such a theory involves the specification of balance sheets in both kinds of banks. These are first assumed to be of the following form:[6]

FEDERAL RESERVE SYSTEM

Assets		*Liabilities*	
"Investments,"	B_1	Reserve accounts,	R

PRIVATE BANKS

Assets		*Liabilities*	
Reserves,	R	Deposits,	D
Loans,	L		
"Investments,"	B_2		

"Investments" consist of bonds; in practice these are mainly government bonds. The term is put into quotation marks because it is used in the special sense that appears in banking terminology. In terms of the terminology of this book (see Chapter 1), the investments (*not* in quotation marks) made by the Federal Reserve System would be ΔB_1; those made by private banks would be $\Delta(L + B_2)$. This chapter will refer to ΔB_1 as "open market operations," because that is what the Federal Reserve System calls them. The System buys and sells bonds through private brokers and does not deal directly with the Treasury, except in unusual circumstances. When it buys, it pays by check, and these checks are deposited in banks' reserve accounts. When the System sells, it is paid by checks which are then charged to banks' reserve accounts. Such transactions may not occur at all for considerable periods, but if the System wants to intervene in the bond market, it may buy or sell several hundred million dollars of bonds in a week's time.

In this simple system, therefore, $\Delta R = \Delta B_1$. Federal Reserve open market *purchases* of (government) bonds add to member bank reserves, and open

[6] Federal Reserve notes, our paper money, are on the liabilities side of the balance sheet. We disregard them for the present.

market *sales* of such bonds reduce member bank reserves. These operation are the most important means of day-to-day control over the banks that th System can use. The changes in reserve requirements (r) are relatively in frequent, although they can be made to serve much the same kinds of purpose as open market operations. (See, however, Problem 5.6.)

These two balance sheets, expressed symbolically, state that

$$0 = B_1 - R$$
$$0 = R + L + B_2 - D$$

In addition, suppose the total earning assets of the banking system (that is debt of the nonbanking system) consist either of loans by banks (L) or bond (B), and that

$$B = B_1 + B_2$$

(all bonds are held by the Federal Reserve System or the private banks). Th sale of bonds by borrowing firms or the government, in any period, is ΔB

Let the banks' demand for reserves be the same as in the Tiny Model:

$$R = rD + F_R$$

where F_R, as before is *excess reserves*, rD is *required reserves*, and r th *reserve ratio*.

Finally, suppose that Federal Reserve can vary its "investments" at wil Then,

$$F_F = B_1$$

The variable-into-factor mapping of this theory is therefore written:

$$(\mathbf{F_F}, \mathbf{0}, \mathbf{B}, \mathbf{F_R}, \mathbf{0}) = (\mathbf{B_1}, \mathbf{B_2}, \mathbf{R}, \mathbf{L}, \mathbf{D}) \begin{pmatrix} 1 & 1 & 1 & 0 & 0 \\ 0 & 0 & 1 & 0 & 1 \\ 0 & -1 & 0 & 1 & 1 \\ 0 & 0 & 0 & 0 & 1 \\ 0 & 0 & 0 & -r & -1 \end{pmatrix}$$

The inverse form of this theory is

$$(\mathbf{F_F}, \mathbf{0}, \mathbf{B}, \mathbf{F_R}, \mathbf{0}) \begin{pmatrix} 1 & -1 & 1 & \frac{1}{r} & \frac{1}{r} \\ 0 & 0 & -1 & \frac{r-1}{r} & -\frac{1}{r} \\ 0 & 1 & 0 & -1 & 0 \\ 0 & 0 & 0 & -\frac{1}{r} & -\frac{1}{r} \\ 0 & 0 & 0 & 1 & 0 \end{pmatrix} = (\mathbf{B_1}, \mathbf{B_2}, \mathbf{R}, \mathbf{L}, \mathbf{D})$$

TABLE 5.2

THE IMPLICATIONS OF THEORY 6

THE EFFECT OF A UNIT CHANGE ON	THE EFFECT OF A UNIT CHANGE IN		
	F_F (Open market operations)	B (New bond issues)	F_R (Excess reserves)
B_2 (Bank holdings of Bonds)	-1	1	0
R (Bank reserves)	1	0	0
L (Bank loans)	$\frac{1}{r}$	-1	$-\frac{1}{r}$
D (Bank deposits)	$\frac{1}{r}$	0	$-\frac{1}{r}$

Table 5.2 interprets this simple monetary system. When the Federal Reserve System buys bonds, it reduces bank "investments" by the same amount, because all bonds are assumed to be held by Federal Reserve and banks. These purchases increase bank reserves by an equal amount; and the banks increase their loans and deposits by $1/r$. This quantity is greater than 1, because r, the reserve ratio, is less than 1. (Remember that deposits are the only kind of money.)

The money supply (D) is unaffected by the sale of new bonds. When new bonds are sold, the banks buy them and reduce their direct loans to customers by an equal amount. This particular feature of the theory is of some interest in terms of government policy. If the bonds are issued because of a government deficit, the sale of bonds automatically reduces bank loans to business (and/or mortgage loans to households) and does *not* lead to an expansion of the money supply. Indeed, if investment is financed from bank loans, government deficits bring about automatic declines in investment by business. For example, in 1966, when government spending on the Viet Nam war rose sharply, the Federal Reserve System was anxious to prevent increases in the money supply. The increased government borrowing led to considerable shortages of credit for business and a major drop in housing construction. With only moderate oversimplification, the decline in housing construction in 1966 can be explained in this fashion.

A change in the banks' desire to have more reserves than Federal Reserve requirements does not affect total reserves. Taken alone, it does not affect the bond holdings of banks. It does affect loans and the amount of deposits.

Of course, this discussion deals with the banking system without any reference to the nonbanking sector. Consequently, it can deal with the nonbanking system only indirectly—as the discussion of the 1966 situation indicates. It is natural to see what happens to the rest of the economy.

Problem 5.1 Suppose the reserve requirement is changed from r to r'. If excess reserves are unchanged, what will be the direction of the effect on D? On L?

Problem 5.2 Suppose F_F, B, F_R are all given, and the reserve requirement is increased from r to r'. What will happen to the variables?

Problem 5.3 Suppose Federal Reserve sees an increase of \$1 in excess reserves and decides to stabilize the amount of bank deposits. What can it do?

Problem 5.4 Suppose Federal Reserve sees an increase of \$1 in excess reserves. It says to itself, "Ames says changes in money and changes in credit go together. Let us therefore offset the change in reserves in such a way as to stabilize both bank holdings of bonds and bank loans." What can it do?

Problem 5.5 Suppose a current government deficit of \$1. Federal Reserve decides that this deficit should not be allowed to change the total amount of bank lending (of all kinds). What must it do?

Problem 5.6 Suppose excess reserves to be constant. The Federal Reserve can produce a given effect $\overline{\Delta D}$ on bank deposits *either* by a sale of \$$X$ in government bonds, *or* by an increase in reserve requirements from r to r'. Compare the effects of the two changes upon the variables of this theory.

Problem 5.7 The paper currency of the United States consists almost entirely of Federal Reserve notes. A more realistic balance sheet for the Federal Reserve System would have the form

"Investments," B_1	Reserve accounts, R
	Notes, N

When the depositors of commercial banks collectively cash checks, these banks write checks on their reserve accounts, and Federal Reserve gives the banks the currency they need. Use the information in Theory 6 to show the effects on the banking system of an increase of \$1 in the amount of *currency* that the public wants to hold. What happens to the total money supply (currency plus deposits) when the amount of currency rises by \$1?

THEORY 7. BANKING AND THE INTEREST RATE

Nothing has been heard about the interest rate since Theory 1, although some fairly plausible reasons were given for treating it as something that affected investment and hence the whole economy. By making one small change in Theory 6, we can make it into a theory involving the rate of interest. But first, let us consider the strategy to be pursued.

Banks have two kinds of earning assets. They make loans directly to individual customers and they buy bonds (mostly United States Government, state, and local government bonds) on the open market. The interest rates that banks charge their customers are clearly stated on the IOU signed by the customer. The rate of interest earned by banks (or anyone else, for that matter) on bonds purchased in the market requires more explanation.

Government and business bonds are traded every day in the bond market. Their prices vary from day to day also. These price changes do not affect the books of the issuer at all, for his obligations are written, once and for all, on the bond itself.

Why should the price of bonds vary? The answer, obviously, is that some days people will pay more for a given bond issue than other days. The reason is that some days they have more alternative uses for their free cash than other days.

Let us return to Tiny Model 3, which was concerned with prices. This theory supposed that the quantity of any goods that people were willing to buy depended on the price of those goods. For bonds, in particular,

$$B = ep + F_D$$

The theory also said that the quantity of any goods that people were willing to sell depended on the price of those goods. For bonds, in particular,

$$B = fp + F_S$$

But this "supply" of bonds relates to the total amount of this kind of debt that businesses and government wish to have. Suppose that we take the bonds in the market as given (on any particular day they may be). Then the supply equation is replaced by the fixed number:

$$B = \bar{B}$$

Bond prices, then, are given by substitution:

$$\bar{B} = ep + F_D$$

$$p = \frac{\bar{B} - F_D}{e}$$

Changes in bond prices, then, will follow the rule

$$\Delta p = \frac{\Delta\bar{B} - \Delta F_D}{e}$$

Since the higher bond prices are, the fewer bonds people will presumably wish to hold, $e < 0$. Consequently, if $\bar{B}$ increases, p will decrease; and if F_D increases, p will increase.

When the price of bonds changes, the interest rate also changes. This statement at first seems surprising, but it is clear enough on reflection. Suppose that a bond has a face value V, that it matures in t years, and that its holder (whoever he may happen to be at the time) receives \$$C$ in income for each year it was outstanding. Then a purchaser supposes, when he buys the bond, that he will receive a total of $V + Ct$ if he holds it until maturity. Suppose he pays a price of \$$P$ for the bond. Then the return on his investment will be given by the formula[7]

$$P(1 + i)^t = V + Ct$$

Here i is the interest rate, and $(1 + i)^t$ is the ordinary compound interest formula, measuring the rate of return on a \$1 investment held t years. Thus, if the market price, P, is known, one may evaluate i:

$$(1 + i)^t = \frac{V + Ct}{P}$$

$$i = \left(\frac{V + Ct}{P}\right)^{1/t} - 1$$

If the market rate of interest is known, one may evaluate the price:

$$P = \frac{V + Ct}{(1 + i)^t}$$

In other words, the higher the rate of interest, the smaller the price that an investor will pay for his bond. Alternatively, the higher the market price of bonds, the smaller the rate of return an investor gets from buying them.

Thus, the interest rate and the price of bonds move in opposite directions, for purely arithmetical reasons. Now let us look back at Theory 5. This theory stated that bonds were issued by nonbank businesses, and that the total bonds issued (B) were equal to the bond holdings of Federal Reserve (B_1) and the banks (B_2). But the statement $B = B_1 + B_2$ means that the evaluation of the bond issues by nonbanks is the same as that of the bondholders. In other words, the price of bonds is fixed. For if the price of bonds varies, bondholders may pay more or less for their bonds than the amount that the bonds are carried at in the books of the issuers.

So we shall drop the statement $B = B_1 + B_2$ and replace it by the statement

$$B_2 = gD + F_B$$

which says that banks decide on their bondholdings by looking at their

---

[7] This approximation says that the coupon return is not invested. If it is reinvested, a more exact formula is

$$P(1 + i)^t = V + \frac{c}{t}[(1 + i)^t - 1]$$

deposits. This statement makes decisions about bondholdings analogous to decisions about reserves in Tiny Model 4. Combining this statement with the other four statements of Theory 6, we have

$$(\mathbf{F_F}, \mathbf{0}, \mathbf{F_B}, \mathbf{R}, \mathbf{0}) = (\mathbf{B_1}, \mathbf{B_2}, \mathbf{R}, \mathbf{L}, \mathbf{D}) \begin{pmatrix} 1 & 1 & 0 & 0 & 0 \\ 0 & 0 & 1 & 0 & 1 \\ 0 & -1 & 0 & 1 & 1 \\ 0 & 0 & 0 & 0 & 1 \\ 0 & 0 & -g & -r & -1 \end{pmatrix}$$

The only difference between this matrix and that of Theory 6 is that here $-g$, rather than zero, appears in row 5, column 3. The inverse mapping is

$$(\mathbf{B_1}, \mathbf{B_2}, \mathbf{R}, \mathbf{L}, \mathbf{D}) = (\mathbf{F_F}, \mathbf{0}, \mathbf{F_B}, \mathbf{L}, \mathbf{0}) \begin{pmatrix} 1 & \frac{g}{r} & 1 & \frac{1-r-g}{r} & \frac{1}{r} \\ 0 & -\frac{g}{r} & -1 & \frac{-1-r-g}{r} & \frac{-1}{r} \\ 0 & 1 & 0 & -1 & 0 \\ 0 & -\frac{g}{r} & 0 & \frac{-1-g}{r} & \frac{-1}{r} \\ 0 & 0 & 0 & 1 & 0 \end{pmatrix}$$

The implications of Theory 7 are given in Table 5.3.

If banks increase their loans when their deposits rise, then $(1 - r - g) > 0$, since this number measures the effect on loans of a \$1 increase in bank deposits. The signs of all the elements in the inverse matrix are therefore determined.

In this system $B_1 + B_2$ measures the value of all bonds held as assets. This value is given by

$$B_1 = F_F$$

$$B_2 = \frac{g}{r} F_F + F_B - \frac{g}{r} R$$

so

$$B_1 + B_2 = \left(1 + \frac{g}{r}\right) F_F + F_B - \frac{g}{r} R$$

$$= F_F + F_B \qquad (\text{since } F_F = B_1 = R)$$

TABLE 5.3

THE IMPLICATIONS OF THEORY 7

THE EFFECT UPON	THE EFFECT OF		
	Open market operators (ΔF_F)	Increased bank demand for bonds	Increased excess reserves (ΔF_B)
Federal Reserve bondholding (ΔB_1)	1	0	0
Private bank bondholdings (ΔB_2)	g/r	1	$-g/r$
Bank reserves (ΔR)	1	0	0
Bank loans (ΔL)	$\frac{1-r-g}{r}$	-1	$\frac{-1-g}{r}$
Bank deposits (ΔD)	$\frac{1}{r}$	0	$-\frac{1}{r}$

The interest rate, then, is given (approximately) by

$$i = \left(\frac{V + Ct}{P}\right)^{1/t} - 1$$

Here P is the market value of the bonds $B_1 + B_2$. Thus,

$$i = \left(\frac{V + Ct}{F_F + F_B}\right)^{1/t} - 1$$

The interest rate falls when F_F (Federal Reserve holdings of bonds) or F_B (the level of bank demand for bonds) rises.

In this expression V is the face value of the total bonds outstanding in the market. If V increases, new bonds are issued. Given F_F and F_B, the interest rate rises. The interest rate is also affected by t, the length to maturity of the bonds, and the coupon rate C.

The symbols C and t are well defined in the macroeconomic theoretical sense, for there is only one kind of bond. Needless to say, in real bond markets, there are many kinds of bonds and many maturity dates.

The relation between the interest rate and the factors F_F and F_B is nonlinear. Students with the calculus may determine the effect of changes in F_F, F_t, C, t and V upon the interest rate, but exact formulae will not be given here.[8]

[8] In Chapter 5 of the author's *Introduction to Macroeconomic Theory* (Holt, Rinehart, Winston, Inc., 1968) a slightly different form of this theory is given. The behavioral statement used is $B_2 = gR + F_B$, so that bondholdings depend on the reserves of the banking system. This statement is consistent with the common view that Treasury Bills, with short maturities, are almost the same as cash, from the banker's point of view. Thus bills and reserves should vary in much the same way. The discussion in the *Introduction* now seems to the author to be less neat than that given here.

Remark. The discussion of Theory 1 raised the point that, from the point of view of general principle, it was desirable to have as many dimension-free behavioral coefficients as possible in a theory. Theory 7 has two such coefficients. It also has the advantage of deriving the interest rate from other economic variables, all of which (except t, which is expressed in calendar years) are dollar values. It is natural to prefer this formulation of the way the capital market determines the interest rate to a theory in which this rate is an explicit variable. It would have been possible, of course, to have made bank reserves, loans, and bondholdings linear functions of an interest rate, the level of which was determined in the market. But this procedure would have introduced one more variable into the theory, and a further behavioral assumption would have been needed. Moreover, it would have been necessary to introduce *dimensional* behavioral coefficients, relating percentage points in the interest rate to dollars of assets held. It would not have been clear *a priori* within what limits such coefficients might vary.

Problem 5.8 Go through 5.2–5.7. Which of these are *not* answerable in the context of Theory 7? Answer each answerable question, and determine the direction of change of the interest rate under the assumed conditions.

MONETARY THEORIES AND INCOME THEORIES

This chapter has presented a Tiny Model and Theories 6 and 7. The variables whose values are determined by the three are as follows:

Tiny Model 4 determined	Money
	Bank loans
Theories 6 and 7 determined	Bank holdings of bonds
	Bank reserves
	Bank loans
	Bank deposits

Theory 7 also implicitly determined the interest rate. No explicit calculation of the interest rate was given, for the formula would be complicated.

These variables are quite different from the variables determined in Theories 1 through 5: consumption, investment, the interest rate, tax revenue, the national product. At first guess, one might be tempted to say that the theories in this chapter really have nothing to do with those in Chapter 3, because, after all, they are concerned with quite different variables.

However, let us recall what has been said about investment. In Tiny Model 2 we said, suppose that the amount of plant that businesses want to have depends on their total assets. If something is done to change the money supply, total assets will change, and therefore the volume of plant desired by business will change. Investment is the change in plant, so a change in the money supply creates a demand for investment.

Theory 1 reasoned that the demand for investment depends partly on the interest rate. The demand for consumer goods depends partly on the money supply. If there is a change in the banking sector, so that the interest rate and bank deposits both change, then these changes are bound to have an effect on the variables of Theory 1.

Theories 3 and 4 would seem to have no such direct connection with the banking theories. But if the government has a deficit, then *either* it must borrow the sum needed to pay for its purchases, *or* it must print paper money. Once credit and money enter the discussion, a connection has been made to the theories in this chapter.

The conclusions drawn from monetary theories, therefore, are related to the subjects in the income theories. At this point, however, readers may be able to see a relation but not be able to specify just how the connection might work out. It is the function of the next chapter to fit the two ways of thought into a single system.

6

Money and the National Income

This chapter presents a set of theories that demonstrate several distinct ways of relating the subject matter of the last three chapters. It will prove confusing to readers who do not understand its purposes. Therefore, it begins with a statement of what will be done in it.

(1) Each theory in this book consists of propositions about that part of the social accounting system relevant to the subject under discussion, and other propositions about the behavior of the economic units that figure in the theory. Chapters 3 and 4 were mainly concerned with theories about the national product. Chapter 5 was mainly concerned with theories about the balance sheets of banks. This chapter presents a set of theories involving (1) the *national product* accounts; (2) *nonbank balance sheet* accounts; and (3) *bank balance sheet* accounts. That is, this chapter assembles the various parts of the economy into a single unified whole. This assembling requires some care and thought.

(2) Theories are proposed explanations of some set of phenomena. It is usually possible to advance more than one explanation for an event.

The skillful theorist is able to propose alternative possibilities. This chapter is in part an illustration of how to go about presenting alternative explanations. The question under consideration is the following one: What is the connection (if any) between money and the national income? Such a question is answered in two steps. The first step involves *proposing* several possible explanations. The second step involves *selecting* the best of these in terms of the conditions known to exist in (say) the United States economy of the 1960s.

(3) The question under discussion has been studied in great detail for forty years. Economists have not, however, reached any agreement as to which answer is the most suited to the economy of the United States. For this reason, it is necessary to present the discussion in terms of *possible* explanations. But even if there were agreement as to which explanation of this question were best, it would still be useful to learn how to construct alternative explanations. People become interested in any subject (including economics) because they want to discover answers to questions. Answers that are already known may simply be memorized, and for this reason they are not very interesting. A subject is interesting precisely because it is full of unanswered questions. At the moment one meets an unanswered question, there is a need for learning some procedure such as that illustrated in this chapter.

(4) Readers will find this chapter confusing if they are used to textbooks that claim to present them "the truth, the whole truth, and nothing but the truth." They will be unable to memorize ready-made conclusions; instead, they will be required to understand simple interpretations of the views of several groups of thoughtful men who do not agree about the question under discussion.

All of the theories presented in this chapter represent an economy consisting of (1) consumers, (2) businesses, (3) commercial banks, and (4) the Federal Reserve System. (The last two sectors are called "the banking system.") They differ, however, in the nature of the interrelations that they assume to exist among them. Specifically, and in somewhat simplified form:

Theory 8A says that the Federal Reserve System influences the commercial banks, consumers, and businesses. Businesses influence consumers but not the banking system. Consumers influence nobody.

Theory 8B says that the Federal Reserve System and the commercial banks both influence consumers and businesses. Consumers and businesses influence nobody.

Theory 8C says that the banking system influences nobody, but consumers and businesses influence each other.

Theory 8D says that the Federal Reserve System influences commercial banks, consumers, and businesses. Businesses influence consumers and commercial banks. Consumers influence commercial banks but not businesses.

These four possibilities are not the only ones that might have been considered. They do, however, represent the most common views of economists.

They can all be formulated within the general context of the linear macroeconomic systems that have already been developed. The fact that the general approach of this book yields such a rich variety of possible applications constitutes powerful evidence of its usefulness as a starting point for macroeconomic analysis. The fact that these main trends of economic thought can all be formulated consistently within a single framework is powerful evidence that theoretical discussion is not enough to lead economists to a selection of theories applicable to any given economy. Careful study of the facts is also required to select the most suitable variant from families of theories (such as the four theories presented here).

AN EXPURGATED HISTORY OF THE SUBJECT

The literature on the connection between income and money has gone through a number of stages. It is useful to summarize these stages, for they contain useful ideas. The first stage is associated with the so-called monetary identity:

$$MV = PQ$$

Imagine that the money supply consists of dollar bills, and that whenever they change hands, the person making the payment signs his name on the bill. Every time there is a business transaction, some quantity of goods is sold at a certain price, and also dollar bills are signed by the buyers of goods. At the end of the day (or week or month), we determine the average number of signatures on the dollar bills. This number measures the "velocity" (V) with which money changes hands; the product of V and the number of dollars M, therefore, is a precise measure of the value of the goods that changed hands.

It is also the case that $1/V$ measures the average length of time that people hold a dollar bill. The greater $1/V$ is, the longer people hold onto their money before spending it. Of course, the greater $1/V$ is, the less velocity is. We may therefore associate, very roughly, $1/V$ with the tendency of people to hold their cash rather than to spend it. Thus, $1/V$ may be associated with what has been called saving in connection with income accounting. Obviously the association is indirect, but it is real.

For any particular kind of goods, if Q units are sold at a price of P then PQ represents the money value of the goods sold. We may interpret the right-hand side of the monetary identity in two ways. We may take P as a measure of the price level for all goods, and Q as a measure of the level of output (such as the "real gross national product," which is the national product measured in constant prices). Alternatively, as theorists, we may suppose that only one commodity (called "goods") is produced, in amount

Q, and that it is sold at price P. Chapter 9 will discuss the difficulties associated with these concepts. For the present we will assume that the second alternative is correct: There is one commodity, "goods," some of which is consumed and the rest used to build factories. Starting from the proposition that PQ corresponds to the gross national product of earlier chapters, we use the monetary identity to theorize about the connection between money and income.

In Tiny Model 1, it was shown that

$$Y = \frac{1}{1-a}(I + F_C)$$

If money were used only for income transactions (so that there were no purchases or sales of any assets), velocity would be

$$V = \frac{Y}{M} = \frac{(I + F_C)}{(1-a)M}$$

In this case, increases in investment (I), or in autonomous consumption (F_C), or in the marginal propensity to consume $(1 - a)$ would all increase velocity, given any amount of money. Since holding money is (in this theory) an alternative to spending (whether on investment or consumption), increases in a "generalized willingness to spend" can be associated with increases in velocity (V) and with decreases in the average time ($1/V$) a dollar is held.

In Theory 1, it was shown that

$$Y = \frac{1}{1-a}\left(F_C + F_I - \frac{b+d}{e}F_L + \frac{b+ev+d}{e}M\right)$$

So that (again assuming no asset transactions)

$$V = \frac{Y}{M} = \frac{b+ev+d}{e(1-a)} + \frac{\left(F_C + F_I - \frac{b+d}{e}F_L\right)}{(1-a)M}$$

This case is consistent with Tiny Model 1, but we now see directly that an increase in the demand for money ($\Delta F_L > 0$) means a decrease in velocity, because $(b + d)/e > 0$. Consequently, $1/V$ decreases as F_L increases.

These two theories are both more precise and more simple than the literature on velocity. They are more precise in the sense that they are based on explicit national income theories, which did not exist in the 1920s. These theories show that for any vector of factors, a numerical value for V may be calculated. They are simpler in two respects. First, all the relations involved are linear. Second, they ignore the existence of transactions involving assets. Even if the total assets of the community were constant, we should expect that there would be transfers of these assets among businesses and individuals.

Thus the formulas given here relate only to "income velocity." They serve, however, to emphasize the fact that velocity, in principle, increases with increases in autonomous consumption or investment. We can only conjecture that velocity depends also on events in the capital markets given the particular two theories used here.

The formulas used here take velocity as something to be explained. The earlier literature tended to regard velocity as a given number. That is, V was taken as a given number, just as, in the relation between consumption and the amount of money of Theory 1,

$$C = aY + vL + bR + F_C$$

v was taken to be a given number. If velocity is a given number V, then one may theorize about the effects of changes in the money supply (M) on the rest of the monetary identity $MV = PQ$.

Problem 6.1 If V is indeed a constant, then the factors in Tiny Model 1 and in Theory 1 are not all independent of each other. Suppose that F_C is uniquely determined by M and the other factors. Reconstruct the tables of interpretations for these theories on this assumption.

Suppose that the quantity of money (M) is changed, but that V (the willingness, roughly speaking, of people to hold money) is fixed. Then either the price level (P) or output (Q) must change. If the economy is operating at capacity, so that there is no unemployment, output cannot increase as money increases. Thus, with fixed $V = \bar{V}$ and $Q = \bar{Q}$,

$$M\bar{V} = \bar{Q}P$$

$$M = \left(\frac{\bar{Q}}{\bar{V}}\right)P$$

and prices will vary in proportion to the quantity of money.

If there is idle capacity, and unemployment, then (it was said), prices may be taken as given ($P = \bar{P}$); if V is constant, then

$$M\bar{V} = \bar{P}Q$$

$$M = \left(\frac{\bar{P}}{\bar{V}}\right)Q$$

so that output varies with the money supply.

This form of the relation between money and income was seen to be unsatisfactory when the first measures of the national income were developed. For not all business transactions relate to income. Some payments of money are associated with transfers of assets. To surmount this difficulty, it was assumed (in effect) that transfers of assets were proportional to income transactions, and therefore,

$$MV = Y$$

Here V must be redefined as "income velocity," and Y is the national product. In this form, the "quantity theory" asserts a relation between national income and quantity of money. If velocity is constant, then the two vary proportionately. If V is related to national income in some suitable way, then it is still possible to express income in terms of the quantity of money. Assume, for instance, that for some reason

$$V = aY + b$$

Then

$$M(aY + b) = Y$$

$$Mb = Y(1 - aM)$$

$$Y = \frac{bM}{1 - aM}$$

If M increases, it may be shown that Y will increase, providing a and b are both positive or both negative and both fixed. The second case may be ruled out since both M and Y are inherently positive.

Actually, it turned out to be relatively simple to disentangle these matters, once the idea of including the social accounts as a systematic part of a theory became accepted. There are three relevant pieces to the economy: the income accounts, the balance sheets of nonbanks, and the balance sheets of banks. Money certainly appears as a component of the last two sets of accounts, and the assertion to be studied is that the banks may affect national income.

The earlier chapters have shown that we may have simple or complicated theories pertaining to each of the sets of accounts. It is natural in considering any new problem, however, to return to the simplest theory possible. Therefore, the connection between money and the national income will be considered in its very simplest form. This approach is justified because a new "operation" is being undertaken: the combination of related theories. So far, the only modifications made in theories has been the "enlargement" of a theory to include more variables and more complicated assumptions about economic behavior. It is therefore useful to look at the operation of combining theories.

COMBINING THE INCOME AND MONETARY ACCOUNTS

Most macroeconomics starts with some very simple notion, which may then be elaborated into a more complicated structure. Three very simple starting points have been presented: Tiny Model 1, dealing with the national income; Tiny Model 2, dealing with (nonbank) balance sheets; and Tiny Model 4, dealing with bank balance sheets. These three Tiny Models all have the same structure. That is, with each model there is associated a matrix having the form

$$\begin{pmatrix} 1 & -x \\ -1 & 1 \end{pmatrix}$$

The symbol designated x here is in each case a number between 0 and 1; each number has a different economic interpretation in each of the Tiny Models. In Tiny Model 1, x was replaced by a, the "marginal propensity to consume," which designates the proportion of a dollar's increase in income that is consumed. In Tiny Model 2, x was replaced by b, which designates the proportion of a dollar's increase in assets that is used to buy more plant. In Tiny Model 4, x was replaced by $(1 - r)$, where r is the "reserve requirement," designating the proportion of a dollar's increase in deposits that the banks must hold in the form of cash (reserves).

In each of the chapters so far, a Tiny Model has been imbedded in some larger system. Additional factors and variables have been taken into the theory, so as to make it closer to ordinary experience and able to account for larger classes of observable events.

Each chapter, however, has tended to be isolated from the others. There is some overlap in subject matter, as is shown by overlap in the list of factors and variables. But this overlap is not really a combination of theories into a uniform way of looking at the economy. This combination may be effected at various levels of complexity. For example, the theories about the national income were of various degrees of difficulty. Tiny Model 1 was the simplest version; Theory 1 involved the interest rate, but not government; Theories 2 and 3 involved government, but not the interest rate. It would have been possible to present a theory involving the interest rate and also government. To combine theories about income with theories about bank and nonbank balance sheets, some level of complexity must be specified.

The following discussion will show how to combine the three Tiny Models, rather than the more complicated theories which have been considered. The simpler models will be complicated enough to bring out some fundamental problems in the combination of theories.

At the end of Chapter 2, block notation was described. This notation is a compact way of writing down theories which otherwise might have large and complicated matrices. The use of block notation will considerably simplify the present discussion, for it is possible to represent the Tiny Models as blocks, which are to be combined to form a theory about an entire economy.

The three Tiny Models may be written down separately as

$$\mathbf{F}_1 = \mathbf{V}_1\mathbf{M}_1$$

in the case of Tiny Model 1,

$$\mathbf{F}_2 = \mathbf{V}_2\mathbf{M}_2$$

in the case of Tiny Model 2,

$$\mathbf{F}_4 = \mathbf{V}_4\mathbf{M}_4$$

in the case of Tiny Model 4.

Each M_i stands for a matrix of the form:

$$\begin{pmatrix} 1 & -x \\ -1 & 1 \end{pmatrix}$$

Each F_i and V_i stands for a vector with two components. If the three Tiny Models were really independent of each other, we could write a single theory to encompass them all:

$$(\mathbf{F}_1, \mathbf{F}_2, \mathbf{F}_4) = (\mathbf{V}_1, \mathbf{V}_2, \mathbf{V}_4)\begin{pmatrix} M_1 & 0 & 0 \\ 0 & M_2 & 0 \\ 0 & 0 & M_4 \end{pmatrix} = (\mathbf{V}_1\mathbf{M}_1, \mathbf{V}_2\mathbf{M}_2, \mathbf{V}_4\mathbf{M}_4)$$

For each block F_i on the left, there would be a block $V_i M_i$ on the right. These would each represent, respectively, each of the Tiny Models.

(1) If this procedure were adopted, then when block notation was replaced by ordinary vector notation,

$$(\mathbf{F}_1, \mathbf{F}_2, \mathbf{F}_4) = (\mathbf{I}, \mathbf{F_C}, \mathbf{M}, \mathbf{F_K}, \mathbf{R}, \mathbf{F_L})$$

$$(\mathbf{V}_1, \mathbf{V}_2, \mathbf{V}_4) = (\mathbf{Y}, \mathbf{C}, \mathbf{W}, \mathbf{K}, \mathbf{M}, \mathbf{L})$$

An obvious difficulty is that M, the amount of money, appears both as a factor and as a variable. There is no reason why there should not be some theories (such as Tiny Model 2) in which M is a factor, and others (such as Tiny Model 4), in which M is a variable, providing that these theories are recognized as distinct. But when theories are put together, the "product" must exhibit a systematic and consistent treatment of the parts. Therefore, M cannot be on both sides of the equation.

It is possible to take care of this difficulty by treating M solely as a variable. This means rewriting the system:

$$(\mathbf{I}, \mathbf{F_C}, \mathbf{0}, \mathbf{F_K}, \mathbf{R}, \mathbf{F_L}) = (\mathbf{Y}, \mathbf{C}, \mathbf{W}, \mathbf{K}, \mathbf{M}, \mathbf{L}) \begin{pmatrix} 1 & -a & 0 & 0 & 0 & 0 \\ -1 & 1 & 0 & 0 & 0 & 0 \\ 0 & 0 & 1 & -b & 0 & 0 \\ 0 & 0 & -1 & 1 & 0 & 0 \\ 0 & 0 & -1 & 0 & 1 & -s \\ 0 & 0 & 0 & 0 & -1 & 1 \end{pmatrix}$$

Note: In this chapter, we will use the notation $s = 1 - r$, where r is the reserve requirement.

(2) Now an inconsistency appears in the balance sheet sector of the economy. The banks make loans, which appear as part of their assets. These loans presumably represent debts of the nonbanks, but, as now defined, the nonbanks do not have any debts. When this inconsistency is removed

$$(\mathbf{I}, \mathbf{F_C}, \mathbf{0}, \mathbf{F_K}, \mathbf{R}, \mathbf{F_L}) = (\mathbf{Y}, \mathbf{C}, \mathbf{W}, \mathbf{K}, \mathbf{M}, \mathbf{L}) \begin{pmatrix} 1 & -a & 0 & 0 & 0 & 0 \\ -1 & 1 & 0 & 0 & 0 & 0 \\ 0 & 0 & 1 & -b & 0 & 0 \\ 0 & 0 & -1 & 1 & 0 & 0 \\ 0 & 0 & -1 & 0 & 1 & -s \\ 0 & 0 & 1 & 0 & -1 & 1 \end{pmatrix}$$

In block form, this theory is

$$(\mathbf{F}_1, \mathbf{F}_2, \mathbf{F}_4) = (\mathbf{V}_1, \mathbf{V}_2, \mathbf{V}_4) \begin{pmatrix} M_1 & 0 & 0 \\ 0 & M_2 & 0 \\ 0 & M_{42} & M_4 \end{pmatrix}$$

The inverse form of this system is

$$(\mathbf{Y}, \mathbf{C}, \mathbf{W}, \mathbf{K}, \mathbf{M}, \mathbf{L}) = (\mathbf{I}, \mathbf{F_C}, \mathbf{0}, \mathbf{F_K}, \mathbf{R}, \mathbf{F_L}) \begin{pmatrix} \frac{1}{1-a} & \frac{a}{1-a} & 0 & 0 & 0 & 0 \\ \frac{1}{1-a} & \frac{1}{1-a} & 0 & 0 & 0 & 0 \\ 0 & 0 & \frac{1}{1-b} & \frac{b}{1-b} & 0 & 0 \\ 0 & 0 & \frac{1}{1-b} & \frac{1}{1-b} & 0 & 0 \\ 0 & 0 & \frac{1}{1-b} & \frac{b}{1-b} & \frac{1}{1-s} & \frac{s}{1-s} \\ 0 & 0 & 0 & 0 & \frac{1}{1-s} & \frac{1}{1-s} \end{pmatrix}$$

TABLE 6.1

THE IMPLICATIONS OF THEORY 8

THE EFFECT OF A UNIT INCREASE OF	THE EFFECT UPON					
	National product	Consumption	Net worth	Plant	Money	Bank loans
Investment (ΔI)	$\frac{1}{1-a}$	$\frac{a}{1-a}$	0	0	0	0
Consumer demand (ΔF_C)	$\frac{1}{1-a}$	$\frac{1}{1-a}$	0	0	0	0
Demand for plant (ΔF_K)	0	0	$\frac{1}{1-b}$	$\frac{1-b}{1-b}$	0	0
Bank reserves (ΔR)	0	0	$\frac{1}{1-b}$	$\frac{b}{1-b}$	$\frac{1}{1-s}$	$\frac{s}{1-s}$
Supply of bank loans (ΔF_L)	0	0	0	0	$\frac{1}{1-s}$	$\frac{1}{1-s}$

NOTE: From Chapter 4, remember that if the demand for reserves is $R = rM + F_R$, the supply of loans is $L = (1 - r)M + F_L$, where $F_L = -F_R$.

And the interpretation of this inverse form is given in Table 6.1. For convenience, we shall label this theory as Theory 8.

Theory 8 seems to have some curious implications, as Table 6.1 indicates.

(1) If investment rises, plant remains fixed. But in Chapter 1 it was shown that investment is the change in plant; an increase in investment must increase the amount of plant.

(2) Investment is presumably financed either from saving (an increase in net worth), or by a reduction in cash balances, or by an increase in debt. But Table 6.1 says that it is possible to increase investment with no change in *any* of these variables.

(3) If the amount of plant increases (as was shown in Chapter 1), there is investment, and investment is a part of the national product. But in Table 6.1, the factor changes that affect the national product do not affect the total level of plant; and the factor changes that affect the level of plant do not affect the national product.

These various difficulties all involve investment, in one way or another. So far, there is nothing that explicitly links investment to the balance sheet system of Tiny Model 2. If we introduce the definition $K = K_0 + I$, which says that plant in the given period (K) is equal to plant in the previous period (K_0) plus new plant ($\Delta K \equiv I$), and if we make investment, like plant (a variable), then system 8A is obtained:

$$(\mathbf{0}, \mathbf{F_C}, \mathbf{K_O}, \mathbf{0}, \mathbf{F_K}, \mathbf{R}, \mathbf{F_L}) = (\mathbf{Y}, \mathbf{C}, \mathbf{I}, \mathbf{W}, \mathbf{K}, \mathbf{M}, \mathbf{L}) \times \begin{pmatrix} 1 & -a & 0 & 0 & 0 & 0 & 0 \\ -1 & 1 & 0 & 0 & 0 & 0 & 0 \\ -1 & 0 & -1 & 0 & 0 & 0 & 0 \\ 0 & 0 & 0 & 1 & -b & 0 & 0 \\ 0 & 0 & 1 & -1 & 1 & 0 & 0 \\ 0 & 0 & 0 & -1 & 0 & 1 & -s \\ 0 & 0 & 0 & 1 & 0 & -1 & 1 \end{pmatrix}$$

The number of variables and factors has been increased from six to seven. In block form, Theory 8A is not quite like Theory 8:

$$(\mathbf{F}_1, \mathbf{F}_2, \mathbf{F}_4) = (\mathbf{V}_1, \mathbf{V}_2, \mathbf{V}_4) \begin{pmatrix} M_1 & 0 & 0 \\ M_{21} & M_2 & 0 \\ 0 & M_{42} & M_4 \end{pmatrix}$$

This is because the block M_{21} is zero in 8 and not zero in 8A. Moreover, M_2 has become a 3×3 matrix, so that the second row and the second column of blocks is different in 8A from 8.

Has any improvement in performance been brought about? The inverse form of Theory 8A is

$$(\mathbf{Y}, \mathbf{C}, \mathbf{I}, \mathbf{W}, \mathbf{K}, \mathbf{M}, \mathbf{L}) = (\mathbf{0}, \mathbf{F_C}, \mathbf{K_O}, \mathbf{0}, \mathbf{F_K}, \mathbf{R}, \mathbf{F_L}) \times \begin{pmatrix} \frac{1}{1-a} & \frac{a}{1-a} & 0 & 0 & 0 & 0 & 0 \\ \frac{1}{1-a} & \frac{1}{1-a} & 0 & 0 & 0 & 0 & 0 \\ \frac{-1}{1-a} & \frac{-a}{1-a} & -1 & 0 & 0 & 0 & 0 \\ \frac{b}{(1-a)(1-b)} & \frac{ab}{(1-a)(1-b)} & \frac{b}{1-b} & \frac{1}{1-b} & \frac{b}{1-b} & 0 & 0 \\ \frac{1}{(1-a)(1-b)} & \frac{a}{(1-a)(1-b)} & \frac{1}{1-b} & \frac{1}{1-b} & \frac{1}{1-b} & 0 & 0 \\ \frac{b}{(1-a)(1-b)} & \frac{ab}{(1-a)(1-b)} & \frac{b}{1-b} & \frac{1}{1-b} & \frac{b}{1-b} & \frac{1}{1-s} & \frac{s}{1-s} \\ 0 & 0 & 0 & 0 & 0 & \frac{1}{1-s} & \frac{1}{1-s} \end{pmatrix}$$

From this inverse form, we deduce the implications given in Table 6.2. This table shows that the particular troubles found in Table 6.1 have indeed been

TABLE 6.2

THE IMPLICATIONS OF THEORY 8A

THE EFFECT OF A UNIT INCREASE IN	THE EFFECT UPON					
	National product	Consumption	Investment	Net worth	Plant	Money
Consumer demand (ΔF_C)	$\frac{1}{1-a}$	$\frac{1}{1-a}$	0	0	0	0
Demand for plant (ΔF_K)	$\frac{1}{(1-a)(1-b)}$	$\frac{a}{(1-a)(1-b)}$	$\frac{1}{1-b}$	$\frac{1}{1-b}$	$\frac{1}{1-b}$	0
Bank reserves (ΔR)	$\frac{b}{(1-a)(1-b)}$	$\frac{ab}{(1-a)(1-b)}$	$\frac{b}{1-b}$	$\frac{1}{1-b}$	$\frac{b}{1-b}$	$\frac{1}{1-s}$
Supply of loans (ΔF_L)	0	0	0	0	0	$\frac{1}{1-s}$

cleared up. Changes in investment are indeed associated with equal changes in plant. Changes in investment are always associated with changes in national product.

Consider the question of financing investment. If F_K, the level of demand for plant, rises by 1, actual plant and investment increase by $1/1 - b$, and net worth increases by an equal amount. Savings was shown in Chapter 1 to be the same as the change in net worth, so in this case savings equals investment. The banking system is unaffected.

However, when the supply of loans increases by 1, loans increase by $1/(1 - s) = 1/r$ (where r is the reserve requirement). The quantity of money (bank deposits) rises by $1/(1 - s)$. The increase in cash assets causes nonbanks to want more plant, in the amount of $b/1 - b$. Total assets thus rise by $(1 - bs)/(1 - s)(1 - b)$; this increase is financed from loans in the amount of $s/(1 - s)$ and savings (net worth) in the amount of $1/(1 - b)$.

An interesting feature of Theory 8A is the following: The Federal Reserve System could affect the national product, but the private banks could not. Changes in bank reserves (which are carried out by the Federal Reserve System) affect all parts of the social accounts. But changes in the supply of loans have only the effect of changing loans and the amount of money by equal amounts. In other words, the private banks would be "neutral," insofar as the level of current output and income are concerned.

This feature of Theory 8A will be unsatisfactory to most monetary theorists. They may argue, in part, that by omitting bond financing, the theory has omitted one of the important features of investment finance. Theory 5 certainly made the private banks influence the level of plant, and hence the amount of investment—a component of output.

But it is not necessary to make Theory 8A more complicated to satisfy this criticism. It is merely necessary to alter the behavioral assumptions of the theory and to start off, so to speak, with a different collection of Tiny Models. It might have been difficult to devise Theory 8A starting from scratch. Given the structure of the theory, however, it is relatively easy to alter it in such a way as to see how the economy would behave if people and businesses acted in somewhat different ways from those specified so far.

Historical Remark. In Tiny Model 2, the coefficient b appears in the equation $K = bW + F_K$. This says that the amount of plant businesses want to hold depends on their total assets. An increase of $1 in total assets will produce an investment of b in new plant.

In Theory 8A, and in some other variants of this theory, the Federal Reserve System is able to influence the national product if $b > 0$; if $b = 0$, the banking system has no effect on the national product variables. This situation exists when businesses do not invest in response to changes in the money supply.

During the great depression of the 1930s, the Federal Reserve System allowed bank reserves to grow, so as to encourage investment. But in fact investment was very small, and excess reserves were quite large. There was a very common view among economists that a "liquidity trap" existed. That is, businesses simply absorbed any cash they could, without using their increased assets for investment purposes. This argument says that in periods of depression, the coefficient b of Tiny Model 1, Theory 8A, and so forth, becomes zero. (The "liquidity trap" is analyzed again, from a different point of view, in Chapter 9.)

The special case in which $b = 0$ is not very interesting analytically, but it has an important place in the history of economics. The important group of economists who argue that government spending and tax policy would be able to combat depressions got their start from the conviction that in depressions $b = 0$, so that the monetary authorities would be unable to bring about improvements in business conditions. Modern theory of the national product started off from this point.

Problem 6.2 In Chapter 5, it was shown that changes in the value of bonds in asset accounts could take place even if there were no changes in the number of bonds outstanding. These changes would be interpreted as changes in the interest rate. Is there any corresponding interpretation of Theory 8 that would explain differences between investment and changes in plant?

Problem 6.3 Interpret the effects of changes in bank reserves and the supply of loans in the case where there is a liquidity trap. Specifically, explain what businesses do in response to changes in their environment.

ALTERNATIVE PATTERNS OF NONBANK BEHAVIOR

Tiny Model 1 contains a statement about consumer behavior: Consumers look at their incomes and then decide how much to spend. An alternate, but equally simple theory would be the following: Consumers look at the balance in their bank accounts and decide how much to spend. This alternative behavior would be given by the equation

$$C = vM + F_C$$

or equivalently

$$F_C = C - vM$$

This statement is not unrelated to that in Tiny Model 1. Suppose that Mr. Consumer is paid on each Friday, say an amount of \$98.00. If Mrs. Consumer spends exactly \$15.00 per day, then she will have exactly nothing in her bank account when her husband gets home on Friday evening. To put it differently, when half the week is gone, she will have \$49.00 in her bank account; this sum is her average balance over the course of the week. Looking at her spending, we can say either (1) she spends her entire income in the course of the week ($C = Y$), or (2) during the week she spends twice her average bank balance ($v = 2$, $F_C = 0$). Obviously, if she keeps a minimum cash balance, or if she saves a part of her weekly income, then different relations will prevail between consumption and income, and also between consumption and bank balances.

Observationally, in any given case, one can make either a statement relating consumer spending to income, or a statement relating consumer spending to cash balances. But one can distinguish two quite different ways in which Mrs. Consumer might decide whether to buy a new dress. (1) She may say, "I will buy the dress, because I have enough money in the bank to pay for it." (That is the decision we are now suggesting.) (2) She may say "My husband will bring home his check next Friday, and I can therefore afford this dress." (That is the decision suggested by Tiny Model 1.) There is, as we shall see, an important distinction between the two kinds of decisions.

Tiny Model 2 contains a statement about business behavior: Businesses look at their total assets and decide how much plant to acquire. Their decision relates to the division of assets between cash and plant. An alternate, but equally simple theory would be the following: Businesses look at their cash balances and decide how much plant they can afford. (If they want more plant, they may either borrow or use their own funds to pay for it.) This alternative behavior would be given by the equation

$$K = wM + F_K$$

or equivalently,

$$F_K = K - wM$$

In this case, the business decides whether or not to buy a new factory or a new piece of equipment by looking at its bank account. In this respect, its behavior would be analogous to the behavior of Mrs. Consumer.

Nobody would argue that either the behavior implied by the Tiny Models or the behavior being investigated here matches the complexity of human actions in the real world. Even so, however, it turns out that it makes quite a bit of difference in the workings of the economy whether human behavior is more like that of the Tiny Models or more like that in the present theory. For when these two statements are substituted for the corresponding statements of Theory 8A, there is obtained a new theory, which will be called Theory 8B:

$$(\mathbf{0}, \mathbf{F_C}, \mathbf{K_0}, \mathbf{0}, \mathbf{F_K}, \mathbf{R}, \mathbf{F_L}) = (\mathbf{Y}, \mathbf{C}, \mathbf{I}, \mathbf{W}, \mathbf{K}, \mathbf{M}, \mathbf{L}) \times \begin{pmatrix} 1 & 0 & 0 & 0 & 0 & 0 & 0 \\ -1 & 1 & 0 & 0 & 0 & 0 & 0 \\ -1 & 0 & -1 & 0 & 0 & 0 & 0 \\ 0 & 0 & 0 & 1 & 0 & 0 & 0 \\ 0 & 0 & 1 & -1 & 1 & 0 & 0 \\ 0 & -v & 0 & -1 & -w & 1 & -s \\ 0 & 0 & 0 & 1 & 0 & -1 & 1 \end{pmatrix}$$

The inverse of this equation turns out to be

$$(\mathbf{Y}, \mathbf{C}, \mathbf{I}, \mathbf{W}, \mathbf{K}, \mathbf{M}, \mathbf{L}) = (\mathbf{0}, \mathbf{F_C}, \mathbf{K_0}, \mathbf{0}, \mathbf{F_K}, \mathbf{R}, \mathbf{F_L}) \times \begin{pmatrix} 1 & 0 & 0 & 0 & 0 & 0 & 0 \\ 1 & 1 & 0 & 0 & 0 & 0 & 0 \\ -1 & 0 & -1 & 0 & 0 & 0 & 0 \\ 0 & 0 & 0 & 1 & 0 & 0 & 0 \\ 1 & 0 & 1 & 1 & 1 & 0 & 0 \\ \frac{w+v}{1-s} & \frac{v}{1-s} & \frac{w}{1-s} & \frac{1-s+w}{1-s} & \frac{w}{1-s} & \frac{1}{1-s} & \frac{s}{1-s} \\ \frac{w+v}{1-s} & \frac{v}{1-s} & \frac{w}{1-s} & \frac{w}{1-s} & \frac{w}{1-s} & \frac{1}{1-s} & \frac{1}{1-s} \end{pmatrix}$$

One obvious difference between the implications of Theory 8A and Theory 8B (as given in Table 6.3) is that in 8B the commercial banks can influence the national product. That is, the elements of the last row of Table 8B are nonzero. The first five elements of the last row of Table 8A were all zeros.

In this theory, velocity of cash balances of consumers (v) and businesses (w) have replaced the marginal propensity to consume (a) and the plant coefficient (b) of Theory 8A. Consequently, when investment rises, there is no induced effect on consumer spending; and when the demand for plant rises, there is no induced effect upon cash balances demanded. Thus, terms in $(1 - a)$ and $(1 - b)$ appearing in the denominator of terms in Table 6.2 do not appear here. Generally speaking, this system is insensitive to changes in the nonmonetary variables, because that is the way it was constructed.

Problem 6.4 Theory 8A states that a \$1 increase in bank reserves will increase the national product by $b/(1-a)(1-b)$; Theory 8B says the increase will be $(w+v)/(1-s)$. Compare the different reactions of consumers and of businesses that explain the differences in result. Why is it that s does not appear in the first expression, even though s appears in Theory 8A?

Problem 6.5 Theory 3 shows that under certain conditions an increase in government spending has the same effect on the economy as an increase in investment. Would that conclusion necessarily hold in the context of Theory 8? (*Hint:* Consider your answer to problem 6.2).

Problem 6.6 Suppose that government spending is used exclusively to build bridges, roads, and other "productive assets," and that the conditions of Theory 3 apply. Then government spending acts on the economy in the same way as investment. Suppose that an increase in national product equal to ΔY is sought, and this increase may be obtained either by increasing government spending or by increasing bank reserves. Compare the magnitudes of the two that would be needed (1) under conditions of Theory 8A; (2) under conditions of Theory 8B.

TABLE 6.3

THE IMPLICATIONS OF THEORY 8B

THE EFFECT OF A UNIT INCREASE IN	THE EFFECT UPON						
	National product	Consumption	Investment	Net worth	Plant	Money	Bank loans
Consumer demand (ΔF_C)	1	1	0	0	0	0	0
Demand for plant (ΔF_K)	1	0	1	1	1	0	0
Bank reserves (ΔR)	$\frac{w+v}{1-s}$	$\frac{v}{1-s}$	$\frac{w}{1-s}$	$\frac{1-s+w}{1-s}$	$\frac{w}{1-s}$	$\frac{1}{1-s}$	$\frac{s}{1-s}$
Supply of loans (ΔF_L)	$\frac{w+v}{1-s}$	$\frac{v}{1-s}$	$\frac{w}{1-s}$	$\frac{w}{1-s}$	$\frac{w}{1-s}$	$\frac{1}{1-s}$	$\frac{1}{1-s}$

Historical Remark. Table 6.3 makes it possible to explain why economists have abandoned theories like Theory 1, in which money appears as a factor, in favor of theories in which all balance sheets accounts appear as variables.

When World War II began, there was large-scale unemployment in the United States. Between the German occupation of France (June 1940) and Pearl Harbor (December 1941) there was a large increase in government spending. By the spring of 1942, unemployment had disappeared, and the government began to try to persuade housewives to take jobs. As the end of the war approached in 1944–1945, professional economists, who then thought in terms of Theory 3, predicted as follows: Government spending rose from \$9 billion in 1939 to \$95 billion in 1944, and unemployment disappeared. When the war ends, this spending will certainly drop. If it dropped back to the prewar level, we should expect (by Theory 3) a return to prewar unemployment levels.

Of course, this did not happen. In particular, consumers spent much more in 1946–1947 than anyone would have predicted. Some people said, "Aha! F_C has increased." But others said the the reason consumers were spending so much more was that they had so much *cash*. Why? Because during the war, automobiles and other durable goods had not been available, so consumers had saved more than usual; some of this saving was in cash. Moreover, the Federal Reserve System had bought large amounts of government bonds, so the money supply had greatly increased. If Theory 8B were true, then an increase in bank reserves would increase the national product. Even if government spending should fall, the economy would not return to its prewar condition because Federal Reserve action during the war would make such a return impossible.

This account, as usual, is oversimplified. However, the unification of income and balance sheet theories was greatly speeded by the puzzle that economists found in our unexpected prosperity after World War II. Theory 3 simply turned out to be wrong, and theories such as Theory 8 (although more complicated) have come to replace it.

Many economists have been reluctant to give the banking system as much importance as it has in Theory 8B. For them, money is merely a tool, and they cannot imagine its influencing "real" things like the production of goods. It is natural to show, in the context of Theory 8, a theory with "neutral money," which will be numbered Theory 8C.

In Theory 8C, consumer spending depends on income, as in Tiny Model 1:

$$C = aY + F_C$$

The demand for plant, however, will be different from any of the statements made so far:

$$K = xY + F_K$$

That is, the amount of plant that businesses want will depend partly on the level of output. It is easy to interpret the amount of plant in terms of "industrial capacity," so that the amount of capacity needed by businesses depend on the volume of output (Y) that businesses are called on to supply to the public.

If these two behavioral statements were true, then the theory as a whole would be

$$(\mathbf{0, F_C, K_0, 0, F_K, R, F_L}) = (\mathbf{Y, C, I, W, K, M, L})$$

$$\times \begin{pmatrix} 1 & -a & 0 & 0 & -x & 0 & 0 \\ -1 & 1 & 0 & 0 & 0 & 0 & 0 \\ -1 & 0 & -1 & 0 & 0 & 0 & 0 \\ 0 & 0 & 0 & 1 & 0 & 0 & 0 \\ 0 & 0 & 1 & -1 & 1 & 0 & 0 \\ 0 & 0 & 0 & -1 & 0 & 1 & -s \\ 0 & 0 & 0 & 1 & 0 & -1 & 1 \end{pmatrix}$$

The inverse form of this theory is

$$(\mathbf{Y, C, I, W, K, M, L}) = (\mathbf{0, F_C, K_0, 0, F_K, R, F_L})$$

$$\times \begin{pmatrix} \frac{1}{1-x-a} & \frac{a}{1-x-a} & \frac{+x}{1-x-a} & \frac{+x}{1-x-a} & \frac{+x}{1-x-a} & 0 & 0 \\ \frac{1}{1-x-a} & \frac{1-x}{1-x-a} & \frac{+x}{1-x-a} & \frac{+x}{1-x-a} & \frac{+x}{1-x-a} & 0 & 0 \\ \frac{-1}{1-x-a} & \frac{-a}{1-x-a} & \frac{-(1-a)}{1-x-a} & \frac{-x}{1-x-a} & \frac{-x}{1-x-a} & 0 & 0 \\ 0 & 0 & 0 & 1 & 0 & 0 & 0 \\ \frac{1}{1-x-a} & \frac{a}{1-x-a} & \frac{1-a}{1-x-a} & \frac{1-a}{1-x-a} & \frac{1-a}{1-x-a} & 0 & 0 \\ 0 & 0 & 0 & 1 & 0 & \frac{1}{1-s} & \frac{s}{1-s} \\ 0 & 0 & 0 & 0 & 0 & \frac{1}{1-s} & \frac{1}{1-s} \end{pmatrix}$$

The implications of Theory 8C are summarized in Table 6.4.

If consumers and businesses behaved as postulated by Theory 8C, then both Federal Reserve and the private banks would be quite unable to influence the level of the national product. Moreover, the banking system would be unaffected by changes in consumer demand and in the demand for plant. Because changes in the banking factors have no effect on the nonbank variables, and because changes in nonbank factors do not affect banking variables, the banking sector is effectively isolated from the rest of the economy.

All four of the theories presented in this chapter have one feature in common: Changes in consumer demand (F_C) and in the demand for plant (F_K) have no effect upon the banking system. Bank decisions about loans (and hence about excess reserves) are made entirely without reference to the level of business activity. But, in real life, bankers could not afford to ignore business conditions. They must consider the likelihood that borrowers will be able to repay their debts. When the national income is low, we might expect banks to be less optimistic about this likelihood than in times when the national income is high. Theory 8D will take this possibility into account.

TABLE 6.4

THE IMPLICATIONS OF THEORY 8C

THE EFFECT OF A UNIT INCREASE IN	THE EFFECT UPON						
	National product	Consumption	Investment	Net worth	Plant	Money	Bank loans
Consumer demand (ΔF_C)	$\frac{1}{1-x-a}$	$\frac{1-x}{1-x-a}$	$\frac{+x}{1-x-a}$	$\frac{+x}{1-x-a}$	$\frac{+x}{1-x-a}$	0	0
Demand for plant (ΔF_K)	$\frac{1}{1-x-a}$	$\frac{1}{1-x-a}$	$\frac{1-a}{1-x-a}$	$\frac{1-a}{1-x-a}$	$\frac{1-a}{1-x-a}$	0	0
Bank reserves (ΔR)	0	0	0	1	0	$\frac{1}{1-s}$	$\frac{s}{1-s}$
Supply of loans (ΔF_L)	0	0	0	0	0	$\frac{1}{1-s}$	$\frac{s}{1-s}$

Problem 6.7 The "multiplier" of Tiny Model 1 and Theory 8A says tha if investment increases by \$1 the national product rises by $1/(1-a)$. In Theory 8C the corresponding multiplier is $1/(1+x-a)$. Which of the two is larger? How do you account for the difference?

Problem 6.8 What is the effect on business debt of increases in the supply o loans and in bank reserves? To what extent do businesses finance investment from bank credit? For what purposes dc they borrow from banks?

Problem 6.9 Compare the efficacy of changes in government spending and in Federal Reserve policy as a means of affecting the national product in Theory 8C, under the conditions assumed for problem 6.6

The easiest way of asserting that the banks look at business conditions in deciding how many loans to make is to say that

$$L = (1-r)M + zY + F_L \qquad z > 0$$

where r is the reserve requirement. In this case, since $M = R + L$, the supply of loans is

$$M - R = (1-r)M + zY + F_L$$

and the demand for bank reserves therefore goes *down* as the national income rises:

$$\begin{aligned} R &= rM - zY - F_L \\ &= rM - zY + F_R \end{aligned}$$

If $z = 0$, the formula reduces to that used in Tiny Model 4.

This theory is more complicated than any of the other variants studied in this chapter, for it contains *four* coefficients (a, b, r, z) rather than three. It would be simple enough to suppress r, to achieve a more simple theory, but the Federal Reserve requirements are so important in practice that serious objections could be made to any theory disregarding them.

If Theory 8A is modified so as to take this form of bank behavior into account, it becomes:

$$(\mathbf{0}, \mathbf{F_C}, \mathbf{K_0}, \mathbf{0}, \mathbf{F_K}, \mathbf{R}, \mathbf{F_L}) = (\mathbf{Y}, \mathbf{C}, \mathbf{I}, \mathbf{W}, \mathbf{K}, \mathbf{M}, \mathbf{L})$$

$$\times \begin{pmatrix} 1 & -a & 0 & 0 & 0 & 0 & -z \\ -1 & 1 & 0 & 0 & 0 & 0 & 0 \\ -1 & 0 & -1 & 0 & 0 & 0 & 0 \\ 0 & 0 & 0 & 1 & -b & 0 & 0 \\ 0 & 0 & 1 & -1 & 1 & 0 & 0 \\ 0 & 0 & 0 & -1 & 0 & 1 & -s \\ 0 & 0 & 0 & 1 & 0 & -1 & 1 \end{pmatrix}$$

The inverse form of Theory 8D is

$$
(\mathbf{Y}, \mathbf{C}, \mathbf{I}, \mathbf{W}, \mathbf{K}, \mathbf{M}, \mathbf{L}) = (\mathbf{0}, \mathbf{F_C}, \mathbf{K_0}, \mathbf{0}, \mathbf{F_K}, \mathbf{R}, \mathbf{F_L})
$$

$$
\times \begin{pmatrix}
\frac{1}{1-a} & \frac{a}{1-a} & 0 & 0 & 0 & \frac{z(1-b)}{(1-a)(1-b)(1-s)} & \frac{z(1-b)}{(1-a)(1-b)(1-s)} \\
\frac{1}{1-a} & \frac{1}{1-a} & 0 & 0 & 0 & \frac{z(1-b)}{(1-a)(1-b)(1-s)} & \frac{z(1-b)}{(1-a)(1-b)(1-s)} \\
\frac{-1}{1-a} & \frac{a}{1-a} & -1 & 0 & 0 & \frac{-z(1-b)}{(1-a)(1-b)(1-s)} & \frac{-z(1-b)}{(1-a)(1-b)(1-s)} \\
\frac{b}{(1-a)(1-b)} & \frac{ab}{(1-a)(1-b)} & \frac{b}{1-b} & \frac{1}{1-b} & \frac{b}{1-b} & \frac{bz}{(1-a)(1-b)(1-s)} & \frac{bz}{(1-a)(1-b)(1-s)} \\
\frac{1}{(1-a)(1-b)} & \frac{a}{(1-a)(1-b)} & \frac{1}{1-b} & \frac{1}{1-b} & \frac{1}{1-b} & \frac{z}{(1-a)(1-b)(1-s)} & \frac{z}{(1-a)(1-b)(1-s)} \\
\frac{b}{(1-a)(1-b)} & \frac{ab}{(1-a)(1-b)} & \frac{b}{1-b} & \frac{1}{1-b} & \frac{1}{1-b} & \frac{bz+(1-a)(1-b)}{(1-a)(1-b)(1-s)} & \frac{bz+s(1-a)(1-b)}{(1-a)(1-b)(1-s)} \\
0 & 0 & 0 & 0 & 0 & \frac{1}{1-s} & \frac{1}{1-s}
\end{pmatrix}
$$

TABLE 6.5

THE IMPLICATIONS OF THEORY 8D

THE EFFECT OF A UNIT INCREASE IN	THE EFFECT UPON						
	National product	Consumption	Investment	Net worth	Plant	Money	Bank loans
Consumer demand (ΔF_C)	$\frac{1}{1-a}$	$\frac{1}{1-a}$	0	0	0	$\frac{z(1-b)}{(1-a)(1-b)(1-s)}$	$\frac{z(1-b)}{(1-a)(1-b)(1-s)}$
Demand for plant (ΔF_K)	$\frac{1}{(1-a)(1-b)}$	$\frac{a}{(1-a)(1-b)}$	$\frac{1}{1-b}$	$\frac{1}{1-b}$	$\frac{1}{1-b}$	$\frac{z}{(1-a)(1-b)(1-s)}$	$\frac{z}{(1-s)(1-b)(1-s)}$
Bank reserves (ΔR)	$\frac{b}{(1-a)(1-b)}$	$\frac{ab}{(1-a)(1-b)}$	$\frac{b}{1-b}$	$\frac{b}{1-b}$	$\frac{1}{1-b}$	$\frac{bz+(1-a)(1-b)}{(1-a)(1-b)(1-s)}$	$\frac{bz+s(1-a)(1-b)}{(1-a)(1-b)(1-s)}$
Supply of loans (ΔF_L)	0	0	0	0	0	$\frac{1}{1-s}$	$\frac{1}{1-s}$

The implications of Theory 8D are given above in Table 6.5.

Problem 6.10 The historical note on Theory 8A referred to the theory of the "liquidity trap." In Theory 8D, a liquidity trap for businesses exists if $b = 0$; it exists for banks if $s = 0$. (1) What behavioral interpretations do you make for these assertions? (2) Construct Table 6.5 for the cases when $b = 0$, $s \neq 0$; where $s = 0$, $b \neq 0$; where $s = 0$, $b = 0$. Discuss the effects of Federal Reserve policies in these three cases.

Problem 6.11 Suppose Theory 8D is valid, and that the interest rate is (for some reason) fixed. Suppose Federal Reserve wishes to stabilize bank credit as a means of stabilizing the earnings of the commercial banks. What will it do to offset the effects of a \$1 decreases in consumer demand (F_C) and the demand for plant (F_K)?

Theory 8D, then, says that if banks lend *more* as the national income rises, so that $z > 0$, then increases in consumer demand (F_C) and in the demand for plant (F_K) increase the amount of money and of bank credit. This theory implies that the banking sector is influenced by nonbank conditions.

One interesting application of this theory involves a little "cheating." Usually we have treated all coefficients in our matrices as given numbers. Now suppose that z is not simply a given number, but that it changes according to the following rule:

(1) Banks have some estimate of what a proper, or "normal" level of the national product would be. Call this Y_N.

(2) If the national income is below Y_N, banks expect it to rise, and as it rises, they increase their loans. That is, $z > 0$, if $Y < Y_N$. If $Y = Y_N$, then $L = L_N$ is what banks consider to be a "normal" level of credit.

(3) If the national income is above Y_N, banks expect it to fall. As Y rises, they decrease their loans, because they expect that borrowers will be caught by a recession and unable to repay. That is, $z < 0$ if $Y > Y_N$.

If this theory were true, then when the national product went above Y_N, the money supply would start to drop. Literally, money would become "scarce" relative to goods, for all the other parts of the economy would continue to grow.

Actually, one of the things that has happened in all periods of prosperity since the World War II (1953, 1958, 1966, for example), is that it has become difficult for would-be borrowers to obtain loans. The amount of lending and credit do not actually decline, but they do not rise fast enough to satisfy borrowers. The Federal Reserve System has usually been blamed for this situation. The System usually replies that it is not to blame—it is not doing anything. This response is literally true. It does not satisfy the critics who say that if the System is doing nothing, then it should be doing something.

If, in fact, z changed sign in the manner suggested, there would exist a theory that explained why money became scarce when the national income rose "too much." This theory does not fully explain the "tight money" phenomenon: Businesses complain, in periods of tight money, that they actually must reduce investment. In Theory 8D, z does not appear in the first five columns of Table 6.5, so this effect would not occur. But the fact that we have $1/1 - a$ positive, and $z(1 - b)$ negative if $Y > Y_N$ suggests that one could develop a "tight money theory" by, for instance, putting $-z$ in place of a zero in row 1, column 7 of the matrix of Theory 8D.

SUMMARY AND CONCLUSIONS

This chapter has been concerned with putting together into the simplest possible form a theory involving the national product, nonbank balance sheets, and bank balance sheets. Taking Tiny Models 1, 2, and 4 as the starting point, it showed how to present simple theories based on the following social accounting scheme:

1. The national product equals consumption plus investment.
2. Nonbank assets consist of money and plant; the nonbank liabilities side of the balance sheet consists of bank loans and net worth.
3. Investment is the change in plant.
4. Bank assets consist of reserves and loans; bank liabilities consist of money (checking accounts).

There are seven variables to be accounted for, and, in addition to the four accounting definitions, it was necessary to supply statements describing the behavior of

5. Households (as buyers of consumer goods)
6. Businesses (as buyers of plant)
7. Banks (as lenders, and by inference, as holders of bank reserves)

In this very simple collection of theories, many interesting variables were omitted. Government, for example, is not mentioned. The bond market is not mentioned. Federal Reserve is not explicitly a part of the system. The interest rate was not considered. Clearly these theories have presented only the barest skeleton of an economy. But they have certain virtues: They all are about the same economic system, and the differences among them can therefore be precisely stated, as they are in Table 6.6.

TABLE 6.6

COMPARISON OF THE ASSUMPTIONS IN THEORIES 8A TO 8D

THEORY	CONSUMER SPENDING DEPENDS ON	BUSINESS DEMAND FOR PLANT DEPENDS ON	BANK SUPPLY OF LOAN DEPENDS ON
8A	Income	Assets	Money
8B	Money	Money	Money
8C	Income	Income	Money
8D	Income	Net worth	Money and income

The four theories presented do not exhaust all the possible permutations and combinations that could be prepared, but they do have rather different implications. In each theory, these are the same four independent factors: consumer demand (F_C), business demand for plant (F_K), bank reserves (R), which are assumed to be determined by Federal Reserve action, and the level of supply of loans (F_L), which is the "opposite" of the demand for excess reserves ($F_L = -F_R$, in terms of Tiny Model 4). Table 6.7 is a comparison of these four theories in one particular respect. It shows the theories for which a particular variable is affected by each of the four factors in the system.

TABLE 6.7

COMPARISON OF THE IMPLICATIONS OF THEORIES 8A TO 8D

Theories in which the given variable is affected by changes in the listed factor

CHANGES IN	NATIONAL PRODUCT	CON-SUMP-TION	INVEST-MENT	NET WORTH	PLANT	MONEY	BANK LOANS
sumer demand (F_C)	All	All	C	C	C	D	D
and for plant (F_K)	All	Not B	All	All	All	D	D
reserves R	Not C	Not C	Not C	All	Not C	All	All
ly of loans (F_L)	B	B	B	B	B	All	All

This particular collection of theories was selected for special study because they all involved the same variables and the same factors; and in each theory there are three behavioral coefficients in the matrix.[1] But the conclusions drawn are not the same. To claim that some one of these theories applies (say)

[1] Actually Theory 8D had four coefficients. We could suppress the fourth (reserve requirements) so that bank loans did not depend on reserves, and we would not alter the present conclusions.

to the United States economy of 1968, it is necessary to show that the implications of that theory are more applicable to that economy in that year. Then the implications of the alternatives consider the following possibilities: Either the supply of loans affects the national income, or it does not. If it does, 8B is the relevant theory, and the others are not. Either consumer demand and the demand for plant affect the banks, or they do not. If they do, 8D is the relevant theory and the others are not. Either consumer demand affects business investment or it does not. If it does, 8C is the relevant theory, and the others are not.

Again, suppose an increase of $1 in autonomous demand for plant, F_K. According to 8A, the national product will increase by $1/(1 - a)$; 8B states that it will increase by 1; 8C that it will increase by $1/(1 + x - a)$; and 8D that it will increase by $1/(1 - a)$. These numbers are all different, and even if $1/(1 - a) > 1$, it may be that $1/(1 + x - a) < 1$. Consequently, the prediction about the effect of an increase in the demand for plant is by no means independent of the behavioral assumptions made in the theory.

In this chapter, economic theory has made several proposed explanations of economic life. They are rather different proposals, and within the domain of economic theory it is not possible to prove that one of them is more relevant to a discussion of (say) the United States economy of the 1970s than the others.

This conclusion is a particularly important one for readers of economic theory textbooks to remember. Theorists have a tendency to feel that their theory is relevant because it has been worked out properly. Many textbook writers suggest that the answers to practical questions—including questions of government policy—can be decided on purely abstract grounds, merely because the assumptions made are plausible ones. Students who use such textbooks may not believe these conclusions, but they find them handy when it comes to preparing for tests.

Table 6.7 provides a handy first step toward checking on the universality of conclusions that might be reached on purely abstract grounds. Consider the question, "Does an increase in consumer demand (F_C) affect the national product?" In all four of the theories presented here, it does. Likewise an increase in the demand for plant (F_K) affects the national product in all cases. There are ten noncontroversial statements of this sort that can be made on the basis of Table 6.7.

Unfortunately this set of noncontroversial statements is not a very exciting one. Many economists and their students would like to make simple, straightforward statements about the effects of government policies on the economy. (Unfortunately, they are apt to select their favorite policy first, and find reasons to justify it later.) Arguments resembling various versions of Theory 8 are frequently used to justify or oppose programs of government spending and of Federal Reserve operations on purely abstract grounds.

Suppose that the reader has worked out Problems 6.2 and 6.5 and reached the conclusion that government spending is basically like investment. He then decides to ask whether increased government spending or additions to bank reserves will increase the level of consumption in an underdeveloped country.[2] What will he conclude?

Table 6.7 casts some light on this question. Increases in government spending will increase consumption unless Theory 8B holds. Increases in bank reserves will increase consumption unless Theory 8C holds. The peculiarity of Theory 8B is that consumer and business demand depends solely on the quantity of money and not on total income or total assets. The pecularity of Theory 8C is that consumer and business demand depends only on income and not on the money supply or total assets.

Table 6.7 thus indicates that the choice of a policy to achieve a particular objective depends in a meaningful way upon the behavior of consumers and businesses. It indicates that a policy that is suitable in one country or under one set of conditions may not be suitable for other countries or under other conditions. If several internally consistent theories can be constructed to represent an economy having a given set of social accounts, then the effectiveness of a policy recommendation cannot be decided on abstract, theoretical grounds alone. It is also necessary to have a knowledge of empirical economics —that is, a knowledge of how consumers, businesses, and banks actually behave.

Apart from the particular conclusions discussed in the last few paragraphs and the problems associated with them, this discussion should suggest a more general conclusion. Given any particular set of social accounts, it is possible to construct a collection of quite diverse theories about the variables in those accounts. For this reason, one must be suspicious of purely theoretical arguments that purport to explain the behavior of these variables. A particular theory may be ingenious and seem to be full of insight into the workings of the economy, but one must usually conclude that it is only one of a number of possible explanations. To determine which of the possibilities is the best explanation of the behavior of a given economy involves a study of the performance of that economy. In this chapter, Theories 8A, 8B, 8C, and 8D are possible explanations of the connection between money and the national product of an economy. But one would hesitate to select any one of them as relevant to the United States economy of 1970 without some detailed information of how the United States economy functioned in the period immediately before 1970. Theorists do not make that selection, but leave that task to specialists in economic history and statistics.

---

[2] Or he may be interested in finding a wartime policy that requires a reduction in consumption with an accompanying increase in government spending.

Problem 6.12 Discuss the questions "under what conditions are changes in government spending effective in bringing about changes in the national product?" and "under what conditions are changes in bank reserves effective in bringing about changes in the national product?" You cannot answer these questions conclusively, but Theories 8A to 8D offer various clues to the answer.

Problem 6.13 Suppose that Theory 8B is reformulated in such a way as to make consumer spending and business demand for plant depend on total assets, rather than on money supply. Construct a theory that says so, derive the inverse matrix, and tabulate the implications of this theory. Does this difference in assumptions lead to important differences in the conclusions reached in 8B about the workings of the economy?

Problem 6.14 Suppose that Theory 8D is reformulated in such a way as to make business demand for plant depend on total assets rather than on net worth. Construct a theory that says so, derive the inverse matrix, and tabulate the implications of this theory. Does this difference in assumptions lead to important differences in the conclusions reached in 8D about the workings of the economy?

Problem 6.15 At the beginning of this chapter, Theories 8A-8D were characterized in terms of the "influences" exerted by the various sectors upon the workings of the economy. Compare these characterizations with the Tables giving their respective implications, and give a precise definition of statements of the form "Sector X influences Sector Y."

Problem 6.16 Go back to the discussion of block matrices in Chapter 2, and note what is said about the inverses of block-triangular matrices. Formulate the statements you discussed in problem 6.15 in terms of block-triangular matrices. (*Hint:* In Theories 8A–8D the blocks are listed in the following order: income, nonbank balance sheet, bank balance sheet. But you can rearrange this ordering, provided you also rearrange the contents of the matrix.)

Problem 6.17 Bankers are never very popular, because everyone owes them money. But there are two current views about the commercial banks. (1) Money is indeed the root of all evil, and the banks are able to manipulate all economic affairs to their own ends. (2) Banks are really quite passive creatures, whose function is merely to respond to the changing needs which business has for money. Use Tables 6.6 and 6.7 to cast light on the conditions in which each of these views is defensible.

Problem 6.18 Under what conditions can a country devise some combination of changes in government spending and bank reserves that will hold the national income constant, increase investment, and decrease consumption. (This is a common objective of underdeveloped countries.)

Appendix to Chapter 6

THE INTEREST RATE AND THEORY 8

None of the versions of Theory 8 involved the interest rate, for the purpose of the chapter lay elsewhere. But it is a relatively simple matter to enlarge the theory a little, so as to permit an evaluation of the role of the interest rate. There are two ways to introduce it. It might be made an explicit variable, as in Theory 1. But it is unnecessary to introduce it in this fashion, if we play according to the rules of Theory 7, and derive it from other information contained in the theory. This second procedure will be followed here. In the first place, it is neater; in the second, it will be argued in Chapters 9 and 10 that theories of the kind we have been using do not handle prices very neatly. Even if this one price could be introduced explicitly, then, it seems better not to do so. The theory presented in this appendix is part of a larger theory invented by Mr. Atif Kubursi, and is included here with his permission. It has been put into a form resembling Theory 8A. It would also have been possible to use one of the other variants of Theory 8 as basis for it.

The essential feature of Theory 7 was its treatment of bond market prices as a measure of the interest rate. In this theory all credit is to be in the form of a *discount*. In this common banking arrangement, the borrower will sign a promise to pay the bank (say) $1,000 in one year's time. The bank then credits his account with (say) $940. The difference of $60.00 then represents the interest on the loan. If the interest rate were lower, the borrower would receive a larger amount in cash at the time the loan is made. In this arrangement, the bank acquires an asset of $940, the borrower a liability of $1,000.

The interest rate i on this hypothetical loan is given by the formula $(1 + i) = 100/940$. More generally we shall use the formula of Chapter 5,

$$(1 + i) = \left(\frac{L}{L'}\right)^{1/t}$$

where L is the borrower's liability and L' the bank's asset.

There are two lenders in this theory, the commercial banks and Federal Reserve. Since the government does not appear in this theory, we assume that Federal Reserve assets consist of discounts. That is, Federal Reserve buys a part of the loan paper owned originally by commercial banks.[3] We designate by L_B the earning assets of the commercial banks, by L_F the earning assets of Federal Reserve, and by L the debts of nonbank borrowers. Then the interest rate is given by

$$(1 + i) = \left(\frac{L}{L_B + L_F}\right)^{1/t}$$

The theory will tell the way L, L_B, and L_F are determined by the factors in the theory, and thus the interest can be given in terms of the factors.[4] The relation between the factors and the interest rate will not, of course, be linear.

The balance sheets in this theory will be the following

NONBANKS

Cash,	M	Debt,	L
Plant,	K	Net worth,	W

COMMERCIAL BANKS

Reserves,	R	Deposits,	M
Loans,	L_B		

FEDERAL RESERVE

Credit,	L_C	Reserves,	R

---

[3] Actually there is a "commercial paper" market in New York that functions in much the same way (for private borrowers) as does the Treasury Bill market. Federal Reserve does not participate actively in this market. In contrast, British firms do a large amount of borrowing by selling discount type, short-term obligations on an open market. The bank of England carries out large open-market operations in such discounts as well as in short-term Treasury bills. So the arrangements described here are more British than American. The difference, in this context, is not important.

[4] This formula contains the parameter t, the length of life of the loans. This is taken as given (a sort of factor). It is assumed that borrowing goes on in such a way as to leave the average length that loans remain outstanding unchanged. This is a simplification of the problem, of course.

'hus there are three accounting identities,

$$L + W = K + M$$
$$M = R + L_B$$
$$R = L_C$$

[he income identity of the model is familiar:

$$Y = C + I$$

[he statement about nonbank asset behavior is also familiar:

$$K = b(L + W) + F_K \qquad \text{from Tiny Model 2}$$

'lant and investment are related by the identity

$$I = K - K_0 \qquad \text{of Theory 8}$$

The remaining parts of the theory are a little different from what has gone)efore.

The banks are assumed to allocate a fraction, c, of their new loans to con- ;umers. The rest, $(1 - c)$, goes to businesses. Consumers do not borrow ınless they intend to buy goods with the proceeds of the loan. Thus consump- :ion is given by

$$C = aY + c(\Delta L_B + \Delta L_c) + F_c$$
$$= aY + c(L_B + L_c) - c(L_{BO} + L_{c0}) + F_c$$

Here L_B and L_c are the amount of loans held by the commercial banks and by Federal Reserve at the end of the period (year), and L_{BO} and L_{c0} are the cor- responding accounts at the beginning of the year. The latter are factors in the same sense as K_0, the initial stock of plant.

Nonbanks make a decision as to the amount of debt (L) they are willing to show on their balance sheet. This will be written

$$L = v(K + M) + F_L$$

This statement implies that there is a connection between savings and increase in debt. For

$$L + W = K + M,$$

so that

$$L = v(L + W) + F_L$$

$$L = \frac{v}{1 - v} W + \frac{1}{1 - v} F_L$$

and

$$\Delta L = \frac{v}{1 - v} \Delta W = \frac{v}{1 - v} S$$

If people used a part of their savings to *reduce* their debts, $v/1 - v$ would be negative. This would happen in one of two cases:

(1) $v < 0$. In this case, as people's assets rise, their debt declines.
(2) $v > 1$. In this case, as people's assets rise, their net worth declines.

The second possibility seems implausible. The first is possible, but it runs contrary to ordinary observation about consumer credit. Consumer credit, indeed, is a variable that has tended to rise steadily; in a period when consumer assets (cars, houses, appliances, and so on) have risen steadily, one would expect, if $v < 0$, for such loans to have fallen. The author's guess (it is no more than that) is that v is between zero and one. We will see that this guess is a useful one; it makes the interest rate, in this theory, conform to Tin Model 3.

In Theory 8, commercial banks were said to be governed by a need for reserves:

$$R = rM + F_R$$

where r is the reserve requirement and F_R is excess reserves. From this, w deduce that

$$L_B = (1 - r)M + F_{LB} = (1 - r)M - F_R$$

For computational reasons, it is simpler to use the relation $M = L_B + R$, s as to obtain

$$L_B = (1 - r)(L_B + R) + F_{LB}$$

$$rL_B = (1 - r)R + F_{LB}$$

$$L_B = \frac{1 - r}{r} R + \frac{1}{r} F_{LB}$$

$$= sR + F_B$$

thus

$$s = \frac{(1 - r)}{r}, (s + 1) = \frac{1}{r} \quad \text{and} \quad F_L = -\frac{1}{r} F_R.$$

In interpreting the results of the matrix inversion, an increase in F_L means a decrease in the excess reserves of the banking system.

Finally, Federal Reserve's open-market operations are given "from outside." That is, we simply write

$$F_F = L_e$$

Since $R = L_c$, this equivalent to Theory 8, where bank reserves were also determined from outside the system. Thus, rearranging these statements so as to obtain a block-triangular matrix,

$$(\mathbf{0}, \mathbf{F_c} - \mathbf{c}(\mathbf{L_{B0}} + \mathbf{L_{c0}}), \mathbf{K_0}, \mathbf{F_K}, \mathbf{0}, \mathbf{F_L}, \mathbf{0}, \mathbf{0}, \mathbf{F_B}, \mathbf{F_F})$$
$$= (\mathbf{Y}, \mathbf{C}, \mathbf{I}, \mathbf{K}, \mathbf{M}, \mathbf{L}, \mathbf{W}, \mathbf{R}, \mathbf{L_B}, \mathbf{L_c})$$
$$\times \begin{pmatrix} 1 & -a & 0 & 0 & 0 & 0 & 0 & 0 & 0 & 0 \\ -1 & 1 & 0 & 0 & 0 & 0 & 0 & 0 & 0 & 0 \\ -1 & 0 & -1 & 0 & 0 & 0 & 0 & 0 & 0 & 0 \\ 0 & 0 & 1 & 1 & -1 & -v & 0 & 0 & 0 & 0 \\ 0 & 0 & 0 & 0 & -1 & -v & 1 & 0 & 0 & 0 \\ 0 & 0 & 0 & -b & 1 & 1 & 0 & 0 & 0 & 0 \\ 0 & 0 & 0 & -b & 1 & 0 & 0 & 0 & 0 & 0 \\ 0 & 0 & 0 & 0 & 0 & 0 & -1 & -1 & -s & 0 \\ 0 & -c & 0 & 0 & 0 & 0 & -1 & 0 & 1 & 0 \\ 0 & -c & 0 & 0 & 0 & 0 & 0 & 1 & 0 & 1 \end{pmatrix}$$

It will be noted that the second component of the factor vector is the sum $F_c - cL_{B0} - cL_{c0}$. This will cause no complication, since if F_c changes while L_{B0} and L_{c0} are constant, it is as if L_{B0} and L_{c0} were not there.

The inverse form of the theory may then be calculated. This is straightforward enough, and it turns out that

$$
(\mathbf{Y}, \mathbf{C}, \mathbf{I}, \mathbf{K}, \mathbf{M}, \mathbf{L}, \mathbf{W}, \mathbf{R}, \mathbf{L_B}, \mathbf{L_c}) = (\mathbf{0}, \mathbf{F_c} - \mathbf{c}(\mathbf{L_{B0}} + \mathbf{L_{c0}}), \mathbf{K_0}, \mathbf{F_k}, \mathbf{0}, \mathbf{F_L}, \mathbf{0}, \mathbf{0}, \mathbf{F_B}, \mathbf{F_F})
$$

$$
\times \begin{pmatrix}
\frac{1}{1-a} & \frac{a}{1-a} & 0 & 0 & 0 & 0 & 0 & 0 & 0 & 0 \\
\frac{1}{1-a} & \frac{1}{1-a} & 0 & 0 & 0 & 0 & 0 & 0 & 0 & 0 \\
\frac{-1}{1-a} & \frac{-a}{1-a} & -1 & 0 & 0 & 0 & 0 & 0 & 0 & 0 \\
\frac{1}{(1-a)(1-b)} & \frac{a}{(1-a)(1-b)} & \frac{1}{1-b} & \frac{1}{1-b} & 0 & \frac{v}{1-b} & \frac{1-v}{1-b} & 0 & 0 & 0 \\
\frac{b}{(1-a)(1-b)} & \frac{ab}{(1-a)(1-b)} & \frac{b}{1-b} & \frac{b}{1-b} & 0 & \frac{bv}{1-b} & \frac{1-bv}{1-b} & 0 & 0 & 0 \\
0 & 0 & 0 & 0 & 0 & 1 & -1 & 0 & 0 & 0 \\
\frac{b}{(1-a)(1-b)} & \frac{ab}{(1-a)(1-b)} & \frac{b}{1-b} & \frac{b}{1-b} & 1 & \frac{v}{1-b} & \frac{1-v}{1-b} & 0 & 0 & 0 \\
\frac{-(1+s)[b+c(1-b)]}{(1-a)(1-b)} & \frac{-(1+s)[ab+c(1-b)]}{(1-a)(1-b)} & \frac{-b(1+s)}{1-b} & \frac{-b(1+s)}{1-b} & -(1+s) & \frac{-v(1+s)}{1-b} & \frac{-(1-v)(1+s)}{1-b} & -1 & -s & 0 \\
\frac{-b+c(1-b)}{(1-a)(1-b)} & \frac{c(1-b)-ab}{(1-a)(1-b)} & \frac{b}{1-b} & \frac{b}{1-b} & 1 & \frac{v}{1-b} & \frac{1-v}{1-b} & 0 & 1 & 0 \\
\frac{(1+s)[b+c(1-b)]}{(1-a)(1-b)} & \frac{(1+s[ab+c(1-b)]}{(1-a)(1-b)} & \frac{b(1+s)}{1-b} & \frac{b(1+s)}{1-b} & (1+s) & \frac{v(1+s)}{1-b} & \frac{(1-v)(1+s)}{1-b} & 1 & s & 1
\end{pmatrix}
$$

In preparing the table of implications, it is easy to replace $(1 + s)$ by $1/r$. It will be noted that this table closely resembles the table of implications of Theory 8A, as indeed is to be expected from its behavioral assumptions.

TABLE A6.1

THE IMPLICATIONS OF THE THEORY[a]

THE EFFECT UPON	THE EFFECT OF A UNIT CHANGE IN			
	Consumer demand (ΔF_C)	Demand for plant (ΔF_K)	Supply of loans (ΔF_B)	Open market operations (ΔF_F)
Y	$\frac{1}{1-a}$	$\frac{1}{(1-a)(1-b)}$	$\frac{b-c(1-b)}{(1-a)(1-b)}$	$\frac{b+c(1-b)}{r(1-a)(1-b)}$
C	$\frac{1}{1-a}$	$\frac{a}{(1-a)(1-b)}$	$\frac{c(1-b)-ab}{(1-a)(1-b)}$	$\frac{(ab+c)}{r(1-a)(1-b)}$
I	0	$\frac{1}{1-b}$	$\frac{b}{1-b}$	$\frac{b}{r(1-b)}$
K	0	$\frac{1}{1-b}$	$\frac{b}{1-b}$	$\frac{b}{r(1-b)}$
M	0	0	1	$\frac{1}{r}$
L	0	$\frac{v}{1-b}$	$\frac{v}{1-b}$	$\frac{v}{r(1-b)}$
W	0	$\frac{1-v}{1-b}$	$\frac{1-v}{1-b}$	$\frac{1-v}{r(1-b)}$
R	0	0	0	1
L_B	0	0	1	$\frac{r}{1-r}$
L_C	0	0	0	1

[a] A unit increase in F_L increases L by 1, decreases W by 1 and affects nothing else.

The interest rate can now be expressed in terms of the factors:

$$(1 + i) = \left(\frac{L}{L_B + L_c}\right)^{1/t}$$

becomes

$$(1 + i) = \left(\frac{\frac{v}{1-b} F_K + F_L + \frac{v}{1-b} F_B + \frac{v}{(1-b)r} F_F}{F_L + (1 + s)F_F}\right)^{1/t}$$

If excess reserves (F_R) are now inserted into this formula in place of F_B,

$$(1+i) = \left(\frac{\frac{v}{1-b} F_K + F_L + \frac{v}{r(1-b)}(F_F - F_R)}{\frac{1}{r}[F_F - F_R]} \right)^{1/t}$$

$$= \left(\frac{\frac{vr}{1-b} F_K + rF_L}{F_F - F_R} + \frac{v}{1-b} \right)^{1/t}$$

From this formula, we conclude that the interest rate will *increase* if there is

(1) an increase in the demand for plant (F_K)
(2) an increase in the willingness of nonbanks to go into debt (F_L)
(3) a decrease in the assets of Federal Reserve (F_F)
(4) an increase in excess reserves (F_R)

This result is quite consistent with Tiny Model 3, and with economic thinking generally. To obtain it, it was not necessary to introduce the interest rate as a separate variable. The economy will behave as if Tiny Model 3 were valid, even though none of the behavioral statements of the theory made any mention of the interest rate.

Even though this theory makes exactly the predictions about the interest rate that most economists would expect, it is a theory that they would not like. The reason is that no behavioral statement contains the interest rate; no part of the economy explicitly considers the interest rate in making its decisions. It is a well-established economic doctrine that investment decisions, lending decisions, and borrowing decisions do take the interest rate into account.

This theory, then, is placed in an appendix so as to spare the sensibilities of professors. It is worth including to show students (who have not yet formed strong attachments) that we can explain variations in the interest rate in a theory that does not seem to discuss it. This is a useful piece of knowledge. It is particularly useful, since (as we shall see in Chapter 9) theories that include prices are generally messy theories. Macroeconomics has not learned how to handle prices in any neat way. It is most useful to know that within a purely macroeconomic context, where only values are ostensibly involved, one can deduce something about the behavior of interest rates, which are one of the prices most discussed by economists.

7

An Interim Review

The preceding chapters have presented a systematic approach to macroeconomic analysis. An orderly method has been devised:

(1) A section of the social accounting system is selected for study;

(2) The accounting identities are supplemented by behavioral assertions, presented as linear equations;

(3) The variable-into-factor mappings, which are formulations with intuitive economic content, are inverted by a calculation on the matrices in question.

(4) From the factor-into-variable mappings, it is possible to tabulate all the (comparative statics) implications of the theory, and hence to determine the effect of a change in any factor upon any variable of the system.

(5) Where partial theories exist for individual sections of the social accounts, it is possible to prepare unified theories that treat the individual sectors as parts of an integrated economy.

Naturally, the amount of detail in any portion of the social accounts has been kept small. Large and complicated classifications of expenditures, assets, and so on are necessary for advanced research. Details, however, frequently obscure the basic structure of arguments, and an attempt has been made to hold down the number of variables in any theory.

Because the work in these chapters has been extremely compact and formal, some readers may get a feeling that everything has been said that could be said; others may feel that all the interesting material has been left out, because of the nature of the treatment. It is therefore worth exploring in a little more depth several aspects of what has been done, so as to make clear what has not yet been done.

THEORETICAL DEFINITIONS AND SOCIAL ACCOUNTING

Every macroeconomic theory includes a system of social accounts. Each system of social accounts involves aggregation of economic units. Whenever economic units are aggregated into groups, a rule is applied that defines "final" income and product in the income statement and the assets and liabilities accounts in the balance sheet. When the income or balance sheet is the subject of a theory, the subtotals of the account in question are added together in a purely arithmetical operation. As examples of such addition, we note

$$Y = C + I \qquad \text{(in Tiny Model 1 and Theories 1 and 2)}$$

$$Y = C + I + G \qquad \text{(in Theories 3, 4, 5)}$$

If foreign trade were taken into account, we might have

$$Y = C + I + G + X \qquad (X = \text{exports})$$

If banks were considered to be distinct from other businesses, we would have

$$Y = C + I + G + X + B \qquad (B = \text{purchases by banks of national product})$$

Theorists are free to perform such additions, because they simply *define* the national product as the sum of the outputs of individual sectors. The moment that economists try to confirm a theory by matching it against the record of economic events, they must associate a symbol (for instance Y) with some set of statistical data. Naturally, it is then important to know how the data were assembled, since it is important that the data be as close as possible to theoretical specifications. A trivial example would be the following: If theory asserts that

$$C = a(Y - T) + F_c$$

o that consumption depends on personal income after taxes, it is important that data be as close to $(Y - T)$ as possible. Naturally, it may not always be easy to determine which taxes are paid by households and which are not.

In some cases, datà specified by theory are not available at all. It has been assumed in some of our theories that

$$C = vM + F_c$$

That is, consumption depends on cash balances in the hands of households. In fact, it may be difficult or impossible to separate the cash balances of households from the cash balances of the rest of the economy. In this case, one might be able to use the *total* money supply as a "surrogate" or "proxy" variable for the unknown variable "money held by households." It would not be sensible to follow this procedure if the theory in question predicted that money held by households and money held by businesses was expected to change in opposite directions in response to factor changes.

One important fact to bear in mind is that the *measure* one obtains of total income or of total assets is not independent of the sectoral structure of the theory. As an example, consider the national product. This total is derived by an aggregation process, in which sales by one economic unit to other economic units *in the same sector* are eliminated as double-counting. (Coal used by steel mills is subtracted from the sum of "sales by coal mines" plus "sales by steel mills" in obtaining "sales by coal and steel mills viewed as a single industry.") The items that would be double-counted are then considered as "intermediate" products, not the "final products," which appear in the gross national product.

The effect of reducing the number of sectors listed explicitly in a theory should therefore be to increase the amount of "intermediate product" and to reduce the "final product" of the gross national product. Thus, suppose that "business" consists of three industries, A, B and C. The total sales of industry i (i = A, B, C) is S_i, and sales by i to j (i, j = A, B, C) is S_{ij}. If the theory specifies that each industry is a separate sector, then their combined final output is

$$S_A + S_B + S_C$$

If another theory combines industries A and B into a single sector, then the measure of their final output is

$$(S_A - S_{AB}) + (S_B - S_{BA}) + S_C$$

which is obviously less than the first sum. Finally, if industries A, B, C are all in the same sector, their final output is

$$(S - S_{AB} - S_{AC}) + (S_B - S_{BA} - S_{BC}) + (S_C - S_{CA} - S_{CB})$$

which is obviously less than the second sum.

For this reason, published social accounting statistics are never suitable for every theory. In practice, those who prepare the statistics use the most common theoretical structure as the basis for their tabulations. Economists working on any other theoretical structure must therefore reconstruct the social accounting statistics to suit the specifications of their theory.

The details of the statistical adjustments are apt to be intricate. The conceptual adjustments are much easier to understand, although they are not usually discussed in theoretical books. Nevertheless, theorists should be aware that when they alter the sectoral composition of an economy, they alter the set of data needed to test any theory. The variable designated (say) by Y is not always the same in all theories.

Problem 7.1 Usually, national income theories deal with "consumption." Suppose a particular theory assumes that there are two kinds of consumer goods, "durable goods" and "nondurable goods." What adjustments would have to be made in the social accounts?

Problem 7.2 The United States national income statistics include banks as part of the business sector. (The theories in this book assume that banks have balance sheets but no income statements. This is the usual practice.) Suppose an income theory required a discussion of banks' contribution to national income. How would the national income statistics have to be adjusted?

MACROECONOMICS AND ECONOMIC DEVELOPMENT

Macroeconomic theory was developed in large part because economists needed a way of predicting the short-run effects of consumer, business, government, and bank behavior. The variants of Theory 8 indicate that this sort of prediction can be accomplished in a number of ways. There is no virtue in taking a Gallup Poll of economists to determine which view is the most popular. Presumably, at most one of these views is right. It is not now possible to say which one is right.

The social accounting system is in some respects a measure of the development of an economy. Suppose the population of a country to be P; then C/P, consumption per person, is a measure of the standard of individual welfare.[1] Since, for the economy as a whole, income equals output, Y/P, or output per person, is a measure of "productivity."[2]

---

[1] It is not a perfect measure, for not all individuals have the same consumption. Barring questions of income distribution, however, C/P is an indicator of the standard of living.

[2] It is not a perfect measure. If population grew by a small amount, $\Delta P = kP$, where k indicates the proportion of increase in population, it is not at all clear that Y would change so that $\Delta Y = kY$.

The development of a country can also be measured by its assets. For instance, the United States is more developed than (say) Brazil not only because it *makes* more goods per year than Brazil, but also because it *has* more plant and equipment (and more houses, automobiles, and so on) in its assets than Brazil.

It is natural, then, to want to use the social accounting system as a basis for the analysis of economic development. Since the various theories presented here deal with social accounting systems, it is natural to wonder to what extent they can be applied to development problems. The answer is simple: The macroeconomic theories in this book do not apply to development problems in any simple way (this is a pity, because development seems a natural extension of the analysis prescribed here). It is instructive to consider the various versions of Theory 8 in the context of economic development.

All versions of Theory 8 make use of the statement that $K = K_0 + I$, which asserts that investment is the same thing as the change in plant. This statement would not be realistic if the theories dealt with the national income accounts in detail. Investment in those accounts includes changes in inventory as well as changes in plant. It would not be a realistic statement unless it specified some treatment of depreciation, for plant changes because of depreciation as well as because of investment. Still, the definition has been a useful one, for it has provided the simplest possible link between the income and nonbank balance sheet accounts.

At successive periods of time, the numbers represented in the statement $K = K_0 + I$ would naturally change. For the years 1968, 1969, and 1970, for example, we would have

$$K_{1968} = K_{1967} + I_{1968}$$
$$K_{1969} = K_{1968} + I_{1969}$$
$$K_{1970} = K_{1969} + I_{1970}$$

in every theory containing K_0 as the ith component of its vector of factors, a comparison of the factors in these three years would yield

$$(\mathbf{F}_{1,1968} \cdots \mathbf{K}_{1967}, \mathbf{F}_{i+1,1968} \cdots \mathbf{F}_{n,1968})$$
$$(\mathbf{F}_{1,1969} \cdots \mathbf{K}_{1968}, \mathbf{F}_{i+1,1969} \cdots \mathbf{F}_{n,1969})$$
$$(\mathbf{F}_{1,1970} \cdots \mathbf{K}_{1969}, \mathbf{F}_{i+1,1970} \cdots \mathbf{F}_{n,1970})$$

Suppose that all other factors affecting the economy are constant, but investment takes place, so that $K_{1969} > K_{1968} > K_{1967}$. Then as the amount of plant in the economy changes, the variables in the economy will also change. In this sense, the growth of the economy affects economic processes.

Roughly speaking, the reason for this phenomenon is the following. Suppose that businesses want some particular amount of plant, $\bar{K}$. To obtain it, they must supplement what they have, K_0, by new investment. The more plant they have already, the less they must buy to obtain what they want. The less they must buy, the less investment there will be, and therefore the less will be the national product.

This proposition may be stated more exactly. In theories 8A to 8D, K_0 appears as a factor. The other factors were consumer demand (F_C), demand for plant (F_K), bank reserves (R), and the supply of loans (F_L). Suppose that all of these other factors are fixed, and that in 1968 there is investment equal to I_{1968}. Then the economy in 1969 will be different from that in 1968 because (and only because) K_0 has changed. Moreover, $\Delta K_0 = I_{1968}$. The effect of this change on all the variables of the system is measured by the elements in row 3 of the inverse matrix of the four respective variants of the theory. These elements are given in Table 7.1. Obviously, if any investment takes place in period t, then unless at least one factor rises in period $(t + 1)$, the level of economic activity will fall in period $(t + 1)$

TABLE 7.1

EFFECT OF ONE DOLLAR'S INVESTMENT IN PERIOD t UPON THE VARIABLES OF THE ECONOMY IN PERIOD $(t+1)$, ACCORDING TO THEORIES 8A TO 8D.

THEORY	THE EFFECT UPON						
	National product	Consumption	Investment	Net worth	Plant	Money	Ba[nk] loa[ns]
8A	$\frac{-1}{1-a}$	$\frac{-a}{1-a}$	-1	0	0	0	0
8B	-1	0	-1	0	0	0	0
8C	$\frac{-1}{1+x-a}$	$\frac{-a}{1+x-a}$	$\frac{-(1-a)}{1+x-a}$	$\frac{-x}{1+x-a}$	$\frac{-x}{1+x-a}$	0	0
8D	$\frac{-1}{1-a}$	$\frac{a}{1-a}$	-1	0	0	$\frac{-z}{(1-a)(1-s)}$	$\frac{z}{(1-a)(}$

Suppose Theory 8A holds. Then if investment in period t is I_t, $\Delta K_{t+1} = I_t$, and $\Delta Y_{t+1} = \frac{-1}{1-a} I_t$, if all other factors are constant. If Theory 8B holds, $\Delta Y_{t+1} = -I_t$, and so on. The magnitude of the decline varies from theory to theory, but a decline is nevertheless present in all of the theories. Of course, the factor K_0 is not the only factor in the theory. If the levels of consumption (F_C), demand for plant (F_K), bank reserves (R) or supply of loans (F_L) increased, the decrease brought about by the increase in plant (K_0) might be offset. But the whole point of our classification of objects into factors and variables was to list those things (the factors) that could be considered capable of independent variation. It is a change in the underlying argument if now we supplement our theory to say that these factors vary in such a way as to offset changes in plant. Why should they?

To explain why the factors should (or rather, why they might) change in such a way is to introduce a bit more depth into theories than we have so far had. All of the theories so far considered have been most useful in talking about month-to-month and year-to-year changes. But Table 7.1 raises a big historical problem: We look at the world today, and compare it with the world in 1900. Obviously our cities, and our factories have grown enormously in numbers and in size. Our farms now use vast amounts of machinery. Plant, which is K_0 in Theory 8, has grown tremendously. If Theory 8 were correct, income should have dropped enormously since 1900. Since it has not dropped, should we discard Theory 8?

The answer to this question is simple: Of course we should drop Theory 8, when we have a better one to take its place. But it is not easy to construct new and better theories. This book is supposed to be a book for beginners, and the publisher feels it should be kept simple. For this reason, we leave the more difficult subjects for more advanced courses. It is possible, nevertheless, to speak in a simple way about what a more satisfactory theory would have to explain. As it turns out, this discussion gives some ideas about what happens when an economy like that of the United States turns from being a rural to being an urban society, and when it absorbs a vast increase in knowledge such as that which has taken place during the course of this century.

Decreases in national product are associated with decreases in employment. Why did not the vast increase in American plant after 1900 bring about an enormous increase in unemployment? As a matter of fact, this is just what happened, from one point of view. When a business reduces its output, it may either lay some workers off, or make all workers work shorter hours. In 1900, American workers had a 60-hour week and in the 1960s a 40-hour week. This reduction in employment is "as if" one-third of the 1900 labor force had been discharged, but with the social effects distributed among everyone.

In 1900 most children left school after a few years. In the 1960s most children completed high school. In 1900 fewer people lived until age 65, but those who did continued to be employed. In the 1960s most people of age 65 and over were retired on some sort of pension.

In other words, one of the predictions of Table 7.1 is not wrong. The increase in American plant has in fact reduced employment very considerably. It has not produced hardship, because, in the main, people have been willing to stay in school longer, to work shorter hours, and to retire sooner than formerly. Is this rise in "laziness" a good thing? It has certainly avoided the problems associated with unemployment.

When Table 7.1 was discussed, it was shown that not all investment decreased income, but only "net" investment—the difference between total construction of new plant and depreciation on existing plant. If one could imagine that whenever investment increased there was a corresponding increase in the wearing out of plant, it would be impossible to increase the amount of plant in existence. Why might this sort of thing come about?

Problem 7.3 Consider the consumption function $C = aY + fM + F_C$. Make a plausible argument about how a, f, and F_C might change in an economy with a growing population. Would these changes accentuate or reduce the downward tendency of the national income produced by increases in K_0?

Problem 7.4 In Theory 5 the factor vector includes the symbol M_0, the quantity of money in the preceding period; and B_0, the amount of bonds outstanding in the preceding period. Use the reasoning of this section concerning K_0 to interpret the meaning of "changes in M_0 and in B_0." What practical questions of government policy may be discussed in terms of these changes?

The theories in this book have associated the demand for plant with the demand for investment, since investment is the same thing as the change in plant. But can there be an economic event that causes business to say, "I do not necessarily want more plant than formerly, but I do want to tear down Factory A and build Factory B in its place"? If such decisions could be made, then investment today would not decrease income tomorrow, as Table 7.1 says it should.

The kind of decision described does occur whenever an invention is put to economic use. Such events are called *innovations*. Usually, an innovation introduces a new kind of output or a new kind of process. The accounting system used here does not report innovations. It says merely that new goods will either be part of consumption, part of investment, or part of government purchases. Moreover, the business that introduces a new product may have no intention of tearing down any factory buildings itself—indeed, it may be a new firm with no old assets. But if the new firm is making something better than what was available formerly, the effect may be to close down older firms. From the economy's point of view, the innovation meant setting up a new factory and knocking down an old factory. Moreover, from the economy's point of view, the "old factory" that is knocked down is not necessarily of exactly the same size as the new factory. It might be "larger" or "smaller."

The statements about consumption made in the various theories considered in earlier chapters all consist of two parts. In part, consumption is said to vary with income, or cash balances, or wealth. In part, consumption is autonomous, simply independent of anything else. In this sense, the term F_C

appearing in all the statements about consumption is a measure of the standard of living that Americans "insist upon," whether they can "afford" it or not. The circumstances in which Americans live are today very different from those of 1900. Houses are no longer simply large, waterproof boxes, but rather containers for considerable amounts of complicated machinery, which replaces the labor of domestic servants and even alters the climate of the dwelling. Americans are today notoriously devoted to automobiles—in a way that seems to be independent of income or wealth. In 1900 they were not. This list of twentieth-century changes could be multiplied. It seems to amount to a long list of reasons why F_C is larger than it used to be. To some extent, these changes in F_C have to do with scientific advance. As new products have been introduced into the economy, consumer demand has changed. If this view is correct, scientific advance is something that affects both consumers and businesses. But in the earlier discussions, F_C and F_K, or F_C and F_I were thought of as being quite independent of each other. Perhaps this view is too simple.

Finally, the various versions of Theory 8 all list bank reserves as an independent factor. (Other theories have listed government spending and tax rates as independent factors.) This way of treating government makes sense if we want to isolate the response pattern of the economy in order to examine it. In principle, government agencies operate in quite different ways from businesses. When we treat these agencies as "factors" rather than as "variables" we merely recognize this fact.

But look back to the simplest version of the theory of money: $MV = PQ$. If the economy is growing, then Q is increasing. If savings tend to decline, as is suggested by the increase in consumption (F_C), then V will tend to rise. But it may well be that V does not rise as fast as Q. In this case, unless the quantity of money (M) rises, prices (P) will fall. It seems to be a well established political fact that the community objects to falling prices.

Problem 7.5 Explain why people who have debts may be worse off if their incomes and the prices of goods decline proportionately.

If the conditions of the last paragraph hold, then one may regard the Federal Reserve System as under pressure to expand bank reserves as growth takes place. If the System does not do so, then prices may fall, and political difficulties may arise. But to say this is to say that this government agency, and perhaps other government agencies, too, are not really independent factors. Perhaps a good deal of their activity is merely a response to changes in the environment. It is certainly true that in the early 1930s increased government spending took place because the government "had to" do something about the unemployed. President Hoover, in fact, was defeated in the election of 1932 because he had evidently "not done enough." Later presidents have been much more attentive to economic conditions, and in fact an act passed in 1946 created a Council of Economic Advisors to the president to try to make sure that the government would respond to changes in economic conditions.

Where government responds more-or-less automatically to changes in the economy, its actions are like those of a variable in the theory and not like those of a factor. The theories presented so far have treated the Federal Reserve System and the government as if they were able to take action without being forced to do so, or without being impeded by anything else in the economy. This assumption is oversimplified, as every elected and appointed government official knows. And it may be another reason why our theories do not work well in the analysis of development.

Theory 8 was an improvement over the earlier theories in the book, in the sense that it combines income, asset, and banking system accounts into a single theory. In this sense it is "complete," even though it is less detailed than the "sectoral" theories, such as those dealing with fiscal policy, the banking system, and so on. The great virtue of such a complete theory is that it enables one to determine separately the influences of the consumer, business, banking, and Federal Reserve sectors on all parts of the economy. Moreover, the structure of Theory 8 is so flexible that a variety of behavior patterns can be examined.

But despite this formal improvement, there is no version of Theory 8 that will explain economic development. It does not really make sense to say that as the productive capacity (K_0) of a country rises, its income falls. The experience of the United States since 1900 is just the opposite; and international comparisons of developed and undeveloped countries at any date (say 1968) do not bear out the prediction. It must therefore be that the macroeconomics useful in analyzing economic development must proceed along quite different lines.

Let us return to Table 7.1 and consider depreciation (a subject on which very little has been said). If some fraction d of plant wears out during the period, then in period t depreciation will be dK_t; if I_t of new plant is bought during this period, then the increase in plant is given by $\Delta K_{t+1} = I_t - dK_t$. In this case, $\Delta Y_{t+1} = \frac{-1}{1-a}(I_t - dK_t)$ for Theory 8A. The more rapidly plant depreciates, the greater will d be, and the less the decline in income resulting from a given investment program. Indeed, if investment is represented as a rate of growth in plant ($I_t = eK_t$), then $\Delta Y_{t+1} = \frac{-(e-d)}{1-a} K_t = \frac{d-e}{1-a} K_t$. For any given plant K_t, the greater d is, and the less e is, the smaller will be the fall in Y.

Naturally, one does not advise business to let its plant wear out as rapidly as possible (so that d will be large). That advice would not be in the interests of business. Naturally, business's costs are lower (and profits higher) if plant wears out slowly than if it wears out fast. And one does not advise business to invest as little as possible. For the individual business, small investment means little growth. For the economy as a whole, small investment *today* means low incomes *today*. Rather, the point is that if the various versions of Theory 8 are correct, the more investment is carried on today, the lower income may be expected to be in the future.

Problem 7.6 The identity $K_0 = K - I$ appears in all versions of Theory 8. Replace this identity by $(1 - d) K_0 = K - I$, where d is the rate of depreciation; and construct new versions of the tables of implications of Theories, 8A–8D. What difference does it make to the theories, now that the depreciation rate has been taken into account?

Observe that this result is not stated as an observed fact, but rather as a theoretical prediction. It is an example of a certain number of gloomy propositions in economics, which have led it to be called the "dismal science" by Carlyle. Carlyle was talking about another gloomy proposition by Thomas Malthus—perhaps the most famous of its kind. Malthus said in the early 1800s that if the population started off from a level of P_0 and grew at a *rate* of r per year for t years, it would be $P_0(1 + r)^t$. If the food supply started off from a level of F_0, and grew by an amount of f per year, then at the end of t years it would be $F_0 + ft$. The food supply per person would be

$$F/P = (F_0 + ft)/P_0(1 + r)^t$$

The larger t becomes, the less F/P will be, so that eventually we will all be at the brink of starvation.

This proposition led Malthus to advocate birth control, and his opponents to suffer greatly. The main objection to it is that it is not true. In fact, food production has not grown more slowly than population over the past few centuries. Only in recent years have demographers been able to point to a real danger of food shortages for the world—and even here, the imbalance is concentrated in Latin America and certain parts of Asia.

But even if Malthus's proposition has not proved valid, it has stimulated a great deal of study of population problems by raising an interesting question.

The assertion that the more investment there is today the less income there will be tomorrow has also raised an interesting question. Known as the Harrod-Domar question, after the two economists who first discovered it, this question has helped to integrate income and balance sheet analysis, and thus has played an important part in the development of macroeconomics. Because it shows that macroeconomics does not explain some important aspects of the economic development of countries over prolonged periods of time, it helps to set forth a program for future economic research.

MACROECONOMIC ADJUSTMENTS

The general view of a theory in this book is that it provides a one-to-one mapping of factors into variables. Given a theory with behavioral content, say

$$\mathbf{M} : \mathbf{V} \to \mathbf{F}$$

there is an associated "inverse" mapping,

$$\mathbf{M}^{-1} : \mathbf{F} \to \mathbf{V}$$

which gives the implications of the theory. In particular, where the mappings $\mathbf{M}$ and $\mathbf{M}^{-1}$ are linear, then

$$\mathbf{M}^{-1} : \Delta\mathbf{F} \to \Delta\mathbf{V}$$

The theorist can thus predict the consequences of each change in factors upon the variables of the theory. This is a very tidy way to organize macroeconomic reasoning.

This general reasoning is open to strong objections. The most cogent of these are that

(1) This specification of a theory does not take any account of timing requirements, and

(2) This specification assumes that adjustments to factor changes are instantaneous.

It is instructive to see what these objections do to the calm certainty with which we have reached conclusions in earlier theories.

Consider two propositions that have appeared in various places so far:

$$C = aY + F_c$$

$$C = vM + F_c$$

These say, respectively, that consumers look at their income and at their cash balances when they decide on their current consumption. How are these statements to be interpreted?

Suppose consumers look at their incomes. Income is actually received on stipulated days (for example, Friday afternoon, the last day of the month, and so on). It is not true that spending on any day depends on income earned that day, for on most days no income is actually received. Moreover, many people do not have fixed incomes: they may have variable amounts of overtime pay, they may be paid on a piecework basis. In either case, a worker may not know with certainty what his next paycheck will be. In this case, his current spending must depend either on his *last* paycheck or on some *expectations* concerning the next one.

Suppose consumers look at their cash balances. In this case, their cash balance will vary between high points (on days when paychecks are received) and low points (the day before paychecks are received). However, their daily spending will not ordinarily be bunched according to this particular pattern. Consequently, the expression $C = vM + F_c$ will not ordinarily apply well to daily spending, as related to daily bank balances. It may apply with more precision to monthly spending and some "average cash balance" or "minimum cash balance."

Consequently, when theorists try to say what they really mean by statements such as these consumption functions, they necessarily become involved in specifying something about the timing of the several variables that appear in the statements. The more complicated the timing problems involved, the more the theory will differ from the very simple statements given in the theories of Chapters 3 to 7.

Now consider the effects of a change in factors. At some date t there is a vector $\mathbf{F}_t$ of factors. At some later date t' there is another vector $\mathbf{F}_{t'}$. Shall one assume that the economy makes an abrupt jump from $\mathbf{F}_t$ to $\mathbf{F}_{t'}$? Or is it rather the case that at some intermediate date t'', there is an intermediate vector $\mathbf{F}_{t''}$, somewhere "between" $\mathbf{F}_t$ and $\mathbf{F}_{t'}$?

If the change from $\mathbf{F}_t$ to $\mathbf{F}_{t'}$ is gradual, then there will presumably be some gradual change in the variables, from $\mathbf{V}_t$ to $\mathbf{V}_{t'}$. But even if the change in $\mathbf{F}$ is abrupt, it might still be the case that the variables change only gradually. In this case, at time t'', we would observe variables $\mathbf{V}_{t''}$, which differ both from the old equilibrium $\mathbf{V}_t$ and the new equilibrium $\mathbf{V}_{t'}$.

If the change from $\mathbf{F}_t$ to $\mathbf{F}_{t'}$ is gradual, there may be no objection to saying that if we observe a factor vector $\mathbf{F}_{t''}$ and an associated variable $\mathbf{V}_{t''}$, then these two are related by the relation $\mathbf{M}^{-1}$. The economy moves gradually along a set of equilibrium points. But if the economy has an adjustment process which takes time to work itself out, then some observations (perhaps all observations) we might make are of disequilibrium values of $\mathbf{V}$. That is, at an intermediate date t'', we observe a $\mathbf{V}_{t''}$ which is *not* the image $\mathbf{F}_{t''}\mathbf{M}^{-1}$ of the factor vector $\mathbf{F}_{t''}$. Rather, it is the resultant of two separate forces: the equilibrium $\mathbf{F}_{t'}\mathbf{M}^{-1}$, toward which it is moving, and also some adjustment mechanism which acts to determine the speed at which the variables move toward the new equilibrium.

Theorists also recognize that "events that never happen" can appear as factors influencing economic activity. Imagine that investment is influenced by taxes (Theory 4). Congress is debating a law to reduce taxes. Expecting the passage of the law, business increases investment. At the last moment, Congress votes down the reduction. Investment will presumably fall again. Meanwhile, however, a law that was never passed will have influenced business spending, through an expectations mechanism.

The theories presented here have bypassed all questions of timing and expectations. The appendix to this chapter will show a variant of Theory 8 that takes timing problems into account in a very simple way.

Meanwhile, consider a very simple example of how timing problems might interfere with the interpretation one makes of a theory. Suppose that the Federal Government (for some foolish reason) based its decisions on Theory 8. That is, the Federal Government changes its spending, and Federal Reserve the level of bank reserves on the basis of that theory. One day, then, all these important people come to work, and observe that an increase in productive capacity (K) is taking place. They look at Table 7.1 to determine what will happen. They therefore predict a decline in national product. Knowing Theory 3 and Theory 8, they say that increased government spending will increase the national product; so will increases in bank reserves—unless 8C is valid. We suppose 8C to be invalid.

The other variants of Theory 8 all say that the more investment there is in period t, the more the national product falls in period $(t + 1)$. That is, the change in plant in period t is associated with changes in product in period $(t + 1)$. If Federal Reserve wants to stabilize income, it must make changes in reserves proportional to changes in plant. That is, changes in reserves should be proportional to investment. The more investment there is in period t, the more reserves should be increased in period $(t + 1)$.

Now let us go back to the theory of fiscal policy. The discussion of Theory 3 led us to the conclusion that if the government wishes to stabilize the national product, one way of doing so is to vary government spending so as to offset declines in investment. In other words, when investment falls, government spending should rise. When investment rises, government spending should fall.

The prescription of Theory 3 is almost exactly the opposite of that given in the preceding paragraph. One argument says that if investment rises in period t, reserves and/or government spending should *rise* in period $(t + 1)$; the other says that if investment rises in period t, reserves and/or government spending should *fall* in period (t). We have to say "almost," because one argument relates to time period t, the other to period $(t + 1)$.

Should bank reserves rise or fall when investment rises, if the economy is to be stabilized?

This question enables us to clarify the difference between theoretical economists and applied economists. The theoretical economist will think: "Aha! I need a theory in which time plays a part. Presumably, I should not think of bank reserves as a number R, but as something that varies with time, $R(t)$; and I want a time pattern for $R(t)$ that will leave Y a constant (or maybe increasing at a steady rate), even though plant (K_0) is increasing. Is there any $R(t)$ with this property?"

The applied economist will think along different lines. Suppose, for example, that he is advising the Federal Reserve System. Then he will use a theory such as Theory 8B as a guide, but as nothing more. This theory tells him to buy government bonds when the national product is falling, in order to offset the decline, or to sell if it is rising "too fast." A theory such as Theory 7 will tell him what to do *if* he wants certain changes in interest rates. But he does not need to know the numerical values of the coefficients in the theories (a, b, s, x, z, and so on). He does not have to know whether the coefficients are fixed or whether they are changing. He judges when to start (and stop) making purchases by looking directly at the variables in the economy. In the particular example under discussion, the dynamic process underlying changes may not particularly matter to central bankers.

It is of scientific interest to know what the numerical values of the coefficients of a theory may be and how they have changed. But for many practical purposes, these coefficients are "only" of scientific interest. Applied economists can frequently work quite effectively with a rather bad theory, simply because the defects in the theory do not happen (at the moment) to be of practical importance. It may be more important, in practical terms, for the applied economist to have up-to-date information than to have an elegant theory.

The reason is a simple one. The theorist regards a theory as something to be carefully worked out and tested against some body of experience. The theory is then accepted, modified, or rejected. The applied economist is concerned with affecting some part of economic life, using a specified set of actions (for Federal Reserve, buying and selling bonds). We may regard him as looking at a vector of variables and deciding that he wants a particular variable to be larger (or smaller) than it actually is. Generally it is clear, in principle, whether "buying" or "selling" tend to increase or to decrease this variable. The question then is, "Have I bought, or sold enough *today* to move the variable to the level I want?" If the answer is "no," then further action is required tomorrow. If the answer is "yes," he waits until tomorrow to see whether the variable has "stuck" at the desired value. In this respect, today's errors can be corrected tomorrow—in most cases.

The applied economist has a competence of his own, for he has watched the course of events with care and thought. If he knows his trade, he has a theory to guide him. This theory is usually formulated in terms of adjustment mechanisms. That is, it supposes a certain sequence of responses to actions by the government authorities. Like the general or the quarterback, the applied economist tries to formulate the elements of a successful strategy, and to do so he relies on studies of what has happened in the past. But his objective is not to understand how the economy works, but to learn how he may make it work differently.

Because of this difference in objective, there is a gap between theoretical and applied economics. Theoretical economists feel that applied economics lacks understanding, and applied economists feel that theoretical economics is not useful. There is merit in both observations. This book is not concerned with applied economics, and it need not comment on it. The theories presented here do, of course, suffer from a lack of precision. This defect does occur precisely at the point where questions of timing and of adjustment processes appear. The theories given here may be useful in calculating the end product of an adjustment process—this is one way to interpret the table of implications that accompanies each theory. The intermediate steps in economic adjustment, however, cannot now be studied analytically. The reason is that "dynamic" theories (an example of which appears in the appendix to this chapter) are still in a much more primitive state than "static" and "comparative static" analyses such as those in this book. Applied economists, then, are wise to regard any theory as still very incomplete. They are not equally wise, however, if they fail to use the understanding that can be gained from existing macroeconomic concepts.

AN OUTLINE OF THE FINAL CHAPTERS

There is some point in expanding Theory 8. That theory is based on three Tiny Models; these models are much too compact to be used to represent any real economy. The theories in Chapters 3 to 5 represent expansions of the Tiny Models; it is natural, then, to put those theories together, just as the Tiny Models were put together. The difficulty is that theories with large numbers of variables become clumsy to work with. For this reason, students may well turn pale if asked to work with systems having large, messy matrices. On the other hand, they may well be able to understand, in an intuitive way, at least, some of the problems associated with large systems. The next chapter presents a theory that puts together the material in Chapters 3 to 5. The point of view of the chapter is somewhat more general than that of those chapters. The task is not merely the exploration of a big, messy matrix; it is rather to consider the ways in which the economist can use simple analysis to construct larger theories, with more "realism" than that which appeared in Theory 8. Just as Theory 8 had several variants, leading to rather different economic mechanisms, so does this larger theory. The economist who understands something of the "strategy" of theory construction can approach the large theory more efficiently than the economist who merely blunders into a large theory. And so Chapter 8 deals with strategy as well as with "hard analysis" and the mechanics of matrix inversion.

It was noted in the Introduction, and again in Chapter 5, that the variables we have been discussing may be thought of as *values* or as *quantities*. There is indeed a major unsolved problem in all of the preceding work. What does macroeconomics have to say about prices? Chapters 9 and 10 are concerned with adding a "price part" to the analysis given above. For the only price that has so far been discussed is the interest rate (which in some circumstances is measured by the price of securities). Economists are generally convinced the price changes are not determined solely by the special circumstances of particular industries. They tend to agree that macroeconomic events have a "price dimension" as well as a "quantity dimension." Macroeconomics must ultimately be able to deal with both "dimensions" of economic activity. Chapters 9 and 10 explain what can now be done to analyze prices in macroeconomic terms.

Finally, in Chapter 11, we come to a question that bothers most students: Why are there so many theories? Most of them, after all, must be inapplicable to any given economy. The reason why there are so many theories is that economists have been unable to agree on one of them. The disagreement is in part on questions of fact: Which theory actually explains economic events *best*? To understand why it is hard to agree on a theory, it is necessary to know something about how one can test theories against the record. Chapter 11 is concerned, therefore, with testing theories.

All of the chapters so far have been compact and straightforward, because the subjects under discussion seem to be clearly defined and capable of complete treatment. The remaining chapters deal with portions of macroeconomics where work is still in progress, and where a good deal remains to be done. In the Introduction, it was observed that the older macroeconomics had to be abandoned because it did not explain price changes well. Modern macroeconomics is still in the process of developing a workable approach to price variations. Since the work is incomplete, the theoretical analysis is not as neat as one would like it to be. Perhaps some reader will be sufficiently interested by the problems raised to be led to solve them.

Appendix to Chapter 7

A DYNAMIC VERSION OF THEORY 8

This appendix will constitute a very small-scale introduction to dynamic theories. Such theories involve time in some essential way. A simple way to introduce time into a theory is to assert that all behavioral relations exist with *lags*. That is, we suppose that if a relation between a variable $\mathbf{V}$ and a variable $\mathbf{W}$ exists it has the form

$$\mathbf{V_t = kW_{t-1} + F}$$

The economic unit, in other words, makes a decision about $\mathbf{V}$ at time t; this decision does not depend on the current value of $\mathbf{W}$, which would be designated $\mathbf{W_t}$; instead it depends on the value of $\mathbf{W}$ in the preceding period, $\mathbf{W_{t-1}}$. Time is supposed to consist of discrete dates $0, 1, 2, \ldots, t, t+1, \ldots$. The unit of time may be the day, week, month, or year. Decisions are made once every time period. For instance, consumer spending in week t may depend on the size of last week's paycheck, not on the expected size of this week's paycheck.

Two vectors of variables appear in the theory: $\mathbf{V_t}$, the current observation, and $\mathbf{V_{t-1}}$, the preceding observation. A more general formulation of a dynamic theory would involve more than two vectors; it might involve the vectors $\mathbf{V_t}, \mathbf{V_{t-1}}, \mathbf{V_{t-2}}, \ldots, \mathbf{V_{t-m}}$ for some arbitrary number m. A solution to a dynamic theory is a vector $\mathbf{V}$, the components of which are functions of time. Thus $\mathbf{V}$ might have the the general form $(\mathbf{V}_1^t, \mathbf{V}_1^t, \mathbf{V}_3^t, \ldots, \mathbf{V}_n^t)$, where each component $\mathbf{V}_i^t$ is a function of time, assuming the values $\mathbf{V}_i^1, \mathbf{V}_i^2, \mathbf{V}_i^3, \ldots$

at successive dates. (The superscript denotes the date; the subscript denotes the name of the variable.) In this respect a solution to a dynamic theory prescribes a "history" for the economy.

This theory appears in an appendix because it makes use of matrix addition and multiplication. It is thus more difficult mathematically than the theories in the text.

The four variations of Theory 8 may be transformed into dynamic equations of the form

$$\mathbf{V_t A} = \mathbf{V_{t-1} B} + \mathbf{F_t}$$

This transformation involves two matrices, **A** and **B**. The matrix **A** is the same for all versions of the theory:

$$\mathbf{A} = \begin{pmatrix} 1 & 0 & 0 & 0 & 0 & 0 & 0 \\ 1 & 1 & 0 & 0 & 0 & 0 & 0 \\ -1 & 0 & -1 & 0 & 0 & 0 & 0 \\ 0 & 0 & 0 & 1 & 0 & 0 & 0 \\ 0 & 0 & 1 & -1 & 1 & 0 & 0 \\ 0 & 0 & 0 & -1 & 0 & 1 & 0 \\ 0 & 0 & 0 & 1 & 0 & -1 & 1 \end{pmatrix}$$

Thus **A** is the matrix that is obtained by setting the behavioral coefficients in each version of Theory 8 equal to zero (these are the coefficients that are not 0, +1 or −1). **A** is the same in all versions of Theory 8. The matrix **B** differs from one version to the next. In the dynamic version of Theory 8A,

$$\mathbf{B} = \begin{pmatrix} 0 & a & 0 & 0 & 0 & 0 & 0 \\ 0 & 0 & 0 & 0 & 0 & 0 & 0 \\ 0 & 0 & 0 & 0 & 0 & 0 & 0 \\ 0 & 0 & 0 & 0 & b & 0 & 0 \\ 0 & 0 & 0 & 0 & 0 & 0 & 0 \\ 0 & 0 & 0 & 0 & 0 & 0 & s \\ 0 & 0 & 0 & 0 & 0 & 0 & 0 \end{pmatrix}$$

Thus the matrix **B** consists of zeros, except in the positions where some version of Theory 8 has a behavioral coefficient. Readers can verify that (**A** − **B**) is a matrix in the static version of Theory 8.

Since **A** has an inverse, it is possible to replace the equation

$$\mathbf{V_t A} = \mathbf{V_{t-1} B} + \mathbf{F_t}$$

with the equation

$$\mathbf{V_t = V_{t-1} BA^{-1} + F_t A^{-1}}$$

by multiplying both sides of the equation by $\mathbf{A^{-1}}$. Observe that if $\mathbf{V_t}$ can equal $\mathbf{V_{t-1}}$—in other words, if it is possible for there to be a solution of the sort given in Theory 8—then

$$\mathbf{V_t A = V_{t-1} B + F_t}$$

becomes

$$\mathbf{V_t A = V_t B + F_t}$$

$$\mathbf{V_t(A - B) = F_t}$$

$$\mathbf{V_t = F_t(A - B)^{-1}}$$

This is precisely the theory given in Chapter 6. This solution is the *static equilibrium* solution.

Now let us suppose that $\mathbf{F_t = F_{t-1} = F}$, so that the factors are unchanged at two successive periods. It follows that

$$\mathbf{V_t = V_{t-1} BA^{-1} + FA^{-1}}$$

$$\mathbf{V_{t-1} = V_{t-2} BA^{-1} + FA^{-1}}$$

Subtracting, therefore,

$$\mathbf{V_t - V_{t-1} = V_{t-1} BA^{-1} - V_{t-2} BA^{-1}}$$

So that

$$\mathbf{\Theta = V_t - V_{t-1}(E + BA^{-1}) + V_{t-2} BA^{-1}}$$

where $\mathbf{\Theta}$ is the zero vector and $\mathbf{E}$ the unit matrix.

Let us now ask whether there exists a matrix $\mathbf{M}$ of constants having the property that $\mathbf{V_{t+1} = V_t M}$ for every value of t. If such a matrix exists, then

$$\mathbf{V_{t+2} = V_t M^2}$$

$$\mathbf{V_{t+3} = V_t M^3}$$

$$\cdots$$

$$\mathbf{V_{t+t'} = V_t M^{t'}}$$

$$\cdots$$

and so on. The *powers of* $\mathbf{M}$ are defined as products of $\mathbf{M}$ multiplied by itself an appropriate number of times $= \mathbf{M^2 = MM}$; $\mathbf{M^3 = MMM}$; $\ldots \mathbf{M^{t'} = MM^{t'-1}}$.

If there exists such an $\mathbf{M}$, then

$$\Theta = \mathbf{V_t} - \mathbf{V_{t-1}}(\mathbf{E} + \mathbf{BA^{-1}}) + \mathbf{V_{t-2}}\,\mathbf{BA^{-1}}$$

could be rewritten in the form

$$\begin{aligned}\Theta &= \mathbf{V_{t-2}}\,\mathbf{M^2} - \mathbf{V_{t-2}}\,\mathbf{M}(\mathbf{E} + \mathbf{BA^{-1}}) + \mathbf{V_{t-2}}\,\mathbf{BA^{-1}} \\ &= \mathbf{V_{t-2}}[\mathbf{M^2} - \mathbf{M}(\mathbf{E} + \mathbf{BA^{-1}}) + \mathbf{BA^{-1}}]\end{aligned}$$

Since this equation holds for every value of t, we may replace $t - 2$ by t:

$$\Theta = \mathbf{V_t}[\mathbf{M^2} - \mathbf{M}(\mathbf{E} + \mathbf{BA^{-1}}) + \mathbf{BA^{-1}}]$$

The product of the two matrices $(\mathbf{M} - \mathbf{E})$ and $(\mathbf{M} - \mathbf{BA^{-1}})$ is

$$\mathbf{M^2} - \mathbf{EM} - \mathbf{M}\,\mathbf{BA^{-1}} + \mathbf{E}\,\mathbf{BA^{-1}}$$

For every matrix $\mathbf{X}$, $\mathbf{X} = \mathbf{EX} = \mathbf{XE}$. Thus, this last result

$$\begin{aligned}&= \mathbf{M^2} - \mathbf{ME} - \mathbf{M}\,\mathbf{BA^{-1}} + \mathbf{BA^{-1}} \\ &= \mathbf{M^2} - \mathbf{M}(\mathbf{E} + \mathbf{BA^{-1}}) + \mathbf{BA^{-1}}\end{aligned}$$

and thus,

$$\theta = \mathbf{V_t}(\mathbf{M} - \mathbf{E})(\mathbf{M} - \mathbf{BA^{-1}})$$

Since $\mathbf{M}$ takes $\mathbf{V_t}$ into $\mathbf{V_{t+1}}$ regardless of what the starting point $\mathbf{V_t}$ may be, we must specify

either that

$\mathbf{M} - \mathbf{E} = \mathbf{0}$ (the zero matrix). In this case,

$$\mathbf{M} = \mathbf{E}$$

or that

$\mathbf{M} - \mathbf{BA^{-1}} = \mathbf{0}$ (the zero matrix). In this case,

$$\mathbf{M} = \mathbf{BA^{-1}}$$

Consider the two possibilities separately:

if $\mathbf{M} = \mathbf{E}$, then $\mathbf{V_t} = \mathbf{V_{t-1}}$. In this case (7.1)

$$\begin{aligned}&\mathbf{V_t} = \mathbf{V_{t-1}}\mathbf{M} = \mathbf{V_{t-1}} = \mathbf{V_{t-1}}(\mathbf{BA^{-1}}) + \mathbf{F_t}\,\mathbf{A^{-1}} \\ &\mathbf{V_{t-1}}\mathbf{A} = \mathbf{V_{t-1}}\,\mathbf{B} + \mathbf{F_t} \\ &\mathbf{V_{t-1}}(\mathbf{A} - \mathbf{B}) = \mathbf{V_t}(\mathbf{A} - \mathbf{B}) = \mathbf{F_t}\end{aligned}$$

which is precisely the static form of Theory 8, which has already been studied.

if $\mathbf{M} = \mathbf{BA^{-1}}$, then (7.2)

$$\mathbf{V_t} = \mathbf{V_{t-1}}\mathbf{BA^{-1}} = \mathbf{V_{t-1}}\,\mathbf{BA^{-1}} + \mathbf{F_t}\,\mathbf{A^{-1}}$$

Subtract $\mathbf{V_t BA^{-1}}$ from both sides of the equation,

$$\Theta = \mathbf{F_t A^{-1}}$$

and multiply both sides of the equation by **A**,

$$\Theta\mathbf{A} = \Theta = \mathbf{F_t}$$

It follows that if $\mathbf{M} = \mathbf{BA^{-1}}$, the condition $\Theta = \mathbf{V_t(M - E)(M - BA^{-1})}$ is satisfied. Then $\mathbf{F_t} = \mathbf{F_{t-1}} = \mathbf{F}$, if and only if $\mathbf{F} = \theta$. We rule this possibility out as trivial.

Thus, in order that $\mathbf{F_t} = \mathbf{F_{t-1}} = \mathbf{F} \neq \mathbf{0}$, it must be the case that $\mathbf{M} = \mathbf{E}$. This amounts to saying that if **F** is constant, the economy behaves as if a static version of Theory 8 were true.

It is more interesting to see what happens when **V** varies. In this case, $\mathbf{M} = \mathbf{BA^{-1}}$. How does **V** change? Observe, first, that

$$\mathbf{V_t} = \mathbf{V_{t-1} BA^{-1}} + \mathbf{F_t}$$
$$\mathbf{V_{t-1}} = \mathbf{V_{t-2} BA^{-1}} + \mathbf{F_{t-1}}$$

so that

$$\Delta\mathbf{V}_t = \Delta\mathbf{V}_{t-1}\mathbf{BA}^{-1} + \Delta\mathbf{F}_t$$

It now simplifies notation to write $\mathbf{BA^{-1}} = \mathbf{X}$.

Suppose that prior to time $t = 0$, $\Delta\mathbf{V_0} = 0$, that is, $\mathbf{V}_{-1} = \mathbf{V_0}$. Then the static solution holds:

$$\mathbf{V_0} = \mathbf{F_0(B - A)^{-1}} \text{ and } \Delta\mathbf{V_0} = \mathbf{0}$$
$$\Delta\mathbf{V}_1 = \Delta\mathbf{V_0 X} + \Delta\mathbf{F}_1 = \Delta\mathbf{F}_1$$
$$\Delta\mathbf{V}_2 = \Delta\mathbf{V}_1\mathbf{X} + \Delta\mathbf{F}_2 = \Delta\mathbf{F}_1\mathbf{X} + \Delta\mathbf{F}_2$$
$$\Delta\mathbf{V}_3 = \Delta\mathbf{V}_2\mathbf{X} + \Delta\mathbf{F}_3 = (\Delta\mathbf{F}_1\mathbf{X} + \Delta\mathbf{F}_2)\mathbf{X} + \Delta\mathbf{F}_3$$
$$= \Delta\mathbf{F}_1\mathbf{X}^2 + \Delta\mathbf{F}_2\mathbf{X} + \Delta\mathbf{F}_3$$
$$\Delta\mathbf{V}_4 = \Delta\mathbf{V}_3\mathbf{X} + \Delta\mathbf{F}_4$$
$$= \Delta\mathbf{F}_1\mathbf{X}^3 + \Delta\mathbf{F}_2\mathbf{X}^2 + \Delta\mathbf{F}_3\mathbf{X} + \Delta\mathbf{F}_4$$

and so on, so that for arbitrary t

$$\Delta\mathbf{V}_t = \Delta\mathbf{F}_1\mathbf{X}^{t-1} + \Delta\mathbf{F}_2\mathbf{X}^{t-2} + \Delta\mathbf{F}_3\mathbf{X}^{t-3} + \cdots + \Delta\mathbf{F}_t$$

or, in summation notation,

$$\Delta\mathbf{V}_t = \sum_{i=1}^{t} \Delta\mathbf{F}_i\mathbf{X}^{t-i}$$

Since $\Delta\mathbf{V}_t = \mathbf{V}_t - \mathbf{V}_{t-1}$,

$$\mathbf{V}_t = \mathbf{V}_{t-1} + \sum_{i=1}^{t} \Delta\mathbf{F}_i\mathbf{X}^{t-i}$$

or, in the original notation

$$\mathbf{V}_t = \mathbf{V}_{t-1} + \sum_{i=1}^{t} \Delta\mathbf{F}_i(\mathbf{BA}^{-1})^{t-i}$$

Every history of the factors may be written as a sequence

$$\mathbf{F}_0, \mathbf{F}_1, \mathbf{F}_2 \cdots, \mathbf{F}_{t-1}, \mathbf{F}_t$$

and each such sequence implies a sequence of factor *changes*,

$$\Delta\mathbf{F}_1, \Delta\mathbf{F}_2, \ldots \Delta\mathbf{F}_{t-1}, \Delta\mathbf{F}_t$$

Given any sequence of factor changes, and a vector $\mathbf{V}_{t-1}$, the value of the vector $\mathbf{V}_t$ is uniquely determined. The matrix $(\mathbf{BA}^{-1})$ is given by the initial assumptions.

In particular, suppose that the vector $\mathbf{F}_t$ is fixed at $\mathbf{F}$ for all t up to $t = -1$; then it changes to $\mathbf{F} + \Delta\mathbf{F}$ at $t = 0$, and remains fixed thereafter. Then $\Delta\mathbf{F}_t = \mathbf{\Theta}$ for all t except $t = 0$, then it is $\Delta\mathbf{F}$. This hypothetical sequence corresponds to a single change in $\mathbf{F}$, of the kind described in Chapters 3 to 7.

However, the dynamic adjustment mechanism follows the general formula

$$\Delta\mathbf{V}_t = \sum_{0}^{t} \Delta\mathbf{F}_i \mathbf{X}^{t-i}$$

In this instance, only $\Delta\mathbf{F}_0$ differs from Θ. Thus

$$\Delta\mathbf{V}_t = \Delta\mathbf{F}_0 \mathbf{X}^t$$

The adjustment process stops if and only if $\Delta\mathbf{V}_t = \mathbf{\Theta}$. In general, this condition will hold only if $\mathbf{X}^t = 0$ for some power of t.

It can be the case that $\mathbf{X}^t$ approaches zero as t becomes larger. As an example, consider the dynamic version of Theory 8A.[3] The first three powers of $\mathbf{BA}^{-1}$ for this theory are

$$\mathbf{BA}^{-1} = \begin{pmatrix} -a & a & 0 & 0 & 0 & 0 & 0 \\ 0 & 0 & 0 & 0 & 0 & 0 & 0 \\ 0 & 0 & 0 & 0 & 0 & 0 & 0 \\ b & 0 & b & b & b & 0 & 0 \\ 0 & 0 & 0 & 0 & 0 & 0 & 0 \\ 0 & 0 & 0 & 0 & 0 & s & s \\ 0 & 0 & 0 & 0 & 0 & 0 & 0 \end{pmatrix}$$

[3] Not all matrices will go to zero as t increases. The condition that must be satisfied for this condition to hold are that the characteristic values of the matrix must all be of absolute value less than one. (This condition will not mean anything to readers who have not studied matrix algebra.)

$$(\mathbf{BA}^{-1})^2 = \begin{pmatrix} a^2 & -a^2 & 0 & 0 & 0 & 0 & 0 \\ 0 & 0 & 0 & 0 & 0 & 0 & 0 \\ 0 & 0 & 0 & 0 & 0 & 0 & 0 \\ b^2 - ab & ab & b^2 & b^2 & b^2 & 0 & 0 \\ 0 & 0 & 0 & 0 & 0 & 0 & 0 \\ 0 & 0 & 0 & 0 & 0 & s^2 & s^2 \\ 0 & 0 & 0 & 0 & 0 & 0 & 0 \end{pmatrix}$$

$$(\mathbf{BA}^{-1})^3 = \begin{pmatrix} -a^3 & a^3 & 0 & 0 & 0 & 0 & 0 \\ 0 & 0 & 0 & 0 & 0 & 0 & 0 \\ 0 & 0 & 0 & 0 & 0 & 0 & 0 \\ (b^3 + b^3 - ab^2 + a^2b) & (b^3 + ab^2 - a^2b) & b^3 & b^3 & b^3 & 0 & 0 \\ 0 & 0 & 0 & 0 & 0 & 0 & 0 \\ 0 & 0 & 0 & 0 & 0 & s^3 & s^3 \\ 0 & 0 & 0 & 0 & 0 & 0 & 0 \end{pmatrix}$$

and so on. Since a, b, and s are all between zero and one, a^t, b^t, and c^t go to zero as t increases. If a and b are close to equality, then ab is close to b^2, ab^2, and a^2b are close to b^3, and so forth. This means that the unpleasant-looking terms in columns 1 and 2 of row four get smaller as higher powers of $\mathbf{BA}^{-1}$ are taken. Indeed, in this particular case, it might be quite reasonable to assume that all powers of $\mathbf{BA}^{-1}$ above some moderately small value of t would exert a completely negligible influence on $\Delta\mathbf{V}_t$.

The point is the following: If the static theory held, then the changes in variables in any period of time would depend only on the changes in factors taking place at that time, so $\Delta\mathbf{V}_t = \Delta\mathbf{F}_t(\mathbf{A} - \mathbf{B})^{-1}$. But if a dynamic process is taking place, $\Delta\mathbf{V}_t$, the present changes in the variables, may depend on the entire history $\Delta\mathbf{F}_t$, $\Delta\mathbf{F}_{t-1}$, $\Delta\mathbf{F}_{t-2} \ldots$ of the factors. It is possible that events sufficiently remote in time are of no practical consequence to present changes, but this is a proposition that would have to be verified in each case. If dynamic processes exist in the economy (as most economists suspect), it is misleading to look only at present changes in factors when one is trying to explain present changes in variables.

The entire subject of dynamic processes is a difficult one, and it is not discussed as thoroughly in this book as static and comparative static analysis. This appendix merely sketches a beginning of the subject.

8

Moderate and Large-Scale Theories

The discussion in Chapter 6 had to be somewhat roundabout because it had no very good way of talking about government spending and taxation. In a general way it was safe to treat government spending as being akin to investment, but we know from Theory 5 that some complications arise when attempts are made to combine models involving government spending with elements of balance sheet accounts. These complications arise because government deficits involve the sale of bonds or printing of paper money, and hence activities in balance sheets. In Theory 8 money and plant were the only assets of nonbanks. If the government had a surplus or deficit, this theory says it would have borrowed (or reduced borrowings) from banks. In Theory 8 individuals and businesses do not hold government bonds.

Readers may feel that the issues raised by Theory 8 are perhaps interesting, but not very helpful in seeing how the capital markets are related to the rest of the economy. This chapter will therefore present a theory that is basically a larger-scale version of Theory 8. Instead of bypassing government and the capital markets, it will put them into the theory. Instead of being an assemblage of three Tiny Models, with seven variables, the new theory will assemble the larger theories already studied, and end up with a fifteen-variable model.

Theories that become as large as this have a strong tendency to become obscure. Even patient and hardworking economists may have trouble in seeing the matrix and its inverse as more than a messy collection of symbols. One of the purposes of a theory is to bring order and clarity into a discussion. For this reason, the users of theories involving many variables have to seek special ways of producing clarity. In particular, they may use block-matrix notation to bring out the internal structure of the theory more forcibly to their readers. This method of thinking will be familiar to readers from Chapter 6. There, the various alternate hypotheses amounted to the different arrangement of zero and nonzero blocks in a theory. Since the blocks were small, there was no reason to dwell on this aspect of the theory. But where blocks associated with income, with nonbank balance sheets, and with bank balance sheets become, roughly, of order 5 each, then it becomes much easier to think in terms of blocks than in terms of single equations.

The theories presented here will not (the author promises) have more than fifteen variables, and considerable efforts will be made to keep them intelligible. In the past decade, progress in the compilation of statistics and in the use of computers has encouraged the school of thought called *econometrics* to make numerical estimates of coefficients appearing in very large theories. The largest theory in print in 1969[1] involved something in the order of 180 variables, and its creators felt a need for a theory perhaps twice as large to represent the economy in adequate detail.

The present value of such very large models is much disputed. The issue in large part revolves about the adequacy of data. We learn in high school that a straight line will run through any two points and a circle can be made to fit any three points. If a linear theory contains N variables, it may be shown that there exist coefficients that will give a perfect fit to any N observations. Statisticians are reluctant to put any faith in estimates, unless the number of observations of each variable considerably exceeds the number of variables in the system. Their reluctance reflects the fact that every theory (good, bad, or indifferent) must fit well unless these conditions are met.

Quarterly data on the national product accounts go back to 1946—about 80 quarters. Good annual data go back to 1929—about 40 years. Some annual data go back 100 years to 1870. These facts put severe limits on the size of theories that can be tested by existing statistical techniques.

---

[1] J. S. Duesenberry, G. Fromm, L. R. Klein, and E. Kuh (eds.), *The Brookings Quarterly Model of the United States*, Chicago (Rand McNally & Company, 1965).

On the other hand, it is quite clear that the small- to medium-sized theory presented in this book (five to fifteen variables) contains too few variables to satisfy the hard-nosed realists. In particular it would be of great help in business and government forecasting if large-scale theories could be tested and used. An important practical obstacle at the moment is the absence of a statistical methodology to cope with such theories. This obstacle can perhaps be overcome. If it is, the large theory will doubtless find many uses.

In asking beginners to look at larger theories than they like, this author makes the forecast that, in coming years, business and government will use larger theories than those in this book. For practical reasons, then, it would be well for beginners to get a preview of the coming attractions in applied economics.

The procedure used will be the following. We first present Theory 9, which is a balance sheet theory, replacing Tiny Models 2 and 4 by more complicated and, we hope, more realistic systems. Then Theory 10 combines Theory 9 and Theory 4, which is a more complicated version of Tiny Model 1. Thus, Theory 10 can be thought of in much the same way as Theory 8. It contains three sets of accounts: income, nonbank balance sheets, and bank balance sheets. Unlike Theory 8, it explicitly contains the fiscal system as well as a (more complicated) monetary system, so that problems of the bond market begin to emerge more clearly in the context of the economy.

The purpose of these theories is not merely to invert big matrices—this is neither much fun nor very informative. Rather it is to show how theories are built up and how careful theorists must be in examining the details of their system. Thus, Theory 9 starts off rather cheerfully with a number of plausible assumptions. When the matrix is inverted, it will turn out that if the interest rate is to vary consistently with the reasoning in Tiny Model 3, some rather unexpected modifications of the starting point must be made. And Theory 10 is an elaboration of one of the points that underlay Chapter 6: There is more than one way to make a theory to account for changes in some set of variables; and theorists can often set up block-triangular theories in several quite different ways. In this way, they can find (for example) ingenious arguments to rationalize the platform of their favorite politician.

THEORY 9. BANKING AND THE ASSETS OF THE ECONOMY

Balance sheet analysis is puzzling because one man's asset is another's liability. Thus money—one of our assets when we have it—appears as a liability of the banks as well as an asset of nonbanks. The debts of business and government are also assets belonging to the banks and the Federal Reserve System. In Theory 9, all the balance sheets of the economy are represented. They are more detailed than those of Theory 8, though they are still (as usual) in simplified form.

The balance sheet of the Federal Reserve System is now assumed to take the form

FEDERAL RESERVE SYSTEM

Assets		*Liabilities*	
Gold certificates,	A	Reserve accounts,	R
"Investments,"	B_1	Federal reserve notes,	N

Gold certificates exist because the United States Treasury is committed to buy and sell gold at $35.00 per ounce. It will buy from United States gold mines, and it will buy from or sell to foreign governments. (The latter transactions are the only important ones, for United States gold output is small.) The Treasury does not pay for gold from tax revenues. Instead, it borrows from Federal Reserve, and the gold certificates are the "IOUs" it gives when it borrows. When the Treasury sells gold, it uses the proceeds to pay off a part of this debt. Gold transactions settle obligations arising in international trade and investment operations. Since this book does not deal with international trade and finance, these transactions are basically independent "factors." They take place, and are sometimes important, and for this reason a limited recognition of them is made here. If this book were written for European students, it would be ridiculous to be so brief in the discussion, since European countries are very much more affected by international transactions than is the United States.

Federal Reserve notes are the paper money in circulation in the United States. Earlier theories raised the question "Where does the money come from?" The only answer they gave was, "If the government has a deficit, it prints paper money and uses it to pay its bills" (Theory 5). Now, however, a better answer can be given: If people, collectively, take money "out of" the banks, the banks may "buy" paper money from Federal Reserve, paying for it by writing checks against the balances in their reserve accounts.

The balance sheet of the private banks in this theory will be like that used in Theory 8:

PRIVATE BANKS

Assets		*Liabilities*	
Reserves,	R	Deposits,	D
Loans,	L		
"Investments,"	B_2		

The balance sheet for the nonbank sector has three additional variables (1) plant and equipment owned by business (K); (2) bonds held by non-banks (B_3); and (3) the total bonded debt of the community (B). The balance sheet of this sector, then, is the following:

NONBANK SECTOR

HOUSEHOLDS, BUSINESS, GOVERNMENT

Assets		*Liabilities*	
Deposits,	D	Bank loans,	L
Federal reserve notes,	N	Bonds,	B
Bonds,	B_3		
Plant and equipment,	K		

In a real economy, business and households do not have debts equal to their assets. Net worth (capital stock) for United States business as a whole is about 2/3 of total assets. But in this particular theory, the main object of interest is money and debt. The relationships being discussed are not materially affected by the presence of a constant net worth account. For the present, it is simpler to talk as if all assets were financed by borrowing, either directly from banks (in the case of loans) or by sale of bonds.[2] Since there is no income account from which to add to net worth, one would include savings (net worth) by the statement $W = F_N$, which is not very exciting.

The nonbank sector includes bonds on both sides of its balance sheet. Some bonds issued by some nonbanks are owned by other nonbanks. It is desirable to list B_3 as a nonbank asset. The alternative procedure would be to list nonbank debts as $B - B_3$. In this case it would be impossible to distinguish between the sale of new bond issues (ΔB) and the purchase of bonds by nonbank security holders (ΔB_3).

Theory 9 thus includes the three balance sheets, and four familiar behavioral statements:

1. For the Federal Reserve System:

$$A + B_1 = R + N$$

2. For the private banks:

$$D = R + L + B_2$$

[2] In Chapter 1, it was pointed out that stocks and bonds could be treated in very much the same way for purposes of macroeconomic analysis. Readers who wish to may consider "Bonds" in this theory as being "stocks and bonds." They should remember, however, that neither the Federal Reserve System nor the private banks are owners of stock, so that all stock is included in B_3.

3. For nonbanks:

$$L + B = D + N + B_3 + K$$

4. The demand for reserves by private banks:

$$R = rD + F_R$$

5. The Federal Reserve System decides "from outside the system" what its bond holdings will be:

$$B_1 = F_F$$

[*Note:* Open-market operations are the same as ΔB_1.]

6. Banks decide on the amount of loans they are willing to make by considering the size of their deposits:

$$L = qD + F_L$$

[*Note:* q should be positive, since the more deposits banks have, the more loan we should expect them to make. But q should be less than 1, since, when deposits go up, banks must keep more reserves, and should also want to hold more bonds.]

7. Nonbanks choose between having bank deposits and having Federal Reserve notes. It is assumed that the following very simple relation holds:

$$N = nD + F_N$$

[*Note:* n should be positive. Since notes are a small part of all cash assets, we should expect n to be less than 1.]

This statement is a rule for dividing cash assets into two parts. It says that there is no direct connection between the demand for notes and the amount of noncash assets held.[3]

The following two statements have several virtues: (1) They complete the theory, so that it becomes a one-to-one mapping. (2) They sound like statements made in earlier theories. (3) They even sound plausible. It will turn out that they lead to very curious conclusions. Unraveling these conclusions will give some insight into what constitutes an acceptable hypothesis.

---

[3] The only circumstances when the demand for notes is of importance are either seasonal (at Christmas time people draw notes in order to do their seasonal shopping) or in time of bank panic (when people want cash in their pockets because they are afraid the banks will fail). The most recent United States bank panic was in early 1933. A number of earlier panics play a respectable part in our monetary history.

8. Nonbanks decide on the amount of plant they want by considering the total funds they have been able to raise. That is, this decision is basically like that of banks—and it is also the same rule that has been used in Theories 2 and 5:

$$K = k(L + B) + F_K$$

[*Note:* k should be positive, since the more funds nonbanks can raise, the more plant we should expect them to want. But k should be less than 1, since nonbanks will want to increase other assets, too.]

9. Nonbank demand for bonds, like nonbank demand for plant and equipment, depends on the total funds available to nonbanks:

$$B_3 = p(L + B) + F_B$$

[*Note:* We should expect p to be between zero and 1, just as k is between zero and one. In fact, $(k + p)$ should be less than one.]

In Theory 6, the statement $(B = B_1 + B_2)$ said that all bonds were held either by the Federal Reserve System or by private banks. In this theory, the corresponding statement would be $(B = B_1 + B_2 + B_3)$. This statement was not made here, and readers may well wonder whether the bonds issued (B) will equal the number of bonds owned $(B_1 + B_2 + B_3)$. This question will be dealt with later, once the factor-into-variable mapping has been obtained.

When the nine statements are put together into a theory,

$$(\mathbf{F_F}, \mathbf{A}, \mathbf{0}, \mathbf{F_R}, \mathbf{F_L}, \mathbf{F_N}, \mathbf{0}, \mathbf{F_K}, \mathbf{F_B}) = (\mathbf{B_1}, \mathbf{R}, \mathbf{B_2}, \mathbf{N}, \mathbf{L}, \mathbf{D}, \mathbf{B}, \mathbf{K}, \mathbf{B_3})$$

$$\times \begin{pmatrix} 1 & -1 & 0 & 0 & 0 & 0 & 0 & 0 & 0 \\ 0 & 1 & 1 & 1 & 0 & 0 & 0 & 0 & 0 \\ 0 & 0 & 1 & 0 & 0 & 0 & 0 & 0 & 0 \\ 0 & 1 & 0 & 0 & 0 & 1 & 1 & 0 & 0 \\ 0 & 0 & 1 & 0 & 1 & 0 & -1 & -k & -p \\ 0 & 0 & -1 & -r & -q & -n & 1 & 0 & 0 \\ 0 & 0 & 0 & 0 & 0 & 0 & -1 & -k & -p \\ 0 & 0 & 0 & 0 & 0 & 0 & 1 & 1 & 0 \\ 0 & 0 & 0 & 0 & 0 & 0 & 1 & 0 & 1 \end{pmatrix}$$

As usual, the order of the individual statements and variables has been changed, so as to bring together blocks of zeros, and thereby make possible simpler ways of inverting the matrix. This particular arrangement makes clear that the system can be written in block form as a collection of 3×3 blocks:

$$\begin{pmatrix} M_{11} & M_{12} & 0 \\ M_{21} & M_{22} & M_{23} \\ 0 & 0 & M_{33} \end{pmatrix}$$

Moreover, there is a 6 × 6 block in this system that is block-triangular:

$$\begin{pmatrix} M_{22} & M_{23} \\ 0 & M_{33} \end{pmatrix}$$

And the fact that two other blocks,

$$(M_{12} \quad 0) \quad \text{and} \quad \begin{pmatrix} M_{21} \\ 0 \end{pmatrix}$$

contain zeros means that when the matrix is inverted, it will not be necessary to conduct as large-scale operations as were necessary, say, in Theory 5. In fact,

$$\begin{pmatrix} M_{11} & M_{12} & 0 \\ M_{21} & M_{22} & M_{23} \\ 0 & 0 & M_{33} \end{pmatrix}^{-1} =$$

$$\begin{pmatrix} [M_{11} - M_{12} M_{22}^{-1} M_{21}]^{-1} & -M_{11}^{-1} M_{12} [M_{22} - M_{21} M_{11} M_{12}]^{-1} & M_{11}^{-1} M_{12} [M_{22} - M_{21} M_{11}^{-1} M_{12}]^{-1} M_{23} M_{33}^{-1} \\ -M_{22}^{-1} M_{21} [M_{11} - M_{12} M_{22}^{-1} M_{21}]^{-1} & [M_{22} - M_{21} M_{11}^{-1} M_{12}]^{-1} & -[M_{22} - M_{21} M_{11}^{-1} M_{12}]^{-1} M_{23} M_{33}^{-1} \\ 0 & 0 & M_{33}^{-1} \end{pmatrix}$$

All the diagonal blocks in this inverse are 3 × 3 and are relatively easy to handle:

$$\mathbf{M}_{11}^{-1} = \begin{pmatrix} 1 & -1 & 0 \\ 0 & 1 & 1 \\ 0 & 0 & 1 \end{pmatrix}^{-1} = \begin{pmatrix} 1 & 1 & -1 \\ 0 & 1 & -1 \\ 0 & 0 & 1 \end{pmatrix}$$

$$\mathbf{M}_{22}^{-1} = \begin{pmatrix} 0 & 0 & 1 \\ 0 & 1 & 0 \\ -r & -q & -n \end{pmatrix}^{-1} = \begin{pmatrix} -\frac{n}{r} & -\frac{q}{r} & -\frac{1}{r} \\ 0 & 1 & 0 \\ 1 & 0 & 0 \end{pmatrix}$$

$$\mathbf{M}_{33}^{-1} = \begin{pmatrix} -1 & -k & -p \\ 1 & 1 & 0 \\ 1 & 0 & 1 \end{pmatrix}^{-1} = \begin{pmatrix} \frac{-1}{1-k-p} & \frac{-k}{1-k-p} & \frac{-p}{1-k-p} \\ \frac{1}{1-k-p} & \frac{1-p}{1-k-p} & \frac{p}{1-k-p} \\ \frac{1}{1-k-p} & \frac{k}{1-k-p} & \frac{1-k}{1-k-p} \end{pmatrix}$$

The computation of the inverse matrix is straightforward, if a bit tedious, and gives the factor-into-variable mapping:

$$
\begin{aligned}
&(\mathbf{B}_1, \mathbf{R}, \mathbf{B}_2, \mathbf{N}, \mathbf{L}, \mathbf{D}, \mathbf{B}, \mathbf{K}, \mathbf{B}_3,)\\
&\quad = (\mathbf{F_F}, \mathbf{A}, \mathbf{0}, \mathbf{F_R}, \mathbf{F_L}, \mathbf{F_N}, \mathbf{0}, \mathbf{F_K}, \mathbf{F_B})\\
&\quad \times \begin{pmatrix}
1 & \frac{r}{n+r} & \frac{1-q-r}{n+r} & \frac{n}{n+r} & \frac{q}{n+r} & \frac{1}{n+r} & \frac{(n-1)-q(1-k-p)}{(n+r)(1-k-p)} & \frac{k(n+1)}{(n+r)(1-k-p)} & \frac{p(n+1)}{(n+r)(1-k-p)} \\
0 & \frac{r}{n+r} & \frac{1-q-r}{n+r} & \frac{n}{n+r} & \frac{q}{n+r} & \frac{1}{n+r} & \frac{(n+1)-q(1-k-p)}{(n+r)(1-k-p)} & \frac{k(n+1)}{(n+r)(1-k-p)} & \frac{p(n+1)}{(n+r)(1-k-p)} \\
0 & 0 & 1 & 0 & 0 & 0 & 0 & 0 & 0 \\
0 & \frac{n}{n+r} & \frac{q-n-1}{n+r} & \frac{-n}{n+r} & \frac{-q}{n+r} & \frac{-1}{n+r} - & \frac{(n+1)-q(1-k-p)}{(n+r)(1-k-p)} - & \frac{k(n+1)}{(n+r)(1-k-p)} - & \frac{p(n+1)}{(n+r)(1-k-p)} \\
0 & 0 & -1 & 0 & 1 & 0 & -1 & 0 & 0 \\
0 & \frac{-r}{n+r} & \frac{q+r-1}{n+r} & \frac{r}{n+r} & \frac{-q}{n+r} & \frac{-1}{n+r} - & \frac{(1-r)-q(1-k-p)}{(n+r)(1-k-p)} - & \frac{k(1-r)}{(n+r)(1-k-p)} - & \frac{p(1-r)}{(n+r)(1-k-p)} \\
0 & 0 & 0 & 0 & 0 & 0 & \frac{-1}{1-k-p} & \frac{-k}{1-k-p} & \frac{-p}{1-k-p} \\
0 & 0 & 0 & 0 & 0 & 0 & \frac{1}{1-k-p} & \frac{1-p}{1-k-p} & \frac{+p}{1-k-p} \\
0 & 0 & 0 & 0 & 0 & 0 & \frac{1}{1-k-p} & \frac{k}{1-k-p} & \frac{1-k}{1-k-p}
\end{pmatrix}
\end{aligned}
$$

Table 8.1 interprets Theory 9, explaining the effects on the economy of increases in the factors. Several terms have rather natural explanations, which follow the simpler results for Theory 6.

For instance, in Theory 6, a dollar's worth of bonds purchased by the Federal Reserve System (in "open market operations") increased member bank reserves by one dollar, and deposits by $1/r$ (where r was the reserve ratio). In Theory 9, the corresponding values are $r/(n + r)$ (which is less than 1) and $1/(n + r)$ (which is less than $1/r$). The difference is due to the fact that when deposits go up, the amount of paper money in circulation also increases.

The term $(1 - k - p)$ appears in the denominator of all the reactions of the nonbank sector. If we looked no further than the assumptions, we would decide something of the following sort. When total assets of nonbanks increase by one dollar, the amount of plant desired increases by k, and the bonds demanded (to be held as assets, B_3) increase by p. Consequently, $(1 - k - p)$ represents the additional demand for cash (bank deposit plus notes) which accompanies a unit increase in assets. There is an immediate analogy between $(1 - k - p)$ and the "multiplier" $1/(1 - a)$ in Tiny Model 1 or the "money multipliers" $1/(1 - b)$ in Tiny Model 2. The smaller the amount of cash that nonbanks wish to hold when their assets increase (that is, the smaller is $1 - k - p$), the more strongly the system should react to changes in the independent factors.

Table 1 says that an increase in gold certificates has the same effect as a Federal Reserve purchase of bonds. This book does not deal in any detail with international transactions, but certain observations can be easily made:

(1) Gold is purchased by the United States Treasury when sales to foreigners exceed purchases from foreigners; and it is sold when United States purchases abroad exceed sales abroad. Gold transactions take place as a means of settling balances due without causing disturbances on foreign exchange rates. (This assertion will not be proved here.) These transactions have a direct effect upon the assets of the United States—both inside and outside the banking sector.

(2) The Federal Reserve System can offset inflows of gold by selling bonds, or outflows of gold by buying bonds. If it does so, however, it prevents internal adjustments within the economy that would tend to readjust United States buying and selling abroad. (Proof of this proposition would require introducing a new sector, "foreigners" into both income and balance sheet analysis.) The procedure would be an extension of that suggested by the last three problems in Chapter 4.

(3) Imagine that at those times when Federal Reserve is selling bonds in order to reduce bank reserves, it is simultaneously buying gold from foreigners. Then these two actions will offset each other. Such a situation might occur because the bond sales force down bond prices, and the low bond prices

TABLE 8.1

THE IMPLICATIONS OF THEORY 9

THE EFFECT OF A UNIT INCREASE IN	THE EFFECT ON							
	Member bank reserves (R)	Bank "Investments" (B_2)	Federal Reserve notes (N)	Bank loans (L)	Deposits (D)	Bonds issued (B)	Total plant (K)	Nonbank bond holdings (B_3)
Federal Reserve "investments" (F_F)	$\frac{r}{n+r}$	$\frac{1-q-r}{n+r}$	$\frac{n}{n+r}$	$\frac{q}{n+r}$	$\frac{1}{n+r}$	$\frac{(n+1)-q(1-k-p)}{(n+r)(1-k-p)}$	$\frac{k(n+1)}{(n+r)(1-k-p)}$	$\frac{p(n+1)}{(n+r)(1-k-p)}$
Gold certificates (A)	$\frac{r}{n+r}$	$\frac{1-q-r}{n+r}$	$\frac{n}{n+r}$	$\frac{q}{n+r}$	$\frac{1}{n+r}$	$\frac{(n+1)-q(1-k-p)}{(n+r)(1-k-p)}$	$\frac{k(n+1)}{(n+r)(1-k-p)}$	$\frac{p(n+1)}{(n+r)(1-k-p)}$
Excess reserves (F_R)	$\frac{n}{n+r}$	$\frac{q-n-1}{n+r}$	$\frac{-n}{n+r}$	$\frac{-q}{n+r}$	$\frac{-1}{n+r}$	$-\frac{(n+1)-q(1-k-p)}{(n+r)(1-k-p)}$	$-\frac{k(n+1)}{(n+r)(1-k-p)}$	$-\frac{p(n+1)}{(n+r)(1-k-p)}$
Supply of bank loans (F_L)	0	-1	0	1	0	-1	0	0
Demand for paper money (F_N)	$\frac{-r}{n+r}$	$\frac{q+r-1}{n+r}$	$\frac{r}{n+r}$	$\frac{-q}{n+r}$	$\frac{-1}{n+r}$	$-\frac{(1-r)-q(1-k-p)}{(n+r)(1-k-p)}$	$-\frac{k(1-r)}{(n+r)(1-k-p)}$	$-\frac{p(1-r)}{(n+r)(1-k-p)}$
Demand for plant (F_K)	0	0	0	0	0	$\frac{1}{1-k-p}$	$\frac{1-p}{1-k-p}$	$\frac{p}{1-k-p}$
Nonbank demand for bonds (F_B)	0	0	0	0	0	$\frac{1}{1-k-p}$	$\frac{k}{1-k-p}$	$\frac{1-k}{1-k-p}$

encourage foreigners to buy United States securities, paying for them (in effect) in gold. In such a case, Federal Reserve may be unable to affec bank reserves as it wishes to because of offsetting foreign purchases o securities.

Problem 8.1 Turn back to Tiny Model 3 of Chapter 2, and suppose that i applies to the bond market.

(1) Suppose that there is a given total number of bonds in existence. What happens to the price of bonds if there is an increase in the level of Demand (F_D)? What happens to the rate of interest?

(2) Suppose that there is a given initial number of bonds What is the effect of a new issue of bonds on bond prices and on the interest rate?

(3) Interpret the analysis of interest and investment of Theory 1 in terms of Tiny Model 3, assuming that all investment is financed by bond issues.

(4) Suppose that the private part of the bond market is describable by Tiny Model 3. How would you interpret (in this model) a decision by the Federal Reserve System to make open market purchases? Open market sales?

(5) Suppose that Federal Reserve policy is to stabilize the interest rate. Describe this policy in terms of Tiny Model 3.

In Theory 9 there are three kinds of bondholders, and hence three variables, B_1, B_2, B_3; but there is no provision that the sum of these is equal to B, the total bonded debt of the nonbank sector. In contrast, Theory 5 had two kinds of bondholders, and it specified that their holdings equaled the total bonded debt ($B_1 + B_2 = B$ was a statement of the theory).

Table 8.1 lists changes in bank and nonbank holdings of bonds (B_2 and B_3). Implicitly, it also lists changes in Federal Reserve bond holdings, for changes in B_1 take place if and only if F_F changes. It also lists changes in B, the total bonded debt. Table 8.2 shows that in general the equality $\Delta B_1 + \Delta B_2 + \Delta B_3 = \Delta B$ does not hold.

It is possible to construct an exact expression for the interest rate, using the formula

$$1 + i = \left(\frac{B}{B_1 + B_2 + B_3}\right)^{1/t}$$

One simply substitutes for the variables, using the factor-into-variable mapping. But this expression turns out to be rather clumsy, and it will be convenient to use a simplification, which can be constructed as follows. The interest rate, in practice, is a small number, so that neither $(1 + i)$ nor

$B/(B_1 + B_2 + B_3)$ is very different from one. Roughly speaking, then, when a single factor changes, we calculate a new value of i, say

$$1 + i + \Delta i = \left(\frac{B + \Delta B}{B_1 + B_2 + B_3 + \Delta B_1 + \Delta B_2 + \Delta B_3}\right)^{1/t}$$

$$\Delta i \approx \left(\frac{\Delta B}{B + \Delta B_1 + \Delta B_2 + \Delta B_3}\right)^{1/t}$$

Still speaking very roughly, Δi will be positive if ΔB is greater than $\Delta B_1 + \Delta B_2 + \Delta B_3$. One can get a first approximation of a measure of the effect of a change in any one factor F on the interest rate by saying

$$\text{Sign}(\Delta i) \neq \text{Sign}(\Delta B_1 + \Delta B_2 + \Delta B_3 - \Delta B)$$

The right hand side is rather easy to calculate (see Table 8.2). We therefore use it as a guide. Nobody should consider this formula to be anything but a timesaver. We use it here to point out interesting and puzzling implications of the assumptions made above. They looked innocent, but it turns out they are not.

TABLE 8.2

THE EFFECT ON THE INTEREST RATE OF CHANGES IN THE INDEPENDENT FACTORS OF THEORY 9—A ROUGH GUESS

UNIT FACTOR INCREASE	$\Delta B_1 + \Delta B_2 + \Delta B_3 - \Delta B$	EFFECT ON THE INTEREST RATE IF $K > 0$, $P > 0$
Open market purchase by F.R.S. (ΔF_F)	$\frac{-k(n+1)}{(n+r)(1-k-p)}$	+
Gold certificates bought by F.R.S. (ΔA)	$\frac{-k(n+1)}{(n+r)(1-k-p)} - 1$	+
Demand for excess reserves (ΔF_R)	$\frac{k(n+1)}{(n+r)(1-k-p)}$	−
Supply of bank loans (ΔF_L)	0	0
Demand for F.R. notes (ΔF_N)	$\frac{k(1-r)}{(n+r)(1-k-p)}$	+
Demand for plant (ΔF_K)	$-\frac{(1-p)}{1-k-p}$	−
Nonbank demand for bonds (ΔB_3)	$-\frac{k}{1-k-p}$	−

Table 8.2 will have a strong impact on monetary economists: They will say it looks crazy. For in setting up the theory, we assumed that $k > 0$, $p > 0$ and $(1 - k - p) > 0$. If this were true, then when Federal Reserve bought government bonds, the interest rate would *increase*. From Tiny Model 3, we know that an increase in open market operations is an increase in the *demand* for bonds. The price of bonds should rise, and the interest rate should fall. If the demand for excess reserves rises, then banks are less willing to make loans and buy bonds. From Tiny Model 3, we would say there is a decline in the demand for bonds. The price of bonds should fall and the interest rate should rise. If nonbank demand for bonds rises, the price of bonds should rise and the interest rate should fall. None of these propositions follows from Table 8.2.

In other words, if the "plausible" assumptions made in statements 8 and 9 of the theory are kept $[k > 0,\ p > 0,\ (1 - k - p) > 0]$, some very strange conclusions would be reached about interest rate changes—at least so far as the adherents of Tiny Model 3 are concerned. If Tiny Model 3 fails, all of microeconomics totters. To make Theory 8 compatible with Tiny Model 3 and with the theory of price and markets, it will be necessary to reconsider these two statements.

The theory said that the assets of the nonbanking system consist of deposits (D), paper money (N), bonds (B_3) and plant (K), and that all of these deposits are acquired either from bank loans (L) or bond sales (B). It was assumed that

$$\begin{aligned} K &= k(L + B) + F_K \\ B_3 &= p(L + B) + F_B \end{aligned} \tag{8.1}$$

Presumably, if K and B_3 depend on total liabilities, they may also depend on total assets, since the two are equal:

$$\begin{aligned} K &= k(D + N + K + B_3) + F_K \\ B_3 &= p(D + N + K + B_3) + F_B \end{aligned} \tag{8.2}$$

Consequently, collecting terms,

$$\begin{aligned} K(1 - k) &= k(D + N + B_3) + F_K \\ B_3(1 - p) &= p(D + N + K) + F_B \end{aligned} \tag{8.3}$$

Substituting for B_3 in the first of these expressions and for K in the second,

$$\begin{aligned} K(1 - k) &= k\left(D + N + \frac{p}{1 - p}(D + N + K) + \frac{1}{1 - p}F_B\right) + F_K \\ B_3(1 - p) &= p\left(D + N + \frac{k}{1 - k}(D + N + B_3) + \frac{1}{1 - k}F_K\right) + F_B \end{aligned} \tag{8.4}$$

Collecting terms again,

$$K\left(1 - k - \frac{kp}{1-p}\right) = \left(k + \frac{p}{1-p}\right)(D+N) + \frac{k}{1-p}F_B + F_K$$
$$B_3\left(1 - p - \frac{kp}{1-k}\right) = \left(p + \frac{k}{1-k}\right)(D+N) + \frac{p}{1-k}F_K + F_B \tag{8.5}$$

So, finally, if (8.1) is true, K and B_3 may be shown to depend on the quantity of money $(D + N)$, on F_B and on F_K:

$$K = \frac{k+p-kp}{1-k-p}(D+N) + \frac{k}{1-k-p}F_B + \frac{1}{1-k-p}F_K$$
$$B_3 = \frac{k+p-kp}{1-k-p}(D+N) + \frac{p}{1-k-p}F_K + \frac{1}{1-k-p}F_B \tag{8.6}$$

The form of this statement is rather different from the starting point. We must now ask about the values of the coefficients k and p. The term F_B measures the level of demand for bonds by nonbanks; the term F_K measures the level of demand for plant. Since bonds and plant are substitutes for each other, it is natural to suppose that an increase in F_B reduces the amount of plant desired, and that an increase in F_K reduces the amount of bonds desired. Finally, if more money is available, nonbanks will want more plant and also more bonds. These three considerations, taken together, state that

$$\frac{k}{1-k-p} < 0 \qquad \text{(if } F_B \text{ increases, } K \text{ decreases)}$$

$$\frac{p}{1-k-p} < 0 \qquad \text{(if } F_K \text{ increases, } B_3 \text{ decreases)}$$

$$\frac{k+p-kp}{1-k-p} > 0 \qquad \text{(if } D+N \text{ increases, } K \text{ and } B_3 \text{ increase)}$$

Observe that (1) if $1 > k > 0, 1 > p > 0, k + p > 1$, then all three conditions are satisfied. Alternatively, (2) if $k < 0, p < 0, k + p < -1$, all three conditions are also satisfied. We must choose one of these two cases.

Turning to Table 8.2 again, consider the effect of open-market operations (ΔF_F) on the interest rate.[4] The expression $[-k(n+1)/(n+r)(1-k-p)]$

---

[4] Only the direction of change of the interest rate is discussed here. The formula relating interest rates and bond prices requires additional information that is not discussed in this theory: the annual coupon payment per bond, the average number of years to maturity, and so on. The introduction of these variables (which are important to businesses using the bond market) would complicate the mathematics of the theory.

is equal to $[-k/(1-k-p)] \times [(n+1)/(n+r)]$. It will be positive if $k/(1-k-p)$ is negative; and if it is positive, the interest rate will *fall*, just as Tiny Model 3 predicted.

Likewise, if $k/(1-k-p)$ is negative, an increase in the demand for excess reserves (ΔF_R) will cause the interest rate to rise. Again, this result is consistent with Tiny Model 3. We expect that if banks want more reserves, they want fewer bonds, so the price of bonds should fall and the interest rate should rise.

If $k/(1-k-p)$ is negative, an increase in the demand for Federal Reserve notes (ΔF_N) will increase the interest rate; this occurs because the banks, having fewer reserves and deposits, will hold fewer bonds.

So far, it has been said that $k/(1-k-p)$ was negative, but it has not been made clear which of (1) or (2) held. If there is increased demand for new plant (ΔF_K), we should expect more bonds to be issued, and also that the interest rate should rise. The new bond issues in this case are $1/(1-k-p)$; they will be positive if $(k+p) < -1$, but not if $(k+p) > 1$. The effect on the interest rate is given by the sign of $(1-p)/(1-k-p)$, and this fraction is the sum of $1/(1-k-p)$ and $-p/(1-k-p)$. The first term has just been declared positive; the second is also positive, since $-p > 0$. Thus we can reject possibility (1) in favor of (2).

Finally, if nonbank demand for bonds rises (ΔB_3), the interest rate will fall, providing $k/(1-k-p)$ is negative.

Now consider what has been achieved by the derivation of statements (8.6). Starting from Tiny Model 3, we could deduce from very simple propositions what should happen to the interest rate if various changes occurred in the bond market. It is natural to expect that a more complicated theory should be more or less consistent with these findings. But although statements 8 and 9 of Theory 9 seemed plausible, they led to findings that might well be inconsistent with Tiny Model 3. But from statements (8.6) a different, equally plausible pair of statements can be derived, which yield results consistent with Tiny Model 3.

To construct a theory which will be consistent with Tiny Model 3—and with microeconomics generally—we would have to take into account the results summarized in statement (6). The original formulation of statements 8 and 9 thus turns out to yield a set of predictions inconsistent with what economists think they know about the behavior of prices and markets.

It was not obvious that this particular pair of statements would have consequences of this sort. (Indeed, the author was surprised when he found them.) They have been retained in the text precisely because they illustrate the fact that theorizing is a difficult business. Theorists must be careful to explore as carefully as they can the implications of their assumptions. If no inquiry had been made into the implications of Theory 9 concerning the interest rate (which is not even mentioned in the theory), one would never have been able to guess that there were real difficulties underlying the apparently innocuous assumptions of the theory.

The larger the theory the larger the chance of failing to investigate conclusions such as these. It is for this reason that many economists are suspicious of attempts to date to construct large theories in the hope of creating "realism." The gain in realism is achieved only when the implications of the theory have been thoroughly explored.

A mathematical peculiarity of the reasoning in statements (1)–(6) is that a theory of our standard form $F = VM$ is replaced by one of the form $FN = VM$, involving two matrices, **N** and **M**. A characteristic of such theories is that two or more factors may appear in a single behavioral equation—just as in (6). Theories of the form $FN = VM$ have more general properties than those studied here. (The number of factors may exceed the number of variables, for instance.) And such theories may turn out to be more solidly related to the theory of individual behavior (microeconomics) than the theories presented here. We do not, however, discuss this more general type of theory, because it requires more advanced mathematics and economics than the theories we do discuss.

THEORY 10. FISCAL AND MONETARY POLICY

Differences of opinion among economists have been referred to at various places in this discussion. One group tends to think of the economy in terms of balance sheets, a second in terms of income statements. Consequently, when the first group seeks governmental remedies to macroeconomic disorders, it turns naturally to an analysis like Theory 9, and to a government agency like the Federal Reserve System to implement this analysis. The second group, in a similar situation, turns naturally to an analysis like Theories 3 or 4, and it seeks a remedy in changes in government spending or taxation.

As this book has progressed, the theories have tended to become larger—that is, to take more variables into account. The "larger" a theory, the more bothersome it is to handle; and the more difficult is it to interpret the results. In Tiny Model 1, the inverse matrix consisted of elements $1/(1 - a)$ and $a/(1 - a)$, the sign and meaning of which was fairly obvious. Theory 9, on the other hand, involves 5 coefficients, k, q, n, p, r. The precise content of a term such as

$$\frac{\Delta B}{\Delta F_F} = \frac{(n + 1) - q(1 - k - p)}{(n + r)(1 - k - p)}$$

is certainly not easy to interpret.

Chapter 4 showed how government spending and taxation may influence the rest of the economy. Theory 9 shows how the Federal Reserve System (by open-market and gold certificate transactions) can influence the balance sheet accounts. It is natural to devise a theory in which the System would also affect the national income accounts.

Theory 9 involves nine variables; Theories 3 and 4 involved five additional variables. To combine these theories would therefore involve at least fourteen variables. A prudent person avoids inverting 14 × 14 matrices more often than he has to.

Let us consider a topic that has come up before: the block-triangular matrix. To make things simpler, we introduce the following notation: The inverse of a matrix with blocks $\mathbf{M}_{ij}$, will have blocks $\overline{\mathbf{m}}_{ij}$. That is,

$$\begin{pmatrix} M_{11} & M_{12} \\ M_{21} & M_{22} \end{pmatrix}^{-1} = \begin{pmatrix} \overline{m}_{11} & \overline{m}_{12} \\ \overline{m}_{21} & \overline{m}_{22} \end{pmatrix}$$

The numbers of rows and columns in a block $\overline{\mathbf{m}}_{ij}$ are the same as in the corresponding block $\mathbf{M}_{ij}$.

From Chapter 2, we know that if a matrix is block-triangular, its inverse is also block-triangular. That is,

$$\begin{pmatrix} M_{11} & M_{12} \\ 0 & M_{22} \end{pmatrix}^{-1} = \begin{pmatrix} \overline{m}_{11} & \overline{m}_{12} \\ 0 & \overline{m}_{22} \end{pmatrix}$$

$$\begin{pmatrix} M_{11} & 0 \\ M_{21} & M_{22} \end{pmatrix}^{-1} = \begin{pmatrix} \overline{m}_{11} & 0 \\ \overline{m}_{21} & \overline{m}_{22} \end{pmatrix}$$

Suppose that Theory 3 or Theory 4 was a basis for the "income part" of a theory, and Theory 9 the basis for the "balance sheet part." Then there would be a variable-into-factor mapping

$$(\mathbf{F_W}, \mathbf{F_Y}) = (\mathbf{V_W}, \mathbf{V_Y}) \begin{pmatrix} M_{11} & M_{12} \\ M_{21} & M_{22} \end{pmatrix}$$

such that $\mathbf{M}_{11}$ resembled the matrix of Theory 9, and $\mathbf{M}_{22}$ resembled the matrix of Theory 3 (or 4).

It is much easier to invert a matrix that is block triangular than one that is not. We might construct a theory:

$$(\mathbf{F_W}, \mathbf{F_Y}) = (\mathbf{V_W}, \mathbf{V_Y}) \begin{pmatrix} M_{11} & M_{12} \\ 0 & M_{22} \end{pmatrix}$$

or we might construct a theory:

$$(\mathbf{F_W}, \mathbf{F_Y}) = (\mathbf{V_W}, \mathbf{V_Y}) \begin{pmatrix} M'_{11} & 0 \\ M'_{21} & M'_{22} \end{pmatrix}$$

Would this matter? Consider the factor-into-variable mappings:

$$(\mathbf{V_W}, \mathbf{V_Y}) = (\mathbf{F_W}, \mathbf{F_Y})\begin{pmatrix} \overline{m}_{11} & \overline{m}_{12} \\ 0 & \overline{m}_{22} \end{pmatrix}$$

$$(\mathbf{V_W}, \mathbf{V_Y}) = (\mathbf{F_W}, \mathbf{F_Y})\begin{pmatrix} \overline{m}'_{21} & 0 \\ \overline{m}'_{21} & \overline{m}'_{22} \end{pmatrix}$$

The elements of $(\overline{\mathbf{m}}_{ij})$ may be interpreted as $\left(\frac{\Delta V_j}{\Delta F_i}\right)$. Therefore, in the first case, $\overline{\mathbf{m}}_{21} = 0$ means that

$$\frac{\Delta V_j}{\Delta F_i} = 0$$

whenever F_i is a *factor* appearing in Theory 3, and V_j a *variable* appearing in Theory 9. In the second case, $\overline{\mathbf{m}}'_{12} = 0$ means that $\frac{\Delta V_j}{\Delta F_i} = 0$ whenever F_i is a *factor* appearing in Theory 9 and V_j a *variable* appearing in Theory 3.

In terms of economic policy, $\overline{\mathbf{m}}_{21} = 0$ $\overline{\mathbf{m}}_{12} \neq 0$ means that changes in government spending and taxation may affect the national income accounts but not the balance sheet accounts. In contrast, changes in Federal Reserve holdings of either government bonds or gold certificates affect both the national income and the national wealth.

On the other hand, $\overline{\mathbf{m}}'_{12} = 0$ $\overline{\mathbf{m}}'_{21} \neq 0$ means that changes in government spending and taxation affect both the income and the balance sheet (wealth) accounts. In contrast, changes in Federal Reserve holdings of either government bonds or gold certificates will affect the balance sheet accounts but not the national income accounts.

It is possible to construct both kinds of theories. There follows now a pair of theories involving fifteen variables, such that

(1) in each theory, the block $\mathbf{M}_{11}$ is basically like Theory 9
(2) in each theory, the block $\mathbf{M}_{22}$ is basically like Theory 3 or Theory 4.

However, in Theory 10A changes in the factors associated with income accounts have no effect on wealth variables; in Theory 10B changes in the factors associated with wealth accounts have no effect on income variables. Theory 10A is a theory to please the advocates of Federal Reserve policies; Theory 10B is a theory to please the advocates of "fiscal policies"—changes in government spending and taxation.

The two theories will differ in what seems at first to be rather minor ways—ten out of the fifteen statements in each theory are exactly the same. It is interesting, therefore, to see the way in which a small change in statements may affect the workings of a theory.

If it is possible to construct theories that contradict each other in important respects (after all, $\overline{\mathbf{m}}'_{12} = 0$ and $\overline{\mathbf{m}}_{21} = 0$ are propositions with important policy consequences), then economists could not decide, on theoretical grounds *alone*, what economic policies should be used to attain given objectives. They must know what the economy is really like, so as to verify which assertions like "$\overline{\mathbf{m}}'_{12} = 0$" or "$\overline{\mathbf{m}}_{21} = 0$" seem actually to be valid. So long as economists were content with Tiny Models 1 and 2, many economic questions (particularly policy questions) could be answered in principle. But if two theories give different predictions (the statements "$\mathbf{m}_{12} \neq 0$" and "$\mathbf{m}'_{21} \neq 0$" are predictions), then general answers to policy questions do not exist. A surprising number of people who should know better believe statements such as "Increases in government spending increase the national product," "Federal Reserve purchases of government securities increase the national product," "government deficits are bad," "Federal Reserve cannot really affect business conditions, except to make them worse." If they do not believe them, they believe the opposite. But while all such statements are plausible, their truth has not been demonstrated, so far as real economies are concerned.

So let us construct our pair of theories. Each, as noted, contains fifteen statements. Twelve are the same in both theories. Of these twelve, eight come from Theory 9, and the remainder from Chapter 4. They are numbered here in the order in which they appear in the variable-into-factor mapping. The notation is the same as in earlier theories.

(1) The Federal Reserve System is free to decide how many bonds it will hold:

$$F_F = B_1$$

(2) The Federal Reserve balance sheet is

$$A + B_1 = N + R$$

(3) The balance sheet of the banking system is

$$R + L + B_2 = D$$

(4) The demand for reserves by the banking system is

$$R = rD + F_R$$

(5) The supply of loans by the banking system is

$$L = qL + F_L$$

(8) The balance sheet of nonbanks is

$$N + D + B_3 + K = L + B + W$$

(9) The demand for bonds by nonbanks is

$$B_3 = p(L + B + W) + F_B$$

(10) The national product is

$$Y = C + I + G$$

(14) The government deficit is covered by selling bonds:

$$\Delta B = G - T$$

(15) Government is free to decide how much it will spend:

$$G = F_G$$

Now consider the pairs of alternate statements.

Pair 1

(6a) The statement concerning the demand for paper money is taken from Theory 9:

$$N = nD + F_N$$

If this statement is used, column 6 of M_{21} consists entirely of zeros.

(6b) The demand for money depends on the level of economic activity and on taxes:

$$N + D = v(C + I + G) + xT + F_N$$

If this statement is used $n = -1$ in 6a, and column 6 of $\mathbf{M}_{21}$ contains four nonzero elements.

[*Note:* The *purpose* of (6b) is to replace the consumption function $C = a(Y - T) + v(D + N) + F_C$ used in Theory 2. Money and income are linked in such a way that $\mathbf{M}_{12} \neq 0$. The function (6b) relates consumer spending and the amount of money. It is very much like monetary theories popular in the 1920s, in which $1/v$ was called "income velocity"—$1/v$ measures (if $F_N = 0$) how many times on the average "each piece of money" is spent in income-producing transactions.]

Pair 2

(7a) The statement covering the demand for plant and equipment is taken from Theory 9:

$$K = k(L + B + W) + F_K$$

If (7a) is used, the value of k must be tested to see whether it leads to appropriate conclusions about the interest rate. If this statement is used, column 7 of $\mathbf{M}_{21}$ consists entirely of zeros.

(7b) The demand for plant and equipment depends partly on the level of economic activity and on taxation policy:

$$K = k(L + B + W) + \bar{c}C + \bar{h}G + \bar{g}T + F_K$$

Formula (7b) is like Theory 4 in one respect. It revives the controversy about the effects of government actions on business; but it assumes that these actions affect the total demand for plant (K) rather than the demand for investment goods ($I \equiv \Delta K$). If (7b) is used, column 7 of $\mathbf{M}_{21}$ contains nonzero items.

Pair 3

(11a) The statement concerning consumption is taken from Theory 3:

$$C = a(Y - T) + F_C$$

If (11a) is used, column 2 of $\mathbf{M}_{12}$ consists entirely of zeros.

(11b) If consumption is influenced by the quantity of money,

$$C = a(Y - T) + v(N + D) + F_C$$

If (11b) is used, column 2 of $\mathbf{M}_{12}$ contains nonzero entries.

[*Note:* There is clearly a connection between statement (6b) and statement (11b). The first states that the demand for an asset (money) depends partly on income items. The second states that the demand for consumer goods depends partly on an asset item. In some respects, the two are similar. Economists who are seeking to "prove" a particular block-triangular scheme will be tempted to decide which to use according to their personal preferences. It is enough for us to point out that, from the theoretical point of view, the policy recommendations of such economists may be suspect.]

Pair 4

(12a) In Theory 4, investment depended solely on other income accounts.

$$I = cC + LG + gT + F_I$$

If this statement is used, column 3 of $\mathbf{M}_{12}$ consists entirely of zeros.

(12b) In Theory 7, the relation between total plant and investment was defined as

$$K = K_0 + I$$

If (12a) is used, column 3 of $\mathbf{M}_{12}$ contains a nonzero item. Statement (12b) is a means of guaranteeing that the change in plant is equal to investment. If it is not used, then ΔK is not necessarily equal to I. The difference would have to be explained either as a fall in prices of older plant, or as the closing down of certain presumably obsolete factories. The reasoning would resemble the reasoning in Theory 7 about bond prices.

Pair 5

(13a) If tax collections depend only on income,

$$T = tY + F_T$$

If this statement is used, column 4 of $\mathbf{M}_{12}$ consists entirely of zeros. Notice that this statement would not be true if there were taxes on tangible assets (K) or intangible assets (B_2 and B_3). The structure of the tax system may affect the decision to use (13a) rather than another system.

(13b) In Theory 9, the identity

$$B = B_0 + \Delta B$$

established the connection between "new bonds" and "existing bonds." If this expression is used, the only bonds issued will be government bonds, for statement (14) makes $\Delta B = G - T$. If this identity is not used, businesses will issue bonds in the amount $\Delta B - (G - T)$. If this statement is used the fourth column of $\mathbf{M}_{12}$ will contain a nonzero entry.

Problem 8.2 Select one statement from each pair, so as to construct variable-into-factor mappings incorporating Theory 8 of block $\mathbf{M}_{11}$, Theory 3 or Theory 4 as block $\mathbf{M}_{22}$, and having

(1) $\mathbf{M}_{12} = 0$, $\mathbf{M}_{21} \neq 0$
(2) $\mathbf{M}_{12} \neq 0$, $\mathbf{M}_{21} = 0$
(3) $\mathbf{M}_{12} \neq 0$, $\mathbf{M}_{21} \neq 0$

Use the inverses of the matrices to Theories 3, 4, and 7 to construct Tables for variants (1) and (2). Consider the different implications for Federal Reserve and Treasury policies under each of these two theories.

Problem 8.3 Suppose that government spending is always kept equal to tax revenue. What is the effect on the economy of a \$1 increase in spending and tax revenue? What is the effect on the government of unit changes in the other factors?

Problem 8.4 Is there a theory such that $\mathbf{M}_{12} = 0$ and the interest rate is fixed? If so, what are the consequences of changes in the government deficit and of open market operations on the variables in the economy?

Problem 8.5 Is there a theory such that $\mathbf{M}_{21} = 0$ and the interest rate is fixed? If so, what are the consequences of changes in the government deficit and of open market operations on the economy?

Problem 8.6 Suppose that the interest rate is not fixed, but that the Federal Reserve System carries on open market operations in such a way that changes in the government deficit do not affect the interest rate. What conditions does this impose on the factor-into-variable mapping? Consider separately the cases $\mathbf{M}_{12} = 0$ and $\mathbf{M}_{21} = 0$.

Problem 8.7 Suppose that the interest rate is not fixed, and that the Federal Reserve System carries on open market operations in such a way as to keep the level of the national product constant when the demand for investment and/or plant changes. What conditions does this policy impose on the factor-into-variable mapping? Consider separately the cases $\mathbf{M}_{12} = 0$ and $\mathbf{M}_{21} = 0$.

Problem 8.8 Suppose that the Federal Reserve System does nothing, and the government deficit is kept at a level that stabilizes the interest rate. What happens when the demand for investment and/or plant falls? What conditions does this policy impose on the factor-into-variable mapping? Consider separately the cases $\mathbf{M}_{12} = 0$ and $\mathbf{M}_{21} = 0$.

Theory 10 presents a more elaborate form of the problem introduced in Theory 8: What is the connection between income and wealth? Shall the economy be considered as a block-triangular system? If so, shall we say that the factors associated with income have no effect on the variables associated with wealth? Or shall we say that the factors associated with wealth have no effect on income?

Viewed from the point of view of the theorist, the difference does not really matter. Block-triangular matrices are simply easier to invert. The theorist can construct either block-triangular or "irreducible" theories (that is theories that do not have block-triangular matrices). He can even take into account some of the central behavioral controversies without losing his freedom to set up a block-triangular theory.

The two main controversies discussed have related to the connection between investment and government and to the connection between consumption (or investment) and the money supply. Since investment is the same as the change in plant, it is possible to assert either of two very similar propositions: (1) government spending and tax policies affect the total amount of plant (K) desired by businesses; and (2) government spending and tax policies affect the amount of investment ($\Delta K \equiv I$) desired by businesses. By selecting one statement rather than the other, theorists can help make their theory "more block-triangular" in the desired direction.

Theorists can make the connection between money and spending in two ways. First, the consumption function (or the investment function) may have money as one of its arguments: If consumers or businesses have more cash they will naturally spend more. Second, the demand for assets is ordinarily related to the quantity of money; if it is also related to the level of economic activity a linkage between money and spending is created. Thus, businesses use plant to make goods. The larger their current output is, the more plant we should expect them to want; and the more cash they have, the more plant we would expect them to want.

Theorists thus have some freedom to consider alternative formal statements relating the income accounts to the wealth accounts. By selecting among the alternatives in a clever enough way, the theorist can end up with all kinds of block-triangular arrangements. This fact is another illustration of a central proposition running through this book: There are many logically consistent theories, but not all of these apply to any given country. Having done his best, the theorist must hand his theories over to the statistician for testing.

TREASURY BILLS AND COMMON STOCKS

In Chapter 1, reasons were given for treating stocks and bonds as if they were the same. Readers who have worked out Theory 10 are probably grateful that they were lumped together. But, after all, stocks and bonds are different. Moreover, there are many kinds of bonds. It is unfortunately necessary to go into these matters a little, even though no formal theory will be presented.

Government bonds are documents that fall due, and are repaid regularly. Individual issues of bonds are in amounts of a few billion dollars each, and some are smaller. When the bonds are issued in the first place, they are issued for varying periods of time, ranging from three months to twenty years. The reason for this variation is that all sorts of institutions would like to hold government bonds. Some are willing to hold bonds of short life, and others bonds of long life. The Treasury feels it has an easier time selling bonds if it has all kinds of bonds to sell.

The very short-lived bonds—90 to 270 days—are called Treasury Bills. For many years the Treasury has been selling between one and two billion dollars' worth of these every Monday morning. These are handy investments for people who are accumulating cash that they expect to invest in something permanent soon, but not quite yet. They are handy for the Treasury, too. Tax payments fall due on certain dates (everyone knows that the annual tax statement for individuals falls due on April 15), while the government has to make payments all the time. By borrowing a little more on some Mondays and a little less on other Mondays, the Treasury is able to keep its cash balance stable.

Students of the banking system have been particularly interested in the market for Treasury Bills, for they feel that these bills are "very much like" money—indeed they are turned into money after 90 or 180 or 270 days. But these bills are usually *assets* of the banks and *debts* of the nonbanks (that is, government), whereas most forms of money are *debts* of the banks and *assets* of the nonbanks. So if these bills are "nearly" money, they are "nearly" a different kind of money.

In the 1950s, The Federal Reserve System went through a phase when all its operations were in Treasury Bills, and none in longer-term government bonds. At this time, the System felt that interest rates on long-term government bonds were competitive with the interest rates on private bonds and stocks, while interest rates on Treasury Bills were not. If this were true, then the "Bills only" policy would make it possible for the System to affect the reserves of banks without affecting business investment, which (see Theory 1) is affected by the interest rate. This policy was abandoned in 1960–1961, because business activity was by that time falling; Federal Reserve decided that it might be a good idea to stimulate investment by buying long-term government bonds and forcing down the interest rate.

To formulate this theory, or to test it, one has to break the variable "bonds" of Theory 10 into parts. Such a breakup increases the complexity of theory, and is not necessary for present purposes. The reason for carrying it out would be that people who actually do business in "the bond market" feel that Treasury Bills are quite different from other government debt. If such a breakup were undertaken, it would have to specify, for instance, what the difference might be between the demand for bills and the demand for bonds. The result of setting up such a theory would presumably be to enable us to explain why interest rates on bills may change at different rates from interest rates on bonds. This fact has often been observed, and a body of literature about it exists, both in business management and economics.

The depression of 1929 started with a violent fall in stock market prices, and everyone felt that this fall had something important to do with the depression which followed. Usually stock market prices start to fall *before* unemployment begins to rise in recessions, and start to rise *before* recoveries begin. In this sense, it is natural to think of stock market events as "causes" rather than "effects" of the business cycle.

There is still no good theory relating the stock market to the rest of the economy. The stocks fit into the economy much as bonds did in Theory 10 —although banks have not been allowed to own stocks since 1934. That is, stocks are balance sheet items; changes in stock issues are related to investment, just as bond issues are. But it is extremely difficult to theorize systematically about the stock market, because it is difficult to make simple theories about the motives of investors in stock.

The motives of investors are of many kinds. Some of them seek an annual income on their investment, while others seek to resell their investment at a profit. The price of a stock is influenced by its current earning power, but is also influenced by what investors expect its future earning power to be. These expectations may or may not be justified; even if they are not justified, however, they may influence market prices. When one attempts to formulate hypotheses about the assets of the community that are invested in stocks, one must take into account such expectations, even "unreasonable" ones. Thus, if investors expect that prevailing increases or decreases will continue, the statements describing demand consider not only the levels of variables but also the changes that are taking place in these variables.

Mathematically, theories of this sort are called differential or difference equations and are much more complicated than the theories discussed here. From an economic point of view, these theories become much messier because of the variety of expectations that may be involved. Investors in the stock market are partly influenced by the *state* of the economy, and partly by current *changes* in the stock market itself. In the terminology of this book, it is not clear to what extent the stock market should be thought of as a "factor" influencing the economy, and to what extent it is a "variable" determined (along with others) by economic conditions generally.

In mentioning the Treasury Bill market and the stock market, we are merely pointing out two areas that are the object of advanced study. In this book, we have got around them by compressing them into an aggregate called "bonds." This procedure enables us to deal with an economy containing "only" fifteen variables. It is quite reasonable that people who are particularly interested in the securities markets should criticize Theories 9 and 10 for being too simple. They are, of course. They may, however, form the basis for more detailed analysis of the relation between these markets and the rest of the economy.

Problem 8.9 The various versions of these theories contain two initial conditions, B_0, the total debt, and K_0, the stock of plant. Discuss the economic meaning of changes in B_0 and K_0, and show the effects of such changes on the variables of the system. To what extent are they consistent with the discussion in Chapter 6? To what extent are they new?

Problem 8.10 Consider, in particular, the question of why there was no depression after World War II. That is, suppose that government spending rises sharply for several years, and there are therefore several years with large deficits. Then government spending drops to the "prewar" level. Will the national product also drop to the former level; or will the increase in government debt (bonds held by banks and nonbanks) cause an increase in the national product, as compared to prewar?

9

Theories about Values and Theories about Prices and Quantities

PRICE CHANGES AND QUANTITY CHANGES

Each of the theories discussed so far has been about (1) some particular part of the social accounts, and (2) some particular sectors of the economy. None has taken everything at once. When theories grow beyond a certain size, they involve so many variables and factors at once that there is no simple and natural way of looking at them. One important subject, however, can still be treated in a simple way: prices. Various things have been said (for example) about the variable called "consumption": (1) it is a part of national income; (2) it is thought to depend in a linear way on total income, on disposable income or on the size of personal cash balances. The first statement is based on a definition: $Y = C + I + G$. This definition states that it is possible to add together C, I, and G. The second statement, of the form $C = aY + F_C$, says that there can be linear relations between a numerical variable *consumption*, and other numerical variables and factors.

If C, I, G, are the sets of goods bought by households, businesses and government, then $C + I + G$ is the set of goods each element of which has been bought by some household or by some business or by a government unit. But a set is not a number, and it makes no sense, for instance, to write $C = aY + F_C$, as is done in Tiny Model 1. To define such a function, it is necessary to associate a number with any set of goods; then it is necessary to assert that these numbers can be added together. If they can be added, the rules of arithmetic apply, not the rules of set addition. Only if there are *numbers* C, Y can the meaning of $C = aY + F_C$ be defined.

Suppose that family F last Monday bought three pounds of steak, five pounds of potatoes, a washing machine, and a bottle of aspirin. Then the set consisting of these objects can be transformed into a number, if each object is valued at the price that F paid for it. For example, consider the valuation:

three pounds of steak at \$1.19 =	\$ 3.57
five pounds of potatoes at \$.07 =	.35
one washing machine =	179.00
one bottle aspirin =	.29
Total	\$183.21

Family F's consumption on Monday was \$183.21, which is a number. It can be added to similar numbers representing consumption on Tuesday, Wednesday, and so on.

This method of assigning numbers to sets consisting of quantities of goods and services involves the use of prices. The theories presented so far have calculated the changes in variables that are associated with changes in the factors of the system. But such change may occur because the quantities of goods purchased (or owned) have changed, because the prices paid for the goods have changed, or both. To give a complete description of what is going on in an economy, it is necessary to separate changes in quantities of goods from changes in price. A complete theory would specify a connection between quantity changes and price changes. The following example gives an illustration of a simple theory in which price and quantity changes are introduced separately.

Suppose that the economy is as described in Tiny Model 1. That is,

$$(\mathbf{I}, \mathbf{F_C}) = (\mathbf{Y}, \mathbf{C})\begin{pmatrix} 1 & -a \\ -1 & 1 \end{pmatrix}$$

and from this statement, we infer that

$$(\Delta\mathbf{I}, \Delta\mathbf{F_C})\begin{pmatrix} \dfrac{1}{1-a} & \dfrac{a}{1-a} \\[2ex] \dfrac{1}{1-a} & \dfrac{1}{1-a} \end{pmatrix} = (\Delta\mathbf{Y}, \Delta\mathbf{C})$$

It is natural to ask exactly what is meant by $\Delta\mathbf{I}$, $\Delta\mathbf{F_C}$, $\Delta\mathbf{Y}$, $\Delta\mathbf{C}$. If we follow the reasoning given above, then $\Delta\mathbf{C}$, the change in consumption, would be calculated as follows:

$$\begin{aligned} \mathbf{V}'_1 - \mathbf{V}'_1 &= \Delta\mathbf{V}_1 = \text{the change in spending on commodity 1} \\ \mathbf{V}'_2 - \mathbf{V}_2 &= \Delta\mathbf{V}_2 = \text{the change in spending on commodity 2} \\ &\cdots \\ \mathbf{V}'_n - \mathbf{V}_n &= \Delta\mathbf{V}_n = \text{the change in spending on commodity } n \\ \sum(\mathbf{V}'_i - \mathbf{V}_i) &= \Delta\mathbf{C} = \text{the change in consumption} \end{aligned}$$

and similar additions would be used to define the other terms needed by the theory.

In Tiny Model 3, a single market was discussed. The amounts demanded and supplied for any commmodity were said to depend in a linear way on prices, so that for each commodity,

$$(\mathbf{F_D}, \mathbf{F_S}) = (\mathbf{Q}, \mathbf{P})\begin{pmatrix} 1 & 1 \\ -e & -f \end{pmatrix}$$

and hence

$$(\mathbf{Q}, \mathbf{P}) = (\mathbf{F_D}, \mathbf{F_S})\begin{pmatrix} \dfrac{-f}{e-f} & \dfrac{-1}{e-f} \\[2ex] \dfrac{e}{e-f} & \dfrac{1}{e-f} \end{pmatrix}$$

$$(\Delta\mathbf{Q}, \Delta\mathbf{P}) = (\Delta\mathbf{F_D}, \Delta\mathbf{F_S})\begin{pmatrix} \dfrac{-f}{e-f} & \dfrac{-1}{e-f} \\[2ex] \dfrac{e}{e-f} & \dfrac{1}{e-f} \end{pmatrix}$$

Thus changes in quantity ($\Delta\mathbf{Q}$) and in price ($\Delta\mathbf{P}$) depend in a linear way on the changes in the levels of demand ($\Delta\mathbf{F_D}$) and supply ($\Delta\mathbf{F_S}$). Suppose two distinct possibilities:

(1) Only demand changes, so that $(\Delta\mathbf{F_D}, \Delta\mathbf{F_S}) = (\Delta\mathbf{F_D}, \mathbf{0})$.

In this case,

$$(\mathbf{\Delta Q}, \mathbf{\Delta P}) = \mathbf{\Delta F_D}\left(\frac{-\mathbf{f}}{\mathbf{e}-\mathbf{f}}, \frac{-1}{\mathbf{e}-\mathbf{f}}\right)$$

(2) Only supply changes, so that $(\mathbf{\Delta F_D}, \mathbf{\Delta F_S}) = (\mathbf{0}, \mathbf{\Delta F_S})$.
In this case,

$$(\mathbf{\Delta Q}, \mathbf{\Delta P}) = \mathbf{\Delta F_S}\left(\frac{\mathbf{e}}{\mathbf{e}-\mathbf{f}}, \frac{1}{\mathbf{e}-\mathbf{f}}\right)$$

Now consider what happens to total spending:

$$\Delta V = (P + \Delta P)(Q + \Delta Q) - pQ = p\Delta Q + Q\Delta p + \Delta p\Delta Q$$

When ΔP and ΔQ are substituted in this expression, then
(1) if only demand has changed,

$$\Delta V = P\left(\frac{-f}{e-f}\Delta F_D\right) + Q\left(\frac{-1}{e-f}\Delta F_D\right) + \frac{f}{(e-f)^2}(\Delta F_D)^2$$

(2) if only supply has changed,

$$\Delta V = P\left(\frac{e}{e-f}\Delta F_S\right) + Q\left(\frac{1}{e-f}\Delta F_S\right) + \frac{e}{(e-f)^2}(\Delta F_S)^2$$

These expressions are no longer linear. The first involves $(\Delta F_D)^2$ and the second involves $(\Delta F_S)^2$. Thus if Tiny Model 3 is true, it may prevent the construction of linear theories (such as Tiny Model 1) that distinguish between price and quantity changes. In this case, we know that such theories will be more difficult, mathematically, than those described in this book.

Problem 9.1 Assume that both ΔF_D and ΔF_S are different from zero. Derive an expression for ΔV.

PRICE INDICES, QUANTITY INDICES, AND MACROECONOMICS

The variables that have appeared in all theories to date have basically been "values." They could change either in response to price changes or to quantity changes. In a set containing many kinds of goods, very large numbers of possibilities for change exist. Thus a change in the value of consumption from a number C to a number C' may come about literally in an infinite number of ways. But economists often find it convenient to think of a macroeconomic value, such as consumption, as being the product of two *indices*, a *price index* P_C, and a *quantity index* Q_C. Strictly speaking, they do not say that $C = P_C Q_C$, but rather that C varies with the product $P_C Q_C$, or that $C = kP_C Q_C$ for some constant (number) k. An understanding of indices is essential to an understanding of macroeconomic thinking.

Imagine that we look at the prices of individual kinds of consumer goods at two different dates, and that these prices turn out to be P_1 and P_1' for commodity 1, P_2 and P_2' for commodity 2, and so on. In general the prices will not change proportionately. That is, $P_1'/P_1 \neq P_2'/P_2 \neq \cdots \neq P_n'/P_n$. It is not silly, however, to ask how much, *on the average*, prices changed.

Again, imagine that we look at the amounts of individual kinds of consumer goods bought in two different periods, and that these quantities turn out to be q_1 and q_1' for commodity 1, q_2 and q_2' for commodity 2, and so on. In general these quantities do not change proportionately. That is, $q_1'/q_1 \neq q_2'/q_2 \neq \cdots \neq q_n'/q_n$. It is not silly, however, to ask how much, *on the average* the quantities of goods changed.

A *price index* is a measure of the average level of some collection of prices; a *quantity index* is a measure of the average level of some collection of quantities. Both indices are "pure numbers" in a special sense. Both indices are referred to a *base period*, which is ordinarily taken as 100. Thus, for instance, the statement, "The index of consumer prices in 1965 was 109.9 on a 1957–1959 base" means that on the average, prices of goods listed as "consumer goods" in the index in 1965 were 9.9 per cent higher in 1965 than in 1957–1959. The statement, "The index of manufacturing output in 1955 was 264 on a 1929 base" means that when outputs of particular goods called "manufactures" are compared for the years 1929 and 1955, on the average the 1955 outputs are 2.64 times as great as the 1929 outputs.

Actual calculation of indexes do not use all prices or all outputs. A large economy produces literally hundreds of thousands of different kinds of goods, as you can tell by looking at a Sears and Roebuck catalog, or by walking through a supermarket. Thus an index is not a complete enumeration, but a representative selection of goods. To make an index, statisticians select a relatively small list of goods, and "weight" the individual items according to their importance in the economy. The formulas used would be of the following kind:

$$\text{The price index} = \frac{\text{the cost of purchasing a given shopping list in year } Y}{\text{the cost of purchasing that shopping list in the base period}}$$

$$\text{The quantity index} = \frac{\text{the value, in base period prices, of output of a given list of goods in year } Y}{\text{the value of output of the given list of goods in the base period}}$$

Since an index is an "average" change, it is greatly affected by the way in which individual prices and outputs change, and by the nature of the relation between price and quantity changes. The numerical example in Table 9.1 is extreme, but it illustrates why economists do well to be cautious in their use of indices.

TABLE 9.1

ILLUSTRATIVE DATA FOR THE CONSTRUCTION OF PRICE AND QUANTITY INDICES

	YEAR 1	YEAR 2
Raw data		
Price of Commodity 1	1.0	.5
Price of Commodity 2	1.0	2.0
Output of Commodity 1	100	200
Output of Commodity 2	100	50
Value of total output		
In Year 1 prices	200	250
In Year 2 prices	250	200

The price index takes a given shopping list and evaluates it at two different dates. Output of year 1 was worth 200 in prices of year 1, and 250 in prices of year 2; thus this price index for year 2 would be $\frac{250}{200} \times 100 = 125$; on the other hand, output of year 2 was worth 250 in year 1 prices, and 200 in year 2 prices, so that this price index for year 2 would be $\frac{200}{250} \times 100 = 80$. Did prices on the average, go up 25 percent or go down 20 percent between year 1 and year 2? There is no single answer to this question.

Problem 9.2 Compute quantity indexes for output (1) using year 1 prices, and (2) using year 2 prices as weights.

The numerical example just given shows that it may be impossible to decide whether, on the average, prices or outputs have risen or fallen. That is, it may be possible to construct one index showing an increase, and another index, using the same basic data, showing a decrease. This situation is a statistical property of indexes, and one might argue that a theoretical book such as this should not involve itself with statistical problems.

Statisticians are well aware of the uncertainty associated with the use of indexes. They have a variety of formulas for constructing indexes, some of which are relatively less subject to uncertainty than that just used. But the problem of measuring price and quantity changes, in the macroeconomic sense, is one which *in principle* has more than one answer. If it were not so natural to think in macroeconomic terms, we would be tempted to throw out all theories that distinguish between price and quantity changes, on the grounds that these are indefinable concepts.

The theories in this book are quite clear so long as *values* such as business spending, consumer spending, total plant, and so on are under discussion. There may be practical difficulties about measuring these values, but these are not difficulties of principle. When, however, an "aggregated" value such as those listed above, is thought of as the product of a price index and a quantity index, then even in principle it may be impossible to construct indices that give clear answers to the questions "Did prices rise, on the average?" and "Did quantities rise, on the average?"

Macroeconomists recognize this difficulty. Some are more grudging in their recognition than others. Most of them will say that indices are useful within limits:

(1) If prices (or outputs) vary more or less in strict proportion, then the range of possible indices that can be constructed from given data is small;

(2) Over most of our history, such rough proportionality is found in periods of up to 20 years in length;

(3) When a theory is tested over a relatively short period, then, economists usually proceed as if they were theorizing about the production index (or the price index), rather than about the activities for which these indexes stand. This procedure is justified on the grounds that if any other index had been used, the result would not have been very different.

THEORIES ABOUT VALUES AND THEORIES ABOUT QUANTITIES

Let us suppose that it is possible to construct unambiguous price and quantity indices, so that the value of any macroeconomic variable may be written as the product of a price index and a quantity index. Then any theory may be formulated either as a *theory about values* or as a *theory about quantities*. But the two theories are not interchangeable.

This proposition will be illustrated by means of Tiny Model 1. This theory states that

$$Y = C + I$$

$$C = aY + F_C$$

Economists think about this model in two different ways:

$$\left.\begin{aligned} P_Y Q_Y &= P_C Q_C + P_I Q_I \\ P_C Q_C &= aP_Y Q_Y + F_C \end{aligned}\right\} \text{A theory about values}$$

$$\left.\begin{aligned} Q_Y &= Q_C + Q_I \\ Q_C &= aQ_Y + \emptyset_C \end{aligned}\right\} \text{A theory about quantities}$$

where the variables represent indices as follows:

For	The price index is	The quantity index is
Total Output	P_Y	Q_Y
Consumption	P_C	Q_C
Investment	P_I	Q_I

Problem 9.3 These two versions of Tiny Model 1 have consumption functions that are in some respects the same and in some respects different. Compare what they say about the way people spend their incomes.

These two versions of Tiny Model 1 both have a statement that the national product (Y) is the sum of consumption (C) and investment (I). If the three variables are thought of as money values, then they have a common unit, dollars, and it makes sense to add them. If they are thought of as physical quantities, it is not clear that they can be added (just as we are taught that apples and oranges cannot be added).

If Y, C, and I are indexes, then a mixed situation exists: (1) to the extent that the indexes are calculated using prices in "a base year," they are analogous to values and can be added; (2) but the choice of a base year is arbitrary, so that the indexes are ill-defined measures of quantity. That is, the value of the coefficient a in the second statement of the theory, might well depend upon the particular year chosen as base. This would be true because consumers react to changes in the price structure as well as to changes in income. When the variables are thought of as indexes, considerations relating to price structure are all "swept under the rug." In effect, we talk about Y, C, and I as if they were really quantities, although we know that they are not. In this sense, attempts to sort out price effects and quantity effects involve theorizing about numbers that are only uncertainly related to the phenomena the theory is about.

Returning to the consideration of the two versions of the Tiny Model, it is easy to see that P_Y is a sort of mean of P_C and P_I, for

$$P_Y Q_Y = P_C Q_C + P_I Q_I$$

implies that

$$P_Y = P_C\left(\frac{Q_C}{Q_Y}\right) + P_I\left(\frac{Q_I}{Q_Y}\right)$$

If it were true, as the *theory about quantities* states, that $Q_Y = Q_C + Q_I$, then,

$$P_Y = P_C\left(\frac{Q_C}{Q_Y}\right) + P_I\left(1 - \frac{Q_C}{Q_Y}\right)$$

But if the *theory about values* holds, one cannot make this assertion as more than an approximation.

If the *theory about values* holds,

$$P_C Q_C = aP_Y Q_Y + F_C$$
$$= a(P_C Q_C + P_I Q_I) + F_C$$
$$P_C Q_C = \frac{1}{1-a}(P_I Q_I + F_C)$$

Suppose that the value of investment ($P_I Q_I$) and F_C are constant. Then the right hand side of this equation is some number, say W. Thus

$$P_C Q_C = W$$

and

$$Q_C = \frac{W}{P_C}$$

This statement says that the money expenditure on consumer goods does not depend on the price level. Hence it also says that savings does not depend on the price level, but only on money income. This statement might be true, but one would have to know the facts about consumer behavior to assert it.

If the *theory about quantities holds*, then

$$Q_C = aQ_Y + \phi_C$$

relates the quantity of consumer goods purchased to total output. Then,

$$Q_C = a(Q_C + Q_I) + \phi_C$$
$$Q_C = \frac{1}{1-a}(Q_I + \phi_C)$$

Suppose now that

$$P_C = P_I + \Delta P_I$$

Then the value of consumer spending is

$$P_C Q_C = \frac{1}{1-a}(P_I Q_I + P_C \phi_C + Q_I \Delta P_I)$$

This expression is certainly different from the corresponding expression for $P_C Q_C$ in the theory about values. Specifically the right-hand side is *not* independent of the price of consumer goods. In particular, the term $P_C \phi_C$ replaces F_C; it changes automatically as P_C changes. Therefore both spending on consumption ($P_C Q_C$) and savings change as consumer prices change. This statement might be true. Consequently it is a question of fact whether the theory about quantities or the theory about values is a better representation of consumer behavior.

In a theory (either about values or about quantities) that asserts that $C = aY + F_C$, it is true that, given F_C, $\Delta C = a\Delta Y$, and that a is a given number. It is also true that the matrix associated with this system,

$$\begin{pmatrix} 1 & -1 \\ -a & 1 \end{pmatrix}$$

is independent of prices. Suppose that

$$(\mathbf{I}, \mathbf{F_C}) = (\mathbf{Y}, \mathbf{C})\begin{pmatrix} 1 & 1 \\ -a & -1 \end{pmatrix}$$

is a theory about values. Then

$$(\mathbf{I}, \mathbf{F_C}) = (\mathbf{P_I Q_I}, \mathbf{F_C}) = (\mathbf{Q_I}, \mathbf{F_C})\begin{pmatrix} P_I & 0 \\ 0 & 1 \end{pmatrix}$$

and

$$(\mathbf{Y}, \mathbf{C}) = (\mathbf{P_Y Q_Y}, \mathbf{P_C Q_C}) = (\mathbf{Q_Y}, \mathbf{Q_C})\begin{pmatrix} P_Y & 0 \\ 0 & P_C \end{pmatrix}$$

Since

$$\begin{pmatrix} P_I & 0 \\ 0 & 1 \end{pmatrix}^{-1} = \begin{pmatrix} \frac{1}{P_I} & 0 \\ 0 & 1 \end{pmatrix}$$

the relation between the vectors of quantity variables and factors is given by

$$(\mathbf{Q_I}, \mathbf{F_C}) = (\mathbf{Q_Y}, \mathbf{Q_C})\begin{pmatrix} P_Y & 0 \\ 0 & P_C \end{pmatrix}\begin{pmatrix} 1 & 1 \\ -a & -1 \end{pmatrix}\begin{pmatrix} \dfrac{1}{P_I} & 0 \\ 0 & 1 \end{pmatrix}$$

$$= (\mathbf{Q_Y}, \mathbf{Q_C})\begin{pmatrix} P_Y & P_Y \\ -aP_C & -P_C \end{pmatrix}\begin{pmatrix} \dfrac{1}{P_I} & 0 \\ 0 & 1 \end{pmatrix}$$

$$= (\mathbf{Q_Y}, \mathbf{Q_C})\begin{pmatrix} \dfrac{P_Y}{P_I} & P_Y \\ -a\dfrac{P_C}{P_I} & -P_C \end{pmatrix}$$

Here the matrix which maps $(\mathbf{Q_Y}, \mathbf{Q_C})$ into $(\mathbf{Q_I}, \mathbf{F_C})$ is not independent of prices, and its inverse is therefore not independent of prices.

Problem 9.4 Suppose that the theory about the quantities holds:

$$(\mathbf{Q_I}, \mathbf{F_C}) = (\mathbf{Q_Y}, \mathbf{Q_C})\begin{pmatrix} 1 & 1 \\ -a & -1 \end{pmatrix}$$

What is the mapping that takes $(\mathbf{Y}, \mathbf{C})$ into $(\mathbf{I}, \mathbf{F_C})$?

Granted that it makes a difference whether Tiny Model 1 is supposed to relate to values or to quantities, it is natural to ask why the discussion about index numbers in the second section of this chapter matters. The rest of this section is a discussion of this question. It shows that the numerical value we might assign to the marginal propensity to consume (a) in Tiny Model 1 is not independent of the way we measure quantities of output. Consequently, whenever we consider this theory as a theory about quantities, the coefficient in the theory is materially affected by the statistical calculation used to measure quantities. This fact makes it much more difficult to interpret theories about quantities than theories about values.

Suppose that Tiny Model 1 is a theory about quantities, and that we could observe the economy at two dates.[1] Then at each date C, Y, I, and F_C would be given numbers.

At the first date it would be the case that

$$Y_1 = C_1 + I_1$$
$$C_1 = aY_1 + F_{C1}$$

[1] In practice, we would never compute a on the basis of only two observations. However many observations we used, the same problem would exist.

and at the second date it would be the case that

$$Y_2 = C_2 + I_2$$

$$C_2 = aY_2 + F_{C2}$$

We could then solve for a by using the second equation of the model:

$$(1, -\mathbf{a})\begin{pmatrix} C_1 & C_2 \\ Y_1 & Y_2 \end{pmatrix} = (\mathbf{F}_{C1}, \mathbf{F}_{C2})$$

since the matrix can be inverted:

$$(1, -\mathbf{a}) = (\mathbf{F}_{C1}, \mathbf{F}_{C2})\begin{pmatrix} \dfrac{Y_2}{C_1Y_2 - C_2Y_1} & \dfrac{-C_2}{C_1Y_2 - C_2Y_1} \\ \dfrac{-C_1}{C_1Y_2 - C_2Y_1} & \dfrac{Y_1}{C_1Y_2 - C_2Y_1} \end{pmatrix}$$

The first equation of the model may now be substituted for Y_1 and Y_2:

$$(1, -\mathbf{a}) = (\mathbf{F}_{C1}, \mathbf{F}_{C2})$$

$$\times \begin{pmatrix} \dfrac{C_2 + I_2}{C_1(C_2 + I_2) - C_2(C_1 + I_1)} & \dfrac{-C_2}{C_1(C_2 + I_2) - C_2(C_1 + I_1)} \\ \dfrac{-C_1}{C_1(C_2 + I_2) - C_2(C_1 + I_1)} & \dfrac{C_1 + I_1}{C_1(C_2 + I_2) - C_2(C_1 + I_1)} \end{pmatrix}$$

Since

$$1 = \frac{F_{C1}(C_2 + I_2) - F_{C2}C_1}{C_1(C_2 + I_2) - C_2(C_1 + I_1)}$$

The numerator and denominator of the fraction are equal. Therefore it is possible to rewrite

$$-a = \frac{-F_{C1}C_2 + F_{C2}(C_1 + I_1)}{C_1(C_2 + I_2) - C_2(I_1 + C_1)}$$

in the form

$$-a = \frac{-F_{C1}C_2 + F_{C2}(C_1 + I_1)}{F_{C1}(C_2 + I_2) - F_{C2}C_1}$$

$$a = \frac{F_{C2}(C_1 + I_1) - F_{C1}C_2}{F_{C1}(C_2 + I_2) - F_{C2}C_1}$$

To assert that Tiny Model 1 is about quantities is to assert that C_1, C_2, I_1, I_2 and F_C are based upon quantity indices. These indices may be computed using prices of any year as weights. We shall show that our estimate of a, the marginal propensity to consume, depends on the choice of the quantity index.

In the equality

$$F_{C1}(C_2 + I_2) - F_{C2}C_1 = C_1(C_2 + I_2) - C_2(C + I_1)$$

we may set $C_1 + I_1 = 1$, since income in the base year is arbitrary. Then

$$(F_{C1} - C_1)(C_2 + I_2) = C_2 + F_{C2}C_1$$

This means that the larger I_2 is, the larger will be F_{C2}. The choice of a particular index of output thus influences the estimated change in F_{C2}.

In the equality

$$a = \frac{F_{C2} - F_{C1}C_2}{F_{C1}(C_2 + I_2) - F_{C2}C_1}$$

the larger I_2 is, the larger will be the numerator, and the smaller will be the denominator of a; hence the larger will be our estimate of the marginal propensity to consume.

On the other hand, the smaller C_2 is, the larger will be our estimate of the marginal propensity to consume.

If either F_{C2} or C_2 is sufficiently large, it is possible for a to become negative.

From this demonstration, it is clear that the value we might assign to a is not independent of the way in which measurements of the quantity of output are made. It is natural to inquire whether this fact is of importance. On this score, we may say that output of the investment goods industries is particularly uncertain. For example,[2] if United States machinery output is priced in 1899 prices we would conclude that output was 5.5 times as great in 1939 as in 1899. If it is priced in 1939 prices, we would conclude that it had *decreased* 30 percent from 1899 to 1939. On the other hand, over the same period, output of consumer durable goods increased 102 percent or 82 percent, depending on whether 1899 or 1939 prices are used as weights.

These examples are dramatic, mainly because a long period of time is used. But the 1954 Census of Manufactures lists measures of the output of 436 industries in 1954, compared to 1947. In 79 percent of all cases, the production index using 1947 prices gave a higher 1954 "output" than the index using 1954 prices.

---

[2] These facts are presented in more detail in E. Ames and J. A. Carlson, "Production Index Bias as a Measure of Economic Development" (*Oxford Economic Papers*, March 1968).

Thus when macroeconomic theories about quantity are used, it is impossible to consider the values of coefficients appearing in matrices without considering the particular way in which the measurement of quantity was made. This measurement problem stands between the economist and the phenomenon he studies. In contrast, when the theory is about values, the economist has fewer questions about the phenomenon he studies. He may feel that the data are incomplete; but once the data have been collected, they are immediately relevant to the theory.

Problem 9.5 Go back to the beginning of this section, and consider what happens if Tiny Model 1 is used to construct a *theory about prices*, the objective of which is to explain variations in the price of consumer and investment goods.

THEORY 11. A THEORY INVOLVING PRICES

Suppose that we disregard completely the issues raised in the first three sections of this chapter. Let us construct a theory involving prices, and see what practical problems arise. Theory 1 involved income, consumption, investment, and the interest rate, and thus included one price explicitly. Now let us consider an economy consisting of "goods" (Y), labor (N), and money (M). The price of goods is p, the price of labor (the wage rate) is w, and the price of money is r, the interest rate. Ostensibly, then, there are six variables. For each of them, we would construct a statement about desired purchases (demand) and a statement about desired sales (supply). That is, we would proceed in the same spirit as in Tiny Model 4. However, buyers and sellers of each commodity must look at all three prices. Let us consider why this is so.

1. Buyers of goods are either consumers or investors. If they are consumers, they must take into account wages as well as prices, since their money incomes depend partly on wage rates. If they are investors, the profitability of any investment project depends on the interest rate (as in Theory 1), but also on the price at which the output of the project may be sold and the labor cost involved in operating it.
2. Sellers of goods are businesses. Their willingness to supply goods depends partly on the price they receive, and partly on their costs (including wages and interest charges).
3. Sellers of labor, that is, workers, take into account not only the money they receive, but what they can buy with it. Some people also receive income from interest, and their need to seek work depends, therefore, on the interest rate.

4. Buyers of labor take into account the quantity of goods they expect to supply. That is, they take into account the productivity of labor. We could add that they therefore also consider prices of goods and wage rates, but the theory is simpler to handle if we assume that all considerations involving prices, wage rates, and interest are summed up by the statement describing the supply of goods. This is not unreasonable, since the amount of labor demanded is ultimately linked to the quantity of goods supplied.

5. "Buyers of money" are people who hold cash. We know (from Chapter 4) that money and bank loans are generated in the same operation, but we shall pretend that there is no need to bring bank and nonbank balance sheets into the system. The amount that people are willing to borrow depends on the interest rate, and the amount of cash is held to be determined by bank loans. Therefore the amount of money people wish to hold depends on the interest rate. It is also assumed that it is related to the amount of income (for reasons explained in Theory 2 and Theory 6); it is also related to prices and wage rates, since these influence the amount people think they want to borrow.

6. Finally, we assume that Federal Reserve can determine the money supply "from outside," at any arbitrary number.

These conditions may be set down as a set of equations:

The demand for goods is

$$Y = ap + bw + cr + vM + F_Y$$

The supply of goods is

$$Y = mp + nw + jr + kY + \phi_Y$$

The demand for labor is

$$N = dY + F_N$$

The supply of labor is

$$N = sp + ew + fr + wM + \phi_N$$

The demand for money is

$$M = gp + hw + jr + kY + F_M$$

The supply of money is

$$M = \phi_M$$

Here,

Y = the quantity of goods
p = the price of goods
N = the number of workers employed
w = the wage rate
M = the quantity of money
r = the interest rate

This system, in vector-matrix notation, is

$$(\mathbf{Y}, \mathbf{N}, \mathbf{p}, \mathbf{w}, \mathbf{r}, \mathbf{M}) = (\mathbf{F}_y, \phi_y, \mathbf{F}_n, \phi_n, \mathbf{F}_m, \phi_m)\begin{pmatrix} 1 & 1 & -d & 0 & -k & 0 \\ 0 & 0 & 1 & 1 & 0 & 0 \\ -a & -m & 0 & -s & -g & 0 \\ -b & -n & 0 & -e & -h & 0 \\ -c & -q & 0 & -f & -j & 0 \\ -v & 0 & 0 & -w & 1 & 1 \end{pmatrix}$$

Here is a linear system of equations, and it would seem a straightforward matter to go ahead and invert the matrix as was done in earlier theories. But readers who try to invert it will find the operation much more difficult than in any case to date. The reason for this is that only twelve elements of the thirty-six in the matrix are zero; and although there are only six statements in the theory, the matrix contains sixteen coefficients that are not equal to zero or to one. The mechanical difficulties of inversion are matched by difficulties in interpreting the terms in the inverse matrix. In a little while, we shall invert a smaller matrix of this type, and readers can see this problem in more detail. Meanwhile, if they do not believe the author, they may try the inversion for themselves.

There are two reasons for not inverting the matrix as it stands. First, it is not constructed properly in one important respect. Second, it is not the sort of theory generally used by economists working on this particular problem.

The mistake in this theory is that it does not guarantee a result consistent with social accounting principles. It is fundamental that the value of income is equal to the value of output. There are two kinds of income in this theory—wages and interest—and one kind of output. Social accounting principles (Chapter 1) require that

$$pY = wN + rM$$

(since money is evidently the only asset in this economy). It this statement is added, then there will be seven statements and six variables, which is too many statements. Moreover, the social accounting statement is nonlinear. That is,

$$(p + \Delta p)(Y + \Delta Y) = pY + p\Delta Y + Y\Delta p + \Delta p \Delta Y$$

and the change in income, which is the sum of the last three terms, is not independent of p and Y. The same thing may be said about changes in (wN) and in (rM). Consequently, something has been omitted that would make it impossible to use linear methods. This difficulty is a repetition of the problem discussed in the first part of this chapter.

The fact that this theory is not the sort generally used by economists would not be a criticism, if it worked well. But since it contains a basic flaw any-how, it is natural to turn to the more common type of theory. This usual type of theory is subject to the same criticism as that just given, but it is a bit simpler. It has one virtue, which may offset this failing. This virtue is that it attempts to deal with a problem called "money illusion."

Imagine that people are paid a certain wage rate w_1 and that they can buy goods at a price p_1. Given these two, they provide N_1 workers and buy quantity Y_1 of goods. Now suppose that we change wages and prices proportionately, so that the wage rate is $xw_1 = w_2$ and prices are $xp_1 = p_2$. It would appear that since all that has happened is a proportionate change in the "tokens" used, people's activities should be unchanged: They will continue to work N_1 hours and buy Y_1 goods. However, the number of "dollar bills they save" should change. This is because at first, savings is

$$S_1 = w_1 N_1 - p_1 Y_1$$

and later

$$S_2 = xw_1 N_1 - xp_1 Y_1 = x(w_1 N_1 - p_1 Y_1) = xS_1$$

But since all prices and wages have changed proportionately, the money saved, S_2, will buy exactly as many goods as before, and it will represent exactly as many hours of labor as before.

Behavior of this sort is described as having "no money illusion." A *money illusion* is said to exist when people look at dollar amounts of money, rather than measuring money in terms of what it will buy. In the absence of money illusion, the various demand and supply relations in Theory 11 will not directly involve prices. Instead, they will involve "real wages" (w/p), a "real interest rate" (r/p) and a "real quantity of money" (M/p). This is true because if w, r, M, and p all change proportionately, none of these three "real" variables will change. The word "real" means "adjusted for the level of goods prices." It is well established in the literature, although not above reproach, conceptually. The effect is to destroy "money illusion" in behavioral statements. Thus in Theory 11, Statement 1 read

$$Y = ap + bw + cr + vM + F_y$$

This means that if there is no money illusion if all prices change proportionally by a factor x,

$$Y = axp + bxw + cxr + vxM + F_y$$

and, by subtraction

$$0 = x[ap + bw + vM] = [ap + bw + vM]$$

Therefore any one of the prices must depend linearly on the other two:

$$p = -\frac{b}{a} w - \frac{v}{a} M$$

and there is no reason why this should be the case. On the other hand, if

$$Y = b\left(\frac{w}{p}\right) + c\left(\frac{r}{p}\right) + v\left(\frac{M}{p}\right) + F_y$$

there is no money illusion; Y changes only when w, r, or M changes *relative to the price of goods.*[3]

If Theory 11 were used, then in principle we could solve for the price level, p. If the theory is adjusted in this way, the price level is irrelevant, and only the "price structure" and the "real quantity of money" are determined.

The question of money illusion has an important place in macroeconomics. Most economists feel that if there were money illusion, some part of the community would not be interpreting its own best interest in a sensible way. One test that is put forward when a new monetary theory is proposed is therefore, "Does this theory involve money illusion?" Sometimes the illusion is present, but only in a concealed form. For example, Theory 1 is a part of Keynes's *General Theory of Employment, Interest and Money*. The "employment" part was not included in Theory 1. The reason is that it has turned out that if Keynes's theory holds in the labor market, then workers are interested only in money wages, paying no attention to the purchasing power of these wages, when they decide how much to work. In contrast, the "neoclassical" (non-Keynesian) theories assume that workers are interested in real wages, not money wages.

The work done in setting forth Theory 11 was not wasted, even though the author decided not to go into that theory in detail. For we may set up a very similar theory, in which there is no money illusion. In this new Theory 11A,

The demand for goods is

$$Y = b\bar{w} + c\bar{r} + v\overline{M} + F_Y$$

The demand for labor

$$N = dY + F_n$$

The supply of labor is

$$N = e\bar{w} + f\bar{r} + w\overline{M} + \phi_N$$

The demand for money (*real* money) is

$$\overline{M} = h\bar{w} + j\bar{r} + kY + F_M$$

The supply of (real money) is

$$\overline{M} = \phi_M$$

---

[3] Formally, we could introduce the variables p/w, r/w and M/w, putting all variables into "wage units," or the variables p/r, w/r, and M/r. The present usage is, however, the common one.

The new, "real" variables in this system are

$\bar{w} = w/p$, the real wage rate

$\bar{r} = r/p$, the real interest rate

$\bar{M} = m/p$, the real quantity of money

In vector matrix notation, this theory is

$$(\mathbf{F_y}, \mathbf{F_n}, \boldsymbol{\phi}_\mathbf{n}, \mathbf{F_m}, \boldsymbol{\phi}_\mathbf{m}) = (\mathbf{Y}, \mathbf{N}, \bar{\mathbf{w}}, \bar{\mathbf{r}}, \bar{\mathbf{M}}) \begin{pmatrix} 1 & -d & 0 & -k & 0 \\ 0 & 1 & 1 & 0 & 0 \\ -b & 0 & -e & -h & 0 \\ -c & 0 & -f & -j & 0 \\ -v & 0 & -w & 1 & 1 \end{pmatrix}$$

The matrix of this theory is the same as the matrix of Theory 11, except that row 3 and column 2 have been dropped. The meanings of the coefficients, however, are different, for now many of them are associated with "real" variables rather than "money" variables. For example, b measures the impact on the quantity of goods demanded of *real* wages, $\bar{w}$ not of *money* wages, w.

The usual practice in this book has been to make assumptions about the elements of a matrix and to derive from these assumptions conclusions about the elements of the inverse matrix. In this theory, however, it turns out that theorists are not altogether clear about whether some of the elements should be positive or whether they should be negative. On the other hand, the reasoning in Tiny Model 3 appears to be well established. For this reason, economists are as well prepared to make assertions about the signs of some elements in the *inverse* matrix as they are to make assertions directly about the coefficients in the behavioral equation. We shall therefore invert the matrix first, and then make assumptions about signs of coefficients.

The matrix turns out to be somewhat messy to invert, and the details of the computation are therefore omitted. The inverse mapping is given by

$$(\mathbf{Y}, \mathbf{N}, \bar{\mathbf{w}}, \bar{\mathbf{r}}, \bar{\mathbf{M}}) = (\mathbf{F_y}, \mathbf{F_n}, \boldsymbol{\phi}_\mathbf{n}, \mathbf{F_m}, \boldsymbol{\phi}_\mathbf{m})$$

$$\times \begin{pmatrix} \dfrac{hf-ej}{z} & \dfrac{d(hf-ej)}{z} & -\dfrac{kf+dx}{z} & \dfrac{hd+ke}{z} & 0 \\[2ex] \dfrac{ch-bj}{z} & \dfrac{w_{22}}{z} & -\dfrac{j+ck}{z} & \dfrac{h+bk}{z} & 0 \\[2ex] \dfrac{bj-ch}{z} & \dfrac{d(bj-ch)}{z} & \dfrac{j+ck}{z} & -\dfrac{h+bk}{z} & 0 \\[2ex] \dfrac{ce-bf}{z} & \dfrac{d(ce-bf)}{z} & \dfrac{cd-f}{z} & \dfrac{e-bd}{z} & 0 \\[2ex] \dfrac{w_{51}}{z} & \dfrac{w_{52}}{z} & \dfrac{w_{53}}{z} & \dfrac{w_{54}}{z} & 1 \end{pmatrix}$$

where

$$z = (hf - ej) + k(hf - ce) + d(bj - ch)$$
$$w_{22} = (hf - ej) + k(bf - ce)$$
$$w_{51} = v(hf - ej) + w(bj - ch) + (bf - ce)$$
$$w_{52} = vd(hf - ej) + wd(bj - ch) + d(hf - ce) = dw_{51}$$
$$w_{53} = -v(kf + dj) + w(j + ck) - (cd - f)$$
$$w_{54} = v(kd + ke) - w(h + bk) - (e - bd)$$

Let us assume that the following sign conditions hold:

$b > 0 \quad c < 0 \quad v > 0$
$d > 0$
$e > 0 \quad f < 0 \quad w > 0$
$h > 0 \quad j < 0 \quad k > 0$

And let us also assume that

f is close to zero
$bj - ch > 0$

[This assignment of signs to the coefficients follows these rules: The amount *demanded* of any commodity falls when its own price rises, and rises when the prices of other commodities rise; the amount *supplied* of any commodity rises when its own price rises, and falls when the prices of other commodities rise. This is a common assumption of microeconomic theory.] It may then be shown that $z > 0$; moreover, the signs of all but three of the elements of the inverse matrix are determinate (see Table 9.2).

The three question marks appear in Table 9.2 because the corresponding elements of the inverse matrix are the sums of positive and negative terms; the assumptions made above are not strong enough to determine their sign. Economists would generally guess that an increase in the supply of money would increase the real interest rate. That is, it would cause the money rate of interest to rise more than the price of goods.

TABLE 9.2

THE IMPLICATIONS OF THEORY 11A.

THE EFFECT OF INCREASES IN	THE EFFECT UPON			
	Output of goods (Y)	Employment (N)	Real wages ($\bar{w}$)	Real interest rate ($\bar{r}$)
Demand for goods (F_y)	Increase	Increase	Increase	Increase
Demand for labor (F_n)	Decrease	Increase	Increase	Increase
Supply of labor (ϕ_n)	Increase	Increase	Decrease	Decrease
Demand for money (F_m)	Decrease	Decrease	Decrease	?
Supply of money (ϕ_m)	Increase	Increase	?	?

The assumptions made about signs of coefficients were those usually made by economists. But two of them deserve fuller discussion. These are the coefficients c and j, appearing respectively in Statements 1 and 4 describing the demand for goods and the demand for money. Money and goods are substitutes in economics, in the sense that income not used to buy goods is taken to be held as cash, while assets other than earning assets consist of cash. It would seem natural, therefore, that if increases in the real interest rate cause the quantity of goods to change in one direction, they should also cause the quantity of money demanded to change in the opposite direction. In this theory this condition is not met.

The demand for goods, in earlier theories, was differentiated into demand for consumption goods and demand for investment goods. In Theory 1, increases in the (money) interest rate gave consumers an incentive to lend more to business, and hence to buy less from current income. They gave investors less incentive to buy new plant, for they increased the cost of new projects. Thus if both kinds of demand for goods declines as the interest rate rises, total demand for goods should decline as the interest rate rises.

In this theory, the variable used is $\bar{r} = r/p$, the real interest rate. $\bar{r}$ increases if r increases, but it also increases if p, the price level, falls. This circumstance does not affect our statement about investors. If the price of goods falls, the profitability of investment projects will also fall, and investment should decrease. But if prices fall, we should expect the quantity of consumer goods purchased to *rise*. Thus in asserting that $c < 0$, we assert that the investment component of demand is more important than the consumption component, so far as changes in r/p are concerned.

The reverse, of course, is implied by the assertion $b > 0$. For b is the coefficient associated with $\bar{w} = w/p$. So far as consumers are concerned, a decrease in prices should increase the quantity of goods they buy. But if prices fall and wages remain constant, the profitability of investment projects will fall, and the amount of investment should also fall. To assert that $b > 0$ is to say that the consumption component of demand is more important than the investment component, so far as changes in w/p are concerned.

Finally, when c and b are of different signs, a difference in point of view is observed. The reason $b > 0$ is that when wages rise relative to prices, wage-earners will buy more goods because they have increased "real incomes." But if interest rates rise relative to prices, interest-earners can buy more goods because they have increased "real incomes." In placing $c < 0$, Theory 11A says, in effect, that income from interest is not a significant source of purchasing power for goods.

The way to keep all these various elements straight would be to list them separately. Ideally, there would be separate demand statements for consumer goods by wage-earners, for consumer goods by interest-earners, and for investment goods. But such a theory would be considerably more complicated than Theory 11A, and it would certainly involve the use of nonlinear statements, so as to keep it consistent with the social accounts.

The fourth statement of Theory 11A relates to the demand for money. In this statement $j < 0$, so that increases in the "real interest rate" r/p decrease the amount of money demanded in the economy. So far as consumers are concerned, the choice lies between buying consumer goods, lending money, and holding cash. A rise in the interest rate is taken to mean that the cost of holding cash rises. That is, the consumer loses income (in the form of interest) when he holds cash rather than lending. But so far as businesses go, a rise in interest rates means that it is more costly than before to borrow money. Businesses will desire less new plant in consequence, as stated. But it is also true that if businesses reduce their debts, they will reduce their total costs. One way to reduce debt is to use part of their cash balances to repay the debt.

To take this chain of circumstances fully into account, it would be necessary to introduce balance sheet accounts into Theory 11A. There would have to be explicit account taken of the banking system, since "money" is in the form of bank deposits. But money, in a balance sheet, is not "real money," $\overline{M} = M/p$, but rather M. Even if, from the point of view of "money illusion," it is natural to talk about $\overline{M}$, it is not necessarily reasonable to adjust all balance sheet items by the same price level. When consumers are separated from investors in the income (goods) accounts, two "real wages" appear. One is the "real wages" w/p_C, or ratio between wages and consumer goods prices, p_C. This ratio may well be important to consumers. The other is the "real wages" w/p_I, or ratio between wages and investment goods prices p_I. This ratio may well be important to investors.

To introduce considerations of price and quantity into macroeconomic theory seems to introduce a great deal of complexity. So long as only values were involved, it was possible to develop fairly large theories with only moderate complications. But even a three-part theory like Theory 11A (goods, labor, money) becomes messy if prices and quantities are to be taken into account separately. The following chapter shows a way out of this difficulty, which some economists consider to be the way macroeconomics is to develop in the future. Meanwhile, to conclude this chapter, a series of rules of thumb will be presented to show how in fact many economists seek to avoid the difficulties inherent in the full-blown price theories in the spirit of Theory 11A.

RESERVATION PRICES AND CAPACITY LIMITS

Because theories that list both prices and quantities as variables tend to be rather intricate, economists in practice use simplifying devices of several kinds. These devices are based on observation of the economy, and are grafted onto value theories in such a way as to make separate conclusions about prices and quantities possible. These devices have the important advantage of resembling the behavior of the economy. They have the important disadvantage that there is no explanation of why they should "work."

The Phillips Curve

A useful rule of thumb is given by the so-called Phillips curve. This curve is derived in the following way. For any country, we prepare a chart showing the annual (or quarterly) change in wage rates on one axis and the percentage of the labor force that is unemployed on the other axis. In many countries, one is able to construct a nice curve which shows that the larger the percentage of the labor force unemployed, the less wage rates increase. There is, in fact, a level of unemployment at which wage rates, on the average, remain constant.

It is also the case that if changes in prices are plotted against the rate of unemployment, one often finds a nice curve which shows that the larger the percentage of the labor force unemployed, the smaller the increase in the price level. This second chart is related to the first, because the larger price increases are, the larger wage increases tend to be, and vice versa.

The rate of unemployment "needed" to stabilize either the wage rate or the price level varies from one country to another. In part this variation is a statistical illusion—each country has its own way of measuring unemployment. But it also seems to be true that each country (for whatever reason) has a special way of looking at price and wage increases. The statistical records of some countries produce charts that look as if workers had fixed money wages, so that changes in the standard of living took place mainly as a result of price changes. The records of other countries produce charts which look as if businesses sold at fixed prices, so that changes in the standard of living took place mainly as a result of changes in wage rates. And in some countries prices and wages both increase steadily (with, of course, variations in rates).

For example, France and Germany and the United States are frequently contrasted, over the twenty years from 1947 to 1967. In France, the price level has risen almost without interruption and wages have risen also. Germany has had a tendency toward very stable prices and wages. The United States always has a rising wage rate, but prices have sometimes been virtually unchanged for years at a time. (Naturally in periods like the Korean and Viet Nam wars, prices have risen in the United States.)

Assume that the Phillips curve represents the way economics behave. Then there is a level of unemployment that will stabilize prices, and/or wage rates. Then if Tiny Model 1 is valid, as a theory about values,

$$Y = \frac{1}{1-a} I + \frac{1}{1-a} F_c$$

$$C = \frac{a}{1-a} I + \frac{1}{1-a} F_c$$

we may write

$$Y = pQ_y$$
$$C = pQ_c$$
$$I = pQ_I$$

where p measures the price level and Q_y, Q_c, Q_I are indexes of the quantity of output, consumption, and investment in the economy. If the relation between output and employment is

$$N = kQ_y + F_n \qquad k > 0$$

and unemployment is $N0 - N$, where N is the size of the labor force, and the Phillips curve says that the change in the price level is

$$\Delta p = b(N_0 - N) + F_u \qquad b < 0$$

we may write

$$\begin{aligned}\Delta p &= b(N_0 - kQ_y - F_n) + F_u \\ &= b\left(N_0 - \frac{kY}{p} - F_n\right) + F_u \\ &= bN_0 - \frac{bk}{p}\left(\frac{1}{1-a}I + \frac{1}{1-a}F_c\right) - bF_n + F_u \\ &= -\frac{bk}{1-a}Q_I - \frac{bk}{1-a}\frac{F_c}{p} - bF_n + F_u\end{aligned}$$

If there is an increase in the productivity of labor, F_n declines. This is true because

$$Q_y = \frac{1}{k}N - \frac{1}{k}F_n$$

and the average product of labor is

$$\frac{Q_Y}{N} = \frac{1}{k} - \frac{1}{Nk}F_n$$

which obviously rises as F_n declines. Since $-\dfrac{bk}{1-a} > 0$, we conclude that Δp, the increase in prices, is larger,

(1) The larger is investment (Q_I)
(2) The larger is the level of consumption (F_C)
(3) The lower is the level of labor productivity (F_n)
(4) The greater is the constant term in the Phillips curve (F_u)

To apply the hypothesis of the Phillips curve, then, it is necessary first to apply a theory of the sort given in earlier chapters, and then, in a second stage, to calculate price changes which will take place. In this sense, the hypothesis is not a part of Tiny Model 1—or of any other general macroeconomic theory. It is for this reason that the hypothesis is called a "rule of thumb." So far, it remains outside of macroeconomic theory, and is applied at the end of the theory, to give a special answer to a problem not covered in the theory. The phenomenon recorded by the Phillips curve is a genuine one, however, and it is a defect of theory that there is no good explanation of why the economy works this way.

One curious feature of the Phillips curve is the following: Suppose at time t,

$$\Delta p_t = -\frac{bk}{1-a} Q_{It} - \frac{bk}{1-a} \frac{F_{ct}}{P_t} - bF_{nt} - F_{ut}$$

then let Q_I, F_C, F_n, F_u all remain unchanged. The next time around, at time $t+1$, we will see

$$\Delta p_{t+1} = -\frac{bk}{1-a} Q_{It} - \frac{bk}{1-a} \frac{F_{ct}}{P_t + \Delta p_t} - bF_{nt} - F_{ut}$$

This is a different price increase because the denominator of the second term on the right has changed, even though no factor has changed.

In this sense, the Phillips curve involves a dynamic process—the variables in the theory depend explicitly on time. As was stated in Chapter 6, dynamic processes are more difficult to formulate than the (static) theories in this book. The theory underlying the Phillips curve, in particular, has never been worked out in detail.

The Reservation Price of Labor

Sellers in a market are said to have a reservation price $\bar{p}$, if they would rather take their goods home unsold than sell them at a price less than $\bar{p}$. The existence of a reservation price alters the performance of a market from the standard used in Tiny Model 3. This change takes place because the (supply) statement about sellers,

$$q_S = fp_S + F_S$$

applies only if $p_S \geq \bar{p}$. If $p_S < \bar{p}$, then

$$q_S = 0$$

Let us suppose that demand for the product is described by

$$q_D = ep_D + F_D \qquad e < 0$$

Then the solution given by Tiny Model 3 said

$$q_S = q_D = q$$

$$p_S = p_D = p$$

$$q = \frac{-f}{e-f} F_D + \frac{e}{e-f} F_S$$

$$p = \frac{-1}{e-f} F_D + \frac{1}{e-f} F_S$$

This solution, however, applies only for $p \geq \bar{p}$. Otherwise

$$q_D = q$$
$$p_S = p_D = \bar{p}$$
$$q = e\bar{p} + F_D$$

The amount that sellers are willing to sell at price $\bar{p}$ is

$$q_S = f\bar{p} + F_S$$

and since they can only sell q, they must "take home" the surplus,

$$q_S - q = (f - e)\bar{p} + F_S - F_D$$

and the price is given by

$$\left.\begin{aligned} p &= \frac{-1}{e-f} F_D + \frac{1}{e-f} F_S \\ p &= \bar{p} \end{aligned}\right\} \text{if and only if } q_D = q_S \geq e\bar{p} + F_D$$

If, in particular, the market described is the labor market, then the hypothesis is that workers will not work for a wage below $\bar{w}$. The surplus labor, or unemployment is given by

$$U = q_S - q = (f - e)\,\bar{w} + F_S - F_D$$

If the demand for labor rises, F_D rises, and U therefore falls. But until U

reaches zero, wages will remain at $\overline{w}$. At that point, the usual analysis of Tiny Model 3 becomes operative.

This sort of theory has a place in the history of macroeconomics; also it is related to, but not the same as the Phillips curve hypothesis.

In discussing unemployment in Chapter 3, we observed that at the time of the great depression of the 1930s, one prescription for unemployment was based on Tiny Model 3. If there is unemployment (it was said), wages are not given by the formula of Tiny Model 3. Instead, they are held "too high" by unions, minimum wage laws, and the like. If a way could be found to force down wages, it was said that unemployment would disappear. Partly it would disappear because employers would hire more workers at lower wages (after all $e < 0$); partly it would disappear because fewer people would seek work at lower pay, so that the size of the labor force would drop.

The answer given by opponents of this view was given by Tiny Model 1. If wages are reduced, earnings will drop, and the demand for goods will also drop, because $C = aY + F_C$. Consequently, at lower wages, employers will sell fewer goods and hence hire fewer workers rather than more workers. But this argument produced two inconsistent ways of talking about a single phenomenon. Ultimately, the proposal to consider wage-earners as having a reservation price came to be accepted by many economists as a theory.

There are two basic reasons for using this particular version of Tiny Model 3 in connection with the labor market. The first reason is that there is usually some unemployment, and sometimes quite a lot of it. Price theory (of which Tiny Model 3 is the starting point) says that price and quantity are components of a vector that represents the solution to some equation. There is no explanation of these variables unless the solution exists. If unemployment exists because the vector of price and quantity is not a solution to the theory, then what is this vector? After all, there is an infinity of vectors $\mathbf{Y}$ such that $\mathbf{Y} \neq \mathbf{XM}$ for any matrix $\mathbf{M}$! By formulating the theory of unemployment as has been done here, economists can explain why wages can be fixed at $\overline{w}$ even if there is unemployment.

This theory puts some strain on the imagination. It says that all workers stop work completely the moment the wage rate drops below $\overline{w}$. If there were even one worker who would work for a weekly wage of one cent less than $\overline{w}$, the theory, strictly speaking, would not hold. Pressed upon this issue, economists would blush, and mumble that a theory is after all a simplification of a complex world. And so it is. But some simplifications leave us happier than others.

A second reason for using the reservation price hypothesis in the labor market has to do with price changes. If the reservation wage rate, $\overline{w}$, exists, then employment changes without any changes in wages whenever employment is less than $e\overline{w} + F_D$. But when employment rises above this level, then wages rise above $\overline{w}$.

The reservation wage theory differs from the Phillips curve in several respects:

(1) Both say that there is a level of employment, and hence a level of unemployment, at which wages will remain fixed. The reservation wage theory says that if the demand for labor drops, employment will fall, but wages will not fall. The Phillips curve says that if the demand for labor drops, employment will fall and wages will fall.

(2) The reservation wage theory says that if F_D and F_S are given, the quantity of labor employed and the level of wages are given. The Phillips curve says that F_D and F_S might determine the quantity of labor employed and the *change* in the wage rate, but they do not, evidently, determine the wage rate itself.

(3) Consequently, the reservation wage theory makes a prediction about the level of wages under given conditions, while the Phillips curve predicts changes only.

The Capacity Limits of Output

Sellers in a market are said to have a capacity limit $\bar{q}$, if they will never put more than quantity $\bar{q}$ on the market, no matter what the price in the market may be. When there is a capacity limit, the (supply) statement about sellers of Tiny Model 3,

$$q_S = fp_S + F_S$$

applies only if $q_S \leq \bar{q}$. Designate, in particular by $\bar{p}$, the price such that

$$\bar{q} = f\bar{p} + F_S$$

Then the solution given by Tiny Model 3, that

$$q = \frac{-f}{e - f} F_D + \frac{e}{e - f} F_S$$

$$p = \frac{-1}{e - f} F_D + \frac{1}{e - f} F_S$$

holds only if $q \geq \bar{q}$. If $q > \bar{q}$, then the first statement drops out. The quantity traded is given by $\bar{q}$, and price is given by

$$p = \frac{1}{e}(\bar{q} - F_D)$$

which is obtained from the demand statement of Tiny Model 3:

$$q_D = ep_D + F_D$$

Since $e < 0$, increases in the level of demand (F_D) increase price, but of course they do not increase quantity above $\bar{q}$.

The notion of a capacity limit seems to be clear, applied to the economy as a whole: Everybody has a job, and all the machines in all the factories are busy. But the clarity of the notion disappears on closer examination. The "labor force" includes people who sometimes take jobs and sometimes do not. Many housewives, for example, take part-time jobs from time to time; and there is no clear indication that the upper limit to the number of hours they would work is well defined. Moreover, most businesses have quantities of old, and relatively inefficient equipment which is not ordinarily in use, but which can be used if business is active enough. Taking into account all the possibilities for overtime work, extra shifts, use of standby equipment, and so on, it is very difficult to assert that there is really an upper limit beyond which output simply cannot go.

The Phillips curve deals, strictly speaking, with the labor market. But it has an analog in terms of output. Many economists think in terms of "potential (real) gross national product." This "potential gross national product" is a capacity concept: it is the maximum level that total output could reach at any given moment, if the labor force were fully employed. Calculations of potential gross national product are, in fact, regularly made by government agencies.[4] It is then observed that when actual output is close to potential output, prices rise more than if output is not close to potential output.

Indeed, advocates of the use of fiscal policy as a means of controlling economic activity are apt to start agitation for tax increases when they observe actual output approaching the "potential gross national product." Their reasoning closely resembles the Phillips curve thinking: The less "slack" in the economy, the more prices will rise.

But the capacity limit theory differs from the "capacity analog" of the Phillips curve in several respects:

(1) The Phillips curve analog says that the farther actual output is from potential, the *less* prices will *rise*. The capacity limit theory says that the farther actual output is from potential, the *lower* prices will *be*.

(2) The Phillips curve analog does not actually need to suppose that there is a maximum level above which output cannot rise. The "potential GNP" level may be defined simply as a level of output such that prices will not rise. In

[4] These calculations yield "potential" output that is less than actual output on some occasions. It is hard to imagine output being greater than it can possibly be. However, the calculations are concerned with determining a more modest figure: what output would be if unemployment were "small" and there was "not much" overtime work going on. If unemployment drops below this "small" level, if housewives take jobs in unusual numbers, or if overtime is above the "not much" level, then output may well rise above its calculated "potential."

contrast, a capacity limit, strictly speaking, is an upper limit, beyond which output cannot rise.[5]

(3) The Phillips curve analog says what the change in price will be, and is thus part of a dynamic theory, the exact workings of which are not known. The capacity limit theory can be precisely stated, but it is open to objections—chiefly the objection that there is, strictly speaking, no capacity limit.

If a capacity limit theory is used, then it may be grafted onto Tiny Model 1, as follows. If Tiny Model 1 holds, as a theory about values, then

$$Y = \frac{1}{1-a} I + \frac{1}{1-a} F_C$$

and

$$Y = pQ_y = \frac{1}{1-a} pQ_I + \frac{1}{1-a} F_C$$

then either

$Q_y = \bar{Q}_y$ is capacity output, or in the first case, the price level is
$Q_y < \bar{Q}_y$

given by

$$p\left(\bar{Q}_y - \frac{1}{1-a} Q_I\right) = \frac{1}{1-a} F_C$$

$$p = \frac{\dfrac{1}{1-a} F_C}{\bar{Q}_y - \dfrac{1}{1-a} Q_I}$$

In the second case, the equation

$$pQ_y = \frac{1}{1-a} pQ_I + \frac{1}{1-a} F_C$$

is interpreted as representing the demand for goods; and the supply of goods is given by

$$Q_y = fp + F_S$$

---

[5] Remember that this book is mainly concerned with linear theories. In a more complicated mathematical context, one could assume that the coefficients *e* and *f* of Tiny Model 3 varied with output; if output were "small," *f*, for instance, might be "large," and *f* might decline as output rose. This possibility would "take care of" some objections to the concept of "capacity limit."

so that

$$p(fp + F_S) = \frac{1}{1-a} pQ_I + F_S$$

$$fp^2 + p\left(F_S - \frac{1}{1-a} Q_I\right) - F_S = 0$$

This expression is quadratic and has two solutions. But since p must be positive, it may be shown that only one of the solutions has economic meaning. Given this solution, Q_y may then be determined.

The Liquidity Trap

The concept of "liquidity trap" was mentioned in a historical note to Theory 8A. It will be recalled that it was there related to banks and applied to the situation where banks do not expand their loans as their reserves rise. In this form, it attracted considerable attention in the 1930s. British and American banks failed to lend as much as they could have during this period, even though central banks were trying to encourage them to expand credit.

One of the important contributions of Keynes to discussions of this period was his suggestion that the banks were not the only institutions to blame; the trouble was that the entire economy was unresponsive to changes in the monetary sector. One of the important residual influences of Keynes is found in the commonly accepted doctrine that central banks can stop inflations, but they cannot stop depressions. They can prevent credit from growing, but they cannot force businesses to borrow if they do not want to.

This doctrine says that there are two possible states of the economy: In prosperity, an interest-sensitive state; and in depressions an interest-unresponsive state. Because of this doctrine many economists hold that monetary policy is good in booms, but only fiscal policy will work in busts. The following discussion will explain this notion; it is closely related to reservation-price concepts. Since the doctrine originated with Keynes, it is natural to present it in the context of Theory 1, which is a Keynesian theory. But it will be useful to eliminate the technical defect in the statement presented there. So Theory 1 will first be written in a better form.

The *interest-sensitive* state of the economy exists if the rate of interest is greater than some rate $\bar{R}$. In this state, the economy consists of

1. A national product of the usual sort

$$Y = C + I$$

2. A consumption function

$$C = aY + bR + vL + F_C$$

which depends on the interest rate (R), and the quantity of money (L) as well as on income.

3. An investment function

$$I = dR + F_I$$

which depends on the interest rate.

4. A part of income is hoarded. The demand for additional hoards is given by

$$\Delta L = eR + fY + F_L$$

The quantity ΔL is for *increased* cash balances. Thus $\Delta L = L - L_0$, where L is the present, and L_0 the initial cash balance. We may therefore rewrite this statement as

$$L = eR + fY + F_L + L_0$$

5. Finally, the authorities decide on the total amount of money they will create:

$$\Delta L = F_M$$

or, alternatively

$$L = F_M + L_0$$

In the interest-sensitive state, the quantity of money people wish to hold, given by formula 4, must equal the quantity of money supplied by the authorities. The economy adjusts income, interest rate, and so forth, to suit the money supply.

Out of respect for J. M. Keynes, this theory contains one coefficient (f) that did not appear in Theory 1. He asserted that one of the motives people had for holding cash was a "transactions motive." That is, in order to maintain their spending at a given rate, people will wish to have a corresponding, and suitable amount of cash on hand. Spending, in total, is given by Y; and fY, a multiple of this spending, represents the "transactions demand" for money.

In the interest-sensitive state, then, the economy is represented by the system

$$(\mathbf{0}, \mathbf{F_C}, \mathbf{F_I}, \mathbf{F_L} + \mathbf{L_0}, \mathbf{F_M} + \mathbf{L_0}) = (\mathbf{Y}, \mathbf{C}, \mathbf{I}, \mathbf{R}, \mathbf{L}) \begin{pmatrix} 1 & -a & 0 & -f & 0 \\ -1 & 1 & 0 & 0 & 0 \\ -1 & 0 & 1 & 0 & 0 \\ 0 & -b & -d & -e & 0 \\ 0 & -v & 0 & 1 & 1 \end{pmatrix}$$

which in inverse form is

$$
(\mathbf{0}, \mathbf{F_C}, \mathbf{F_I}, \mathbf{F_L} + \mathbf{L_0}, \mathbf{F_M} + \mathbf{L_0})
\begin{pmatrix}
\frac{e}{D} & \frac{ea + bf}{D} & \frac{-df}{D} & \frac{-f}{D} & 0 \\
\frac{e}{D} & \frac{e - df}{D} & \frac{-df}{D} & \frac{-f}{D} & 0 \\
\frac{e}{D} & \frac{ea + bf}{D} & \frac{e(1 + a) + bf}{D} & \frac{-f}{D} & 0 \\
\frac{-(b + d)}{D} & \frac{-a(b + d) - b(1 - a)}{D} & \frac{-d(1 - a)}{D} & \frac{-(1 - a)}{D} & 0 \\
\frac{b + d + ev}{D} & \frac{v(e - df) + a(b + d) + b(1 - a)}{D} & \frac{-d[vf - (1 - a)]}{D} & \frac{-vf + (1 - a)}{D} & 1
\end{pmatrix}
$$

$$
= (\mathbf{Y}, \mathbf{C}, \mathbf{I}, \mathbf{R}, \mathbf{L})
$$

We have set $D = a(1 - a) + f(b + d)$. The implications of this system are given in the upper half of Table 9.3.

The usual assumptions about the signs of the coefficients are

$$\begin{array}{lll} a > 0 & b < 0 & d < 0 \\ e < 0 & f > 0 & v > 0 \end{array}$$

From these, it is possible to determine that $D < 0$. Consequently, the signs of the elements in the inverse matrix are different from the signs of their numerators. (See the upper half of Table 9.3.)

In the "liquidity trap," the same functions are assumed to exist. But the demand for money (L) is no longer equal to the supply of money ($F_M + L_0$). Instead, the interest rate has dropped to some floor, $\bar{R}$, from which it will not rise so long as $L > F_M + L_0$. Thus the theory consists of the statements

$$\left.\begin{array}{l} Y = C + I \\ C = aY + bR + vL + F_c \\ I = dR + F_I \end{array}\right\} \text{as before}$$

plus the two statements about the money market

$$\begin{array}{l} R = \bar{R} \\ L = F_M + L_0 \end{array}$$

That is to say,

$$(\mathbf{Y, C, I, R, L})\begin{pmatrix} 1 & -a & 0 & 0 & 0 \\ -1 & 1 & 0 & 0 & 0 \\ -1 & 0 & 1 & 0 & 0 \\ 0 & -b & -d & 1 & 0 \\ 0 & -v & 0 & 1 & 1 \end{pmatrix} = (\mathbf{0, F_C, F_I, \bar{R}, F_M + L_0})$$

In inverse form this becomes

$$(\mathbf{0, F_C, F_I, \bar{R}, F_M + L_0})\begin{pmatrix} \frac{1}{1-a} & \frac{a}{1-a} & 0 & 0 & 0 \\ \frac{1}{1-a} & \frac{1}{1-a} & 0 & 0 & 0 \\ \frac{1}{1-a} & \frac{a}{1-a} & 1 & 0 & 0 \\ \frac{b+d}{1-a} & \frac{b+ad}{1-a} & d & 1 & 0 \\ \frac{v}{1-a} & \frac{v}{1-a} & 0 & 0 & 1 \end{pmatrix} = (\mathbf{Y, C, I, R, L})$$

TABLE 9.3

THE IMPLICATIONS OF THE LIQUIDITY TRAP HYPOTHESIS

THE EFFECT UPON	THE EFFECT OF A UNIT CHANGE IN			
	The level of consumption (ΔF_c)	Autonomous investment (ΔF_I)	Demand for money (ΔF_L)	Supply of money (ΔF_M)
Case A. Interest-Sensitive Case				
Income (ΔY)	e/D	e/D	$-(h+d)/D$	$(b+d+ev)/D$
Consumption (ΔC)	$(e-df)/D$	$(ea+bf)/D$	$-[a(b+d)+b(1-a)]/D$	$[v(e-df)+a(b+d)+b(1-a)]/D$
Investment (ΔI)	$-df/D$	$[e(1-a)+bf]/D$	$-d(1-a)/D$	$-d[vf-(1-a)]/D$
Interest rate (ΔR)	$-f/D$	$-f/D$	$-(1-a)/D$	$-[vf-(1-a)]/D$
Excess demand for money (ΔX)	0	0	0	0
Case B. Liquidity Trap Case				
Income (ΔY)	$1/(1-a)$	$1/(1-a)$	$(b+d)/(1-a)$	$v/(1-a)$
Consumption (ΔC)	$1/(1-a)$	$a/(1-a)$	$(b+ad)/(1-a)$	$v/(1-a)$
Investment (ΔI)	0	1	0	0
Interest rate (ΔR)	0	0	0	0
Excess demand for money (ΔX)	$f/(1-a)$	$f/(1-a)$	1	$-(1-a-fv)/(1-a)$

The implications of this system are given in the lower half of Table 9.3. If there is a liquidity trap, there is an excess demand for money, which is expressed as follows: If the demand for money is given by the statement used in the interest-sensitive case,

$$L = eR + fY + F_L + L_0$$

and the supply of money is

$$F_M + L_0$$

Then excess demand is given by

$$X \equiv L - M - L_0 = e\bar{R} + fY + F_L - F_M$$

If there were no transactions demand, then

$$X = F_L - F_M$$

regardless of other variables in the system. The authorities can reduce the excess demand for money in either event by increasing the quantity of money. At the point where $X = 0$, the system would shift back into an interest-sensitive state.

Substituting for Y, and taking differences,

$$\Delta X = \frac{f}{1-a}\,\Delta F_c + \frac{f}{1-a}\,\Delta F_1 + F_L + \left(\frac{fv}{1-a} - 1\right)\Delta F_M$$

Notice that the difference between the two cases is in the set of statements used to determine the values of the variables. In an economy with a declining interest rate, something happens when the rate reaches $\bar{R}$. The economy "knows" it should drop one statement and add another in the list making up the theory. (Some writers talk as if the values of b, d and/or f drop to zero at $\bar{R}$, but that is not the essential feature.)

Consequently, if this theory is true, then a unit increase in the quantity of money will change investment by $d(1 - a)/D > 0$, in the absence of a liquidity trap. It will not affect investment at all if there is a liquidity trap. A unit increase in the quantity of money will increase the national income by $(b + d + ev)/D > 0$ if there is no liquidity trap, and by $v/(1 - a)$ if there is a liquidity trap. From this observation, we see again how important it is to know what consumer behavior actually is. If consumption is unaffected by the size of the money supply ($v = 0$), then monetary policy would not affect the national income if there is a liquidity trap. This is one reason why the proponents of monetary policy are most insistent in their conjecture that v is greater than zero.

The great question with this theory, like other reservation price theories is this: How does the economy know that the time has come to shift from one state to the other? While the importance of the liquidity trap in the history of economics is great, it appears today to be in the nature of a stopgap, in a case where no theory existed to explain the great depression of the 1930s.

Problem 9.6 Reread the Appendix to Chapter 3 on the so-called *IS-LM* analysis. Now construct an *IS* and an *LM* curve for each of the two cases discussed in this section. What are the signs of the coefficients of the interest rate? How do changes in each factor affect the equilibrium?

Problem 9.7 Construct *IS* and *LM* curves for Theory 11A. What are the signs of coefficients of the interest rate? How do changes in each factor affect the equilibrium?

CONCLUSIONS

The methods discussed in this last section are quite commonly used. They tend to produce arguments that are consistent with experience, and they are much easier to explain to undergraduates than the more complicated theories such as Theory 11A. Readers will have understood by now that the writer does not like them much. The reason is basically that they must be used as a "second stage," to supplement the conclusions of some theory about values, such as those given in Chapters 3 to 8.

If one had to choose between intricate theories like Theory 11A and "two state" theories like those in this last section, one would conclude that macroeconomics is not well able to suggest good explanations of the price and quantity changes taking place in the economy as a whole. Indeed, macroeconomics has a good deal of unfinished business.

But there is one further approach to macroeconomics, which does offer some promise as a means of taking separate account of price changes and quantity changes. The next chapter will introduce this alternative method, which avoids the complexity of Theory 11A without introducing the arbitrariness of the special rules just discussed.

10

A Programming-Type Theory

PROGRAMMING-TYPE THEORIES

The theory presented in this chapter will introduce a new and different approach to the construction of macroeconomic theories. This theory will be a special type of linear theory related to the mathematical theory of *linear programming.* This subject was invented independently by Kontorovich and by von Neumann around 1940. It became of tremendous practical importance with the development of computer technology, for it gave a ready way to deal with many engineering, scientific, and management problems that it had hitherto been impossible to answer because of the great number of variables involved.

Programming has various economic interpretations. Indeed, von Neumann came upon the notion in writing (with Morgenstern) *The Theory of Games and Economic Behavior,*[1] the economic content of which has to do with business competition. Furthermore, programming theory is closely related to input-output analysis, which

---

[1] Princeton, N.J., 1943.

was invented by Leontief in his *Structure of the American Economy*[2] as a way of studying the way in which the technological relations among different industries help to determine the structure of prices and the commodity composition of the national product.

Many economists consider that programming and these related methods offer, in the long run, better prospects for economic analysis than the sort of theory presented in the earlier chapters of this book. This judgement rests in part upon the superior treatment of prices which exists in programming theories. This opinion is a guess, for the detailed use of such methods in macroeconomics is only beginning. This chapter gives an example of the application of programming to a macroeconomic problem. The example is a small one, but it illustrates a way of thought that will probably have increasing impact on economics.[3]

All of the theories presented in Chapters 3 to 8 represented elaborations and combinations of Tiny Models 1 to 4. Each of them contained behavioral statements built up from four general kinds of assumptions:

(1) The value of the income that any economic group spends for any particular purpose depends on the total money income of the group.

(2) The value of the assets that an economic group holds in a particular form depends on the total money value of the assets of the group.

(3) The value of the income spent for some particular purpose by an economic group depends on the cash balances of that group.

(4) The value of a particular kind of assets depends on the money income of some group in the community.

By selecting appropriately from among these hypotheses, it has been possible to present explanations of the workings of quite complicated economic systems. In this respect, the four assumptions—which may be called *allocative*—are a useful set of rules for setting up macroeconomic theories. They could be used in problems considerably more complicated than Theory 10. We gave up at that point only because we had no compelling reason to get into bigger theories.

The programming theories are based upon a different set of basic assumptions. These assumptions have mathematical content, but we are here interested mainly in their economic interpretation. The basic economic assumption may be expressed in the following form:

The quantity of goods that any economic group buys from any other economic

---

[2] Cambridge, Mass., 1941.

[3] David Gale, *The Theory of Linear Economic Models*, New York (McGraw-Hill) 1960 is an introduction to programming theories. Its economics is based on the articles in T. C. Koopmans (ed.) *Activity Analysis of Production and Allocation*. New York (John Wiley & Sons, Inc.), 1951. A simple introduction to this branch of economics is C.S. Yan, *An Introduction to Input-Output Economics*, New York (Holt, Rinehart and Winston) 1969.

group is proportional to the quantity of goods that the buyer is currently producing.

For example, the "output" of labor is measured in man-hours (or maybe man-years) of work. It is assumed that labor's purchases of goods are proportionate to the level of employment.

For example, the "output" of the consumer goods industry is measured by some index of production. It is assumed that the amount of labor used by makers of consumer goods is proportional to the output of consumer goods in any given set of conditions.

This basic type of assumption relates quantities to quantities. In contrast, the basic assumptions of the earlier theories worked well only when values were related to values.

So long as allocative theories dealt with values, it was a simple matter to disaggregate them—so as to divide the economy into larger numbers of sectors. In this sense, the allocative theory is a natural way to theorize about values.

The programming theories, in principle, deal with relations among quantities. The particular theory presented in this chapter involves four quantities and four prices. But it would be a simple matter conceptually to disaggregate this theory, so that it involved larger numbers of smaller sectors of the economy. In this sense the programming theory is a natural way to theorize about prices and quantities.

Readers may say with justice that the particular theory given in this chapter uses price indices and quantity indices, and in this respect it is no better than the theories of Chapter 9. But the writer could say with justice that if he chose to, he could present a theory in which the sectors had been disaggregated to a point where the reader would not object. He would have practical difficulty gathering the data to test such a theory, and equal difficulty with computer programs, if the number of sectors in the economy were very large. But his difficulty is not a difficulty of principle, as it is with the allocative theory about quantities.[4]

Finally, the programming theory does away with an element of artificiality in the earlier theories. The allocative theory was described as a one-to-one mapping of factors into variables. But the distinction between factors and variables was in some cases not easy to make. Some economic values (for example, the quantity of money) appeared as factors in some theories and as variables in other theories. Other factors, such as "the level of consumer demand," F_C, in the consumption statement $C = aY + F_C$ are never variables, but are "constant terms" in a linear equation. Variations in these "constant

---

[4] A different difficulty will, however, turn up. This difficulty will be discussed below. The programming theory is not the answer to all problems.

terms" have interesting economic implications. But it is artificial to distinguish between the symbol a and the symbol F_C in the consumption statement, even though the distinction proved useful in the context of allocative theory. In the programming theory, there are no "factors" as such. There are only variables, and coefficients in matrices.

To illustrate these matters, we now set forth an example of a programming theory. The development of such theories is not so far advanced as that of the allocative theories, and therefore the example is a simple one.

The variables that appear in the following theory are listed in Table 10.1.

TABLE 10.1

VARIABLES USED IN THEORY 12

SECTOR OF THE ECONOMY	QUANTITY	UNIT OF MEASURE	PRICE	UNIT OF MEASURE	VALUE (INCOME OF SECTOR)
Consumer goods	q_C	index	p_C	index	$v_C = p_C q_C$
Investment goods	q_I	index	p_I	index	$v_I = p_I q_I$
Labor	q_L	man-years	p_L	yearly wage	$v_L = p_L q_L$
Plant and equipment	q_K	machine-years	p_K	yearly rent	$v_K = p_K q_K$

This theory assumes that manufacturers of consumer goods and investment goods hire labor and rent plant and equipment. The owners of the plant are different from the managers of businesses, and their (rental) income is treated as a business cost. Managers are paid wages for their services. It is assumed that businesses do not buy any goods (either consumption or investment goods) and suppliers of services (labor and plant rentals) do not buy any services. All of these assumptions are made in order to enable us to construct as simple a theory as possible.

Readers will note that this theory involves "social classes"—managers, workers, and property-owners. In this respect it harks back to the nineteenth-century theories mentioned in Chapter 1.

AN INPUT-OUTPUT MACROECONOMY

Consider sales by sector i to sector j. Here i and j stand for two of the subscripts C, I, L, K, which denote the four sectors of the economy. Sales *by i to j* will be denoted by v_{ij}. The set of all transactions in the economy, then, is representable by the matrix

$$\begin{pmatrix} 0 & 0 & v_{CL} & v_{CK} \\ 0 & 0 & v_{IL} & v_{IK} \\ v_{LC} & v_{LI} & 0 & 0 \\ v_{KC} & v_{KI} & 0 & 0 \end{pmatrix}$$

Problem 10.1 What is the meaning of each of the eight symbols in this matrix?

Now observe certain sums, all in money values:

$v_{CL} + v_{CK} = v_C =$ sales by consumer manufacturers
$v_{IL} + v_{IK} = v_I =$ sales by investment goods manufacturers
$v_{LC} + v_{LI} = v_L =$ sales by labor
$v_{KC} + v_{KI} = v_K =$ rental income of plant owners

These are sums of *rows* of the matrix (v_{ij}). The sums of *columns* are many values:

$v_{LC} + v_{KC} =$ purchases by consumer goods manufacturers
$v_{LI} + v_{KI} =$ purchases by investment goods manufacturers
$v_{CL} + v_{IL} =$ purchases by labor
$v_{CK} + v_{IK} =$ purchases by plant owners

The symbols v_{CL} and v_{CK} stand for the value of consumer goods bought by workers and plant owners, respectively. It is supposed that these values can be determined separately. There are two aspects to this assertion:

(1) It might be difficult to obtain the correct numbers that these symbols represent. If we went to retail stores, for example, we might find that they could not tell whether a given customer was a wage-earner or a property-owner. This is a practical objection.

(2) In this case, however, we could ask individuals whether they were wage-earners or property-owners. Once they had identified themselves, we would ask how much they had spent on consumer goods. In this way, we could obtain numbers for v_{CL} and v_{CK}, *providing* people can identify themselves. But if it turns out that there are people who earn wages and also own plant, there will be people who cannot describe their spending as being a part of v_{CL} or as a part of v_{CK}. This is a difficulty of principle.

This difficulty is a fundamental problem in economic programming theories. Where there are groups that have more than one source of income (or sell more than one kind of goods) it may be impossible to present a matrix of the kind given above. This problem was discussed in Chapter 1. There it was observed that nineteenth-century economics was much concerned with "class"—the allocation of income among workers, landowners, money-lenders, profit-receivers, and so on. Since in fact many individuals earn income in several ways, these issues may not be capable of precise formulation. The existence of "multi-product economic units" is a main theoretical obstacle to "class" theories of economics, and also to programming theories. In contrast, aggregation is not a problem. If we wished to divide "labor" into categories—machinists, Midwesterners, Negroes, and so on—there would be no difficulty, providing each given individual belongs to one and only one category.

The symbols v_{IL} and v_{IK} stand for purchases of investment goods by workers and property-owners. In the context of the national income, such purchases could certainly include housing construction. But v_{IK} in particular, can be thought of in a different way. The theory has specified that businesses do not buy businesses. If investment takes place (in the sense that there is new plant built), it takes place as follows: Property owners buy the plant and lease it to businesses.

If this system is "closed," all income is accounted for by expenditures, and all expenditures are covered by income, then

$$
\begin{aligned}
v_{CL} + v_{CK} &= v_{LC} + v_{KC} = v_C \\
v_{IL} + v_{IK} &= v_{LI} + v_{KI} = v_I \\
v_{LC} + v_{LI} &= v_{CL} + v_{IL} = v_L \\
v_{KC} + v_{KI} &= v_{CK} + v_{IK} = v_K
\end{aligned}
$$

This last state of affairs may be written in matrix-vector form:

$$
(1, 1, 1, 1)\begin{pmatrix} 0 & 0 & v_{CL} & v_{CK} \\ 0 & 0 & v_{IL} & v_{IK} \\ v_{LC} & v_{LI} & 0 & 0 \\ v_{KC} & v_{KI} & 0 & 0 \end{pmatrix} = (\mathbf{v_C}, \mathbf{v_I}, \mathbf{v_L}, \mathbf{v_K}) \tag{10.1}
$$

$$
(1, 1, 1, 1)\begin{pmatrix} 0 & 0 & v_{LC} & v_{KC} \\ 0 & 0 & v_{LI} & v_{KI} \\ v_{CL} & v_{IL} & 0 & 0 \\ v_{CK} & v_{IK} & 0 & 0 \end{pmatrix} = (\mathbf{v_C}, \mathbf{v_I}, \mathbf{v_L}, \mathbf{v_K}) \tag{10.2}
$$

The indices of each element of the second matrix are in reverse order from those in the corresponding position of the first matrix. The elements of any *row* of the first matrix are therefore the elements of the corresponding *column* of the second. The matrices of 10.1 and of 10.2 are said to be *transposed* with respect to each other. This subject will be discussed again below. For the present, it is enough to note that the two matrices have the same elements, but that the elements occur in different places in the two matrices.

Definition If **A** is a matrix then $\mathbf{A_T}$ (**A**-transpose) is the matrix such that row i of **A** has the same elements as column i of $\mathbf{A_T}$ for every i.

Example:

$$
\begin{pmatrix} 1 & 2 & 3 \\ 4 & 5 & 6 \\ 7 & 8 & 9 \end{pmatrix}_{\mathbf{T}} = \begin{pmatrix} 1 & 4 & 7 \\ 2 & 5 & 8 \\ 3 & 6 & 9 \end{pmatrix}
$$

So far, we have merely written down in matrix-vector notation a method of social accounting. This method is related to the national income and product accounts. It is more detailed, however, because it lists the sales made by each sector of the economy to each of the other sectors. In order to have an accounting system of this sort, it is necessary to be able to classify all sales, according to the sector making the purchase and the sector making the sale. It may not be possible, for example, to separate the consumer goods bought by wage-earners from the consumer goods bought by bondholders, because some individuals earn wages and also receive income from interest. Some goods may be used both for consumer goods and for investment goods (lumber is an example). But let us provisionally discard this difficulty.

In order to make this accounting system into a theory, it is necessary to introduce into it assertions about the behavior of each sector of the economy. This will be done in the following way. Each term v_{ij} in the matrix of the theory represents the *value* of the sales by sector i to sector j. We shall now define, for every pair (i, j) of sectors, the number a_{ij}:

$$a_{ij} = \frac{q_{ij}}{q_j}$$

That is, for every unit of j sold, sellers of j buy a_{ij} units of i.

Problem 10.2 Let j equal successively to I, C, L, B. Interpret the meanings of the various terms in the matrix.

The behavioral assumption made in this theory is that the terms a_{ij} are constant. One part of the theorist's problem is to determine whether, given constant values for these eight terms, the prices and quantities in the system are uniquely determined. A further problem is to decide what happens to prices and to quantities when one or more of these terms changes.

We approach this problem by simplifying the matrices. Such simplification is desirable, because, given a_{ij}, $q_{ij} = a_{ij}q_j$ and $v_{ij} = p_i a_{ij} q_j$, which is complicated to look at. With this substitution, the matrix written out becomes

$$\begin{pmatrix} 0 & 0 & p_C a_{LC} q_L & p_C a_{CK} q_K \\ 0 & 0 & p_I a_{IL} q_L & p_I a_{IK} q_K \\ p_L a_{LC} q_C & p_L a_{LI} q_I & 0 & 0 \\ p_K a_{KC} q_C & p_K a_{KI} q_I & 0 & 0 \end{pmatrix}$$

In this matrix, every element of row i contains p_i $(i = C, I, L, K)$. Every element of column j contains q_j $(j = C, I, L, K)$. Consequently, this second matrix may be written as a product of matrices.

$$\begin{pmatrix} P_C & 0 & 0 & 0 \\ 0 & p_I & 0 & 0 \\ 0 & 0 & p_L & 0 \\ 0 & 0 & 0 & p_K \end{pmatrix} \begin{pmatrix} 0 & 0 & a_{CL} & a_{CK} \\ 0 & 0 & a_{IL} & a_{IK} \\ a_{LC} & a_{LI} & 0 & 0 \\ a_{KC} & a_{KI} & 0 & 0 \end{pmatrix} \begin{pmatrix} q_C & 0 & 0 & 0 \\ 0 & q_I & 0 & 0 \\ 0 & 0 & q_L & 0 \\ 0 & 0 & 0 & q_K \end{pmatrix}$$

Problem 10.3 Verify that this expansion is correct.

Since $(\mathbf{v_C}, \mathbf{v_I}, \mathbf{v_L}, \mathbf{v_K}) = (\mathbf{p_C q_C}, \mathbf{p_I q_I}, \mathbf{p_L q_L}, \mathbf{p_K q_K})$.
The right side of equation (10.1) is

$$(\mathbf{v_C}, \mathbf{v_I}, \mathbf{v_L}, \mathbf{v_K}) = (\mathbf{p_C}, \mathbf{p_I}, \mathbf{p_L}, \mathbf{p_K}) \begin{pmatrix} q_C & 0 & 0 & 0 \\ 0 & q_I & 0 & 0 \\ 0 & 0 & q_L & 0 \\ 0 & 0 & 0 & q_K \end{pmatrix}$$

and, the left side of (10.1) is

$$(1, 1, 1, 1) \begin{pmatrix} 0 & 0 & v_{CL} & v_{CK} \\ 0 & 0 & v_{IL} & v_{IK} \\ v_{LC} & v_{LI} & 0 & 0 \\ v_{KC} & v_{KI} & 0 & 0 \end{pmatrix}$$

$$= (1, 1, 1, 1) \begin{pmatrix} p_C & 0 & 0 & 0 \\ 0 & p_I & 0 & 0 \\ 0 & 0 & p_L & 0 \\ 0 & 0 & 0 & p_K \end{pmatrix} \begin{pmatrix} 0 & 0 & a_{CL} & a_{CK} \\ 0 & 0 & a_{IL} & a_{IK} \\ a_{LC} & a_{LI} & 0 & 0 \\ a_{KC} & a_{KI} & 0 & 0 \end{pmatrix} \begin{pmatrix} q_C & 0 & 0 & 0 \\ 0 & q_I & 0 & 0 \\ 0 & 0 & q_L & 0 \\ 0 & 0 & 0 & q_K \end{pmatrix}$$

$$= (\mathbf{p_C}, \mathbf{p_I}, \mathbf{p_L}, \mathbf{p_K}) \begin{pmatrix} 0 & 0 & a_{CL} & a_{CK} \\ 0 & 0 & a_{IL} & a_{IK} \\ a_{LC} & a_{LI} & 0 & 0 \\ a_{KC} & a_{KI} & 0 & 0 \end{pmatrix} \begin{pmatrix} q_C & 0 & 0 & 0 \\ 0 & q_I & 0 & 0 \\ 0 & 0 & q_L & 0 \\ 0 & 0 & 0 & q_K \end{pmatrix} \qquad (10.3)$$

The matrix (10.3)

$$\begin{pmatrix} q_C & 0 & 0 & 0 \\ 0 & q_I & 0 & 0 \\ 0 & 0 & q_L & 0 \\ 0 & 0 & 0 & q_K \end{pmatrix}$$

may be cancelled from both sides of (10.1).

Problem 10.4 Show that this statement is true, by computing the inverse of (10.3) and by multiplying both sides of equation (10.1), on the right, by this inverse.

Thus,

$$(\mathbf{p_C}, \mathbf{p_I}, \mathbf{p_L}, \mathbf{p_K}) \begin{pmatrix} 0 & 0 & a_{CL} & a_{CK} \\ 0 & 0 & a_{IL} & a_{IK} \\ a_{LC} & a_{LI} & 0 & 0 \\ a_{KC} & a_{KI} & 0 & 0 \end{pmatrix} = (\mathbf{p_C}, \mathbf{p_I}, \mathbf{p_L}, \mathbf{p_K}) \qquad (10.4)$$

It is also the case that (10.2) may be written

$$(\mathbf{q_C}, \mathbf{q_I}, \mathbf{q_L}, \mathbf{q_K}) \begin{pmatrix} 0 & 0 & a_{LC} & a_{KC} \\ 0 & 0 & a_{LI} & a_{KI} \\ a_{CL} & a_{IL} & 0 & 0 \\ a_{CK} & a_{IK} & 0 & 0 \end{pmatrix} = (\mathbf{q_C}, \mathbf{q_I}, \mathbf{q_L}, \mathbf{q_K}) \qquad (10.5)$$

Problem 10.5 Verify that (10.2) indeed implies (10.5) by going through steps, comparable to those used in deriving (10.4), from (10.1).

The system includes two prices that may seem to be the same at first glance: the price of investment goods (p_I) and the rental price of plant (p_K). It is not obvious that the price associated with total plant (p_K) is different from the price associated with new plant (that is, investment, p_I). If the two prices were related to the same thing, they would have to be the same, for in a market economy a single price will prevail for any one commodity. But we may establish that the two prices refer to different things by showing that $(p_C q_C + p_I q_I) = (p_L q_L + p_K q_K)$. This is the statement in Chapter 1 that output is always equal to income. Output is the sum of the values of consumption and investment; income is the sum of wages and property income. Property income is a rental charge (p_K) on units of equipment (q_K). This equality will now be demonstrated.

Three of the pairs of variables are easy enough to interpret: q_C, for instance, is the quantity of consumer goods and p_C is the price of consumer goods. The fourth pair presents a slightly greater problem: q_K is a measure of the amount of plant in existence, and p_K is the rental charge on a unit of this plant. From the accounting point of view, q_K is a balance sheet item (a stock), and p_K is an income statement item (a flow). The rental price p_K is related, of course, to the purchase price of a unit of plant p_I. The relation between the two is usually given by a formula such as

$$p_K = p_I\,(d + \pi + \rho)$$

d is the annual rate of depreciation, in percent of original cost
π is an insurance premium against damage
ρ is the net return to the owner.

It is reasonable to suppose that d and ρ are fixed, so that variations in p_K reflect mainly variations in the return on an investment in plant. If there were bonds in our economy, ρ could be associated with an interest rate. Property owners would have a choice of earning interest on bonds or of obtaining a return by renting plant. For this reason ρ is often referred to as an interest rate.

The two equations (10.4) and (10.5) may be written more compactly in the form

$$\mathbf{PA} = \mathbf{P}$$

$$\mathbf{QA_T} = \mathbf{Q}$$

The vectors **P** and **Q** are then special cases of vector equations having the form

$$\mathbf{VA} = \mathbf{nV}$$

$$\mathbf{WA_T} = \mathbf{nW}$$

where n is some number (in this case $n = 1$). Whenever this relationship exists, we say that **V** is a *characteristic vector of* **A** *corresponding to the characteristic value n*. **W** is a characteristic vector of $\mathbf{A_T}$ corresponding to the characteristic value n. Every matrix has characteristic vectors and characteristic values, and these are important ways of describing the mathematical properties of matrices.

For example, the matrix **A** has elements which are zero or positive. An important theorem (which will be called the *Frobenius Theorem*, after its inventor) concerning matrices of this sort says that if a matrix with nonnegative elements is *not* block-triangular, then it has a "maximal" characteristic value, which we will denote by **m**. Then

(1) **m** is positive.

(2) There is one and only one vector satisfying the equation $\mathbf{VA} = \mathbf{mV}$.

(3) This vector has nonnegative components.

(4) All other characteristic values have absolute values less than or equal to **m**.

It may be shown that **A** and $\mathbf{A_T}$ have the same set of characteristic values, and hence the same maximal characteristic value. Another theorem states that the components of the vectors **V** and **W** corresponding to **m** for the matrices **A** and $\mathbf{A_T}$ have strictly positive components if and only if **A** and $\mathbf{A_T}$ are *not* block-triangular.

These theorems[5] have important economic interpretations. It is possible to show that 1 must be the maximal characteristic vector of **A** and $\mathbf{A_T}$. It makes no economic sense to compute input-output matrices **A** that yield maximal characteristic vectors with zero components. A component of one of these vectors is either a price or a quantity. If either of these is zero, the corresponding sector of the economy would have no income, and could not

[5] They are proved in relatively advanced texts on matrix algebra. See, for example, F. R. Gantmacher, *Matrix Theory*, New York (Chelsea) 1959, Vol. 2, Chapter XIII.

have been observed in the first place. And so, if **P** and **Q** satisfy equations (10.4) and (10.5), they are the only ones that do so.[6]

An illustration of how a deeper mathematical analysis may be useful to economists follows. It turns out that the matrices **A** and $\mathbf{A_T}$ have characteristic values of -1 as well as of $+1$. If we write (10.4) and (10.5) in block form, so that

$$(\mathbf{P}_1, \mathbf{P}_2)\begin{pmatrix} 0 & A_1 \\ A_2 & 0 \end{pmatrix} = (\mathbf{P}_2\,\mathbf{A}_2\,, \mathbf{P}_1\mathbf{A}_1) = (\mathbf{P}_1, \mathbf{P}_2)$$

$$(\mathbf{Q}_1, \mathbf{Q}_2)\begin{pmatrix} 0 & A_{2T} \\ A_{1T} & 0 \end{pmatrix} = (-\mathbf{Q}_2\,\mathbf{A}_{1\mathbf{T}}\,, \mathbf{Q}_1\,\mathbf{A}_{2\mathbf{T}}) = (\mathbf{Q}_1, \mathbf{Q}_2)$$

Then it also follows that

$$(\mathbf{Q}_1, -\mathbf{Q}_2)\begin{pmatrix} 0 & A_{2T} \\ A_{lT} & 0 \end{pmatrix} = (-\mathbf{Q}_2\,\mathbf{A}_{l\mathbf{T}}\,, \mathbf{Q}_1\mathbf{A}_{2\mathbf{T}}) = (-1)(\mathbf{Q}_1, -\mathbf{Q}_2)$$

so that $(\mathbf{Q}_1, -\mathbf{Q}_2)$ is a characteristic vector of $\mathbf{A_T}$ corresponding to the characteristic value -1. [For **A**, the corresponding characteristic vector would be $(\mathbf{P}_1, -\mathbf{P}_2)$.]

Now it will be shown that the existence of the two characteristic vectors $(\mathbf{P}_1, \mathbf{P}_2)$ and $(\mathbf{Q}_1, -\mathbf{Q}_2)$ corresponding to the characteristic values $+1$ of **A** and -1 of $\mathbf{A_T}$ enable us to verify the economic concept that the *national income* and the *national product* are equal. It is particularly interesting that this way of looking at the economy should lead to this conclusion. For in this chapter, no use has yet been made of this proposition, which was one of the *assumptions* made by the discussion of social accounting in Chapter 1.

Two vectors, $\mathbf{V}_1$ and $\mathbf{V}_2$ are said to be *orthogonal*, if, for

$$\mathbf{V}_1 = (\mathbf{v}_1 \cdots \mathbf{v}_n)$$

$$\mathbf{V}_2 = (\mathbf{v}'_1 \cdots \mathbf{v}'_n)$$

$$\sum_{i=1}^{n} \mathbf{v}_i \mathbf{v}'_i = 0$$

It may be shown that the vectors $\mathbf{P} = (\mathbf{P}_1, \mathbf{P}_2)$ and $\overline{\mathbf{Q}} = (\mathbf{Q}_1, -\mathbf{Q}_2)$ are orthogonal. But that means that

$$(p_C q_C + p_I q_I) - (p_L q_L + p_K q_K) = 0$$

[6] Caution: If $PA = P$, and m is any number, then $(mP)A = (mP)$. That is, a set of prices (or quantities) may vary strictly proportionately, given a matrix A. Leontief called his book *The Structure of the American Economy* because only the structures of prices and of quantities produced (that is, *relative* prices and quantities) were determined by his theoretical analysis.

Therefore,

$$p_C q_C = \text{the value of consumer goods output}$$

plus

$$p_I q_I = \text{the value of investment goods output equals}$$

$$p_L q_L = \text{the value of wage payments}$$

plus

$$p_K q_K = \text{the value of payments to property owners}$$

The first parenthesis is (in terms of Chapter 1) the national product, while the second is the national income. So far, it has been asserted only that all the income of every sector is accounted for, but no connection has been established between this proposition and the theory of the national accounts. We now prove the orthogonality of **P** and $\overline{\mathbf{Q}}$.

The vector **P** is a characteristic vector of **A** corresponding to the characteristic value 1; $\overline{\mathbf{Q}}$ is a characteristic vector of $\mathbf{A_T}$ corresponding to the characteristic value -1. Suppose, now that for a matrix **M**, there are characteristic vectors **x**, **y** and two distinct characteristic values, λ, μ, such that

$$\mathbf{xM} = \boldsymbol{\lambda}\mathbf{x}$$

$$\mathbf{yM_T} = \boldsymbol{\mu}\mathbf{y}$$

Then we shall show that **x** and **y** are orthogonal. We write

$$\mathbf{x} = (\mathbf{x}_1 \cdots \mathbf{x}_n)$$

$$\mathbf{y} = (\mathbf{y}_1 \cdots \mathbf{y}_n)$$

and the elements of **M** as (m_{ij})

$$\mathbf{Z} = \mathbf{xM} = \left(\sum_j \mathbf{x}_j \mathbf{m}_{j1}, \sum_j \mathbf{x}_j \mathbf{m}_{j2}, \ldots, \sum \mathbf{x}_j \mathbf{m}_{jn}\right)$$

$$\mathbf{W} = \mathbf{yM_T} = \left(\sum_j \mathbf{y}_j \mathbf{m}_{1j}, \sum \mathbf{y}_j \mathbf{m}_{2j}, \ldots, \sum \mathbf{y}_j \mathbf{m}_{nj}\right)$$

Then

$$\boldsymbol{\lambda} \sum_i \mathbf{x}_i \mathbf{y}_i = \sum_i (\boldsymbol{\lambda}\mathbf{x}_i)\mathbf{y}_i = \sum_i \mathbf{z}_i \mathbf{y}_i = \sum_i \sum_j \mathbf{x}_j \mathbf{m}_{ji} \mathbf{m}_{ij} \mathbf{y}_i$$

$$\boldsymbol{\mu} \sum_j \mathbf{x}_j \mathbf{y}_j = \sum_j \mathbf{x}_j(\boldsymbol{\mu}\mathbf{y}_j) = \sum_j \mathbf{x}_j \mathbf{w}_j = \sum_j \sum_j \mathbf{x}_j \mathbf{m}_{ji} \mathbf{m}_{ij} \mathbf{y}_i$$

The two double sums on the right are the same. Therefore,

$$\boldsymbol{\lambda} \sum \mathbf{x}_i \mathbf{y}_i = \boldsymbol{\mu} \sum \mathbf{x}_i \mathbf{y}_i$$

Since $\boldsymbol{\lambda} \neq \boldsymbol{\mu}$, this equality can hold if and only if $\sum \mathbf{x}_i \mathbf{y}_i = \mathbf{0}$. That is, **x** and **y** are orthogonal. Therefore, as a special case of this theorem, **P** and $\overline{\mathbf{Q}}$

are orthogonal, and this theory is consistent with the social accounts of Chapter 1, even though it seems to have no particular connection with them at first glance.

The discussion given in the past few paragraphs has skipped over a number of theorems in matrix algebra which are rather more difficult than anything in this book. It is useful to give this brief mention of characteristic vectors, characteristic values, and orthogonal vectors to indicate that there exists a body of mathematical literature that is closely related to the kind of linear theory represented by equations (10.4) and (10.5). When this literature is interpreted by economists, a natural connection may be made between price changes and output changes. This connection exists because prices may be associated with a characteristic vector of a matrix **A**, and quantities with the corresponding characteristic vector of the transpose $\mathbf{A_T}$ of **A**.

PROGRAMMING THEORIES AND ECONOMIC EFFICIENCY

The foregoing discussion derived the matrix **A** (and its transpose) from social accounting considerations and developed an "input-output theory" from the proposition that in an accounting system everything is accounted for exactly once. The disadvantage of such an approach is that it does not state explicitly what the economic nature of the fixed coefficients of the matrix might be. To many readers, they will seem artificial. It is useful, then, to give a second formulation, which says more than the first about how the various sectors of the economy are assumed to behave. It turns out that the two formulations are equivalent. Nevertheless, one gains an understanding of modern economic theory by looking at both formulations, for both have to do with the relation between prices and quantities produced in the various sectors of an economy. In particular, parts of the discussion that follows have counterparts in some of the theories presented earlier.

The usual price theories are like Tiny Model 3, or like Theories 1 and 11A. In such theories the quantities of goods and services that people are willing to buy or sell depend on the prices charged for these goods and services (and sometimes on other prices as well). In the present theory, a "technological" approach is used to make behavioral assumptions. For two of the statements, the assumption is straightforward: The demand for labor depends on the output of consumer and investment goods:

$$D_L = a_{LC}q_C + a_{LI}q_I$$

The demand for (services of) plant depends on the output of consumer and investment goods:

$$D_K = a_{KC}q_C + a_{KI}q_I$$

If output of both kinds of goods is multiplied by a positive number N, the demands will be multiplied by that same number N.[7] The demand for labor to produce consumer goods is the product $a_{LC}q_C$, which varies proportionately with q_C, the output of consumer goods, and so forth.

The two functions D_L and D_K are supposedly based on engineering relationships. In the present problem, the commodities are so highly aggregated that there is no particular meaning that can be attached to the term "engineering." But if a theory could be expressed in so much detail that the commodities are well defined from an engineer's point of view, in principle one could derive these coefficients from engineering process data.[8] The coefficients a_{ij} relate to the engineering question, "How much j does it take to produce a unit of i?"

The other two statements in the theory relate to the demand for consumer goods and investment goods. They are written in very much the same form as the first two:

The demand for consumer goods depends on the output of labor and services of plant:

$$D_C = a_{CL}q_L + a_{CK}q_K$$

The demand for investment goods depends on the output of labor and services of plant:

$$D_I = a_{IL}q_L + a_{IK}q_K$$

In these equations the demand for goods depends on how much "work" is performed by the suppliers of services. Metaphorically speaking, this work creates an "appetite" for goods which is proportionate to the amount of work performed.

These last two demand functions are unlike those of price theory (since they are independent of price). They also differ from the demand functions of ordinary macroeconomics. There consumers decide how to allocate their income as between consumer goods and increases in net worth; businesses decide how to allocate their assets among plant and other forms of assets. Here demands are strictly proportionate to services performed.

The four demand functions D_L, D_K, D_C, D_I assume numerical values for each set (q_C, q_I, q_L, q_K) of output values. That is, output vectors $\mathbf{Q}' = (\mathbf{q}_C', \mathbf{q}_I', \mathbf{q}_L', \mathbf{q}_K')$ are mapped by the matrix of coefficients (a_{ij}) into vectors $\mathbf{D}' = (\mathbf{D}_C', \mathbf{D}_I', \mathbf{D}_L', \mathbf{D}_K')$ of demands.

---

[7] Mathematicians say that D_L and D_K (as well as D_C and D_I below) are *homogeneous of degree one*. Economists say that they exhibit *constant returns to scale*.

[8] The relation between engineering and economic analysis of production is described in R. K. Davidson, V. L. Smith, and J. W. Wiley, *Economics: An Analytical Approach*, Homewood, Ill. (John Wiley & Sons, Inc.) Revised edition, 1962. At a more advanced level, see V. L. Smith, *Production and Investment*. Cambridge, Mass. (Harvard). Second printing, 1966.

At any moment, there are capacity limitations on the vector **Q**. That is to say, there may be a maximum amount of plant that can be used, a maximum amount of labor that the population can provide, and maximum "capacity" of industry to produce consumer or investment goods. It may be difficult to determine these maximum amounts, because

(1) One might be able to encourage housewives to leave their kitchens, and children to leave their schools to take jobs. The extent to which this is possible is unclear.

(2) One might be able to encourage businesses to put extremely old and worn-out equipment back into operation. The extent to which this is possible is unclear.

(3) One might be able to get factories somehow to force more goods through their assembly lines by speedups. It is not clear how far such a speedup can go.

As theorists, however, we can postulate some sort of upper bound on all the components of the output vectors $\{\mathbf{Q}\}$. And if there are such upper bounds on outputs, there will also be upper bounds on the demand vectors $\{\mathbf{D}\}$. A vector **D** is called *feasible* if it is the image of some vector **Q** none of whose components exceed the capacity limitations. A particular demand vector **D** will be called *efficient* if there is no way of reallocating outputs in such a way as to increase *all* the components of **D**. That is, if we compare **D** with any other feasible vector **D′** (any **D′** which can be generated within the capacity limitations), then $\mathbf{D}' - \mathbf{D} = (\mathbf{D}'_C - \mathbf{D}_C, \mathbf{D}'_I - \mathbf{D}_I, \mathbf{D}'_L - \mathbf{D}_L, \mathbf{D}'_K - \mathbf{D}_K)$ will have at least one negative component if **D** is efficient.[9]

Let us suppose now that there is one *maximal* vector $\mathbf{D}^* = (\mathbf{D}^*_C, \mathbf{D}^*_I, \mathbf{D}^*_L, \mathbf{D}^*_K)$, that is, a vector that maximizes the demands for all the commodities in the system. That is, whatever feasible **D** we consider $\mathbf{D}^* - \mathbf{D}$ has only zero or positive components. That is,

$$D_C^* \geq a_{CL}q_L + a_{CK}q_K$$
$$D_I^* \geq a_{IL}q_L + a_{IK}q_K$$
$$D_L^* \geq a_{LC}q_C + a_{LI}q_I$$
$$D_K^* \geq a_{KC}q_C + a_{KI}q_I$$

for $q_L \leq q_L^*$, $q_K \leq q_K^*$, $q_C \leq q_C^*$, $q_I \leq q_I^*$, where the starred symbols represent capacity limits.

All of this discussion has taken place without any mention of prices. But prices are to be an essential feature of the theory we are considering. They are introduced in the following way. In the economy described by the four demand functions D_C, D_I, D_L, D_K, compute the costs of producing the various commodities. For consumer goods production, the amount of labor

[9] Compare this definition of *efficiency* with the definition of optimality in Chapter 6.

used to produce quantity x_C of consumer goods is $a_{LC}x_C$; if the price of labor is p_L, the cost of this labor is $p_L a_{LC} x_C$, and the labor cost per unit of output is $p_L a_{LC}$. Similarly, the amount of services of plant required to produce x_C is $a_{KC} x_C$; if the price of these services is p_K, these services will cost a total of $p_K a_{KC} x_C$. The cost of these services per unit of output is $p_K a_{KC}$. Thus for consumer goods, there will be a cost function

$$P_C = a_{LC} p_L + a_{KC} p_K$$

Similarly, for investment goods there is a cost function

$$P_I = a_{LI} p_L + a_{KI} p_K$$

This theory regards labor as being "produced" by the use of consumer and investment goods. This method of thought will seem strange to noneconomists, but it results quite naturally from the desire of programming theorists to treat all parts of the economy from a single point of view. Labor services are thus produced by providing labor with consumer and investment goods.[10] Thus the cost of labor is

$$P_L = a_{CL} p_C + a_{IL} p_I$$

Services of plant are also "produced" by the application of consumer and investment goods. That is, the owners of plant will not make plant available unless they receive compensation. Thus the cost of services of plant is

$$P_K = a_{CK} p_C + a_{IK} p_K$$

These cost functions permit the formulation of a *dual* concept of efficiency. An economy, it has been said, is operating efficiently when it generates as much demand as possible for its output. But a *dual* definition of efficiency would be the following. An economy is efficient when its costs are as low as possible. This dual definition will now be formulated more precisely.

The symbols P_C, P_I, P_L, P_K are functions of the prices p_C, p_I, p_L, p_K. That is, the matrix of coefficients (a_{ij}) maps vectors $\mathbf{p} = (\mathbf{p_C}, \mathbf{p_I}, \mathbf{p_L}, \mathbf{p_K})$ into vectors $\mathbf{P} = (\mathbf{P_C}, \mathbf{P_I}, \mathbf{P_L}, \mathbf{P_K})$. For any particular vector $\mathbf{p}$, the components of its image $\mathbf{P}$ becomes particular numbers. If we compare $\mathbf{P}$ with any other vector $\mathbf{P}'$ then $\mathbf{P}' - \mathbf{P} = (\mathbf{p}'_\mathbf{C} - \mathbf{p_C}, \mathbf{p}'_\mathbf{I} - \mathbf{p}'_\mathbf{I}, \mathbf{p}'_\mathbf{L} - \mathbf{p_L}, \mathbf{p}'_\mathbf{K} - \mathbf{p_K})$. If $\mathbf{P}'$ is inefficient relative to $\mathbf{P}$, then all of the components of $\mathbf{P}' - \mathbf{P}$ will be positive. That is, everything will cost less if $\mathbf{P}$ than if $\mathbf{P}'$. Consequently, if $\mathbf{P}'$ and $\mathbf{P}$ are both efficient, the vector $\mathbf{P}' - \mathbf{P}$ will have at least one positive component and at least one negative component.

---

[10] In the extreme, this point of view is completely sensible. If one does not provide people with food, they will become completely and permanently unable to work. The less food provided, the more people will die; the more food provided, the larger the labor force will be. This intuitive explanation does not closely fit "affluent societies," but neither is it completely without appeal.

Let us now suppose that there is one vector $\mathbf{P}^* = (\mathbf{P}_C^*, \mathbf{P}_I^*, \mathbf{P}_L^*, \mathbf{P}_K^*)$ which minimizes all the costs of all the commodities in the economy. Then it is the case that

$$P_C^* \leq a_{LC}\, p_L + a_{KC}\, p_K$$

$$P_I^* \leq a_{LI}\, p_L + a_{KI}\, p_K$$

$$P_L^* \leq a_{CL}\, p_C + a_{IL}\, p_I$$

$$P_K^* \leq a_{CK}\, p_C + a_{IK}\, p_K$$

(Note that there is no ceiling on how high prices may rise, as this problem has been formulated. But prices, like quantities, must be nonnegative if the exercise is to have economic meaning.) The vector $\mathbf{P}^* = (\mathbf{P}_C^*, \mathbf{P}_I^*, \mathbf{P}_L^*, \mathbf{P}_K^*)$. Two concepts of efficiency have now been advanced for this economy. One states that demands are to be maximized, the other that costs are to be minimized. These two definitions are now to be related in the following way:

(1) Suppose one seeks to maximize demands. Then one seeks to select a vector $\mathbf{D}' = (\mathbf{D}_C', \mathbf{D}_I', \mathbf{D}_L', \mathbf{D}_K')$ such that
  (a) $(\mathbf{D}_C', \mathbf{D}_I', \mathbf{D}_L', \mathbf{D}_K')$ is *feasible*. That is, it is the image of some vector $(\mathbf{q}_C', \mathbf{q}_I', \mathbf{q}_L', \mathbf{q}_K')$ which does not exceed any capacity limits.

  (b) If $(\mathbf{D}_C', \mathbf{D}_I', \mathbf{D}_L', \mathbf{D}_K')$ is valued at the most efficient costs $(\mathbf{P}_C^*, \mathbf{P}_I^*, \mathbf{P}_L^*, \mathbf{P}_K^*)$, then the total value of this demand, which is

$$\bar{S} = P_C^* D_C' + P_I^* D_I' + P_L^* D_L' + P_K^* D_K'$$

  is to be as great as possible.

(2) Suppose one seeks to minimize costs. Then one seeks to select a vector $\mathbf{P}' = (\mathbf{P}_C', \mathbf{P}_I', \mathbf{P}_L', \mathbf{P}_K')$ such that
  (a) $(\mathbf{P}_C', \mathbf{P}_I', \mathbf{P}_L', \mathbf{P}_K')$ is the image of some vector of prices $(\mathbf{p}_C', \mathbf{p}_I', \mathbf{p}_L', \mathbf{p}_K')$ under the mapping given above,

  (b) If the maximal demands $(\mathbf{D}_C^*, \mathbf{D}_I^*, \mathbf{D}_L^*, \mathbf{D}_K^*)$ are valued at the costs $(\mathbf{P}_C', \mathbf{P}_I', \mathbf{P}_L', \mathbf{P}_K')$, then the total value of these maximal demands which is

$$\underline{S} = P_C' D_C^* + P_I' D_I^* + P_L' D_L^* + P_K' D_K^*$$

  is to be as small as possible.

Two new statements have now been introduced. These involve assigning *values* to the vectors $\mathbf{P}'$ and $\mathbf{D}'$. Values, of course, involve products of prices and quantities. The vector $\mathbf{P}'$ is then valued at the most efficient set of quantities represented by the vector $\mathbf{D}^*$; the vector $\mathbf{D}'$ is valued at the most efficient set of costs represented by the vector $\mathbf{P}^*$. The two sums $\underline{S}$ and $\bar{S}$

consist of four terms. When the first term of $\underline{S}$ is compared to the first term of $\bar{S}$, it is seen that

$$P'_C D^*_C \geq P^*_C D^*_C \geq P^*_C D'_C$$

Similar inequalities may be formed for the other three terms. If, then, it is possible to select P' and D' in such a way that $\underline{S} = \bar{S}$, then it must be the case (since all of the numbers involved are nonnegative), that $\mathbf{P}' = \mathbf{P}^*$ and $\mathbf{D}' = \mathbf{D}^*$. That is $\mathbf{P}'$ and $\mathbf{D}'$ are optimal. For if $\mathbf{D}''$ is any other feasible vector it will be the case for the first component that

$$P'_C D^*_C \geq P^*_C D^*_C \geq P^*_C D''_C$$

But, by assumption $P'_C D^*_C = P^*_C D'_C$, so $P^*_C D'_C \geq P^*_C D''_C$, so that $D''_C \leq D'_C$.

Theorem: A vector $\mathbf{P}'$ which minimizes $\underline{S}$ (the cost of maximal output) is proportional[11] to $\mathbf{P}^*$. A vector $\mathbf{D}'$ which maximizes $\bar{S}$ (the value of aggregate demand) is equal to $\mathbf{Q}^*$.

Now it will be shown that if an equilibrium exists at the optimum, the prices of all outputs that are used in less than capacity amounts are zero; and the outputs of all commodities produced at greater than minimal costs are zero. This result means that demand equals supply equals capacity for all commodities, and that price equals cost for all commodities.[12]

Suppose $\mathbf{D}'$ is selected in such a way as to maximize

$$\bar{S} = P^*_C D'_C + P^*_I D'_I + P^*_L D'_L + P^*_K D'_K$$

and that P' is selected in such a way as to minimize

$$\underline{S} = P'_C D^*_C + P'_I D^*_I + P'_L D^*_L + P'_K D^*_K$$

Consider these two sums term by term. By hypothesis, the first term,

$$D^*_C \geq a_{CL} q_L + a_{CK} q_K \quad \text{for every} \quad q_L, q'_K$$

Consequently,

$$P'_C D^*_C \geq P'_C a_{CL} q_L + P'_C a_{CK} q_K \geq P^*_C a_{CL} q_L + P^*_C a_{CK} q_K = P^*_C D'_C$$

---

[11] In Chapter 9 it was pointed out that if there is no money illusion, proportional changes in *all* prices should not affect the equilibrium. Mathematically, prices are determined only to within a proportionality factor, for there is nothing akin to a "capacity limit" where prices are concerned.

[12] In this type of reasoning, a sharp distinction is made between accounting profit and economic profit. The dividends to owners of plant (p_K) are an accounting profit. An economic profit would exist only if there were *retained* profit, that is, income that is not paid out to anyone. Indeed, it is possible to construct programming-type theories in which a part of the total income of industries is retained in the industry without violating the "no profit rule" that price equals average cost. This rule really means that all income is distributed according to the rules of the theory.

Likewise,

$$P'_I D^*_C \geq P'_I a_{IL} q_L + P'_I a_{IK} q_K \geq P^*_I a_{IL} q_L + P^*_I a_{IK} q_K = P^*_I D'_I$$
$$P'_L D^*_L \geq P'_L a_{LC} q_C + P'_L a_{LI} q_I \geq P^*_L a_{LC} q_C + P^*_L a_{LI} q_I = P^*_L D'_L$$
$$P'_K D^*_K \geq P'_K a_{KC} q_C + P'_K a_{KI} q_I \geq P^*_K a_{KC} q_C + P^*_K a_{KI} q_I = P^*_K D_K$$

The left side of these inequalities consists of terms in $\underline{S}$; the right side consists of terms in $\bar{S}$. By our theorem, the left side equals the right side. Consequently, both of the inequalities ($\geq$) on each line may be replaced by equalities ($=$). In this case, for the first term,

$$P'_C D^*_C = P'_C(a_{CL} q_L + a_{CK} q_K) = P^*(a_{CL} q_L + a_{CK} q_K) = P^*_C D'_C$$

In this case,

$$\textit{either} \quad P'_C(D^*_C - a_{CL} q_L - a_{CK} q_K) = 0$$
$$\textit{or} \quad P^*_C(D'_C - a_{CL} q_L - a_{CK} q_K) = 0$$

In the first case, if $D^*_C - D'_C \equiv D^*_C - a_{CL} q_L - a_{CK} q_K > 0$, then $P'_C = 0$; otherwise, if $P^*_C > 0$, then $D^*_C - D'_C = 0$. Similar results hold for the other terms in the sums $\underline{S}$ and $\bar{S}$.

Theorem: Any commodity not used in capacity amounts has price zero; any commodity whose price is above cost is produced in zero quantity.

[*Note:* This theorem reminds us what a puzzle the fact of unemployment is. Here is another way of showing that unemployment cannot happen. It does happen, however, quite regularly, and economists cannot be satisfied with their theories for precisely that reason.]

Because of this last theorem, if neither consumer goods, nor capital goods, nor labor, nor the services of plant and equipment are provided free of charge, then the economy works in such a way as to guarantee that

$$D^*_C = a_{CL} q_L + a_{CK} q_K$$
$$D^*_I = a_{IL} q_L + a_{IK} q_K$$
$$D^*_L = a_{LC} q_C + a_{LI} q_I$$
$$D^*_K = a_{KC} q_C + a_{KI} q_I$$

If there is equilibrium, so that quantities demanded equal quantities supplied, then

$$(\mathbf{D}^*_\mathbf{C}, \mathbf{D}^*_\mathbf{I}, \mathbf{D}^*_\mathbf{L}, \mathbf{D}^*_\mathbf{K}) = (\mathbf{q}_\mathbf{C}, \mathbf{q}_\mathbf{I}, \mathbf{q}_\mathbf{L}, \mathbf{q}_\mathbf{K})$$

so that

$$(\mathbf{q}_\mathbf{C}, \mathbf{q}_\mathbf{I}, \mathbf{q}_\mathbf{L}, \mathbf{q}_\mathbf{K}) = (\mathbf{q}_\mathbf{C}, \mathbf{q}_\mathbf{I}, \mathbf{q}_\mathbf{L}, \mathbf{q}_\mathbf{K}) \begin{pmatrix} 0 & 0 & a_{LC} & a_{KC} \\ 0 & 0 & a_{LI} & a_{KI} \\ a_{CL} & a_{IL} & 0 & 0 \\ a_{CK} & a_{IK} & 0 & 0 \end{pmatrix}$$

Moreover, if consumer goods, capital goods, labor, and services of plant and equipment are all used in nonzero amounts, then

$$\begin{aligned} P_C^* &= a_{LC}\,p_L + a_{KC}\,p_K \\ P_I^* &= a_{LI}\,p_L + a_{KI}\,p_K \\ P_L^* &= a_{CL}\,p_C + a_{IL}\,p_I \\ P_K^* &= a_{CK}\,p_C + a_{IK}\,p_I \end{aligned}$$

Finally if the "zero profits" condition holds then

$$(\mathbf{P}_\mathbf{C}^*, \mathbf{P}_\mathbf{I}^*, \mathbf{P}_\mathbf{L}^*, \mathbf{P}_\mathbf{K}^*) = (\mathbf{p}_\mathbf{C}, \mathbf{p}_\mathbf{I}, \mathbf{p}_\mathbf{L}, \mathbf{p}_\mathbf{K})$$

and

$$(\mathbf{p}_\mathbf{C}, \mathbf{p}_\mathbf{I}, \mathbf{p}_\mathbf{L}, \mathbf{p}_\mathbf{K}) = (\mathbf{p}_\mathbf{C}, \mathbf{p}_\mathbf{I}, \mathbf{p}_\mathbf{L}, \mathbf{p}_\mathbf{K}) \begin{pmatrix} 0 & 0 & a_{CL} & a_{CK} \\ 0 & 0 & a_{IL} & a_{IK} \\ a_{LC} & a_{LI} & 0 & 0 \\ a_{KC} & a_{KI} & 0 & 0 \end{pmatrix}$$

The two matrix equations have matrices which are related in the following way: Row i ($i = 1, 2, 3, 4$) of one matrix has the same elements as Column i of the other matrix.

Problem 10.6 Let **A**, **B** be arbitrary 4×4 matrices, Show that

$$\begin{aligned} (\mathbf{A} + \mathbf{B})_\mathbf{T} &= \mathbf{A}_\mathbf{T} + \mathbf{B}_\mathbf{T} \\ (\mathbf{AB})_\mathbf{T} &= \mathbf{B}_\mathbf{T}\mathbf{A}_\mathbf{T} \end{aligned}$$

Also, these two equations turn out to be exactly the same as equations (10.4) and (10.5) of the second part of this chapter. Thus an analytical basis has been provided for the entire input-output way of looking at the economy.

CHANGES IN AN INPUT-OUTPUT ECONOMY

The analysis given in the second section of this chapter relies on a basic proposition in matrix theory. If the matrix **A** has fixed coefficients, all of them nonnegative, if 1 is the maximal characteristic value of **A**, and if **A** is not block-triangular, then the structure of prices and of output is uniquely determined.

In real economies, the structure of prices and of quantities changes all the time—even though these changes are gradual. These changes, then, must reflect changes in the coefficients of the matrix **A**. Discussion of economic change in the context of a programming economy therefore involves determining the effects of changes in the coefficients of **A**, and interpreting the meaning of such changes.

There are eight nonzero elements of **A**. The eight economic changes that can occur in this economy are the following:

(1) Δa_{CL} = a change in the amount of consumer goods bought by workers, per man-year of employment.

(2) Δa_{CK} = a change in the amount of consumer goods bought by property-owners, per unit of property owned.

(3) Δa_{IL} = a change in the amount of investment goods (property) bought by workers, per man-year of employment.

(4) Δa_{IK} = a change in the amount of investment goods, (property) bought by property-owners, per unit of property already owned.

(5) Δa_{LC} = a change in the amount of labor required to produce one unit of consumer goods.

(6) Δa_{LI} = a change in the amount of labor required to produce one unit of investment goods.

(7) Δa_{KC} = a change in the amount of (services of) plant required to produce one unit of consumer goods.

(8) Δa_{KI} = a change in the amount of (services of) plant required to produce one unit of investment goods.

The first four changes involve the spending habits of workers and property-owners. That is to say, they involve "tastes," "habits," "fashions," and so on. The last four changes involve the needs of producers of consumer and investment goods for the services of labor and of property. That is to say, they involve "technology." Generally speaking, economists conjecture that "tastes" may be relatively erratic in the short run. That is, they are subject to more or less random changes in the short run, but relatively stable over longer periods of time. In contrast, they conjecture that "technology" does not change much in short periods of time, but exhibits a steady movement in longer periods. Two views have been expressed: (1) Such changes make it possible to *replace* labor with machinery, so that a_{LC} and a_{LI} tend to fall and a_{KC} and a_{KI} to rise. (2) Such changes make it possible to produce given amounts of goods with less labor and also less machinery, so that all four coefficients tend to drop. It is not clear where the truth of the matter lies.

Let us see what happens to this system when *one* of the eight nonzero coefficients changes. To illustrate, a particular coefficient will be singled out.

Then a general formula will be given, and the results of its application will be tabulated.

Suppose, in particular, that a_{CL} changes. That is, suppose that there is a change in the amount of consumer goods that workers wish to buy for every man-year they work. Before the change occurs, the equilibrium *quantities* in the system are a solution to the equation

$$(0, 0, 0, 0) = (\mathbf{q}_C, \mathbf{q}_I, \mathbf{q}_L, \mathbf{q}_K) \begin{pmatrix} -1 & 0 & a_{LC} & a_{KC} \\ 0 & -1 & a_{LI} & a_{KI} \\ a_{CL} & a_{IL} & -1 & 0 \\ a_{CK} & a_{IK} & 0 & -1 \end{pmatrix}$$

Equilibrium *prices* in the system are a solution to the equation

$$(0, 0, 0, 0) = (\mathbf{p}_C, \mathbf{p}_I, \mathbf{p}_L, \mathbf{p}_K) \begin{pmatrix} -1 & 0 & a_{CL} & a_{KC} \\ 0 & -1 & a_{IL} & a_{IK} \\ a_{LC} & a_{LI} & -1 & 0 \\ a_{KC} & a_{KI} & 0 & -1 \end{pmatrix}$$

These two equations may be rewritten in the form

$$(0, 0, 0, 0) = (\mathbf{q}_C, \mathbf{q}_I, \mathbf{q}_L, \mathbf{q}_K) \begin{pmatrix} -1 & 0 & a_{LC} & a_{KC} \\ 0 & -1 & a_{LI} & a_{KI} \\ 0 & a_{IL} & -1 & 0 \\ a_{CK} & a_{IK} & 0 & -1 \end{pmatrix} + (\mathbf{q}_{CL}, 0, 0, 0)$$

Here $q_{CL} = a_{CL}\, q_L$ is the total demand for consumer goods by workers. It is measured in physical units.

$$(0, 0, 0, 0) = (\mathbf{p}_C, \mathbf{p}_I, \mathbf{p}_L, \mathbf{p}_K) \begin{pmatrix} -1 & 0 & 0 & a_{CK} \\ 0 & -1 & a_{IL} & a_{IK} \\ a_{LC} & a_{LI} & -1 & 0 \\ a_{KC} & a_{KI} & 0 & -1 \end{pmatrix} + (0, 0, \mathbf{p}_{CL}, 0)$$

Here $p_{CL} = a_{CL}\, p_C$ is the money spent on consumer goods by workers, for every man-year worked. It is measured in money units.

In these rewritten equations, the element a_{CL} has been dropped from the matrices. To rewrite this in simpler form, we note that equations (10.4) and (10.5) were

$$\mathbf{PA} = \mathbf{P} = \mathbf{PE}$$
$$\mathbf{QA_T} = \mathbf{Q} = \mathbf{QE}$$

so that

$$\mathbf{P}(\mathbf{A} - \mathbf{E}) = \boldsymbol{\theta}$$
$$\mathbf{Q}(\mathbf{A_T} - \mathbf{E}) = \boldsymbol{\theta}$$

where $\boldsymbol{\theta}$ is the null (zero) vector. Then we denote by $\mathbf{A^{CL}}$ the matrix obtained by *deleting* the element a_{CL} from $\mathbf{A}$. We denote by $\mathbf{Q^{CL}}$ and $\mathbf{P^{CL}}$ the second right-hand vectors of these two equations. The two matrix equations above, then, are

$$\boldsymbol{\theta} = \mathbf{Q}(\mathbf{A_T^{CL}} - \mathbf{E}) + \mathbf{Q^{CL}}$$
$$\boldsymbol{\theta} = \mathbf{P}(\mathbf{A^{CL}} - \mathbf{E}) + \mathbf{P^{CL}}$$

Therefore, if we can invert $(\mathbf{A^{CL}} - \mathbf{E})$, it will be the case that

$$\mathbf{Q} = -\mathbf{Q^{CL}}(\mathbf{A_T^{CL}} - \mathbf{E})^{-1}$$
$$\mathbf{P} = -\mathbf{P^{CL}}(\mathbf{A^{CL}} - \mathbf{E})^{-1}$$

All of this is true of the state of affairs *before* the change in a_{CL}. The matrix $\mathbf{A^{CL}}$ does not change, since all other coefficients of $\mathbf{A}$ are to remain constant. Hence, *after* the change, $\mathbf{Q^{CL}}$ will have become $\overline{\mathbf{Q}}^{\mathbf{CL}}$, $\mathbf{P^{CL}}$ will have become $\overline{\mathbf{P}}^{\mathbf{CL}}$, and the new equilibrium quantities and prices will be

$$\overline{\mathbf{Q}} = -\overline{\mathbf{Q}}^{\mathbf{CL}}(\mathbf{A_T^{CL}} - \mathbf{E})^{-1}$$
$$\overline{\mathbf{P}} = -\overline{\mathbf{P}}^{\mathbf{CL}}(\mathbf{A^{CL}} - \mathbf{E})^{-1}$$

It follows, then, that

$$\Delta\mathbf{Q} = \overline{\mathbf{Q}} - \mathbf{Q} = (\mathbf{Q^{CL}} - \overline{\mathbf{Q}}^{\mathbf{CL}})(\mathbf{A_T^{CL}} - \mathbf{E})^{-1} = -\Delta\mathbf{Q^{CL}}(\mathbf{A_T^{CL}} - \mathbf{E})^{-1}$$
$$\Delta\mathbf{P} = \overline{\mathbf{P}} - \mathbf{P} = (\mathbf{P^{CL}} - \overline{\mathbf{P}}^{\mathbf{CL}})(\mathbf{A^{CL}} - \mathbf{E})^{-1} = -\Delta\mathbf{P^{CL}}(\mathbf{A^{CL}} - \mathbf{E})^{-1}$$

In these equations,

$$\Delta\mathbf{Q^{CL}} = (\Delta\mathbf{q_{CL}}, \mathbf{0}, \mathbf{0}, \mathbf{0}$$

where Δq_{CL} is the change in total demand for consumer goods by workers, in units of goods, and

$$\Delta\mathbf{P^{CL}} = (\mathbf{0}, \mathbf{0}, \Delta\mathbf{p_{CL}}, \mathbf{0})$$

where Δp_{CL} is the change in money expenditures on consumer goods per man-year worked.

Suppose, then, that we have succeeded in inverting $(\mathbf{A}^{\mathbf{CL}} - \mathbf{E})$, and that the elements of the inverse matrix are given by (b_{ij}). Then it would be true that

$$(\Delta \mathbf{q_C}, \Delta \mathbf{q_I}, \Delta \mathbf{q_L}, \Delta \mathbf{q_K}) = (-\Delta \mathbf{q_{CL}}, \mathbf{0}, \mathbf{0}, \mathbf{0}) \begin{pmatrix} b_{CC} & b_{IC} & b_{LC} & b_{KC} \\ b_{CI} & b_{II} & b_{LI} & b_{KI} \\ b_{CL} & b_{IL} & b_{LL} & b_{KL} \\ b_{CK} & b_{IK} & b_{LK} & b_{KK} \end{pmatrix}$$

$$= (-\Delta \mathbf{q_{CL}} \mathbf{b_{CC}}, -\Delta \mathbf{q_{CL}} \mathbf{b_{IC}}, -\Delta \mathbf{q_{CL}} \mathbf{b_{LC}}, -\Delta \mathbf{q_{CL}} \mathbf{b_{KC}})$$
$$= -\Delta \mathbf{q_{CL}}(\mathbf{b_{CC}}, \mathbf{b_{IC}}, \mathbf{b_{LC}}, \mathbf{b_{KC}})$$

And also it would be true that

$$(\Delta \mathbf{p_C}, \Delta \mathbf{p_I}, \Delta \mathbf{p_L}, \Delta \mathbf{p_K}) = (\mathbf{0}, \mathbf{0}, -\Delta \mathbf{p_{CL}}, \mathbf{0}) \begin{pmatrix} b_{CC} & b_{CI} & b_{CL} & b_{CK} \\ b_{IC} & b_{IL} & b_{IL} & b_{IK} \\ b_{LC} & b_{II} & b_{LL} & b_{LK} \\ b_{KC} & b_{IK} & b_{KL} & b_{KK} \end{pmatrix}$$

$$= (-\Delta \mathbf{p_{CL}}, \mathbf{b_{LC}}, -\Delta \mathbf{p_{CL}} \mathbf{b_{LI}}, -\Delta \mathbf{p_{CL}} \mathbf{b_{LL}}, -\Delta \mathbf{p_{CL}} \mathbf{b_{LK}})$$
$$= -\Delta \mathbf{p_{CL}} (\mathbf{b_{LC}}, \mathbf{b_{LI}}, \mathbf{b_{LL}}, \mathbf{b_{LK}})$$

Similar formulas can be devised for changes in each of the eight coefficients. Readers are urged to carry out analogous calculations; for the cases where there are changes (say) in a_{KI} and a_{LC}.

The text has so far been a series of conditional statements of the form "*If* $(\mathbf{A}^{\mathbf{CL}} - \mathbf{E})$ can be inverted *then* **X**." It would be possible to invert $(\mathbf{A}^{\mathbf{CL}} - \mathbf{E})$ directly, but it is simpler, in the long run, to give a formula for inverting every *matrix* $(\mathbf{A}^{ij} - \mathbf{E})$, where $\mathbf{A}^{ij}$ is the matrix obtained by deleting the (nonzero) element a_{ij} from **A**.[13]

It is known that $(\mathbf{A} - \mathbf{E})$ does not have an inverse. If it did, then the equation

$$\mathbf{0} = \mathbf{Q}(\mathbf{A_T} - \mathbf{E})$$

would imply that

$$\mathbf{Q} = \mathbf{0}(\mathbf{A_T} - \mathbf{E})^{-1}$$

But for every matrix **M**, $\mathbf{0M} = \mathbf{0}$. Thus if $(\mathbf{A_T} - \mathbf{E})$ had an inverse, all quantities would be zero. (All prices would also be zero.)

It would be possible to demonstrate this proposition for the particular case of $(\mathbf{A_T} - \mathbf{E})$. Suppose we went through the motions of computing $(\mathbf{A_T} - \mathbf{E})^{-1}$. Then we would emerge with the following rather unpleasant matrix, which will be called the *formal inverse* of $(\mathbf{A_T} - \mathbf{E})$.

---

[13] If $\mathbf{B}^{ij}$ is the inverse of $(\mathbf{A}^{ij} - \mathbf{E})$, then $\mathbf{B}^{ij}_{\mathbf{T}}$ is the inverse of $(\mathbf{A}^{ij}_{\mathbf{T}} - \mathbf{E})$.

$$
\frac{1}{D}\begin{pmatrix}
(a_{LI}a_{IL}+a_{KI}a_{IK}-1) & -(a_{LC}a_{IL}+a_{KC}a_{IK}) & (a_{KC}a_{IK}a_{LI}+a_{LC}-a_{KI}a_{IK}a_{LC}) & (a_{LC}a_{IL}a_{KI}+a_{KC}-a_{LI}a_{IL}a_{KC} \\
-(a_{LI}a_{CL}+a_{KI}a_{CK}) & (a_{LC}a_{CL}+a_{KC}a_{CK}-1) & (a_{KI}a_{IK}a_{LC}+a_{LI}-a_{KC}a_{CK}a_{LI}) & (a_{LI}a_{CL}a_{KC}+a_{KI}-a_{LC}a_{CL}a_{KI} \\
(a_{IL}a_{KI}a_{CK}+a_{CL}-a_{IK}a_{KI}a_{CL}) & (a_{KC}a_{CL}a_{IK}+a_{IC}-a_{KC}a_{CK}a_{IL}) & (a_{KC}a_{CK}+a_{KI}a_{IK}-1) & -(a_{CL}a_{KC}+a_{IL}a_{KI}) \\
(a_{IK}a_{LI}a_{CL}+a_{CK}-a_{IL}a_{LI}a_{CK}) & (a_{CK}a_{LC}a_{IL}+a_{IK}-a_{CL}a_{LC}a_{IK}) & -(a_{CK}a_{LC}+a_{IK}a_{KI}) & (a_{CL}a_{LC}+a_{IL}a_{LI}-1)
\end{pmatrix}
$$

The symbol D, when written out in full is

$$D = 1 - a_{LC}a_{CL} - a_{KC}a_{CK} - a_{LI}a_{IL} - a_{KI}a_{IK} + a_{LC}a_{CL}a_{KI}a_{IK} + a_{KC}a_{CK}a_{LI}a_{IL} - a_{LI}a_{CL}a_{KC}a_{IK} - a_{KI}a_{CK}a_{LC}a_{IL}$$

The matrix is called a "formal inverse" because it is not a true inverse. The reason is that D, which appears in the denominator of every element, is necessarily zero. If D were not zero, then $(\mathbf{A} - \mathbf{E})$ would have been successfully inverted, which has been shown to be impossible. But if $D = 0$, then each element of the so-called matrix $(\mathbf{A} - \mathbf{E})^{-1}$ is a number divided by $D = 0$. Of course, no number may be divided by zero. Thus if $D = 0$, $(\mathbf{A} - \mathbf{E})$ cannot be inverted.

On the other hand, it is *useful* to perform this formal inversion. Having this formula before us, we can readily calculate *every* matrix such as $(\mathbf{A}^{\mathbf{CL}} - \mathbf{E})$. To perform this calculation, we merely set every term containing a_{CL} in the formal inverse equal to zero. Then, of course, terms will drop out in the *numerators* of elements in every element which is not in row 1 (whose elements correspond to a first index C) or in column 3 (whose elements correspond to a second index L). Moreover, the *denominator* common to these elements will be D^{CL}, which is derived from D by suppressing the second, sixth, and eighth terms in D. Stated slightly differently,

$$D = D^{CL} - a_{CL}a_{LC} + a_{LC}a_{CL}a_{KI}a_{IK} - a_{LI}a_{CL}a_{KC}a_{IK} = 0$$

so that

$$\begin{aligned} D^{CL} &= a_{CL}a_{LC} + a_{LI}a_{CL}a_{KC}a_{IK} - a_L a_{CL}a_{KCI}a_{IK} \\ &= a_{CL}[a_{LC}(1 - a_{KI}a_{IK}) + a_{LI}a_{KC}a_{IK}] \end{aligned}$$

This formula is a special case of the general formula

$$D^{ij} = a_{ij}[a_{ji}(1 - a_{mn}a_{nm}) + a_{jm}a_{ni}a_{mn}]$$

in which i and j may be any pair of the indexes C, I, L, K such that $a_{ij} \neq 0$ in the matrix $\mathbf{A_T}$. The pair m, n refers to the pair of indexes *not* appearing in a_{ij}.

Careful readers might observe, at this point, that any particular D^{ij} which we might calculate could turn out to be zero, if we happened to choose the elements of the matrix just right. For example, D^{ij} will be zero if for some particular pair of indexes i, j

$$0 = a_{ji}(1 - a_{mn}a_{nm}) + a_{jm}a_{ni}a_{mn}$$

If this condition happened to hold, then of course there would be no way to invert $(\mathbf{A}_{\mathbf{T}}^{ij} - \mathbf{E})$, and hence no way to determine uniquely the effects on prices and quantities of a change in a_{ij}. Consequently, if we should wish to construct a theory that actually explained these effects, then we should have to specify that for no pair (i, j) of indexes does this equality hold. Unless it is possible to specify this condition, then the theory in question does not do one of the things a programming theory ought to do: to predict the consequences on each quantity and each price of a change in each of the eight coefficients in the matrix. For these eight coefficients correspond to the factors of macroeconomic theories. They are the "givens" of the system. The job of the theorist is to explain the consequences of any change in the "givens."

To show the implications of Theory 12, it is necessary to construct a table, comparable to the tables given in Theories 1 to 10. This table will contain 64 entries, because eight coefficients (a_{ij}) may change, and when each one changes, the four prices and the four quantities of the system must change. The entries will be coefficients which appear in equations of two types. The first type relates to *quantities*. In the example given (in which a_{CL} was assumed to change), the quantity changes were given by the equations

$$\begin{aligned}\Delta q_C &= -\Delta q_{CL} b_{CC}\\ \Delta q_I &= -\Delta q_{CL} b_{IC}\\ \Delta q_L &= -\Delta q_{CL} b_{LC}\\ \Delta q_K &= -\Delta q_{CL} b_{KC}\end{aligned}$$

The second type relates to prices. In the example given, the *price* changes were given by the equations

$$\begin{aligned}\Delta p_C &= -\Delta p_{CL} b_{LC}\\ \Delta p_I &= -\Delta p_{CL} b_{LI}\\ \Delta p_L &= -\Delta p_{CL} b_{LL}\\ \Delta p_K &= -\Delta p_{CL} b_{LK}\end{aligned}$$

That is, the coefficients in the quantity equations were elements of row C of the matrix (b_{ij}). The coefficients in the price equations were elements of Column I of the matrix (b_{ij}). The matrix (b_{ij}) is related to the "formal inverse" of $(\mathbf{A_T} - \mathbf{E})$ in the following way: Any element of (b_{ij}) may be obtained from the "formal inverse" by suppressing any term containing a_{CL} that appears in the corresponding element of the formal inverse.

It would be a waste of effort to compute all of the inverse matrix (b_{ij}), for only one row and one column of this inverse have economic meaning. It would also be convenient to have a rule for expressing compactly how to go about obtaining the coefficients that would be used in connection with *every* possible change in elements a_{ij} of the matrix of Theory 11. This rule may be given as follows:

Definition: b_{ij}^{rs} *is obtained by taking the element in row i, column j of the formal inverse of* $(\mathbf{A_T} - \mathbf{E})$, *and by suppressing, in both the numerator and the denominator, every term that contains* a_{rs}.

Table 10.2 contains a statement of how changes in each of the coefficients a_{rs} will affect each price and each quantity. The table is formulated in terms of coefficients b_{ij}^{rs} to conserve space. The derivation of precise expressions for these coefficients from elements of the formal inverse is left as an exercise.

TABLE 10.2

THE IMPLICATIONS OF THEORY 12

THE EFFECT UPON	THE EFFECT OF A CHANGE IN a_{CL}	a_{CK}	a_{IL}	a_{IK}	a_{LC}	a_{LI}	a_{KC}	a_{KI}
q_C	$-b_{CC}^{CL}$	$-b_{CC}^{CK}$	$-b_{IC}^{IL}$	$-b_{IC}^{IK}$	$-b_{LC}^{LC}$	$-b_{LC}^{LI}$	$-b_{KC}^{KC}$	$-b_{KC}^{KI}$
q_I	$-b_{CI}^{CL}$	$-b_{CI}^{CK}$	$-b_{II}^{IL}$	$-b_{II}^{IK}$	$-b_{LI}^{LC}$	$-b_{LI}^{LI}$	$-b_{KI}^{KC}$	$-b_{KI}^{KI}$
q_L	$-b_{CL}^{CL}$	$-b_{CL}^{CK}$	$-b_{IL}^{IL}$	$-b_{IL}^{IK}$	$-b_{LL}^{LC}$	$-b_{LL}^{LI}$	$-b_{KL}^{KC}$	$-b_{KL}^{KI}$
q_K	$-b_{CK}^{CL}$	$-b_{CK}^{CK}$	$-b_{IK}^{IL}$	$-b_{IK}^{IK}$	$-b_{LK}^{LC}$	$-b_{LK}^{LI}$	$-b_{KK}^{KC}$	$-b_{KK}^{KI}$
p_C	$-b_{CL}^{CL}$	$-b_{CK}^{CK}$	$-b_{CL}^{IL}$	$-b_{CK}^{IK}$	$-b_{CC}^{LC}$	$-b_{CI}^{LI}$	$-b_{CC}^{KC}$	$-b_{CI}^{KI}$
p_I	$-b_{IL}^{CL}$	$-b_{IK}^{CK}$	$-b_{IL}^{IL}$	$-b_{IK}^{IK}$	$-b_{IC}^{LC}$	$-b_{II}^{LI}$	$-b_{IC}^{KC}$	$-b_{II}^{KI}$
p_L	$-b_{LL}^{CL}$	$-b_{LK}^{CK}$	$-b_{LL}^{IL}$	$-b_{LK}^{IK}$	$-b_{LC}^{LC}$	$-b_{LI}^{LI}$	$-b_{LC}^{KC}$	$-b_{LI}^{KI}$
p_K	$-b_{KL}^{CL}$	$-b_{KK}^{CK}$	$-b_{KL}^{IL}$	$-b_{KK}^{IK}$	$-b_{KC}^{LC}$	$-b_{KI}^{LI}$	$-b_{KC}^{KC}$	$-b_{KI}^{KI}$

Given Table 10.2, it is possible to obtain the pair of formulas corresponding to a change in a_{rs} for every relevant pair of indices (r, s):

$$\begin{aligned} \Delta q_i &= -\Delta q_{rs}\, b_{ri}^{rs} \\ \Delta p_i &= -\Delta p_{rs}\, b_{is}^{rs} \end{aligned} \qquad i = C, I, L, K$$

There remains only the question of determining the exact meaning of Δq_{rs} and Δp_{rs}. Since *before* the change in a_{rs},

$$\begin{aligned} q_{rs} &= a_{rs} q_s \\ p_{rs} &= a_{rs} p_r \end{aligned}$$

and after the change,

$$\begin{aligned} q'_{rs} &= (a_{rs} + \Delta a_{rs})(q_s + \Delta q_s) \\ p'_{rs} &= (a_{rs} + \Delta a_{rs})(p_r + \Delta p_r) \end{aligned}$$

it follows (by subtraction) that

$$\begin{aligned} \Delta q_{rs} &= \Delta a_{rs} q_s + a_{rs} \Delta q_s + \Delta a_{rs} \Delta q_s \\ \Delta p_{rs} &= \Delta a_{rs} p_r + a_{rs} \Delta p_r + \Delta a_{rs} \Delta p_r \end{aligned}$$

Table 10.2 may be interpreted in the following way. For any relevant pair of indexes (r, s), there is a change in an input-output coefficient a_{rs}. For this change, quantities and prices in the system change according to the formulas

$$\begin{aligned} \Delta q_i &= -\Delta q_{rs}\, b_{ri}^{rs} \\ \Delta p_j &= -\Delta p_{rs}\, b_{js}^{rs} \end{aligned}$$

The changes in quantity and price are proportionate to Δq_{rs} and to Δp_{rs}, respectively. If these are equal to 1, then $-b_{ri}^{rs}$ and $-b_{js}^{rs}$ are the quantity and price changes. What do Δq_{rs} and Δp_{rs} mean? Returning to our original definitions,

q_{rs} is the amount of commodity r purchased by producers of commodity s.
p_{rs} is the amount spent on r by producers of s per unit of s produced.

Consequently,

Δq_{rs} is a change in the amount of r purchased by producers of s, and
Δp_{rs} is the change in expenditures on r by producers of s, per unit of s produced.

Thus the two terms Δq_{rs} and Δp_{rs} provide unit measures of the magnitude of changes in this economy.

CONCLUSIONS

The programming type theory has several great advantages over the macroeconomic theory. In particular, the same set of factors is used to explain both the prices and the quantities which prevail in the economy. It is not, therefore, necessary to introduce into such a theory one set of coefficients that pertain to household and business response to prices, and a different set that pertain to response to income and asset changes. In this respect, these theories are more "compact" than the theories involving prices which were given in Chapter 9.

A second feature of programming theories is that they admit of a deeper form of analysis than the macroeconomic theory. The introduction noted the division of economics into *microeconomics* (concerned with the behavior of individual economic units and small groups of economic units) and *macroeconomics* (concerned with large groups). A major goal of economists is to show how small group behavior is related to large group behavior. In particular, business behavior is generally taken to be dominated by attempts to make as much profit as possible, and this attempt has profound implications on business demand for inputs. The third section of this chapter discussed a macroeconomic theory in terms of efficiency, which is a central microeconomic concept. The theory presented in this chapter is much closer to microeconomics than the "allocative" theories in earlier chapters. In this sense, economists using programming theories have fewer "loose ends" in their thinking than those who use other macroeconomic theories.

On the other hand, precisely because they are more compact and deeper, the programming-type theories are more difficult than the allocation theories. Theory 12, for instance, ends up with a table of implications which, if written out in full, would seem as messy as that of Theory 10, to which the author objected earlier. There are at least as many uncertainties as to the directions of change indicated by Table 10.2 as there were in the directions of change indicated by the corresponding table for Theory 10. The great virtue of the allocative theory was that it could construct theories about quite elaborate systems of social accounts without introducing matrices that were really difficult to invert or messy to interpret.

Defenders of the programming-type theory argue that it is not reasonable to compare these theories with the allocative-type theories presented earlier in this book. Those theories were about *values*, and these distinguish between prices and quantities. They would argue that allocative theories become unmanageable as soon as they try to distinguish among prices, quantities, and values, and that the relevant comparison is between Theory 10 and Theory 12. There, they say, the advantage of the programming-type theory is quite clear.

The use of programming-type theories in "very macroeconomic" problems is still not very common. This type of theory is currently most used in the context of individual industries—steel, food-producers, retail trade, and so on. In these applications, the coefficients have technological interpretations, rather than interpretations involving consumer demand. A considerable range of problems has been studied in this context. The logic of input-output analysis is, however, applicable to the set of problems considered in this book, and that is why Theory 12 has been presented. It handles a certain kind of problem neatly and naturally.

11

Why So Many Theories?

THE CENTRAL BEHAVIORAL ISSUE OF MACROECONOMICS

The great achievement of modern macroeconomics is its development of working systems of social accounts. Most countries have developed regular methods of reporting at least the national income and product accounts. Macroeconomists realize that the theories they develop are about these social accounts, and there has therefore been a great increase in the sharpness of the subject matter under discussion. The greatest weakness of theoretical macroeconomics lies in its failure to develop a theory in which price and quantity changes can be separately analyzed. The great weakness of empirical macroeconomics lies in its failure to date to develop conclusive tests of behavioral hypotheses. The theoretical uncertainty was illustrated in Chapter 6, where four different sets of behavioral assumptions, each plausible, were embedded into a common social accounting scheme. Each variant led to a special set of conclusions about the economic mechanism.

It is a real achievement to be able to formulate a variety of theories. Theorists even consider a theory as an end product. But most economists (and others) are not interested in theories for their own sake. They want one theory—the best one—for use in solving practical problems. They will be somewhat impatient with the view taken in earlier chapters, for it suggests that the construction of theories is to be pursued for its own sake, whether or not the theories have anything to do with any real economic situation.

The somewhat carefree attitude of the earlier chapters reflects two basic attitudes of the author. First, a theory is interesting mainly when it deals with new and unsolved problems. Then theorists are free to suggest as many variations as they want, for nobody knows the answer. It is good practice for students to learn how to theorize, by practicing on matters that are relatively well understood. From this point of view, they can learn about theorizing by working on theories that need not be relevant to economic life.

Second, it would be foolish to adopt a carefree attitude toward macroeconomic theories if macroeconomists agreed as to what the world was like. But as it is, if the author chose to accept Professor A's view that consumption varied with income, Professor B could always complain that in his opinion, consumption varies with total assets, or something else. In 1969, when this book went to press, the professional journals were full of strife about the validity of the simplest macroeconomic behavioral hypotheses. The author considers it dishonest to conceal this controversy, and has no wish to take sides in it. This chapter explains why the controversy exists.

The central issue of macroeconomics seems to be this: Do households and businesses decide on their actions *mainly* by looking at their income, or *mainly* by looking at their assets? A good deal of this book has been concerned with showing how to set up these two alternative theories. Paralleling theoretical discussions, economists and politicians carry on a controversy about government policies.

If income-oriented theories were valid, government policies should be formulated in terms of the collection and disbursement of tax revenues, and government borrowing. These would be the government policies that most affect current spending if income-oriented theories are valid. If, however, the asset-oriented theories were valid, government policies should be formulated in terms of additions to the stocks of money, bank reserves, security holdings, and plant owned by the economy. These would be the government policies that would most affect the economy if asset-oriented theories are valid. This book has dealt only incidentally with public policy, but readers who have worked out the problems should have a good idea of the issues involved.

Readers are naturally impatient with conclusions of the sort given in the preceding paragraph. Many economists, indeed, are prepared to guess at the way people behave, and to make policy recommendations on the basis of their intuitions. But a glance at the economic journals shows that economists have very different intuitions, and do not, in fact, agree about how people and businesses actually behave.

For this reason, it is presumptuous of an author to pretend that there is a demonstrable answer to this central issue. Rather, he should try to explain why a great deal of scholarly effort has failed to produce agreement on this basic question.

If it were possible to treat the economy as a laboratory, then it would be imaginable for the government to carry out controlled experiments. While maintaining bank reserves at a constant level (for instance), one might vary taxes and government spending, and observe what happened. While the Treasury held tax revenues and spending constant, Federal Reserve might vary bank reserves and see what happened. But such experiments do not take place under controlled conditions. Consumers and businesses would not obligingly keep their behavior patterns fixed while the government experimented. Besides, the government cannot act "irresponsibly"—it has the next election to consider. It might be of great scientific interest to show that certain policies produce "bad" results (major depressions, runaway price inflations, and so on). We can hardly imagine politicians allowing economists to demonstrate these effects on an economy in which they were running for office.

Thus it is necessary to try to find out about economic behavior by studying history—which may be looked at as a vast uncontrolled experiment—and to try to develop defensible interpretations of the historical past. For macroeconomics, "history" is essentially a *statistical* record of the national product and balance sheet accounts. The interpretation must be made on the basis of *statistical* analysis and *statistical* tests. This chapter will discuss such tests, and the reasons why they have so far been inconclusive.

THE NATURE OF A TEST

A theory is a proposed explanation of the form $\mathbf{F} = \mathbf{VM}$ or $\mathbf{V} = \mathbf{FM}^{-1}$. [In this chapter we sometimes write $\mathbf{V} = \mathbf{FM}$, leaving off the exponent, providing no confusion results.] The matrix $\mathbf{M}$ gives the exact relation between a vector of variables and a vector of factors.

Two steps are involved in testing a theory. The first step assigns numerical values to the behavioral coefficients in $\mathbf{M}$. The second step measures the extent to which the economy behaves as if $\mathbf{M}$ indeed described the relation among its parts.

It would be possible to assign numerical values to the behavioral coefficients appearing in $\mathbf{M}$ in all sorts of ways. The researcher may have had a vision which told him what they were. Or he may select their values at random. A number of books exist that consist of tables of numbers selected at random, and the researcher could go to one of these. But these methods are not particularly to be recommended. Instead, the researcher will ordinarily try to use observations of the economy to enable him to *estimate* the coefficients of **M**. One important part of testing a theory is to find a way to calculate the values of the coefficients from information about the actual values of the variables in the economy he is studying, over some period of time.

The second step in testing requires that the student determine whether the theory is a good enough explanation of his observations to be accepted. He does not expect that his explanation will be "perfect." There will always be some discrepancy between the evidence and the theory being proposed. The student wishes to assert that his theory is better than the alternatives. In some cases, he may merely try to show that his theory is better than no theory at all. In other cases, he tries to show that his theory is better than another theory that has been proposed by an earlier writer.

If the theory is written in the form $\mathbf{V} = \mathbf{FM}$, it may be thought of as a set of *predictions*. The theory predicts that if the factors in $\mathbf{F}$ could be observed at t different dates, one could form t different vectors, $\mathbf{F}_1, \mathbf{F}_2, \ldots, \mathbf{F}_t$. If the original vector were written out, it would have the form $\mathbf{F} = (\mathbf{f}_1, \mathbf{f}_2, \ldots, \mathbf{f}_n)$. The symbols $\mathbf{f}_1, \mathbf{f}_2, \ldots, \mathbf{f}_n$ stand for individual factors which at any moment would have numerical values. Hence $\mathbf{F}_1, \mathbf{F}_2, \ldots, \mathbf{F}_t$ would be vectors of numbers, where each number represents the value of the factor at that particular moment. If the theory were exactly correct, then the *predicted* values of $\mathbf{V}$ would be $\mathbf{V}_1 = \mathbf{F}_1\mathbf{M}$, $\mathbf{V}_2 = \mathbf{F}_2\mathbf{M}$, and so on. Actually, we expect the theory to be imperfect, so that when the variables in $\mathbf{V}$ are observed, they are "close to, but not exactly" the predicted values, so that $\mathbf{V}_1 \approx \mathbf{F}_1\mathbf{M}$, $\mathbf{V}_2 \approx \mathbf{F}_2\mathbf{M}$ and so on. The symbol $\approx$ stands for "is not very different from." We have not precisely defined this symbol yet, for no way has been given to tell what is meant by "not very different from." At this point in our discussion, however, we are outlining a plan of attack, and not giving exact formulas.

A *prediction* is not the same as a *forecast*. To *forecast* gross national product one might use a formula such as $Y = K_1 + K_2 t$ (where t is calendar time), which says what Y will be at any date in the future. Indeed, such forecasting formulae often "work" quite well. In contrast, the *predictions* of a macroeconomic consist of statements such as the tables of implications of theories in earlier chapters of this book. Forecasts do not necessarily require understanding of economic processes; predictions may say nothing about the future.

Table 11.1 serves to point out the difference between predictions and forecasts. To the question, "How many national banks are *suspended* (closed because they lack cash assets) annually?" the reader can give the exact answer:

$$S = 2.5 - 1.5(-1)^t$$

where S = the number of suspensions per year and t = the calendar date.

To the question, "How many banks were suspended in 1941 and 1942?", the reader easily answers, "4 and 1." As it happens, for 1941 his answer would be correct. For 1942, however, suspensions numbered 0. The formula broke down in 1942, and has never worked since.

TABLE 11.1

NUMBER OF NATIONAL BANK SUSPENSIONS, 1934–1940

1934	1	1938	1
1935	4	1939	4
1936	1	1940	1
1937	4		

SOURCE: *Banking and Monetary Statistics*. Washington, D.C.: Board of Governors of the Federal Reserve System, 1943, p. 283.

The formula gives an excellent way of forecasting how one part of the economy would function in 1934–1941. But it is purely a descriptive device. It does not enable the user to correct an error, by proposing an explanation of the factors determining the number of national bank suspensions. If it proposed an explanation, one might be led to construct from it a better explanation of events after 1941. It has no behavioral content, for it cannot be interpreted as a general (abstract) statement of the reasons banks fail. Readers can investigate neither why it worked in 1934–1941 nor why it failed to work after 1942. Thus it is a sort of generalization, but it is not an explanation.

In selecting one from among alternative explanations of the workings of an economy, we should like the explanation to be a good one, in the sense that one can approximate the observed course of events by using the statements of the theory. Thus the formula fits the observed course of events excellently for a number of years, but when it breaks down, it breaks down completely. Therefore in addition to approximating the actual course of events a theory should say something else: (1) There is no reason to find systematic error in the theory; (2) there is no reason to suspect that the theory would fail if it were applied to a similar situation in another economy (or at another date).

The biologist is prepared to study genetics on the assumption that rules that hold true of fruit flies are apt to be true of human beings. The physicist is prepared to reason that stars, which are very large and distant objects, obey the same laws as small and nearby objects on earth. Indeed, something like a moral crisis occurs when it is suggested that subatomic particles may not follow the same laws as galaxies of stars. Economists, however, consider that human behavior may well be so unstable that any theory they propose is apt to be valid only for brief periods. Thus it would not be surprising to find economists who assert that the United States economy would be represented by one theory from, say, 1890 to 1914, a second theory from 1920 to 1940, and a third from 1945 to 1965. The differences among these theories might merely be different numerical values in matrices of the same general structure; but they might even involve radical changes in the structure of the matrices.

Thus one finds that for many economists a theory need not specify precise numerical values for behavioral coefficients. In a consumption function $C = aY + F_C$, many economists would be satisfied with *any* value of the marginal propensity to consume, a, between zero and one. They would consider this hypothesis falsified only if statistical calculations suggested that $a \leq 0$ or $a > 1$. The reason is that one has no general *theoretical* reason to choose one value of a rather than another. In contrast, physicists are now "hemmed in" by various physical constants (the gravitational constant, the speed of light, and so forth), which severely limit their theoretical speculations.

At several points in this text, there has been a contrast between coefficients in a behavioral statement that are "pure" and coefficients that are behavioral. Thus in the consumption function,

$$C = aY + vM + F_C$$

which relates consumption to income and the quantity of money, a is a "pure" number, which (if the theory makes sense) is between 0 and 1. However, v relates spending (or use of income) to the quantity of money (a balance sheet entry). There is no particular way, at the moment, to suggest theoretically acceptable values for v, except that v should be positive.

Thus economists, in *calculating from observations* the numerical values for coefficients in their theories, have little enough to guide them in deciding how large these coefficients should be. For this reason, the tests of results in economic statistics often seem loose compared to those in other disciplines.

To test a theory, one has to have a theory to test. Macroeconomic theories are of the form $\mathbf{V} = \mathbf{FM}$. A theory is a set of statements that assigns numbers to the elements of the matrix $\mathbf{M}$, and of course it selects the variables to appear in $\mathbf{V}$. The theory will be accepted if it turns out that the world acts as if $\mathbf{M}$ were valid. That is, it must be possible to say what would have happened if $\mathbf{M}$ had been valid. The theory might, for instance, say that if $\mathbf{M}$ were valid, we would observe a vector $\mathbf{V}_1$. Actually, we observe another vector $\mathbf{V}_2$. If we can show that $\mathbf{V}_1$ is not very different from $\mathbf{V}_2$, we say that $\mathbf{M}$ is "close to reality."

A natural way to select a theory that is close to reality is to make the elements of $\mathbf{M}$ depend upon observations of the variables in question. If the matrix is asserted to be $\hat{\mathbf{M}}$, and if the behavioral elements of $\hat{\mathbf{M}}$ are calculated from observed data, then there must be some function, such as $\hat{\mathbf{M}} = \mathbf{G}(\mathbf{V}, \mathbf{F})$, that is used to make the calculations. Of course, one cannot expect to be able to compute $\hat{\mathbf{M}}$ using only one observation of each vector in the theory. One would also like to be able to compute $\hat{\mathbf{M}}$ using all observations available, so that $\mathbf{G}$ should not require any particular *number* of observations.

The function $\mathbf{G}$ is called an *estimator.* An estimator takes a collection of observations, performs certain calculations on these observations, and interprets the results of these calculations as coefficients in a matrix $\mathbf{M}$. The discussion that follows will illustrate the concept of estimator with examples.

First, we consider an estimator that is not a good one, but it can be easily understood. Suppose we have a theory $\mathbf{V} = \mathbf{FM}$, in which $\mathbf{V}$ and $\mathbf{F}$ have n components. Normally, we would expect a certain amount of error in our theory. That is $\mathbf{V} = \mathbf{FM} + \mathbf{E}$ where $\mathbf{E}$ is a vector of errors—discrepancies, that is, between the observed vector $\mathbf{V}$ and the predicted vector $\mathbf{FM}$. But suppose $\mathbf{E} = 0$, so there are no errors. We observe $\mathbf{V}$ and $\mathbf{F}$ at n different dates. If the theory were valid, it would be the case that

$$\begin{aligned}&\text{at date 1, } \mathbf{V}_1 = \mathbf{F}_1\mathbf{M}\\ &\text{at date 2, } \mathbf{V}_2 = \mathbf{F}_2\mathbf{M}\\ &\qquad\cdots\\ &\text{at date } n,\ \mathbf{V}_n = \mathbf{F}_n\mathbf{M}\end{aligned}$$

Now we can make square matrices $\hat{\mathbf{V}}$ and $\hat{\mathbf{F}}$ as follows:

$$\hat{\mathbf{V}} = \begin{pmatrix} V_1^{(1)} & \cdots & V_n^{(1)} \\ V_1^{(2)} & \cdots & V_n^{(2)} \\ & \cdots & \\ V_1^{(n)} & \cdots & V_n^{(n)} \end{pmatrix} \qquad \hat{\mathbf{F}} = \begin{pmatrix} F_1^{(1)} & \cdots & F_n^{(1)} \\ F_1^{(2)} & \cdots & F_n^{(2)} \\ & \cdots & \\ F_1^{(n)} & \cdots & F_n^{(n)} \end{pmatrix}$$

Here the elements of the ith row of $\hat{\mathbf{V}}$ are the observations V_i, and the elements of the jth row of $\hat{\mathbf{F}}$ are the observations F_j. Thus,

$$\hat{\mathbf{V}} = \hat{\mathbf{F}}\mathbf{M}$$

Now, if $\hat{\mathbf{F}}$ is invertible, $\hat{\mathbf{F}}^{-1}\hat{\mathbf{V}} = \mathbf{M}$. If $\hat{\mathbf{V}}$ is invertible, then $\mathbf{M}^{-1} = \hat{\mathbf{F}}\hat{\mathbf{V}}^{-1}$. In this simple example, we have defined the *estimator of* $\mathbf{M}$ as $(\hat{\mathbf{F}}^{-1}\hat{\mathbf{V}})$. This estimator, of course, is obtained by performing calculations on two square matrices of observed numbers.

Actually, if the theory is only approximately true, there would be errors $\mathbf{E}_1, \mathbf{E}_2, \ldots, \mathbf{E}_n$ measuring the difference between the actual and the predicted values of $\mathbf{V}$ at each observation. We can form a matrix $\hat{\mathbf{E}}$ by arranging these errors in the same way as $\hat{\mathbf{V}}$ and $\hat{\mathbf{F}}$. Then $\hat{\mathbf{V}} = \hat{\mathbf{F}}\mathbf{M} + \hat{\mathbf{E}}$ and $\hat{\mathbf{F}}^{-1}\hat{\mathbf{V}} = \mathbf{M} + \hat{\mathbf{F}}^{-1}\hat{\mathbf{E}}$. Thus $\hat{\mathbf{F}}^{-1}\hat{\mathbf{E}}$ is a measure of the error we make by setting the estimator $\hat{\mathbf{M}} = \hat{\mathbf{F}}^{-1}\hat{\mathbf{V}}$. There is no reason to suppose that $\hat{\mathbf{F}}^{-1}\hat{\mathbf{E}}$ is a matrix of zeros. Indeed, it will not be if $\hat{\mathbf{E}}$ is not zero, that is, if the theory is only approximately true. Thus, in general $\hat{\mathbf{M}} \neq \mathbf{M}$.

The trick used to calculate $\hat{\mathbf{M}}$ was this: If there are n components in the vectors $\mathbf{F}$ and $\mathbf{V}$, then we use exactly n observations in our calculation of $\hat{\mathbf{M}}$. If we actually had more than n observations available, we would not use them all. This fact about $\hat{\mathbf{M}}$ leads to the following observations:

(1) We can select n observations from the total in more than one way. For each way of selecting n observations, we can expect to get a different numerical result from the estimator $\hat{\mathbf{F}}^{-1}\hat{\mathbf{V}}$, simply because the theory is at best only approximately valid.

(2) Whichever way we select n observations, we must discard the remaining observations. Thus we know that we cannot use all the information available about the economy when we use this method.

(3) Suppose that our theory contains accounting identities among the variables. Then we know that some columns of $\hat{\mathbf{F}}$ will consist entirely of zeros. In this case, $\hat{\mathbf{F}}$ cannot be inverted. If $\hat{\mathbf{V}}$ is invertible, then the formula $\hat{\mathbf{F}}\hat{\mathbf{V}}^{-1} = \mathbf{M}^{-1}$ would contain an inconsistency. It may be shown that if $\hat{\mathbf{F}}$ cannot be inverted, then $[\hat{\mathbf{F}}\hat{\mathbf{V}}^{-1}]$ *cannot be* inverted either. But $\mathbf{M}$ *can be* inverted (if our macroeconomic theory is a one-to-one mapping of $\mathbf{F}$ into $\mathbf{V}$). So the estimators $\hat{\mathbf{F}}\hat{\mathbf{V}}^{-1}$ and $\hat{\mathbf{F}}^{-1}\mathbf{V}$ can never be used in theories involving accounting identities.

To introduce a family of estimators that can utilize as much information as is available, suppose a theory involves two vectors $\mathbf{V} = (\mathbf{V}_1 \cdots \mathbf{V}_m)$ and $\mathbf{W} = (\mathbf{W}_1 \cdots \mathbf{W}_n)$. It is not necessary to specify at this point whether $\mathbf{V}$ and $\mathbf{W}$ are vectors of factors or of variables. Suppose also an arbitrary number, t, of observations of these vectors. Then the entire set of observations may be written as the matrices

$$\hat{\mathbf{V}} = \begin{pmatrix} V_1^{(1)} & \cdots & V_m^{(1)} \\ & \cdots & \\ V_1^{(t)} & \cdots & V_m^{(t)} \end{pmatrix} \quad \text{and} \quad \hat{\mathbf{W}} = \begin{pmatrix} W_1^{(1)} & \cdots & W_n^{(1)} \\ & \cdots & \\ W_1^{(t)} & \cdots & W_n^{(t)} \end{pmatrix}$$

Here $V_j^{(i)}$ is the ith observation of $\mathbf{V_j}$; $W_j^{(i)}$ is the ith observation of $\mathbf{W_j}$. These matrices are rectangular, for the number of observations is not necessarily equal to m or to n.

Now form the product $\hat{\mathbf{V}}_{\mathbf{T}}\hat{\mathbf{W}}$:

$$\begin{pmatrix} V_1^{(1)} & \cdots & V_1^{(t)} \\ & \cdots & \\ V_m^{(1)} & \cdots & V_m^{(t)} \end{pmatrix} \begin{pmatrix} W_1^{(1)} & \cdots & W_n^{(1)} \\ & \cdots & \\ W_1^{(t)} & \cdots & W_n^{(t)} \end{pmatrix} = \begin{pmatrix} \sum_{i=1}^{t} V_1^{(i)} W_1^{(i)} & \cdots & \sum_{i=1}^{t} V_1^{(i)} W_n^{(i)} \\ & \cdots & \\ \sum_{i=1}^{t} V_m^{(i)} W_1^{(i)} & \cdots & \sum_{i=1}^{t} V_m^{(i)} W_n^{(i)} \end{pmatrix}$$

The matrix $\hat{\mathbf{V}}_{\mathbf{T}}\hat{\mathbf{W}}$ has as many rows (m) as $\mathbf{V}$ has components; it has as many columns (n) as $\mathbf{W}$ has components. Thus the number of observations (t) may be large or small, but it does not have anything to do with the number of rows and columns in $\hat{\mathbf{V}}_{\mathbf{T}}\hat{\mathbf{W}}$. The matrix $\hat{\mathbf{V}}_{\mathbf{T}}\hat{\mathbf{V}}$, therefore, will have m rows and m columns, regardless of the number of observations available. Likewise, $\hat{\mathbf{V}}_{\mathbf{T}}\hat{\mathbf{W}}$ has n rows and n columns. Consequently, estimators based on matrices such as these can use all observations available, however many there may be. Thus they overcome one of the defects in the method of estimation given above.

The elements of $\hat{\mathbf{V}}_{\mathbf{T}}\hat{\mathbf{W}}$ consist of sums $\sum_{i=1}^{t} V_r^{(i)} W_s^{(i)}$. They are calculated as follows. If the t observations of V_r are

$$V_r^{(1)}, V_r^{(2)}, \ldots, V_r^{(t)}$$

and the observations of W_S are

$$W_s^{(1)}, W_s^{(t)}, \ldots, W_s^{(t)}$$

then the element in row r, column s of $\hat{\mathbf{V}}_{\mathbf{T}}\hat{\mathbf{W}}$ is equal to

$$V_r^{(1)} W_S^{(1)} + V_r^{(2)} W_S^{(2)} + \cdots + V_r^{(t)} W_s^{(t)}$$

In particular if $\hat{\mathbf{V}} = \hat{\mathbf{W}}$ and $r = s$, then this element is

$$(V_r^{(1)})^2 + (V_r^{(2)})^2 + \cdots + (V_r^{(t)})^2$$

Thus the diagonal elements of $\hat{\mathbf{V}}_{\mathbf{T}}\hat{\mathbf{V}}$ or of $\hat{\mathbf{W}}_{\mathbf{T}}\hat{\mathbf{W}}$ are the sums of the squares of the observations of the appropriate variables (factors).

Suppose, now, that the theory says $\mathbf{F} = \mathbf{VM}$, and that the theory includes accounting identities—as macroeconomic theories ordinarily must. Then $\mathbf{F}$ may be written in the form $\mathbf{F} = (\mathbf{0}, \mathbf{F}_2)$, where the symbol $\mathbf{0}$ stands for one or more zeros corresponding to these identities. Then, over the range of observations $\hat{\mathbf{F}} = (\hat{\mathbf{0}}, \hat{\mathbf{F}}_2)$ will be a matrix with columns of zeros associated with the symbol $\hat{\mathbf{0}}$. Thus $\hat{\mathbf{V}}_{\mathbf{T}}\hat{\mathbf{F}}$ will also be a matrix with columns of zeros: $\hat{\mathbf{V}}_{\mathbf{T}}\hat{\mathbf{F}} = (\hat{\mathbf{0}}, \hat{\mathbf{V}}_{\mathbf{T}}\hat{\mathbf{F}}_2)$. Thus $\hat{\mathbf{F}} = \hat{\mathbf{V}}\mathbf{M}$ implies that

$$\hat{\mathbf{V}}_{\mathbf{T}}\hat{\mathbf{F}} = \hat{\mathbf{V}}_{\mathbf{T}}\hat{\mathbf{V}}\mathbf{M}$$

If $\hat{\mathbf{V}}_{\mathbf{T}}\hat{\mathbf{V}}$ had an inverse, we could write

$$[\hat{\mathbf{V}}_{\mathbf{T}}\hat{\mathbf{V}}]^{-1}\hat{\mathbf{V}}_{\mathbf{T}}\hat{\mathbf{F}} = \mathbf{M}$$

But if $\hat{\mathbf{V}}_{\mathbf{T}}\hat{\mathbf{F}} = (\hat{\mathbf{0}}, \hat{\mathbf{V}}_{\mathbf{T}}\hat{\mathbf{F}}_2)$,

$$[\hat{\mathbf{V}}_{\mathbf{T}}\hat{\mathbf{V}}]^{-1}\hat{\mathbf{V}}_{\mathbf{T}}\hat{\mathbf{F}} = (\hat{\mathbf{0}}, [\hat{\mathbf{V}}_{\mathbf{T}}\hat{\mathbf{V}}]^{-1}\hat{\mathbf{V}}_{\mathbf{T}}\hat{\mathbf{F}}) = \mathbf{M}$$

However $\mathbf{M}$ does *not* have any columns of zeros. (If it did, $\mathbf{M}$ would not have an inverse, and $\mathbf{F} = \mathbf{VM}$ would not be a one-to-one mapping.)

It is clear, then, that if $\mathbf{F} = \mathbf{VM}$ is a microeconomic theory, so that a one-to-one mapping of factors into variables exists (namely $\mathbf{V} = \mathbf{FM}^{-1}$), the matrix $\hat{\mathbf{V}}_{\mathbf{T}}\hat{\mathbf{V}}$ cannot have an inverse, and the formula

$$\mathbf{M} = [\hat{\mathbf{V}}_{\mathbf{T}}\hat{\mathbf{V}}]^{-1}\hat{\mathbf{V}}_{\mathbf{T}}\hat{\mathbf{F}}$$

cannot be used as an estimator of $\mathbf{M}$.

Estimators of the general form $[\hat{\mathbf{V}}_{\mathbf{T}}\hat{\mathbf{V}}]^{-1}\hat{\mathbf{V}}_{\mathbf{T}}\hat{\mathbf{W}}$ are called *least-squares estimators*. They play an important role in statistical analysis. These estimators have as many *rows* as there are components of $\mathbf{V}$, they have as many *columns* as there are components of $\mathbf{W}$. Thus if $\mathbf{W}$ is a vector with a single component, $[\hat{\mathbf{V}}_{\mathbf{T}}\hat{\mathbf{V}}]^{-1}\hat{\mathbf{W}}_{\mathbf{T}}\hat{\mathbf{W}}$ is a column of numbers. The number of rows and columns of a least-squares estimator is completely independent of the number of observations.

If the theory says $\mathbf{F} = \mathbf{VM}$, then over some set of observations, it predicts that $\hat{\mathbf{F}} = \hat{\mathbf{V}}\mathbf{M}$. Consequently it also predicts that $\hat{\mathbf{V}}_{\mathbf{T}}\hat{\mathbf{F}} = \hat{\mathbf{V}}_{\mathbf{T}}\hat{\mathbf{V}}\mathbf{M}$ and that $[\hat{\mathbf{V}}_{\mathbf{T}}\hat{\mathbf{V}}]^{-1}\hat{\mathbf{V}}_{\mathbf{T}}\hat{\mathbf{F}} = \mathbf{M}$. This notation also makes it convenient to deal with theories expressed in block form. For if the theory, in block form, says

$$(\mathbf{F}_1, \mathbf{F}_2) = (\mathbf{V}_1, \mathbf{V}_2)\begin{pmatrix} M_{11} & M_{12} \\ M_{21} & M_{22} \end{pmatrix}$$

Then

$$(\hat{\mathbf{F}}_1, \hat{\mathbf{F}}_2) = (\hat{\mathbf{V}}_1, \hat{\mathbf{V}}_2)\begin{pmatrix} M_{11} & M_{12} \\ M_{21} & M_{22} \end{pmatrix}$$

$$\begin{pmatrix} \hat{V}_{1T}\hat{F}_1 & \hat{V}_{1T}\hat{F}_2 \\ \hat{V}_{2T}\hat{F}_1 & \hat{V}_{2T}\hat{F}_2 \end{pmatrix} = \begin{pmatrix} \hat{V}_{1T}\hat{V}_1 & \hat{V}_{1T}\hat{V}_2 \\ \hat{V}_{2T}\hat{V}_1 & \hat{V}_{2T}\hat{V}_2 \end{pmatrix}\begin{pmatrix} M_{11} & M_{12} \\ M_{21} & M_{22} \end{pmatrix}$$

The blocks, such as $\hat{\mathbf{V}}_{i\mathbf{T}}\hat{\mathbf{F}}_j$ or $\hat{\mathbf{V}}_{i\mathbf{T}}\hat{\mathbf{V}}_j$ $(i, j = 1, 2)$ are all constructed according to the same rules as were used above in the expression $\hat{\mathbf{V}}_{\mathbf{T}}\hat{\mathbf{W}}$. Thus a single kind of calculation is used throughout.

But when it was asserted that $\mathbf{F} = \mathbf{VM}$, it was asserted that the theory was exactly right. If the theory is only approximately right, then $\mathbf{F} = \mathbf{VM} + \mathbf{E}$, where $\mathbf{E}$, as before, is a vector of errors. Likewise $\hat{\mathbf{V}} = \hat{\mathbf{F}}\mathbf{M} + \hat{\mathbf{E}}$ and

$$\hat{\mathbf{V}}_{\mathbf{T}}\hat{\mathbf{F}} = \hat{\mathbf{V}}_{\mathbf{T}}\hat{\mathbf{V}}_{\mathbf{M}} + \hat{\mathbf{V}}_{\mathbf{T}}\hat{\mathbf{E}}$$
$$[\hat{\mathbf{V}}_{\mathbf{T}}\hat{\mathbf{V}}]^{-1}\hat{\mathbf{V}}_{\mathbf{T}}\hat{\mathbf{F}} = \mathbf{M} + [\hat{\mathbf{V}}_{\mathbf{T}}\hat{\mathbf{V}}]^{-1}\hat{\mathbf{V}}_{\mathbf{T}}\hat{\mathbf{E}}$$

This last statement is reminiscent of the statement used above in connection with the first estimator discussed. It says that the estimator

$$[\hat{\mathbf{V}}_{\mathbf{T}}\hat{\mathbf{V}}]^{-1}\hat{\mathbf{V}}_{\mathbf{T}}\hat{\mathbf{F}} = \hat{\mathbf{M}}$$

will be equal to $\mathbf{M}$ if and only if the residual

$$[\hat{\mathbf{V}}_{\mathbf{T}}\hat{\mathbf{V}}]^{-1}\hat{\mathbf{V}}_{\mathbf{T}}\hat{\mathbf{E}} = \hat{\mathbf{0}}$$

But there is one important difference. In the earlier statement, in order that

$$\hat{\mathbf{F}}^{-1}\hat{\mathbf{E}} = \mathbf{0}$$

it was necessary that $\hat{\mathbf{E}} = \mathbf{0}$, that is, that there be no errors at all in the theory. But in the present case, $\hat{\mathbf{V}}_{\mathbf{T}}\hat{\mathbf{E}}$ may be zero even if some of the errors are not zero (so that $\hat{\mathbf{E}} \neq \mathbf{0}$). This proposition is explored in a little detail in the appendix to this chapter. The following section will discuss the question in a less technical way.

STATISTICAL CONCEPTS

This book deals with theories—linear one-to-one mappings. Statistics is a different branch of mathematics from linear algebra, and cannot be discussed here in any detail. But it is impossible to discuss the testing of macroeconomic theories without some reference to statistics, since the testing of theories in general is based on statistical concepts.

Statistical theory relates to so-called *random variables*. Let $\mathbf{V} = (\mathbf{V}_1, \ldots, \mathbf{V}_n)$ be a vector of variables. Then $\mathbf{V}$ is a random variable (in an n-dimensional space) if it is possible to define a *probability function* on the space over which $\mathbf{V}$ may range. Specifically, let S be any part of this space. That is, S may be the set of all vectors $\mathbf{V} = (\mathbf{V}_1, \ldots, \mathbf{V}_n)$ such that $\mathbf{V}_1$ is between some lower limit $\underline{\mathbf{V}}_1$ and some upper limit $\overline{\mathbf{V}}_1$, $\mathbf{V}_2$ is between $\underline{\mathbf{V}}_2$ and $\overline{\mathbf{V}}_2$, and so on. Then the probability function $P(S)$ is a number between zero and one. If S and S' are non-overlapping parts of the space, $P(S \cup S') = P(S) + P(S')$. If $S = \underline{V}$, the entire space, $P(\underline{V}) = 1$. The *probability* of S is the proportion of all instances of $\mathbf{V}$ such that $\mathbf{V}$ is in S. Knowing that the ith observation of $\mathbf{V}$ was a vector $\mathbf{V}_i$, we know nothing about the next observation $\mathbf{V}_{i+1}$, except that the probability that $\mathbf{V}_{i+1}$ will be in any part S of the space is given by the function P.

If $\mathbf{V}$ is a random variable then any function $f(V_1 \cdots V_n)$ is also a random variable. In particular, if $\mathbf{VM} = \mathbf{F}$ is a linear theory and $\mathbf{V}$ is a random variable, then $\mathbf{F}$ is a random variable. Similarly if $\mathbf{F}$ is a random variable and $\mathbf{V} = \mathbf{FM}$, then $\mathbf{V}$ is a random variable.

A variable that is not random is said to be deterministic. The usual macroeconomic theory is deterministic. But when the theory is tested, a random element is added to the theory. This addition says that the observed values of the variables will differ from the predicted values. Thus, instead of testing the theory $\mathbf{V} = \mathbf{FM}$, we test the theory $\mathbf{V} = \mathbf{FM} + \mathbf{E}$, where $\mathbf{E}$ is an error. This error is taken to be a random variable. If it were not random, it would be deterministic, so that in principle it would be predictable. If it were predictable, a rule would have to be given to say what it would be. But by hypothesis the theory has taken into account all predictable economic elements. Thus any difference between $\mathbf{V}$ and $\mathbf{FM}$ must be random.

If $\mathbf{V}$ is a random variable, then $\hat{\mathbf{V}}$ is a matrix of observations of the random variable. For any matrix of observations $\hat{\mathbf{V}}$ it is possible to compute a vector $\mathbf{M}(\hat{\mathbf{V}}) = [\mathbf{M}(\mathbf{V}_1), \mathbf{M}(\mathbf{V}_2), \ldots \mathbf{M}(\mathbf{V}_n)]$, where $\mathbf{M}(\mathbf{V}_i)$ is the mean (average) value of the variable $\mathbf{V}_i$. Any particular matrix $\hat{\mathbf{V}}$ has a finite number t of observations (rows). If the probability function P governing $\mathbf{V}$ is well behaved, then as the number of observations in $\hat{\mathbf{V}}$ becomes infinite $\mathsf{M}(\hat{\mathbf{V}})$ approaches a limit, $\mathscr{E}(\mathbf{V})$ called the *expected value* of $\mathbf{V}$. It may be verified that if at each time t,

$$\mathbf{V}_t = \mathbf{F}_t\mathbf{M} + \mathbf{E}_t$$

then over a finite period of time,

$$\mathsf{M}(\mathbf{V}) = \mathsf{M}(\mathbf{F})\mathsf{M} + \mathsf{M}(\mathbf{E})$$

and as the number of observations becomes infinite

$$\mathscr{E}(\mathbf{V}) = \mathscr{E}(\mathbf{F})\mathbf{M} + \mathscr{E}(\mathbf{E})$$

Suppose, in particular, that $\mathscr{E}(\mathbf{E}) = \mathbf{0}$. Then $\mathscr{E}(\mathbf{V}) = \mathscr{E}(\mathbf{F})\mathbf{M}$. This means that the theory $\mathbf{V} = \mathbf{FM}$ (which is deterministic) would hold, on the average, given a sufficiently large number of observations. In any short period of time (in particular, at any moment), however, this theory would be only approximately true. For even if $\mathscr{E}(\mathbf{E}) = \mathbf{0}$, $\mathbf{E}$ itself is in general not zero. If $\mathbf{E}$ is a random variable with expected value $\mathbf{0}$ [$\mathscr{E}(\mathbf{E}) = \mathbf{0}$], then it is possible to define, by means of the probability function P_1, the probability (proportion of cases) that $\mathbf{V}$ will differ from $\mathbf{FM}$ by more than any given amount. For

$$\mathbf{E} = \mathbf{V} - \mathbf{FM}$$

is a random variable. Since $\mathbf{E} = (\mathbf{e}_1, \ldots, \mathbf{e}_n)$, one may define a set of pairs bounds $\underline{e}_1$ and $\bar{e}_1$, $\underline{e}_2$ and $\bar{e}_2$, ... $\underline{e}_n$ and $\bar{e}_n$. Call S the set of vectors $\mathbf{E}$ which fall inside these bounds. Then $P(S)$ is the probability that $\mathbf{E}$ will be *inside* the bounds, and $1 - P(S)$ the probability that $\mathbf{E}$ will fall outside the bounds.

Suppose now, that $\hat{\mathbf{E}} = \hat{\mathbf{V}} - \hat{\mathbf{F}}\mathbf{M}$ describes the difference between observed and predicted values of $\mathbf{V}$. Then

$$\hat{\mathbf{F}}_\mathbf{T}\hat{\mathbf{E}} = \hat{\mathbf{F}}_\mathbf{T}\hat{\mathbf{V}} - \hat{\mathbf{F}}_\mathbf{T}\hat{\mathbf{F}}\mathbf{M}$$

and

$$[\hat{\mathbf{F}}_\mathbf{T}\hat{\mathbf{F}}]^{-1}\hat{\mathbf{F}}_\mathbf{T}\hat{\mathbf{E}} = [\hat{\mathbf{F}}_\mathbf{T}\hat{\mathbf{F}}]^{-1}\hat{\mathbf{F}}_\mathbf{T}\mathbf{V} - \mathbf{M}$$

Thus the left side of the equation measures the discrepancy between $\mathbf{M}$ and the least-squares estimator $[\hat{\mathbf{F}}_\mathbf{T}\hat{\mathbf{F}}]^{-1}\hat{\mathbf{F}}_\mathbf{T}\mathbf{V}$ on some finite set of observations.[1]

If $\mathbf{E}$ is a random variable, then $\hat{\mathbf{E}}$ is also a random variable.[2] In terms of expected values

$$\mathscr{E}(\mathbf{F}_\mathbf{T}\mathbf{E}) = \mathscr{E}[(\hat{\mathbf{F}}_\mathbf{T}\hat{\mathbf{V}}) - (\hat{\mathbf{F}}_\mathbf{T}\hat{\mathbf{F}})\mathbf{M}]$$

so that

$$[\mathscr{E}(\hat{\mathbf{F}}_\mathbf{T}\hat{\mathbf{F}})]^{-1}\mathscr{E}(\hat{\mathbf{F}}_\mathbf{T}\mathbf{E}) = \mathscr{E}(\hat{\mathbf{F}}_\mathbf{T}\hat{\mathbf{F}})^{-1}\mathscr{E}(\hat{\mathbf{F}}_\mathbf{T}\hat{\mathbf{V}}) - \mathbf{M}$$

---

[1] Likewise if the theory were formulated in the form $\mathbf{F} = \mathbf{VM}$, with $\mathbf{E} = \mathbf{F} - \mathbf{VM}$, then $\hat{\mathbf{E}} = \hat{\mathbf{F}} - \hat{\mathbf{V}}\mathbf{M}$ and $[\hat{\mathbf{V}}_\mathbf{T}\hat{\mathbf{V}}]^{-1}\hat{\mathbf{V}}_\mathbf{T}\hat{\mathbf{E}} = [\hat{\mathbf{V}}_\mathbf{T}\hat{\mathbf{V}}]^{-1}\hat{\mathbf{V}}_\mathbf{T}\hat{\mathbf{F}} - \mathbf{M}$. In this case $[\hat{\mathbf{V}}_\mathbf{T}\hat{\mathbf{V}}]^{-1}\hat{\mathbf{V}}_\mathbf{T}\hat{\mathbf{E}}$ is a measure of the discrepancy between $\mathbf{M}$ and the least-squares estimator $[\hat{\mathbf{V}}_\mathbf{T}\hat{\mathbf{V}}]^{-1}\hat{\mathbf{V}}_\mathbf{T}\hat{\mathbf{F}}$.

[2] $\mathbf{E}$ is a vector $(\mathbf{e}_1 \ldots \mathbf{e}_n)$; $\hat{\mathbf{E}}$ is a matrix with t rows and n columns. Thus $\hat{\mathbf{E}}$ must be considered as a vector with $n \times t$ components, whereas $\mathbf{E}$ has n components.

and also

$$\mathscr{E}([\hat{\mathbf{F}}_{\mathbf{T}}\hat{\mathbf{F}}]^{-1}\hat{\mathbf{F}}_{\mathbf{T}}\hat{\mathbf{E}}) = \mathscr{E}[([\hat{\mathbf{F}}_{\mathbf{T}}\hat{\mathbf{F}}]^{-1}\hat{\mathbf{F}}_{\mathbf{T}}\hat{\mathbf{V}}) - \mathbf{M}]$$

In other words, if either of the left-hand side terms vanishes, then, on the average, **M** will equal a suitable least-squares estimator, which appears on the right.

In order that $\mathscr{E}(\hat{\mathbf{F}}_{\mathbf{T}}\hat{\mathbf{E}})$ should be 0, it is necessary that **F** be *independent* of **E**. The notion of statistical independence is discussed in the appendix to this chapter. Essentially the result may be summarized as follows. $\hat{\mathbf{F}}_{\mathbf{T}}\hat{\mathbf{E}}$ is a matrix. The element in row i column j of $\hat{\mathbf{F}}_{\mathbf{T}}\hat{\mathbf{E}}$ is

$$\sum_{K=1}^{t} \mathbf{F}_i^{(K)} E_j^{(K)}$$

and the corresponding element of $\mathscr{E}(\hat{\mathbf{F}}_{\mathbf{T}}\hat{\mathbf{E}})$ is

$$\lim_{t\to\infty} \frac{1}{t} \sum_{K=1}^{t} F_i^{(K)} E_j^{(K)}$$

If F_i and E_j are independent, then these two sums equal

$$\frac{1}{t}(\sum F_i^{(K)})(\sum E_j^{(K)})$$

and

$$\mathscr{E}(\mathbf{F}_i)\mathscr{E}(\mathbf{E}_j)$$

respectively. Since $\mathscr{E}(\mathbf{E}_j) = 0$, we have the result: $\mathscr{E}(\hat{\mathbf{F}}_{\mathbf{T}}\hat{\mathbf{E}}) = \mathbf{0}$. In this case also,

$$\mathscr{E}([\hat{\mathbf{F}}_{\mathbf{T}}\hat{\mathbf{F}}]^{-1}\hat{\mathbf{F}}_{\mathbf{T}}\hat{\mathbf{E}}) = [\hat{\mathbf{F}}_{\mathbf{T}}\hat{\mathbf{F}}]^{-1}\mathscr{E}(\hat{\mathbf{F}}_{\mathbf{T}}\hat{\mathbf{E}}) = [\hat{\mathbf{F}}_{\mathbf{T}}\hat{\mathbf{F}}]^{-1}\mathbf{0} = \mathbf{0}$$

To this statistical summary, there is an economic interpretation. The theory $\mathbf{V} = \mathbf{FM} + \mathbf{E}$ states that the theory $\mathbf{V} = \mathbf{FM}$ holds on the average, but is subject to an error at any particular moment. If this error were related to **V** or to **F**, one would state that the linear deterministic statement $\mathbf{V} = \mathbf{FM}$ should be replaced by some nonlinear deterministic statement $\mathbf{V} = \boldsymbol{\mu}(\mathbf{F})$, where $\boldsymbol{\mu}$ stands for a set of nonlinear functions involving the factors in **F**. But the trouble with $\mathbf{V} = \mathbf{FM}$ is not of this form. It is simply that something else—unrelated to **V** or to **F**—intervenes to prevent this theory from being exactly right at any particular moment. Over sufficiently large numbers of observations, however, the errors **E** cancel each other out, so that on the average $\mathbf{V} = \mathbf{FM}$. Statisticians use this property to construct estimators which are *expected to* yield correct values of **M**. That is, these estimators, on the average, or over long sets of observations, will be correct.

Given a particular set of observations of the vectors **V** and **F**, one proceeds *as if* the errors were of an average sort. That is, one assumes that the average error were actually 0, and that the actual errors were independent of **F**. These can only be assumptions, because by definition the errors cannot be observed. These assumptions are justified by the demonstration that this procedure, on the average, does not yield an error. It is further justified by a demonstration[3] that the probability of making a "large" error is small, if this procedure is followed.

While the foregoing discussion is not technical enough to satisfy a statistician, it does provide a rationale for the procedures discussed below. Essentially, the problem is to develop a way to produce estimators of **M**; these estimators are to yield values for elements of **M** that (1) on the average should be correct, and (2) are unlikely to be very far wrong in individual cases.

ESTIMATION IN MACROECONOMICS

A macroeconomic theory has been described as a one-to-one mapping of factors into variables. Stated in terms of the behavior of economic units, it is written $\mathbf{F} = \mathbf{VM}$, even though its implications may be more thoroughly explored if it is written in the inverse form $\mathbf{V} = \mathbf{FM}^{-1}$. Statistical practice aims primarily at the exploration of behavior, and thus is usually concerned with the variable-into-factor mapping.

The vector of factors consists of three types of components. Some components are zero, because some accounting identity holds among the variables. For instance, in a theory involving the national product, one may have the statement $0 = Y - C - I$. Some components refer to initial conditions, which are based in turn on accounting identities. For instance, in a theory involving both national product and a balance sheet account, the statement $K_0 = K - I$ may be included to relate investment to the change in plant. Finally, some components have to do with autonomous behavior (that is, a component of behavior that has nothing to do with the variables in the system). In saying that investment depends partly on the rate of interest, for example, Theory 1 stated that $I = dR + F_I$. Then F_I postulates a hypothetical amount of investment, called autonomous investment, which would take place if the rate of interest were zero.

The second type of component (such as K_0, the initial stock of plant in the economy) is inextricably bound up with problems of dynamic theory. These theories were briefly discussed in the appendix to Chapter 7. Because they are inherently more complicated than static theories, it is natural to disregard them in this book, and we shall do so.

Suppose, then, that there is a vector of factors that has the form $\mathbf{F} = (\mathbf{0}, \mathbf{F}_2)$, where $\mathbf{0}$ stands, as usual, for a block of zeros. Then $\mathbf{F}_2$ stands for a block of factors that represent autonomous behavior—behavior that does not

---

[3] This demonstration is not given here, so as to keep the discussion within manageable length and difficulty.

depend on the values of the variables in the system, but rather is thought to influence these values. For each component of $\mathbf{F}_2$, there is a behavioral statement, such as the familiar equations of Theory 8:

$$F_C = C - aY$$

$$F_C = C - aY - vM$$

$$F_K = K - bW$$

and so on. Generally speaking, for each sector of the economy there will be at least one behavioral statement. If any sector takes n decisions (regarding its spending, assets, and so forth) there will be $(n - 1)$ factors. (The fact that total income equals uses of income, or total assets equal total liabilities for each sector, limits the number of independent forms of decisions a sector can make. Given $(n - 1)$ independent decisions, the nth is determined.)

Expressions such as $\hat{\mathbf{V}}_\mathbf{T}\hat{\mathbf{V}}$ or $\hat{\mathbf{V}}_\mathbf{T}\hat{\mathbf{W}}$ have one great advantage. The elements of these matrices are numbers which are calculated from collections of observations. In contrast, the estimator discussed on page 327 had elements which were calculated from single observations. In the estimators now under study elements of matrices assume values which are measures of the fluctuation of individual variables (factors) about their means, or of the degree of association between pairs of variables (factors) over the period under observation. For instance, if the factors in $\mathbf{F}_2$ refer to some set of independent decisions, then over a period of time we expect that

$$\hat{\mathbf{F}}_\mathbf{T}\hat{\mathbf{F}} = \frac{1}{t}\begin{pmatrix} \sum F_1^{(i)} \\ \vdots \\ \sum F_m^{(i)} \end{pmatrix} \left(\sum F_1^{(i)} \cdots \sum F_m^{(i)}\right) + \begin{pmatrix} \sigma_{11} & 0 & \cdots & 0 \\ 0 & \sigma_{22} & \cdots & 0 \\ & & \cdots & \\ 0 & 0 & \cdots & \sigma_{mm} \end{pmatrix}$$

Here the nondiagonal elements of the right-hand matrix are zero, because the factors are independent.[4] The terms $\sigma_{jj} = \frac{1}{t}\sum [F_j{}^i - \mathscr{E}(F_j)]^2$ measure the amount of fluctuation of factor j about its mean. Terms in the first right-hand matrix (and its transpose) are sums (that is, means *times* the number of observations).

Now suppose our theory has the form[5]

$$(\mathbf{0}, \mathbf{F}) = (\mathbf{V}_1, \mathbf{V}_2)\begin{pmatrix} M_{11} & M_{12} \\ M_{21} & M_{22} \end{pmatrix}$$

---

[4] In discussing economic development in Chapter 7, we explained why it was unreasonable to suppose that changes in factors were, in fact, completely independent of each other. The present assumptions are made for two reasons. First, they simplify exposition of a difficult subject. Second, they correspond to the case most commonly assumed in statistical work. If we chose to assert that the factors are not independent, we would replace the matrices given here by more suitable ones.

[5] We have dropped the subscript 2 from $\mathbf{F}_2$, for no $\mathbf{F}_1$ is used in this calculation.

Then we consider the system in terms of its block structure. The first block states that

$$\mathbf{0} = \mathbf{V}_1\mathbf{M}_{11} + \mathbf{V}_2\mathbf{M}_{21}$$
$$\mathbf{V}_1 = -\mathbf{V}_2\mathbf{M}_{21}\mathbf{M}_{11}^{-1}$$

The second block states that

$$\mathbf{F} = \mathbf{V}_1\mathbf{M}_{12} + \mathbf{V}_2\mathbf{M}_{22}$$

Substituting for $\mathbf{V}_1$,

$$\begin{aligned}\mathbf{F} &= -\mathbf{V}_2\mathbf{M}_{21}\mathbf{M}_{11}^{-1}\mathbf{M}_{12} + \mathbf{V}_2\mathbf{M}_{22}\\ &= \mathbf{V}_2[\mathbf{M}_{22} - \mathbf{M}_{21}\mathbf{M}_{11}^{-1}\mathbf{M}_{12}]\end{aligned}$$

Over a set of observations, then,

$$\begin{aligned}\hat{\mathbf{F}} &= \hat{\mathbf{V}}_2[\mathbf{M}_{22} - \mathbf{M}_{21}\mathbf{M}_{11}^{-1}\mathbf{M}_{12}]\\ \hat{\mathbf{F}}_{\mathbf{T}}\hat{\mathbf{F}} &= \hat{\mathbf{F}}_{\mathbf{T}}\hat{\mathbf{V}}_2[\mathbf{M}_{22} - \mathbf{M}_{21}\mathbf{M}_{11}^{-1}\mathbf{M}_{12}]\\ &= [\mathbf{M}_{22} - \mathbf{M}_{21}\mathbf{M}_{11}^{-1}\mathbf{M}_{12}]_{\mathbf{T}}[\hat{\mathbf{V}}_{2\mathbf{T}}\hat{\mathbf{V}}_2][\mathbf{M}_{22} - \mathbf{M}_{21}\mathbf{M}_{11}^{-1}\mathbf{M}_{12}]\end{aligned}$$

Then *if* the factors are independent and *if* $\hat{\mathbf{F}}_{\mathbf{T}}\hat{\mathbf{F}} = \mathbf{E}$, a unit matrix,

$$\mathbf{E} = [\mathbf{M}_{22} - \mathbf{M}_{21}\mathbf{M}_{11}^{-1}\mathbf{M}_{12}]_{\mathbf{T}}[\hat{\mathbf{V}}_{2\mathbf{T}}\hat{\mathbf{V}}_2][\mathbf{M}_{22} - \mathbf{M}_{21}\mathbf{M}_{11}^{-1}\mathbf{M}_{12}]$$

In general,

$$\begin{aligned}[\hat{\mathbf{V}}_{2\mathbf{T}}\hat{\mathbf{V}}_2]^{-1} &= [\mathbf{M}_{22} - \mathbf{M}_{21}\mathbf{M}_{11}^{-1}\mathbf{M}_{12}]_{\mathbf{T}}[\hat{\mathbf{F}}_{\mathbf{T}}\hat{\mathbf{F}}]^{-1}\\ &\quad \times [\mathbf{M}_{22} - \mathbf{M}_{21}\mathbf{M}_{11}^{-1}\mathbf{M}_{12}]\end{aligned} \tag{11.1}$$

"In the long run" (with an infinite number of observations) and "on the average" (with an infinite number of short-period observations) we expect $\hat{\mathbf{F}}_{\mathbf{T}}\hat{\mathbf{F}}$ to be a unit matrix, and its inverse, therefore, to be a unit matrix. We can also assign limits beyond which $[\hat{\mathbf{F}}_{\mathbf{T}}\hat{\mathbf{F}}]^{-1}$ is unlikely to deviate, if the factors follow certain laws of random fluctuation, and if the number of observations used in the test is large enough.

A theory proposes that $\mathbf{M}$ is a certain matrix. Hence it predicts that $[\mathbf{M}_{22} - \mathbf{M}_{21}\mathbf{M}_{11}^{-1}\mathbf{M}_{12}]$ will have certain numerical values. Because of this last formula, it makes a prediction about what the matrix $[\hat{\mathbf{V}}_{2\mathbf{T}}\hat{\mathbf{V}}]^{-1}$ will turn out to be, if $\hat{\mathbf{F}}_{\mathbf{T}}\hat{\mathbf{F}}$ is equal to its expected value (the unit matrix $\mathbf{E}$). So if we compute $[\hat{\mathbf{V}}_{2\mathbf{T}}\hat{\mathbf{V}}]^{-1}$, and observe that it is not exactly that predicted from the proposed values of $\mathbf{M}$, then we say one of two things:

(1) $[\hat{\mathbf{V}}_{2\mathbf{T}}\hat{\mathbf{V}}]^{-1}$ is not so far different from the predicted value as to make us conclude that $[\hat{\mathbf{F}}_{\mathbf{T}}\hat{\mathbf{F}}]^{-1}$ differs from $\mathbf{E}$ by an improbably large amount; or

(2) $[\hat{\mathbf{V}}_{2\mathbf{T}}\hat{\mathbf{V}}]^{-1}$ is so different from the predicted value that we conclude that our proposed matrix $\mathbf{M}$ is not the right one.

In the first case, we "accept" **M**, in the latter we "reject" **M** as an explanation of the observations. Commonly, we are able to accept only some group of the elements of $\mathbf{M}_1$ and we must reject the rest.[6]

The foregoing discussion makes use of the entire theory, including accounting identities, to compute the coefficients in the behavioral equations. It is a discussion that many economists would not approve of. For the variables of the theory as a whole formed the vector $\mathbf{V} = (\mathbf{V}_1, \mathbf{V}_2)$, while the calculations involved only the block $\mathbf{V}_2$. These economists would favor a different procedure. The theory $\mathbf{F} = \mathbf{VM}$ can be divided into blocks as before,

$$(\mathbf{0}, \mathbf{F}) = (\mathbf{V}_1, \mathbf{V}_2)\begin{pmatrix} M_{11} & M_{12} \\ M_{21} & M_{22} \end{pmatrix}$$

but the part that deals with accounting identities is said to be irrelevant to the discussion of economic behavior. In this case, we need consider only the block

$$\mathbf{F} = \mathbf{V}_1\mathbf{M}_{12} + \mathbf{V}_2\mathbf{M}_{22} \tag{11.2}$$

In this case, we write[7] the so-called *reduced form*:

$$\mathbf{V}_2 = -\mathbf{V}_1\mathbf{M}_{12}\mathbf{M}_{22}^{-1} + \mathbf{F}\mathbf{M}_{22}^{-1} \tag{11.3}$$

In this case, given a set of observations,[8]

$$\hat{\mathbf{V}}_2 = -\hat{\mathbf{V}}_1\mathbf{M}_{12}\mathbf{M}_{22}^{-1} + \hat{\mathbf{F}}\mathbf{M}_{22}^{-1} \tag{11.4}$$

$$\begin{aligned} \hat{\mathbf{V}}_{1\mathbf{T}}\hat{\mathbf{V}}_2 &= -\hat{\mathbf{V}}_{1\mathbf{T}}\hat{\mathbf{V}}_1\mathbf{M}_{12}\mathbf{M}_{22}^{-1} + \hat{\mathbf{V}}_{1\mathbf{T}}\hat{\mathbf{F}}\mathbf{M}_{22}^{-1} \\ -[\hat{\mathbf{V}}_{1\mathbf{T}}\hat{\mathbf{V}}_1]^{-1}\hat{\mathbf{V}}_{1\mathbf{T}}\hat{\mathbf{V}}_2 &= \mathbf{M}_{12}\mathbf{M}_{22}^{-1} - [\hat{\mathbf{V}}_{1\mathbf{T}}\hat{\mathbf{V}}_1]^{-1}\hat{\mathbf{V}}_{1\mathbf{T}}\hat{\mathbf{F}}\mathbf{M}_{22}^{-1} \end{aligned} \tag{11.5}$$

In this case, *if* the variables in $\mathbf{V}_1$ are independent of the factors **F**, then it is expected that $\hat{\mathbf{V}}_{1\mathbf{T}}\hat{\mathbf{F}} = \mathbf{0}$, so that the *least-squares estimator*

$$-[\hat{\mathbf{V}}_{1\mathbf{T}}\hat{\mathbf{V}}_1]^{-1}\hat{\mathbf{V}}_{1\mathbf{T}}\hat{\mathbf{V}}_2 = \mathbf{M}_{12}\mathbf{M}_{22}^{-1} \tag{11.6}$$

The theory, then, asserts that the elements of $\mathbf{M}_{12}$ and $\mathbf{M}_{22}$ have certain values. It thus predicts that the least-squares estimator [left side of equation (12.6)] will have certain values. Suppose that this prediction is not exactly fulfilled (as is usually the case). Then we say one of two things:

(1) The discrepancy between $\hat{\mathbf{V}}_{1\mathbf{T}}\hat{\mathbf{F}}$ and **0**, "in the long run" is expected to be zero, but over short periods of time it is not zero. The observed discrepancy between the predicted value of $\mathbf{M}_{12}\mathbf{M}_{22}^{1}$ and $-[\hat{\mathbf{V}}_{1\mathbf{T}}\hat{\mathbf{V}}_1]^{-1}\hat{\mathbf{V}}_{1\mathbf{T}}\hat{\mathbf{V}}_2$

---

[6] Acceptance or rejection is made on the basis of a set of observations. On a different set of observations, a different decision might be made.

[7] In the literature on this subject, $\mathbf{V}_2$ is referred to as the set of *jointly determined* variables (sometimes *endogenous* variables) and the set $\mathbf{V}_1$ as the set of *predetermined* variables (sometimes *exogenous* variables).

[8] The product $\mathbf{M}_{12}\mathbf{M}_{22}^{1}$ is called the *reduced form* matrix.

could have been the result of random departures of $\hat{\mathbf{F}}$ from the expected pattern, so that we can accept $\mathbf{M}_{12}\mathbf{M}_{22}^{-1}$ as valid.

(2) The discrepancy between the matrix $\mathbf{M}_{12}\mathbf{M}_{22}^{-1}$ and the predicted observations $-[\hat{\mathbf{V}}_{1\mathbf{T}}\hat{\mathbf{V}}_1]^{-1}\hat{\mathbf{V}}_{1\mathbf{T}}\hat{\mathbf{V}}_2$ is so great that only an improbably large deviation of $\hat{\mathbf{F}}$ from its expected pattern could explain this result. Thus we must conclude that $\mathbf{M}_{12}\mathbf{M}_{22}^{1}$ is not valid.

The two testing procedures, (11.5) and (11.6), have one point in common. One takes an assumed value for a matrix that is related to the matrix $\mathbf{M}$ of the theory. One then says that if the theory were exactly valid, some matrix of calculations performed on observations would have some particular value. The difference between the predicted and the observed value of these calculations is then examined to see how likely it is that such a difference could have occurred by chance—due to random variations among the factors.

There is, however, an important difference between the two methods of procedure. To see where it lies, one must return to the original statement of the theory

$$(\mathbf{0}, \mathbf{F}) = (\mathbf{V}_1, \mathbf{V}_2)\begin{pmatrix} M_{11} & M_{12} \\ M_{21} & M_{22} \end{pmatrix}$$

This theory states that $\mathbf{M}$ is invertible. Suppose we write $\mathbf{M}^{-1} = \mathbf{N}$, so that

$$(\mathbf{V}_1, \mathbf{V}_2) = (\mathbf{0}, \mathbf{F})\begin{pmatrix} N_{11} & N_{12} \\ N_{21} & N_{22} \end{pmatrix}$$

and

$$\mathbf{V}_1 = \mathbf{F}\mathbf{N}_{21}$$
$$\mathbf{V}_2 = \mathbf{F}\mathbf{N}_{22}$$

Then the term that is assumed to vanish, $\hat{\mathbf{V}}_{1\mathbf{T}}\hat{\mathbf{F}}$, may be written

$$\hat{\mathbf{V}}_{1\mathbf{T}}\hat{\mathbf{F}} = \mathbf{N}_{21\mathbf{T}}\hat{\mathbf{F}}_{\mathbf{T}}\hat{\mathbf{F}}$$

In general, $\hat{\mathbf{V}}_{1\mathbf{T}}\hat{\mathbf{F}} = \mathbf{0}$ if and only if $\mathbf{N}_{21\mathbf{T}} = \mathbf{0}$. That means that $\mathbf{N}$ is block triangular, and its inverse, $\mathbf{M}$, must also be block triangular,

$$\mathbf{M} = \begin{pmatrix} M_{11} & M_{12} \\ 0_{21} & M_{22} \end{pmatrix}$$

Thus $\mathbf{0} = \mathbf{V}_1\mathbf{M}_{11}$, which means that the accounting identities which appear in the theory may not involve any of the variables[9] included in $\mathbf{V}_2$. This condition is a restriction on the kinds of behavioral statements that may be estimated by means of (11.6).

In Chapters 3 to 7, special attention was paid to the question of block-triangular matrices. It was shown there that in many cases, block-triangular

[9] That is, they may not involve any of the *jointly determined* variables.

matrices were used as expository devices to obtain special cases in which answers appeared to be simple. Such block-triangular matrices can be interpreted in terms of "causality." For instance, the four versions of Theory 8 juggled blocks around so as to examine conditions in which banks would affect (or be affected by) decisions of households and businesses. Such *theoretical* work helps us to understand the consequences of certain types of economic behavior. But in testing a theory, we should *like* to be able to test a theory without requiring that the theory be expressible in block-triangular form.[10]

In using formula (11.5) the statistician predicts the values of $[\hat{\mathbf{V}}_{2\mathbf{T}}\hat{\mathbf{V}}_2]$; in using formula (11.6) he predicts the values of $[\hat{\mathbf{V}}_{1\mathbf{T}}\hat{\mathbf{V}}_1]^{-1}{}_{\mathbf{T}}\hat{\mathbf{V}}_2$. These two matrices, of course, are quite different in content. The difference arises because in (11.5) the statistician has used accounting identities to "eliminate" certain variables from his system, while in (11.6) he has not taken them into account. For this reason, the testing procedures are different. The test associated with (11.5) deals with hypothetical independence relations existing among factors. That associated with (11.6) deals with hypothetical independence between factors and variables.

It will be useful to consider an example. The matrix of Theory 8A involved three behavioral coefficients:

(1) the marginal propensity to consume, from the statement $C = aY + F_C$

(2) the coefficient relating the desired level of plant to total assets, from $K = bW + F_K$

(3) the coefficient relating bank loans to deposits, from $L = sM + F_L$.

We can write the matrix of this theory as **M(a, b, s)**. For each triple (a, b, s), one matrix of the form of Theory 8A is defined, and a prediction can be made for the observed values of $[\hat{\mathbf{V}}_{2\mathbf{T}}\hat{\mathbf{V}}]$. Economists would say that if Theory 8A is wrong, then **M(0, 0, 0)** is right. That is, the predictions made by **M(0, 0, 0)** will be acceptably close to the observations. If, for example, the first and third behavioral statements are right, but the second is wrong, then **M(a, 0, s)** will be acceptably close to the observations. Thus, at a minimum, to accept Theory 8A as a whole, it would be necessary to reject the following matrices:

M(0, 0, 0), M(a, 0, 0), M(0, b, 0), M(0, 0, s), M(a, b, 0), M(a, 0, s), M(0, b, s)

Moreover, rejection of these matrices should be possible, whatever values of a, b, s appear as nonzero arguments in these various special cases.

---

[10] In the early 1960s, there was a school of economic thought that argued on philosophical grounds that $\mathbf{M}_{22}$ should always be formulated as a triangular or block-triangular matrix. That, however, is a different question from the point made here. (The leading proponents of this view were Herman O. A. Wold and R. L. Strotz; the leading opponent was Robert L. Basmann). See H. O. A. Wold (ed.) *Econometric Model Building*. (Amsterdam: North-Holland, 1964), and papers by R. L. Basmann in *Econometrica* 33 (1965) and in *The Journal of the American Statistical Association* 60 (1965).

Observe that in (11.5) the statistician takes the theory as making a prediction about the values of the matrix $[\hat{\mathbf{V}}_{2\mathbf{T}}\hat{\mathbf{V}}_2]^{-1}$; in (11.6) he takes the theory as making a prediction about the value of the matrix $[\hat{\mathbf{V}}_{1\mathbf{T}}\hat{\mathbf{V}}_1]^{-1}\hat{\mathbf{V}}_{1\mathbf{T}}\hat{\mathbf{V}}_2$. In other words, the estimators are quite different. In (11.5) the statistician takes explicitly into account the accounting identities of his system; in (11.6) he does not take them explicitly into account. Consequently, method (11.6) is consistent only with theories, the matrices of which have a special block-triangular structure. On the other hand, in (11.5) the statistician is concerned with relations among the factors of his system, while in (11.6) he is concerned only with the ways in which factors are related to variables.

One particular problem must be mentioned. In both cases considered, some particular prediction is made concerning the values that some estimator may have. That is, each method maps elements of **M** into elements of a matrix calculated from observations. Consider the inverse problem: We predict perfectly the value $[\hat{\mathbf{V}}_{2\mathbf{T}}\hat{\mathbf{V}}_2]^{-1}$ in (11.5), or the value of $[\hat{\mathbf{V}}_{1\mathbf{T}}\hat{\mathbf{V}}_1]^{-1}\hat{\mathbf{V}}_{1\mathbf{T}}\hat{\mathbf{V}}_2$ in (11.6). Then we can say that we have a theory that fits the observations exactly. But we have not proved that this is the only theory that does so.

Moreover, in the more usual case, our predictions only approximate the observations of $[\hat{\mathbf{V}}_{2\mathbf{T}}\hat{\mathbf{V}}_2]^{-1}$ or $[\hat{\mathbf{V}}_{1\mathbf{T}}\hat{\mathbf{V}}_1]^{-1}\hat{\mathbf{V}}_{1\mathbf{T}}\hat{\mathbf{V}}_2$. In this case, we may be able to find other matrices which fit equally well.

In reporting formulas (11.3) and (11.4) we observe that in both cases, a matrix calculated from observations is said to be equal to a matrix calculated from (but not equal to) the matrix of the theory. Thus formula (11.5) tells us that

$$[\hat{\mathbf{V}}_{2\mathbf{T}}\hat{\mathbf{V}}_2]^{-1} = \mathbf{Q}_{\mathbf{T}}\mathbf{Q}, \text{ where } \mathbf{Q} = [\mathbf{M}_{22} - \mathbf{M}_{21}\mathbf{M}_{11}^{-1}\mathbf{M}_{12}]$$

and formula (11.6) tells us that

$$-[\hat{\mathbf{V}}_{1\mathbf{T}}\hat{\mathbf{V}}_1]^{-1}\hat{\mathbf{V}}_{1\mathbf{T}}\hat{\mathbf{V}}_2 = \mathbf{M}_{12}\mathbf{M}_{22}^{-1}$$

Actually we are not interested in **Q**, but in the elements of $\mathbf{M}_{22}$ and $\mathbf{M}_{12}$. (The elements of $\mathbf{M}_{21}$ and $\mathbf{M}_{11}$ are known, for they depend on accounting identities. These are relations involving logic, not facts. If our logic is sound, these blocks must be correct.) Likewise we are not interested in the product $\mathbf{M}_{12}\mathbf{M}_{22}^{-1}$, but in the separate elements of the two blocks.

There is a rather complicated statistical literature on the *identification problem*. This literature is concerned with the fact that it is possible to construct a mapping from **Q**, or from $\mathbf{M}_{12}\mathbf{M}_{22}^{-1}$, into the elements of $\mathbf{M}_{12}$ and $\mathbf{M}_{22}^{-1}$ only if these two blocks satisfy certain special requirements. There is an economic meaning to this literature: If economic behavior does not satisfy certain identifiability conditions, then it is not possible to discover exactly what this behavior is, using statistical techniques. Space does not permit a full discussion of this topic here. Economists who wish to construct testable hypotheses, however, must make sure that these hypotheses satisfy identifiability conditions.

The test just proposed merely says that Theory 8A is accepted if we can reject any theory that says $a = 0$ or $b = 0$ or $c = 0$. Naturally this test is not as severe as a test that insists (say) that a, b, c must all be at least .5. Suppose, on theoretical grounds, one economist would argue that $a \geq .7$, and another would argue that $.7 \geq a \geq .3$. Then it might turn out that the two could agree that $a \neq 0$, but that they had no test powerful enough to distinguish between their hypotheses.

The foregoing discussion is far too brief to do justice to the problem of obtaining numerical estimates of the elements of a matrix associated with a theory. Only two out of a number of possible estimates have been considered. Formula (11.6) in particular, the "single-stage least-squares estimator," has been supplemented by a variety of other formulas, designed to cope with cases in which the expected value of the matrix $\hat{\mathbf{V}}_{1\mathbf{T}}\hat{\mathbf{F}}$ is not zero. Moreover, the purely statistical problems have not been considered in detail. To assert, for instance, that a particular matrix is (or is not) significantly different from zero is a task in itself.

It has been a major achievement of economic statistics to formulate procedures such as those described here. The idea that entire blocks of coefficients (rather than single coefficients) must be studied simultaneously seems to have originated with economists. The problem of "simultaneous equations estimation," as the study of blocks of coefficients is called, is thus a branch of statistics that came into being because of the problems of economics. It did not arise in the classical problems of biology and physics which provided the original impetus to mathematical statistics, mainly because these problems dealt with controlled laboratory situations in which one theoretical statement at a time could be isolated for study.

Moreover, the statistical study of simultaneous equations systems has become a commonplace in economics. The name *econometrics* is often associated with this study. The name, however, is not emphasized here, for many econometricians are economic theorists as well as empirical statisticians, and it is not wise to associate the whole with merely one (albeit an important one) of its parts.

Despite the considerable volume of testing work that has taken place over the past, the number of conclusions about which economists are agreed remains small. Part of the disagreement has to do with personal matters. Economists (like other scientists) who start out with strong preconceptions which are upset by statistical evidence may find it easier to conclude that their statistical techniques were faulty than to reject their prejudices. Part of the disagreement, however, arises from a more interesting source. The following section will explain why the development of new systems of social accounting data will (and should) lead to the revision of empirical conclusions.

PARTIAL AND MORE GENERAL THEORIES

The history of macroeconomic data is a relatively short one. Prior to the establishment of the Federal Reserve System in 1913, there was no regular system of reporting macroeconomic data. From 1913 to the late 1930s, data on the balance sheets of the banks were the only macroeconomic data available. In the late 1930s, annual national product accounts also became available, and after 1945, quarterly national product data were published. Thus by 1945, it was possible to carry on statistical analysis of the banking system, and also statistical analysis of the national product, but it was not possible to carry on a combined analysis, since no data on nonbank balance sheets were available.

However, in the early 1950s, publication of flow of funds accounts began. It is natural to investigate the effect that such a new source of data has upon the conclusions drawn by statisticians. This question can be studied in the following terms. Suppose two theories, T_1 and T_2, where

$$T_1 : (\mathbf{V}_1, \mathbf{V}_2)\begin{pmatrix} M_{11} & M_{12} \\ M_{21} & M_{22} \end{pmatrix} = (\mathbf{F}_1, \mathbf{F}_2)$$

$$T_2 : \mathbf{V}_1, \mathbf{M}_{11} = \mathbf{F}_1$$

It may be assumed that $\mathbf{M}_{11}$ is the same block in both cases. An example of this sort is given in Theory 8. That theory takes Tiny Models 1, 2, 4 and puts them together into a more comprehensive system. The Tiny Models appear as the diagonal blocks of Theory 8, and the nondiagonal blocks express links between bank balance sheets, nonbank balance sheets, and the income accounts.

What will happen to our assessment of Theory T_2, assuming that it becomes possible to formulate and test Theory T_1? That is the question discussed here.

In raising this question, it is not asserted that statistical data simply drop from the sky, without reference to economic theory. That is not the case. National income statistics came to be published on a current basis, in part because Tiny Model 1 had been invented. This model showed that these statistics would be useful. The flow of funds data came to be published currently, in part because monetary theory in the late 1940s had pointed to the need for data that specifically related the national income accounts to the banking system. Thus there is a definite historical connection between the development of new statistical data and the development of theories about the behavior represented by the data.[11] The data appear because theorists

[11] Another example: Studies of interindustry payments began to be made in the late 1940s, supplementing the periodic Censuses of Business. These new studies came into being because W. W. Leontief had shown, on theoretical grounds, that they would be useful. (W. W. Leontief, *The Structure of the American Economy*, Cambridge (Harvard University Press), 1st edition, 1941.)

suggest they will be useful. Once they appear, they stimulate new work and bring about reconsideration of the value of older work.

The current statistical data, of course, give much better information about changes in balance sheets than they do about balance sheet totals. At some point in the future, balance sheet data will perhaps become available. We must therefore consider what might happen to conclusions that may be made on the basis of data now in existence.

To demonstrate that one should expect different results from testing a smaller theory, like T_2, than from testing a larger theory, like T_1, we consider the two procedures separately.

If account is taken of accounting identities, then it is necessary to use formula (11.5)

$$[\hat{\mathbf{V}}_{2\mathbf{T}}\hat{\mathbf{V}}_2]^{-1} = [\mathbf{M}_{22} - \mathbf{M}_{21}\mathbf{M}_{11}^{-1}\mathbf{M}_{12}]_{\mathbf{T}}[\mathbf{M}_{22} - \mathbf{M}_{21}\mathbf{M}_{11}^{-1}\mathbf{M}_{12}]$$

This expression is messy, owing to the presence of subscripts. It is useful to rewrite it as

$$[\mathbf{V}_{\mathbf{T}}\mathbf{V}]^{-1} = [\mathbf{D} - \mathbf{CA}^{-1}\mathbf{B}]_{\mathbf{T}}[\mathbf{D} - \mathbf{CA}^{-1}\mathbf{B}] \tag{11.7}$$

replacing

$\hat{\mathbf{V}}_2$ by $\mathbf{V}$
$\mathbf{M}_{11}$ by $\mathbf{A}$
$\mathbf{M}_{12}$ by $\mathbf{B}$
$\mathbf{M}_{21}$ by $\mathbf{C}$
$\mathbf{M}_{22}$ by $\mathbf{D}$

If (11.7) is the pair of matrices associated with T_1, the larger theory, then $\mathbf{V}$ may be divided into two parts: $\mathbf{V} = (\mathbf{W}_1, \mathbf{W}_2)$, where $\mathbf{W}_1$ consists of variables appearing in T_2, and $\mathbf{W}_2$ consists of variables appearing in T_1 but not in T_2. Corresponding to this classification of variables, one may form blocks in the matrices **A**, **B**, **C**, **D**:

$$[\mathbf{V}_{\mathbf{T}}\mathbf{V}]^{-1} = \begin{bmatrix} W_{1T}W_1 & W_{1T}W_2 \\ W_{2T}W_1 & W_{2T}W_2 \end{bmatrix}^{-1}$$

$$= \left[\begin{pmatrix} D_{11}D_{12} \\ D_{21}D_{22} \end{pmatrix} - \begin{pmatrix} C_{11}C_{12} \\ C_{21}C_{22} \end{pmatrix}\begin{pmatrix} A_{11}A_{12} \\ A_{21}A_{22} \end{pmatrix}^{-1}\begin{pmatrix} B_{11}B_{12} \\ B_{21}B_{22} \end{pmatrix}\right]_{\mathbf{T}}$$

$$\left[\begin{pmatrix} D_{11}D_{12} \\ D_{21}D_{22} \end{pmatrix} - \begin{pmatrix} C_{11}C_{12} \\ C_{21}C_{22} \end{pmatrix}\begin{pmatrix} A_{11}A_{12} \\ A_{21}A_{22} \end{pmatrix}\begin{pmatrix} B_{11}B_{12} \\ B_{21}B_{22} \end{pmatrix}\right]$$

The economist who uses Theory T_2 will set

$$[\mathbf{W}_{1\mathbf{T}}\mathbf{W}_1]^{-1} = [\mathbf{D}_{11} - C_{11}\mathbf{A}_{11}^{-1}\mathbf{B}_{11}]_{\mathbf{T}}[\mathbf{D}_{11} - C_{11}\mathbf{A}_{11}^{-1}\mathbf{B}_{11}]$$

However, the general formula for the inversion of block matrices, as given in Chapter 2, states that

$$\begin{pmatrix} H & J \\ K & L \end{pmatrix}^{-1} = \begin{pmatrix} (H - JL^{-1}K)^{-1} & -(H - JL^{-1}K)^{-1}JL^{-1} \\ -(L - KH^{-1}J)KH^{-1} & (L - KH^{-1}J)^{-1} \end{pmatrix}$$

Thus, on the left side of the equation, $[\mathbf{W}_{1T}\mathbf{W}]^{-1}$ corresponds to $\mathbf{H}^{-1}$, and not to the correct term $(\mathbf{H} - \mathbf{J}\mathbf{L}^{-1}\mathbf{K})^{-1}$. On the right-hand side, the matrix

$$[\mathbf{D}_{11} - \mathbf{C}_{11}\mathbf{A}_{11}^{-1}\mathbf{B}_{11}]$$

and its transpose appear, instead of the correct matrix:

$$\left[\mathbf{D}_{11} - (\mathbf{C}_{11}\mathbf{C}_{12})\begin{pmatrix} A_{11}A_{12} \\ A_{21}A_{22} \end{pmatrix}^{-1} \begin{pmatrix} \mathbf{B}_{11} \\ B_{21} \end{pmatrix} \right]$$

Clearly the two procedures will lead to different results, unless T_1 is a very special theory, which asserts that there is no connection between the parts of the economy included in T_2 and the new part added by T_1.

Suppose, on the other hand, that the behavioral equations are considered without regard to accounting identities. Then it is necessary to use formula (11.6):

$$-[\hat{\mathbf{V}}_{1T}\hat{\mathbf{V}}_1]^{-1}\hat{\mathbf{V}}_{1T}\hat{\mathbf{V}}_2 = \mathbf{M}_{12}\mathbf{M}_{22}^{-1}$$

As before, we simplify the notation so as to eliminate subscripts:

$$-[\mathbf{V}_T\mathbf{V}]^{-1}\mathbf{V}_T\mathbf{W} = \mathbf{A}\mathbf{B}^{-1} \tag{11.8}$$

If (11.8) is the pair of matrices associated with T_1, the larger theory, then **V** and **W** may be divided into two parts:

V = (**X**, **Y**)
  X = the block of variables of **V** that appear in both T_1 and T_2
  Y = the block of variables of **V** that appears only in T_1
W = (**U**, **Z**)
  U = the block of variables of **V** that appear in both T_1 and T_2
  Z = the block of variables of **V** that appears only in T_1.

Then the economist using Theory T_1 will write (11.8), in block form, as

$$-\begin{bmatrix} \mathbf{X}_T\mathbf{X} & \mathbf{X}_T\mathbf{Y} \\ \mathbf{Y}_T\mathbf{X} & \mathbf{Y}_T\mathbf{Y} \end{bmatrix}^{-1} \begin{bmatrix} \mathbf{X}_T\mathbf{U} & \mathbf{X}_T\mathbf{Z} \\ \mathbf{Y}_T\mathbf{U} & \mathbf{Y}_T\mathbf{Z} \end{bmatrix} = \begin{bmatrix} \mathbf{A}_{11} & \mathbf{A}_{12} \\ \mathbf{A}_{21} & \mathbf{A}_{22} \end{bmatrix} \begin{bmatrix} \mathbf{B}_{11} & \mathbf{B}_{12} \\ \mathbf{B}_{21} & \mathbf{B}_{22} \end{bmatrix}^{-1}$$

In contrast, the theorist using Theory T_2 would write (11.6) as

$$-[\mathbf{X}_T\mathbf{X}]^{-1}\mathbf{X}_T\mathbf{U} = \mathbf{A}_{11}\mathbf{B}_{11}^{-1} \tag{11.9}$$

rather than in the correct form, based on the formula for the inversion of block matrices. The left side of (11.9) should be replaced by:

$$[\mathbf{X}_T\mathbf{X} - \mathbf{X}_T\mathbf{Y}(\mathbf{Y}_T\mathbf{Y})^{-1}\mathbf{Y}_T\mathbf{X}][\mathbf{E} - \mathbf{X}_T\mathbf{Y}(\mathbf{Y}_T\mathbf{Y})^{-1}]\begin{bmatrix} \mathbf{X}_T & \mathbf{U} \\ \mathbf{Y}_T & \mathbf{U} \end{bmatrix}$$

And the right side of (11.7) should be replaced by

$$[\mathbf{A}_{11}\mathbf{A}_{12}]\begin{bmatrix} -(\mathbf{B}_{11} - \mathbf{B}_{12}(\mathbf{B}_{22})^{-1}\mathbf{B}_{21})^{-1}\mathbf{B}_{12}\mathbf{B}_{22}^{-1} \\ (\mathbf{B}_{22} - \mathbf{B}_{21}\mathbf{B}_{11}^{-1}\mathbf{B}_{11})^{-1} \end{bmatrix}$$

The discrepancy between the practice of the economist using Theory T_2 and that of the economist using Theory T_1 arises, of course, from the fact that Theory T_2 omits some of the behavioral statements, some of the identities and some of the variables that appear in Theory T_1.

In general, then, we expect that T_1 will lead to a different assessment of economic behavior than T_2 will.

It would be easy to misinterpret this finding, and to conclude that it is always possible to improve on a theory by "sticking in" more variables. Such a conclusion would be contrary to the spirit of good theorizing, which aims at simple explanations of complicated phenomena. The author is not advocating that theories should explicitly include as many variables as possible.

In Chapter 1, it was pointed out that the records of economic activity of a business or of an economy consist of two interrelated sets of accounts: an income statement and a balance sheet. A macroeconomic theory aims at accounting for changes in the set of social accounts. A theory that deals only with the national income accounts, or only with the national balance sheet accounts is only a partial theory. Consequently, it is to be expected that statistical analysis of that part of the system of social accounts will be more or less misleading, as the foregoing analysis suggests.

Although the two branches of macroeconomics—income theory and monetary theory—have relatively long histories, it is only since 1950 that data have become available in a form that permits a first attempt at the unification of the two. Even today, the data on balance sheets (as compared with changes in balance sheets) are incomplete. Theorists are only beginning the work of proposing explanations of the joint variations in the two sets of accounts. For this reason, most of the statistical work done to date must be regarded as relating to partial theories, using only a part of the relevant accounting system. Thus it is not now possible to point to analysis that formulates the central problem of macroeconomics in the context of a complete system of social accounts. Although a great deal of interesting work has been done in national income analysis and in monetary analysis, readers of this book can at once see that it does not address itself to the central question: Are economic decisions mainly formulated in terms of income and its allocation among various uses, or mainly in terms of total assets and their allocation among various categories of asset?

The quantitative analysis of income and its uses can certainly not cast light on the question of the composition of assets, unless balance sheet data are available. The quantitative analysis of asset holdings cannot cast light on the question of income allocation unless income data are included in the theory. Too little time has elapsed since the appearance of data on changes in balance sheet accounts for empirical economists to explore the potentials of this new set of social accounts in the necessary depth. For this reason, statistical work to date, although suggestive, does not approach the central macroeconomic question. That is why the author has felt free to write as if he were dealing with an unresolved question.

Even if two theories include both income and balance sheet accounts, one theory may include more variables and more behavioral statements than the other. In this case, one would not be able to apply the foregoing argument automatically. Suppose, to take a simple case, Theory T_1 divides consumption into two parts, "durable goods" and "nondurable goods," and bonds into "government" and "private bonds," while Theory T_2 combines the two kinds of consumption and the two kinds of bonds. Then comparison of the two theories must be on different grounds: Does the aggregation of T_1 increase our understanding of the process, or does it conceal significant differences in behavior? There is, however, no difference in principle between the two theories.

Again, suppose that theories T_1 and T_2 are dynamic theories, of the sort described in the appendix to Chapter 6. The difference is that Theory T_1 says that behavior at time t depends on events occurring at times $(t - 1)$ and $(t - 2)$. Theory T_2 says only that behavior at time t depends on events occurring at time $(t - 1)$. Then the choice between these theories cannot be made independently of the statistical tests.

Thus the point raised here relates simply to the completeness of the system. The system of social accounts constrains the behavior of economic units through constraints on both income and balance sheet accounts. Since these constraints are inherent in the logic by which the data are collected, they must be fully reflected in the structure of the theories.

The argument thus far can be summarized in the following propositions:

(1) It is possible to devise estimation techniques that tell us the conditions under which calculations performed on the observations of the variables of a macroeconomic theory will yield correct numerical values of the elements of the matrix of that theory.

(2) The correctness of these calculations depends in part upon whether the calculations take into account everything in the theory, or only certain parts of it.

(3) In particular, the variables in a theory form parts of a social accounting system. This system imposes a set of constraints upon what is observed as economic behavior. Consequently, failure to utilize all information concerning the structure of the social accounting system will lead to errors in our perceptions of economic behavior, and hence in estimates made of the numerical values of the coefficients of a matrix suggested by theory.

(4) The development of flow of funds accounting in the 1950s has broadened our concepts of the social accounts. It therefore makes obsolete the empirical results of earlier studies in the following sense: To continue to assert the validity of results reached from national income accounting method alone, or from monetary methods alone, it would be necessary to re-examine these results in the light of a unified accounting scheme embracing both the national

income and the flow of funds accounts. So far, there has been only a limited amount of work incorporating both concepts.

(5) The flow of funds accounting system gives a good deal of information concerning *changes* in social balance sheets. It gives considerably less information, however, about the total values of accounts appearing in these balance sheets. On theoretical grounds, one can conjecture that certain kinds of economic behavior may depend in important ways upon such total values. It would follow that until data on balance sheet totals become available in adequate quantity and quality, it will be impossible to test these hypotheses. Until these tests are made, however, there are grounds to believe that testable theories, as presently formulated, are subject to error. This error exists for the same reason that the error exists in propositions developed before the flow of funds data became available.

These propositions can be derived directly from a consideration of the structure of the subject matter under discussion. That is, it depends on the fact that macroeconomics is inherently concerned with the behavior of national income and national balance sheets, the elements of which are related by logical considerations, as well as by the concrete behavioral patterns of economic units.

There are other grounds, however, for asserting that the behavior of economic units is still a matter for conjecture. These grounds are derived from direct observation of the economy. The following section will explain why our observations of economic activity (taken in the most general sense) provide a basis for skepticism concerning the conclusions that economists have reached concerning the behavior of economic units.

THE EMPIRICAL BASIS OF MACROECONOMIC CONTROVERSY

The economy itself sometimes seems to behave as if it deliberately wants to encourage economists to believe things which aren't true. Indeed, it is much easier to "prove things" in economics than it should be. Consequently the number of economic propositions which would be accepted, using the rules of ordinary statistical procedures, is remarkably high.

To illustrate this proposition, consider a single behavioral equation, $X = aY + F$. One common test used by statisticians to determine whether X and Y are independent uses the *coefficient of correlation*. This is computed by the formula

$$r = \frac{\sum_{i=1}^{t} x_i y_i}{\left[\frac{1}{t}\sum_{1}^{t} x_i^2\right]^{1/2}\left[\frac{1}{t}\sum_{1}^{t} y_i^2\right]^{1/2}}$$

Here the *observed* values of X are $X_1, X_2 \cdots X_t$; the *observed* values of Y are $Y_1, Y_2 \cdots Y_t$. The symbols $x_1 \cdots x_t, y_1 \cdots y_t$ are the deviations of $X_1 \cdots Y_t$ from the average observed value. The coefficient r is a pure number. It is 0 if X and Y are independent; $+1$ if $a > 0$ and the equation contains *no* random error; -1 if $a < 0$ and the equation contains *no* random error.[12] So, when one asserts that X and Y are not independent, one frequently proceeds by showing that the value of r calculated from the observations of X and Y is so large that it could probably not have been observed by chance. Then, if X and Y are *not* independent, the least-squares estimate of a can be taken as a measure of the true coefficient describing the relation between X and Y.

Tables of this coefficient tell us that if X and Y are independent and normal,[13] then if one calculates r for samples of twenty-five observations, one will find (purely by the operations of blind chance) r with absolute value greater than .32 in ten percent of the samples, greater than .38 in five percent of the samples, greater than .45 in two percent of the samples and greater than .49 in one percent of the samples.

In the early days of economic statistics, economists used such results about r to test their findings. Thus if they made 25 observations of two variables, and found a correlation coefficient of (say) .45, they would conclude that the chances were about 50 to 1 against such a correlation arising by chance; they would conclude that there was convincing evidence that the variables they were studying were really connected by a behavioral relation of some kind.

However, the following experiment has been performed. One of the standard statistical source books is the *Historical Statistics of the United States*, published by the United States Government. A sample of 100 series covering the period 1929–1953 was drawn at random from this book, and the correlation coefficients were computed between successive pairs of series, however foolish it might seem to expect any economic relation to exist between them. If the series had been observations of normal independent random variables, then one would have expected one percent of the coefficients to be as great as .49. Actually, 54 percent of the coefficients calculated were .50 or over.[14]

On this evidence, pairs of economic series are 50 times more likely to be "significantly" correlated than the usual significance test would predict. That

---

[12] The demonstration of *Schwarz's inequality* in the appendix to this chapter explains why $1 \geq r \geq -1$.

[13] *Normal* random variables follow a particular law: The probability that X assumes the value x is given by $k \exp -\frac{1}{2}\left(\frac{X-\mu}{\sigma}\right)^2$ where k is a constant, μ the mean and σ is $\sqrt{(\mathbf{x}, \mathbf{x})}$. Normal random variables are the kind best understood by statistical theorists.

[14] E. Ames and S. Reiter, "Distributions of Correlation Coefficients in Economic Time Series," *Journal of the American Statistical Association* (1961).

is, the usual test proposed by statisticians will presumably lead economists to accept 50 times as many behavioral statements as they "should." Consequently, if we find economists who use the correlation coefficient as a test basis for accepting or rejecting statements in their theories, we can expect to find far too many statements being accepted as valid. From this point of view, there is an easy explanation of why economists disagree: Economists disagree because the test they use is not tough enough. (In fairness, however, we hastily add that the weakness may lie with statisticians, who have not come up with tougher tests.)

But it is interesting to look behind this test, and to try to say what it is about economic activity that brings about this result. For even though the macroeconomists may accept individual statements far too readily (using the usual statistical procedures), the reason for the breakdown of the tests serves as a powerful support to the general macroeconomic view of the economy.

If one makes a chart showing a single economic variable over a longish period of time (twenty-five years or more), one usually sees a clear tendency for this variable to increase or to decrease. As a rule, one has no difficulty drawing a straight line on the chart with a ruler in such a way that the line passes close to every point on the chart. In the 100 randomly selected series selected in the experiment described above, one could account for half or more of the variations in about two-thirds of all the series merely by assuming that the series could be approximated by the function

$$X = aT + b$$

where T was the calendar year of the observation. If this relation held exactly, then the annual increase in X would equal the coefficient a. Thus an important part of the variation in any economic activity is usually a tendency toward a steady annual increase (or decrease) which is maintained for fairly long periods of time.[15]

It is not difficult to show that two different series, each of which can be approximated by a straight line, will necessarily seem to vary in much the same way over time. Granted this general tendency toward steady growth or decline in individual sectors of the economy, it is not surprising that one should find that economic variables generally move more closely together than independent series of randomly selected numbers.

Suppose one disregards (corrects for) this *trend*, or persistent tendency for upward or downward change of economic variables. Suppose, that is, that we replace each variable X by a variable $X' = X - aT - b$, where a and b are

---

[15] Essentially similar results took place if one assumed that $\log X = aT + b$. This hypothesis amounts to asserting a constant "compound interest" rate of growth.

selected so as to make X' approximate a constant rather than a rising or falling straight line on a graph. This change might be thought to correct for the long-run tendency toward growth or decline that is peculiar to that variable. This correction might be enough to guarantee that randomly selected pairs of economic variables would appear to be independent of each other. In the sampling experiment described above, a test of this possibility was made. The hundred randomly selected variables were corrected in the manner indicated. Then the corrected variables were correlated. If they had been independent, one percent of these series would have shown a correlation coefficient of .5 or more; actually 28 percent of the observed coefficients were .5 or more. In other words, there are still 28 times as many apparently correlated variables as one would expect to find by chance.

This finding is consistent with the "business cycle" hypothesis, which dominated macroeconomic thinking from 1920 to 1940. A considerable body of writing exists on this subject. Most of it derives from the efforts of Wesley Mitchell, the creator of American economic statistics.[16] The following discussion summarizes some of the basic findings of Mitchell and of Arthur F. Burns and Geoffrey H. Moore, his associates and successors. The work cited below is mainly concerned with developing methods of characterizing changes in groups of economic variables in such a way as to facilitate forecasting. On the other hand, the evidence serves to explain why it is that it seems extremely easy to find pairs of variables whose variations appear to be related.

The initial observation made by Mitchell in his *Business Cycles* (1913) was that any economic variable shows more or less steady increases for periods of a year or more, followed by more or less steady decreases for similar periods. While the lengths and magnitudes of these sequences of increases and decreases are not constant, some 95 percent of the 830 economic variables he had observed by 1950 exhibited this "cyclical" behavior.[17]

These cycles might reach high and low points at different dates for different economic variables. If this were true, then at any moment, one would be able to see some series reaching high points and other series reaching low points. But in fact, one seldom finds that in a particular month some series will be reaching high points and others low points. Instead, one finds clusterings. Some periods are characterized only (or almost only) by high points; other periods only (or almost only) by low points; and in many periods, there are very few high points or low points reached by any economic variables.

---

[16] Mitchell founded the National Bureau of Economic Research, which has been the creator of most of the systems of American economic statistical reporting. Most of the statistical work now carried on by government agencies was originated in the National Bureau.

[17] Wesley C. Mitchell, *What Happens during Business Cycles* (New York: National Bureau of Economic Research, 1951), p. 10.

It is possible to construct a table that gives the dates of "*peaks* and *troughs*" of economic activity (Table 11.2). For present purposes, it is not necessary to explain exactly how these dates are determined. It is possible, however, to use these dates in an interesting way. We investigate, in particular, the following hypothesis: Most economic variables will be declining in any time interval between a peak and a trough; most will be rising in any interval between a trough and a peak.

TABLE 11.2

THE DURATION OF BUSINESS CYCLE EXPANSIONS AND CONTRACTIONS IN THE UNITED STATES, 1854–1957

BUSINESS CYCLE			DURATION OF	
Trough	Peak	Trough	Expansion (months)	Contraction (months)
Dec. 1854	June 1857	Dec. 1858	30	18
Dec. 1858	Oct. 1860	June 1861	22	8
June 1861	Apr. 1865	Dec. 1867	46	32
Dec. 1867	June 1869	Dec. 1870	18	18
Dec. 1870	Oct. 1873	Mar. 1879	34	65
Mar. 1879	Mar. 1882	May 1885	36	38
May 1885	Mar. 1887	Apr. 1888	22	13
Apr. 1888	July 1890	May 1891	27	10
May 1891	Jan. 1893	June 1894	20	17
June 1894	Dec. 1895	June 1897	18	18
June 1897	June 1899	Dec. 1900	24	18
Dec. 1900	Sep. 1902	Aug. 1904	21	23
Aug. 1904	May 1907	June 1908	33	13
June 1908	Jan. 1910	Jan. 1912	19	24
Jan. 1912	Jan. 1913	Dec. 1914	12	23
Dec. 1914	Aug. 1918	Mar. 1919*	44	7
Mar. 1919*	Jan. 1920	July 1921*	10	18
July 1921*	May 1923	July 1924	22	14
July 1924	Oct. 1926	Nov. 1927*	27	13
Nov. 1927*	Aug 1929*	Mar. 1933	21	43
Mar. 1933	May 1937	June 1938*	50	13
June 1938*	Feb. 1945	Oct. 1945	80	8
Oct. 1945	Nov. 1948	Oct. 1949	37	11
Oct. 1949	July 1953	Aug. 1954	45	13
Aug. 1954	July 1957	Apr. 1958	35	9
	July 1960	Feb. 1961	28	7
Average, 24 cycles, 1854–1954			29.9	19.9

SOURCE: For an explanation of the method used to determine the business cycle peak and trough dates and some tests of their validity, see Arthur F. Burns and Wesley C. Mitchell, *Measuring Business Cycles* (New York; National Bureau of Economic Research, 1946), Chap. 4. A few of these dates (designated by an asterisk) have been revised since the Burns-Mitchell report, and the list has been carried forward to the present.

* Revised.

Mitchell's peaks and troughs represent periods of three months, centering on the month given in the table. The *upswing* connecting a trough to a peak is divided into three equal intervals; and the *downswing* connecting a peak to a trough is also divided into three equal parts. In this way, a *reference cycle* pattern can be defined over the history of the American economy. If any economic variable *conformed* exactly to the reference cycle timing, it would always show increases in all intervals of every upswing, and decreases in all of the intervals of every downswing.

Mitchell was not content with taking samples of economic variables. He used all the data he could find, relating to 794 economic variables. For 345 of these (43.5 percent of the total), he found that the timing of their own variations matched that of the hypothetical reference cycle in the sense of reaching high values at peaks and low values at troughs. Another 158 series (19.9 percent) tended to miss the peak or the trough (but not both). Only 85 series (10.6 percent) varied in a way that did not match the reference cycle timing. Forty percent of all the variables rose in every interval of every upswing and fell in every interval of every downswing. Only twenty percent of the variables failed to rise and fall with the reference cycle at least 75 percent of the time.[18]

Mitchell regarded the "reference cycle" as a central point of departure for the discussion of economic problems. He did not observe it directly, for there is no such variable as "the reference cycle." Rather, he inferred its existence from a tendency for all variables to rise or to fall at the same time. This tendency is illustrated by Table 11.3.

Table 11.3 was constructed in the following fashion. For the period 1919–1940, monthly data were available on 705 economic variables. For each month, it was determined what percentage of these variables showed an increase. Thus if the percentage is close to 100, most series were increasing. If it is close to zero, most series were decreasing.

Table 11.3 indicates that over this 22-year period, 383 variables (54.3 percent of the total on the average) showed an increase in a given month. This means, roughly, that in an "average" month about half of all variables are rising and half falling. But this average tendency is highly misleading. In fact, Table 11.3 shows that there is much more of a tendency for economic variables to rise and fall simultaneously than one would find if the variations were really independent of each other. If economic variables were independent of each other, and if there were no tendency for a change in one month to be followed by a like change the next month, a simple probability law could be constructed to show the frequency with which one would expect to find exactly

[18] Wesley C. Mitchell, *op. cit.*, p. 81.

TABLE 11.3

THE NUMBER OF MONTHS OVER THE PERIOD 1919–1940 IN WHICH GIVEN PERCENTAGES OF 705 ECONOMIC VARIABLES SHOWED INCREASES

PERCENTAGES OF VARIABLES SHOWING INCREASES	NUMBER OF MONTHS IN WHICH THESE PERCENTAGES WERE OBSERVED
0– 9.9	1
10–19.9	34
20–29.9	13
30–39.9	23
40–49.9	34
50–59.9	20
60–69.9	55
70–79.9	52
80–89.9	32
90–99.9	0

SOURCE: G. H. Moore (ed.) *Business Cycle Indicators*, Vol. II (Princeton, N. J.: Princeton University Press, 1961), p. 179.

n series increasing in a given month.[19] If this law were valid, one would have observed that in 261 out of the 264 months (almost 99 percent of all months) between 50 and 60 percent of the series would have shown increases. Actually, in 244 out of the 264 months, the observations fell outside this range. In fact, in half of all months (132 months) 70 percent or more of the series changed in the same direction. This result is particularly impressive, since one might expect all sorts of random short-term events in individual parts of the economy to reduce the similarity of month-to-month changes in these variables.

These observations would be quite conclusive from the statistical point of view. They represent another way of explaining that even if one selects economic variables quite at random, one will tend to find that they vary in very much the same way. That is, the correlation coefficients between pairs of these variables will be much too high to permit the conclusion that they are really independent.

[19] The probability that n variables would increase would be a term in the binomial probability law $(.543 + .457)^{705}$. Specifically, $P(n) = \frac{705!}{n!\,(705-n)!}(.543)^n(.457)^{705-n}$. This function can be very closely approximated by the normal law $N(n) = K\,e-\left(\frac{n-383}{\sqrt{2 \times 13.265}}\right)^2$, for which tables are readily available. The number 383 is the mean, and 13.265 the standard deviation of the binomial probability law: $383 = 705 \times .543$ and $13.265 = \sqrt{705 \times .543 \times .457}$.

These observations can also be made into a criticism of statistical practices: The tests used on economic data are insufficiently strict to sort out insignificant similarities among economic variables. On this basis, we can easily explain why many economic theories seem to pass statistical tests, and therefore why there is so much controversy among economists.

But it is possible also to view these observations as powerful evidence in favor of some sort of macroeconomic hypothesis. For if the economy is really governed by some factor-into-variable mapping $\mathbf{FM} = \mathbf{V}$, and if the economy is really very complicated, both $\mathbf{F}$ and $\mathbf{V}$ will be vectors with very large numbers of components. If indeed there are many factors influencing the economy, and if each variable is influenced more or less equally by very many factors, then there is no particular reason why pairs of variables should vary in much the same way over a period of time. The well-established fact of "business cycles" seems to argue that at any period of time, all variables change in much the same way because only a few factors in the economy are changing, and these change in such a way as to influence all economic activity.[20]

If this view can be accepted, one of the basic features of macroeconomics becomes very much clearer. Macroeconomics speaks of total consumption, total investment, the total stock of government bonds, the total money supply and so forth. It would make no sense at all to consider these totals if their component parts behaved in very different ways. It would make no sense, moreover, to construct any macroeconomic theory if the separate parts of the economy really seemed to vary in quite different ways because they were influenced by quite different factors. But there is very strong evidence that there is a basic similarity in the month-to-month and year-to-year changes in different parts of the economy. That is, the economy acts as if only a few factors were influencing it at any moment. It acts as if all sectors were influenced in very much the same way by any factor.

It is true, then, that economists have not agreed about which of the basic macroeconomic hypotheses is the more defensible. One can explain the disagreement in terms of the lack of certain social accounting data which would be needed to make a conclusive test of the issue. One can also explain

---

[20] In the 1930s there was great interest in dynamic theories that had solutions of the form $X = K \cos nt + \text{const}$. The variable X then has periodic ups and downs because cosine functions do also. Many dynamic theories were constructed for the purpose of explaining "business cycles" mathematically. The author does not intend to support this literature, an excellent example of which is H. T. Davis, *The Analysis of Economic Time Series* (Bloomington, Indiana: Principia, 1941). It was in large part an attempt to borrow from physics certain problems (vibrating strings, pendulums, and so on) which did not naturally fit into economics. But Mitchell's work is not based on such theories. It is, indeed, criticized mainly on the grounds that it is purely descriptive and lacks a theory. (The author considers this charge to be unfair, but can easily see why it arises.) As evidence of the phenomena to be explained, Mitchell's work is uncontroverted.

the disagreement in terms of the failure, to date, to formulate statistical methods that can be applied to sets of variables known to be subjected to a common influence (which, for lack of a better term, we call the business cycle). But these difficulties can probably eventually be overcome.

Macroeconomics continues to have a strong appeal for economists. It is ultimately based on very considerable evidence that there is order and pattern in economic events. Whatever theory turns out to be acceptable, macroeconomists predict that it can be a simple one. If it were not simple, then it would be difficult to assemble an overwhelming body of data showing the existence of "business cycles," as Mitchell and his associates have done. Macroeconomists, then, continue to be encouraged by the inherent plausibility of simple explanations of changes in the "big" variables in the social accounts. They can point to very great progress in their understanding of these accounts, even though they cannot lay claim to being able to demonstrate beyond doubt a simple theory governing them.

Appendix to Chapter 11

STATISTICAL INDEPENDENCE

Least-squares estimators involve matrices such as $\hat{\mathbf{V}}_{\mathbf{T}}\hat{\mathbf{V}}$ and $\mathbf{V}_{\mathbf{T}}\mathbf{F}$. The elements of these matrices were terms of the form $\sum_{i=1}^{t} X^{(i)}Y^{(i)}$, which are constructed from sets (actually vectors) of observations:

$$\mathbf{X} = (\mathbf{X}^{(1)}\mathbf{X}^{(2)} \cdots \mathbf{X}^{(t)})$$
$$\mathbf{Y} = (\mathbf{Y}^{(1)}\mathbf{Y}^{(2)} \cdots \mathbf{Y}^{(t)})$$

These observations were originally written as columns in the last section; written as rows, they would be completely analogous to the vectors we have used elsewhere in this book.[21]

Expressions of the form $\Sigma\mathbf{X}^{(i)}\mathbf{Y}^{(i)}$ play a very important role in statistical theory. They have also an important place in vector theory. The following discussion explains them from the latter point of view.

The expression $\Sigma\mathbf{X}^{(i)}\mathbf{Y}^{(i)}$ takes any two vectors $\mathbf{X}$ and $\mathbf{Y}$ and assigns a number to them. This number is called the *inner product* of $\mathbf{X}$ and $\mathbf{Y}$. If $\mathbf{X}$ and $\mathbf{Y}$ are the same vector, then the expression becomes $\Sigma\mathbf{X}^{(i)2}$. It is convenient to use the notation $(\mathbf{X}, \mathbf{Y})$ for an inner product, and to refer to

[21] Readers will recall from Chapter 2 that many books on matrices write all vectors as columns. Providing care is taken to be consistent, it does not matter which practice is followed.

$\sqrt{(\mathbf{X}, \mathbf{X})}$ as the *norm* of **X**. The norm of every vector is greater than or equal to zero.[22]

Since the norm of **X** is a number, for any vector **X**, there is another vector $\mathbf{X}' = \frac{1}{\sqrt{(\mathbf{X}, \mathbf{X})}} \mathbf{X}$, such that $\sqrt{(\mathbf{X}', \mathbf{X}')} = 1$. If $\mathbf{X}^{(i)}$ is the ith component of **X**, then $\mathbf{X}^{(i)}/\sqrt{(\mathbf{X}, \mathbf{X})}$ is the ith component of $\mathbf{X}'$. This may be verified as follows:

$$(\mathbf{X}', \mathbf{X}') = \sum_{i=1}^{t} \left(\frac{\mathbf{X}^{(i)}}{\sqrt{\sum \mathbf{X}^{(i)2}}} \right)^2 = \frac{\sum \mathbf{X}^{(i)2}}{\sum \mathbf{X}^{(i)2}} = 1$$

so that $\sqrt{(\mathbf{X}', \mathbf{X}')} = 1$.

Suppose, now, that **V** and **W** are two vectors of norm 1. Then the vector $(\mathbf{V} - \mathbf{W})$ is defined, and has a norm also. This norm is given by

$$\begin{aligned}\sqrt{(\mathbf{V} - \mathbf{W}), (\mathbf{V} - \mathbf{W}))} &= [\sum (\mathbf{V}^{(i)} - \mathbf{W}^{(i)})^2]^{1/2} \\ &= [\sum \mathbf{V}^{(i)2} - 2\sum \mathbf{V}^{(i)}\mathbf{W}^{(i)} + \sum \mathbf{W}^{(i)2}]^{1/2} \geq 0\end{aligned}$$

and therefore

$$\sum \mathbf{V}^{(i)2} + \sum \mathbf{W}^{(i)2} - 2\sum \mathbf{V}^{(i)}\mathbf{W}^{(i)} \geq 0$$

But since **V** and **W** are of norm 1, the first two terms on the left equal 1, and therefore

$$1 \geq \sum \mathbf{V}^{(i)}\mathbf{W}^{(i)} = (\mathbf{V},\mathbf{W})$$

More generally, suppose that

$$\mathbf{V} = \frac{\mathbf{X}}{\sqrt{(\mathbf{X}, \mathbf{X})}}, \quad \mathbf{W} = \frac{\mathbf{Y}}{\sqrt{(\mathbf{Y}, \mathbf{Y})}}$$

Then the preceding result may be written as

$$1 \geq \frac{(\mathbf{X}, \mathbf{Y})}{\sqrt{(\mathbf{X}, \mathbf{X})}\sqrt{(\mathbf{Y}, \mathbf{Y})}}$$

There is one important proviso. If **X** is a vector, $-\mathbf{X}$ is also a vector. But $\sqrt{(\mathbf{X}, \mathbf{X})} = \sqrt{(-\mathbf{X}, -\mathbf{X})}$, since for every number n, $n^2 = (-n)^2$. But $(-\mathbf{X}, \mathbf{Y}) = -(\mathbf{X}, \mathbf{Y})$. Consequently,

---

[22] The *norm* of a vector is like its "length." Readers are reminded of the Pythagorean theorem of geometry $a^2 + b^2 = c^2$, so that $c = \sqrt{a^2 + b^2}$ expresses the length of the hypotenuse of a right triangle in terms of the length of the other two sides. The *norm* is analogous expression in many-dimensional space. Hence vector spaces with this inner product are referred to as *Euclidean*.

$$\frac{-(\mathbf{X}, \mathbf{Y})}{\sqrt{(\mathbf{X}, \mathbf{X})}\sqrt{(\mathbf{Y}, \mathbf{Y})}} \leq 1$$

implies

$$\frac{(\mathbf{X}, \mathbf{Y})}{\sqrt{(\mathbf{X}, \mathbf{X})}\sqrt{(\mathbf{Y}, \mathbf{Y})}} \geq -1$$

This particular pair of results is known in algebra as *Schwarz's Inequality*.

The particular case $(\mathbf{X}, \mathbf{Y}) = 0$ is called $\mathbf{X}$ is *orthogonal* to $\mathbf{Y}$.[23] It was discussed in Chapter 10 in connection with other vectors. If the two vectors of observations (1) have mean zero and (2) are orthogonal, then statisticians say that $\mathbf{X}$ and $\mathbf{Y}$ are *independent*. In general the average of the observations of any variable do not equal zero; but for any vector $\mathbf{X}$, there is another vector $\mathbf{X}'$ with mean zero. Let $\mathbf{I} = (1, 1, \ldots, 1)$ be a vector consisting of ones. Then $(\mathbf{X}, \mathbf{I}) = \Sigma \mathbf{X}^{(i)}$, $\frac{1}{t}(\mathbf{X}, \mathbf{I}) = \frac{1}{t}\Sigma \mathbf{X}^{(i)}$ is the mean value of the observations of $\mathbf{X}$, and

$$\mathbf{X}' = \mathbf{X} - \frac{1}{t}(\mathbf{X}, \mathbf{I})\mathbf{I}$$

is a vector with mean zero.

Let $\mathbf{X}'$ and $\mathbf{Y}'$ be orthogonal. Then

$$0 = (\mathbf{X}', \mathbf{Y}') = \left[(\mathbf{X} - \frac{1}{t}(\mathbf{X}, \mathbf{I})\mathbf{I}, \mathbf{Y} - \frac{1}{t}(\mathbf{Y}, \mathbf{I})\mathbf{I})\right]$$

$$= (\mathbf{X}, \mathbf{Y}) - \frac{1}{t}(\mathbf{X}, \mathbf{I})(\mathbf{Y}, \mathbf{I}) - \frac{1}{t}(\mathbf{Y}, \mathbf{I})(\mathbf{X}, \mathbf{I}) + \frac{1}{t^2}(\mathbf{Y}, \mathbf{I})(\mathbf{X}, \mathbf{I})(\mathbf{I}, \mathbf{I})$$

But $(\mathbf{I}, \mathbf{I}) = t$. Therefore, if $(\mathbf{X}', \mathbf{Y}') = 0$, then

$$0 = (\mathbf{X}, \mathbf{Y}) - \frac{1}{t}(\mathbf{X}, \mathbf{I})(\mathbf{Y}, \mathbf{I})$$

That is, if $\mathbf{X}'$ and $\mathbf{Y}'$ are orthogonal,

$$\sum X^{(i)}Y^{(i)} = \frac{1}{t}(\sum X^{i})(\sum Y^{(i)})$$

[23] *Orthogonal* means literally "right-angled." In physics, inner products are thought of as cosines of angles, for vectors are thought of as lines. Thus (X, Y) in 3-dimensional space is the cosine of the angle between lines representing X and Y. (See footnote 22 for another geometrical interpretation.)

Consequently, if the vectors of observations **X**, **Y** do not have mean zero, but if they satisfy this last condition, then they are also called independent by statisticians.[24]

The intuitive meaning of this definition of independence can be given as follows. Suppose a long series of observations of two variables:

$$(\mathbf{X}^{(1)}\mathbf{X}^{(2)} \cdots \mathbf{X}^{(t)})$$
$$(\mathbf{Y}^{(1)}\mathbf{Y}^{(2)} \cdots Y^{(t)})$$

Rearrange the order of these observations so that the smallest value of X is first, followed by the others, in increasing order:

Smallest tenth	*Next-to-smallest tenth*	*Largest tenth*
$\mathbf{X}^{(i_1)}\mathbf{X}^{(i_2)} \ldots \mathbf{X}^{(i_r)}$	$\mathbf{X}^{(i_r+1)}\mathbf{X}^{(i_r+2)} \ldots \mathbf{X}^{(i_s)} \ldots$	$\mathbf{X}^{(i_u+1)} \ldots \mathbf{X}^{(i_t)}$
$\mathbf{Y}^{(i_1)}\mathbf{Y}^{(i_2)} \ldots \mathbf{Y}^{(i_r)}$	$\mathbf{Y}^{(i_r+2)}\mathbf{Y}^{(i_r+2)} \ldots \mathbf{Y}^{(i_s)} \ldots$	$\mathbf{Y}^{(i_u+1)} \ldots \mathbf{Y}^{(i_t)}$

Now, for each tenth of the observations, start calculating sums of products:

$$(\sum \mathbf{X}^{(i)}\mathbf{Y}^{(i)})_{10}(\sum \mathbf{X}^{(i)}\mathbf{Y}^{(i)})_9 \cdots (\sum \mathbf{X}^{(i)}\mathbf{Y}^{(i)})_1$$

There certainly exist ten numbers $\mathbf{Z}_{10}, \mathbf{Z}_9, \cdots, \mathbf{Z}_1$ such that

$$(\sum \mathbf{X}^{(i)}\mathbf{Y}^{(i)})_{10} = (\sum \mathbf{X}^{i})_{10}\,\mathbf{Z}_{10},$$
$$(\sum \mathbf{X}^{(i)}\mathbf{Y}^{(i)})_9 = (\sum \mathbf{X}^{10})_9\,\mathbf{Z}_9, \cdots (\sum \mathbf{X}^{(i)}\mathbf{Y}^{(i)})_1 = (\sum \mathbf{X}^{(i)})\mathbf{Z}_1$$

The successive terms $(\sum \mathbf{X}^{(i)})_{10}$, $(\sum \mathbf{X}^{(i)})_9$, and so on, certainly get larger, because the observations are arranged in sequence. If **X** and **Y** are independent, then of course there is no tendency for $\mathbf{Z}_{10}, \mathbf{Z}_9, \cdots \mathbf{Z}_1$ to get either larger or smaller. If the **Z**s tended to get larger, there would be a direct relation between **X** and **Y**; if they tended to get smaller, there would be an inverse relation between **X** and **Y**. If there is no relation (independence, therefore), then $\mathbf{Z}_{10} = \mathbf{Z}_9 = \cdots = \mathbf{Z}_1$. It is only for convenience that the division into ten parts was made. The number of parts being arbitrary (like the number of observations) we can replace all the $\mathbf{Z}_j$ by the single number **Z**; and the statisticians show that $\mathbf{Z} = \frac{1}{t}\sum \mathbf{Y}^{(i)}$, the mean of **Y**.

---

[24] There are other connections between statistical and algebraic formulae. If **X** and **Y** have zero mean $(\mathbf{X}, \mathbf{I}) = (\mathbf{Y}, \mathbf{I}) = 0$, then in statistical terminology, $(\mathbf{X}, \mathbf{X})$ is called the *variance* of **X** (and is written σ_X^2 or σ_{XX}); $\sqrt{(\mathbf{X}, \mathbf{X})}$ is called the *standard deviation* of **X** (and is written σ_X); $(\mathbf{X}, \mathbf{Y})$ is called the *covariance* of **X** and **Y** (and is written σ_{XY}); $(\mathbf{X}, \mathbf{Y}) \div [\sqrt{(\mathbf{X}, \mathbf{X})}][\sqrt{(\mathbf{Y}, \mathbf{Y})}]$ is called the correlation coefficient of **X** and **Y** (and is written r_{XY}). For statistical variables generally $\lim_{t\to\infty} \frac{1}{t}(\mathbf{I}, \mathbf{X})$ is called the *expected value* of **X**, $\lim_{t\to\infty} \frac{1}{t}(\mathbf{X}, \mathbf{X})$ is called the *expected value* of $\mathbf{X}^2$, and so forth.

These properties of independent distributions have *matrix* interpretations. Suppose the variables $\mathbf{V} = (\mathbf{V}_1 \cdots \mathbf{V}_n)$ are independent of each other. Then the matrix $\hat{\mathbf{V}}_\mathbf{T}\hat{\mathbf{V}}$ formed from observations of these variables will be an $n \times n$ matrix. It will have the form

$$\hat{\mathbf{V}}_\mathbf{T}\hat{\mathbf{V}} = \begin{pmatrix} \sum \mathbf{V}_1^{(i)}\mathbf{V}_1^{(i)} & \cdots & \sum \mathbf{V}_1^{(i)}\mathbf{V}_n^{(i)} \\ \sum \mathbf{V}_2^{(i)}\mathbf{V}_1^{(i)} & \cdots & \sum \mathbf{V}_2^{(i)}\mathbf{V}_n^{(i)} \\ & \cdots & \\ \sum \mathbf{V}_n^{(i)}\mathbf{V}_1^{(i)} & \cdots & \sum \mathbf{V}_n^{(i)}\sum \mathbf{V}_n^{(i)} \end{pmatrix}$$

$$= \frac{1}{t}\begin{pmatrix} (\sum \mathbf{V}_1)(\sum \mathbf{V}_1) & \cdots & (\sum \mathbf{V}_1)(\sum \mathbf{V}_n) \\ (\sum \mathbf{V}_2)(\sum \mathbf{V}_1) & \cdots & (\sum \mathbf{V}_2)(\sum \mathbf{V}_n) \\ & \cdots & \\ (\sum \mathbf{V}_n)(\sum \mathbf{V}_1) & \cdots & (\sum \mathbf{V}_n)(\sum \mathbf{V}_n) \end{pmatrix} + \begin{pmatrix} \operatorname{cov}(\mathbf{V}_1\,\mathbf{V}_1) & \cdots & \operatorname{cov}(\mathbf{V}_1\,\mathbf{V}_n) \\ \operatorname{cov}(\mathbf{V}_2\,\mathbf{V}_1) & \cdots & \operatorname{cov}(\mathbf{V}_2\,\mathbf{V}_n) \\ & \cdots & \\ \operatorname{cov}(\mathbf{V}_n\,\mathbf{V}_1) & \cdots & \operatorname{cov}(\mathbf{V}_n\,\mathbf{V}_n) \end{pmatrix}$$

$$= \frac{1}{t}\begin{pmatrix} \sum \mathbf{V}_1^{(i)} \\ \sum \mathbf{V}_2^{(i)} \\ \vdots \\ \sum \mathbf{V}_n^{(i)} \end{pmatrix} \sum \mathbf{V}_1^{(i)}, \sum \mathbf{V}_2^{(i)}, \cdots \sum \mathbf{V}_n^{(i)}$$

$$+ \begin{pmatrix} \operatorname{cov}(\mathbf{V}_1, \mathbf{V}_1) & 0 & \cdots & 0 \\ 0 & \operatorname{cov}(\mathbf{V}_2, \mathbf{V}_2) & \cdots & 0 \\ & & \cdots & \\ 0 & 0 & \cdots & \operatorname{cov}(\mathbf{V}_n, \mathbf{V}_n) \end{pmatrix}$$

Notice (1) that if the variables $V_1 \cdots V_n$ have mean zero, the first term drops out. (2) The second term has zeros everywhere but on the diagonal. (3) If $\operatorname{cov}(\mathbf{V}_1\mathbf{V}_1) = \cdots = \operatorname{cov}(\mathbf{V}_n\,\mathbf{V}_n) = 1$, the second term is a unit matrix.

And if $\mathbf{V} = (\mathbf{V}_1 \cdots \mathbf{V}_n)$ and $\mathbf{W} = (\mathbf{W}_1 \cdots \mathbf{W}_m)$ are sets of variables such that every V_i is independent of every W_j, then

$$\hat{\mathbf{V}}_\mathbf{T}\hat{\mathbf{F}} = \frac{1}{t}\begin{pmatrix} \sum \mathbf{V}_1^{(i)} \\ \cdots \\ \sum \mathbf{V}_n^{(i)} \end{pmatrix}(\sum \mathbf{W}_1^{(i)} \quad \cdots \quad \sum \mathbf{W}_m^{(i)}) + \begin{pmatrix} 0 & \cdots & 0 \\ & \cdots & \\ 0 & \cdots & 0 \end{pmatrix}$$

It is always possible to replace a given matrix of observations in a theory by another matrix in which the average value of each variable is zero. For if

$$\mathbf{V} = \mathbf{FM}$$

for every observation, then over the set of observations,

$$\hat{\mathbf{V}} = \hat{\mathbf{F}}\mathbf{M}$$

and the average value of the observations is obtained as follows: Let $\mathbf{I} = (1, 1, 1, \ldots, 1)$ be a vector of t components. Then

$$\frac{1}{t}\,\mathbf{I}\hat{\mathbf{V}} \text{ is a vector } [\mathbf{M}(\mathbf{V}_1), \mathbf{M}(\mathbf{V}_2), \ldots, \mathbf{M}(\mathbf{V}_n)]$$

where $\mathbf{M}(\mathbf{V}_j) = \frac{1}{t}\Sigma \mathbf{V}_j^{(i)}$ is the average observed value of the jth variable.

Thus, if

$$\hat{\mathbf{V}} = \hat{\mathbf{F}}\mathbf{M}$$

$$\frac{1}{t}\,\mathbf{I}\hat{\mathbf{V}} = \frac{1}{t}\,\mathbf{I}\hat{\mathbf{F}}\mathbf{M}$$

Then $\frac{1}{t}\,\mathbf{I_T}\mathbf{I}\hat{\mathbf{V}}$ is the matrix

$$\begin{pmatrix} \mathbf{M}(V_1) & \mathbf{M}(V_2) & \cdots & \mathbf{M}(V_n) \\ \mathbf{M}(V_1) & \mathbf{M}(V_2) & \cdots & \mathbf{M}(V_n) \\ & & \cdots & \\ \mathbf{M}(V_1) & \mathbf{M}(V_2) & \cdots & \mathbf{M}(V_n) \end{pmatrix}$$

and $\hat{\mathbf{V}} - \frac{1}{t}\,\mathbf{I_T}\mathbf{I}\hat{\mathbf{V}}$ is the matrix

$$\begin{pmatrix} [V_1^{(1)} - \mathbf{M}(V_1)] & \cdots & [V_n^{(1)} - \mathbf{M}(V_n)] \\ & \cdots & \\ [V_1^{(t)} - \mathbf{M}(V_1)] & \cdots & [V_n^{(t)} - \mathbf{M}(V_n)] \end{pmatrix}$$

But $\left(\hat{\mathbf{V}} - \frac{1}{t}\,\mathbf{I_T}\mathbf{I}\hat{\mathbf{V}}\right) = \left(\mathbf{E} - \frac{1}{t}\,\mathbf{I_T}\mathbf{I}\right)\hat{\mathbf{V}}$, and therefore

$$\hat{\mathbf{V}} = \hat{\mathbf{F}}\mathbf{M}$$

implies

$$\left(\mathbf{E} - \frac{1}{t}\,\mathbf{I_T}\mathbf{I}\right)\hat{\mathbf{V}} = \left(\mathbf{E} - \frac{1}{t}\,\mathbf{I_T}\mathbf{I}\right)\hat{\mathbf{F}}\mathbf{M}$$

In this last expression, each observation of each variable is expressed in deviations from the mean value.

The operations performed so far have the effect of transforming a theory of the form $\mathbf{V} = \mathbf{F}\mathbf{M}$ into an equation involving matrices such as, say $\hat{\mathbf{F}}_\mathbf{T}\hat{\mathbf{V}} = \hat{\mathbf{F}}_\mathbf{T}\hat{\mathbf{F}}\mathbf{M}$. The main problem of statistical theory, then, is to predict the consequences of using matrices such as $\hat{\mathbf{F}}_\mathbf{T}\mathbf{V}$, $\hat{\mathbf{F}}_\mathbf{T}\hat{\mathbf{F}}$ to obtain estimates of $\mathbf{M}$. This problem is solved by ascribing to the factors $\mathbf{F}$ the behavior of mathematical entities called *random variables*; then some or all of the matrices will be made up of random variables. Such matrices are frequently easy to analyze.

A random variable f assumes particular numerical values according to some mathematical rule. This rule usually specifies that if we observe f at time t, its value (f_t) tells us nothing about the value that f will assume at another time, t'. However, there is defined a *probability*, that is, a fraction of all observations that f_t will have any particular value such as f_0, in any infinitely long period of time. This rule can also tell us the *probability* (the relative frequency) with which finite collections of observations ("samples") of f will have certain attributes. For instance, if the mean value of f in an infinite set of observations would be M_f, it may be possible to state the proportion of samples of size σ whose mean will be greater than some particular number M'.

If the elements of a matrix such as $\hat{\mathbf{V}}_{\mathbf{T}}\hat{\mathbf{V}}$ or $\hat{\mathbf{V}}_{\mathbf{T}}\hat{\mathbf{F}}$ are thought of as being derived from observations of random variables of known properties, then the matrices themselves will tend to certain known matrices as the number of observations becomes infinite. Moreover, if the random variables obey certain simple laws it is possible to define probabilities that the matrices will differ from these limiting values by more than given amounts. In these cases, one can answer the following kind of question: Suppose the estimator $\mathbf{X}(\hat{\mathbf{V}}, \hat{\mathbf{F}})$ is used to estimate a matrix $\mathbf{M}$, and suppose that in a set of t observations $\mathbf{X}(\hat{\mathbf{V}}, \hat{\mathbf{F}}) = \mathbf{M}_1$. What is the probability that one would obtain $\mathbf{M}_1$ by chance, assuming that in fact a matrix $\mathbf{M}_2$ is the correct one? If the statistician obtains $\mathbf{M}_1$ he will consider that $\mathbf{M}_2$ could not have been the correct matrix, providing that it would be very unusual for him to obtain $\mathbf{M}_1$ when $\mathbf{M}_2$ was in fact the correct matrix. His hypothesis is that uncommon events are seldom observed. Rather than state that the observations that generated $\mathbf{M}_1$ were the result of an unusual set of circumstances involving $\mathbf{M}_2$, he will say that they are an ordinary occurrence involving $\mathbf{M}_1$.[25]

The foregoing discussion will not do justice to the purely statistical problems that arise in the course of estimating the elements of the matrix of a macroeconomic theory. But it does lead the reader to see the point at which statistical hypotheses must assume an important role in testing macroeconomic theories, and the way that statistical hypotheses must supplement the economic arguments underlying a particular theory. For the problem in macroeconomics is not merely to find equations that fit the observations closely. In addition, it is necessary to establish a set of rules that say that the fit is too good to have come about by chance. The data on bank suspensions in Table 11.1 certainly matched the formula $2.5 - 1.5(-1)^t$ very closely, but one would conclude that this formula worked only by chance.

[25] This is technically termed the *maximum likelihood hypothesis.*

Bibliography

This bibliography does not do justice to the enormous literature on macroeconomics. It is intended to present a short list of books and papers which set forth in more extensive form the main ideas which play a part in this book. The list is classified according to the subjects which have mainly concerned macroeconomists. But many items in this list (particularly the more important ones) cut across many classifications. And the organization of the list does not fit very closely to the chapter structure of this book, which is a synthesis of a problem and not a review of a body of literature. Following the bibliography proper there is, therefore, a "Guide," in which readers are referred to those items in the list which are particularly relevant to the individual chapters of this book.

SUBJECT HEADINGS OF THE BIBLIOGRAPHY

I. Social accounting

II. Macroeconomic analysis

- A. The market for goods and services
  - a. Consumption demand
  - b. Investment demand
  - c. Government spending
- B. The market for financial assets
  - a. Demand for money
  - b. Demand for earning assets
  - c. Supply of money

C. The interest rate

D. The market for labor

E. Dynamic theories
  a. Growth theories
  b. Business cycle theories
  c. Other dynamic theories

III. Empirical studies

A. Econometric studies

B. Business cycles

IV. Mathematical background

A. Linear algebra, finite math, and calculus

B. Programming

C. Statistics and econometrics

SUGGESTED READINGS AND BIBLIOGRAPHY

I. Social accounting

1. Board of Governors of the Federal Reserve System, *Flow of Funds in the U.S., 1939–1953*, Washington, D.C., 1955.
2. Copeland, Morris A., *A Study of Money Flows in the United States*, New York, National Bureau of Economic Research, 1952.
3. Goldsmith, Raymond, *A Study of Saving in the United States*, Princeton, N.J., Princeton University Press, 1955, see especially vol. II, parts I–III.
4. Goldsmith, Raymond, and Robert E. Lipsey, *Studies in the National Balance Sheet of the United States*, Princeton, N.J., Princeton University Press, 1963, see especially vol. I, chapters 1–6.
5. National Bureau of Economic Research, *A Critique of the U.S. Income and Product Accounts*, Studies in Income and Wealth, vol. 22, Princeton, N.J., 1958.
6. National Bureau of Economic Research, *Measuring the Nation's Wealth*, Studies in Income and Wealth, vol. 29, New York, Columbia University Press, 1964, especially Appendix I: Part F.
7. Office of Business Economics, *U.S. Income and Output*, Washington, D.C., Government Printing Office, 1959.
8. Rosen, Sam, *National Income: Its Measurement, Determination, and Relation to Public Policy*, New York, Holt, Rinehart, and Winston, Inc., 1963.

9. Ruggles, Richard, and Nancy D. Ruggles, *National Income Accounts and Income Analysis*, 2nd ed., New York, McGraw-Hill, Inc., 1956.
10. United Nations, *A System in National Accounts and Supporting Tables*, New York, Department of Economic and Social Affairs, 1964.

II. Macroeconomic analysis

A. The market for goods and services

a. Consumption demand

11. Ackley, Gardner, *Macroeconomic Theory*, New York, The Macmillan Co., 1961, (chapters 10–12).
12. Ando, Albert, and Franco Modigliani, "The Life Cycle Hypothesis of Saving," *American Economic Review*, vol. 53, 1963, pp. 55–84.
13. Duesenberry, James S., "Income-Consumption Relations and Their Implications," in *Income, Employment, and Public Policy, Essays in Honor of Alvin H. Hansen*, New York, W. W. Norton & Co., Inc., 1948.
14. Farrell, M. J., "The New Theories of the Consumption Function," *Economic Journal*, vol. 69, 1959, pp. 678–696.
15. Ferber, Robert, "Researches in Household Behavior," *American Economic Review*, vol. 52, 1962, pp. 19–63.
16. Friedman, Milton, *A Theory of the Consumption Function*, National Bureau of Economic Research, Princeton, N.J., Princeton University Press, 1957.

b. Investment demand

17. Ackley, Gardner, *Macroeconomic Theory*, New York, The Macmillan Co., 1961, chapter 17.
18. Duesenberry, James, *Business Cycles and Economic Growth*, New York, McGraw-Hill, Inc., 1958.
19. Jorgenson, Dale W., and Calvin D. Siebert, "A Comparison of Alternative Theories of Corporate Investment Behavior," *American Economic Review*, vol. 58, 1968, pp. 681–712.
20. Keynes, John M., *The General Theory of Employment, Interest, and Money*, New York, Harbinger, 1964.
21. Knox, A. D., "The Acceleration Principle and the Theory of Investment: A Survey," *Economica*, New Series, vol. 19, 1952, pp. 269–297.
22. Meyer, John R., and Edwin Kuh, *The Investment Decision—An Empirical Study*, Cambridge, Harvard University Press, 1959.
23. White, William H., "Interest Inelasticity of Investment Demand—The Case from Business Attitude Surveys Re-examined," *American Economic Review*, vol. 46, 1956, pp. 565–587.

24. Witte, James G., Jr., "The Microfoundations of the Social Investment Function," *Journal of Political Economy*, vol. 71, 1963, pp. 441–456.

c. Government spending

25. Bator, Francis M., *The Question of Government Spending*, New York, Macmillan & Co., Inc., 1960.
26. Council of Economic Advisors, "Fiscal Policy in Perspective," reprinted in Warren L. Smith and Ronald L. Teigen, *Readings in Money, National Income, and Stabilization Policy*, Homewood, Ill., Richard D. Irwin, Inc., 1965, pp. 316–329.
27. Council of Economic Advisors, "The Full Employment Surplus Concept," reprinted in Warren L. Smith and Ronald L. Teigen, *Readings in Money, National Income, and Stabilization Policy*, Homewood, Ill., Richard D. Irwin, Inc., 1965, pp. 281–284.
28. Heller, Walter W., *New Dimensions of Political Economy*, Cambridge, Harvard University Press, 1966.
29. Joint Economic Committee, *Economic Report of the President, Hearings before the Joint Economic Council*, Washington, D.C., Government Printing Office, annual.
30. Lewis, Wilfred, *Federal Fiscal Policy in the Postwar Recessions*, Washington, D.C., Brookings Institution, 1962.
31. Musgrave, Richard A., *The Theory of Public Finance*, New York, McGraw-Hill, Inc., 1959.
32. U.S. Senate, Committee on Finance, *Hearings on the Revenue Act of 1963*, 88th Congress, 1st Session.
33. U.S. Senate, Committee on Finance, *Hearings on the Tax Adjustment Act of 1968*, 90th Congress, 2nd Session.

B. The market for financial assets

a. Demand for money

34. American Economic Association, *Readings in Monetary Theory*, Homewood, Ill., Richard D. Irwin, Inc., 1951.
35. Baumol, William J., "The Transactions Demand for Cash: An Inventory Theoretic Approach," *Quarterly Journal of Economics*, vol. 66, 1952, pp. 545–556.
36. Fisher, Irving, *The Purchasing Power of Money*, New York, The Macmillan Co., 1922.
37. Friedman, Milton, "The Demand for Money: Some Theoretical and Empirical Results," *Journal of Political Economy*, vol. 67, 1959, pp. 327–351.
38. Friedman, Milton, "The Quantity Theory of Money: A Restatement," in *Studies in The Quantity Theory of Money*, Chicago, University of Chicago Press, 1956, pp. 3–21.
39. Hansen, Alvin H., *Monetary Theory and Fiscal Policy*, New York, McGraw-Hill, Inc., 1949.

40. Keynes, John M., *A Treatise on Money*, 2 vols., New York, Harcourt, Brace, & World, Inc., 1930.
41. Patinkin, Don, *Money, Interest, and Prices*, 2nd ed., New York, Harper & Row, 1965.
42. Tobin, James, "The Interest-Elasticity of Transactions Demand for Cash," *Review of Economics and Statistics*, vol. 38, 1956, pp. 241–247.
43. Wicksell, Knut, *Lectures on Political Economy*, vol. II: "Money," New York, The Macmillan Co., 1935, Part IV.

b. Demand for earning assets

44. Chase, Samuel B., *Asset Prices in Economic Analysis*, Berkeley, University of California Press, 1963.
45. Horwich, George, *Money, Capital, and Prices*, Homewood, Ill., Richard D. Irwin, Inc., 1964.
46. Musgrave, Richard A., "Money, Liquidity, and the Valuation of Assets," in *Money, Trade, and Economic Growth, in Honor of John Henry Williams*, New York, The Macmillan Co., 1957.
47. Tobin, James, "Liquidity Preference as Behavior Towards Risk," *Review of Economic Studies*, vol. 25, 1958, pp. 65–86.

c. Supply of money

48. Board of Governors of the Federal Reserve System, *The Federal Reserve System—Purposes and Functions*, Washington, D.C., 1963.
49. Brunner, Karl, "A Schema for the Supply of Money," *International Economic Review*, vol. 2, 1961, pp. 79–109.
50. Brunner, Karl, and Allan H. Meltzer, "Some Further Investigations of Demand and Supply Functions for Money," *Journal of Finance*, vol. 19, 1964, pp. 240–283.
51. Chandler, Lester V., *The Economics of Money and Banking*, 4th ed., New York, Harper & Row, 1964.
52. Gurley, John G., and Edward S. Shaw, *Money in a Theory of Finance*, Washington, D.C., Brookings Institution, 1960.
53. Teigen, Ronald L., "Demand and Supply Functions for Money in the U.S.: Some Structural Estimates," *Econometrica*, vol. 32, 1964, pp. 476–509.

C. The interest rate

54. Ackley, Gardner, *Macroeconomic Theory*, New York, The Macmillan Co., 1961, chapter 7.
55. Bailey, Martin J., *National Income and the Price Level*, New York, McGraw-Hill, Inc., 1962.
56. Conard, Joseph W., *An Introduction to the Theory of Interest*, Berkeley, University of California Press, 1959.
57. Fisher, Irving, *The Theory of Interest*, New York, Kelley and Millman, Inc., 1954.

58. Hicks, J. R., "Mr. Keynes and the Classics: A Suggested Interpretation," reprinted in *Macroeconomic Readings*, John Lindauer, ed., New York, The Free Press, 1968.
59. Patinkin, Don, *Money, Interest, and Prices*, 2nd ed., New York, Harper & Row, 1965.
60. Wicksell, Knut, *Lectures on Political Economy*, vol. II: "Money," New York, The Macmillan Co., 1935, Part IV.

D. The market for labor

61. Davidson, Paul, and Eugene Smolensky, *Aggregate Supply and Demand Analysis*, New York, Harper & Row, 1964, chapters 11–14.
62. Douglas, Paul H., *The Theory of Wages*, New York, The Macmillan Co., 1957.
63. Keynes, John M., *The General Theory of Employment, Interest, and Money*, London, Macmillan & Co., Ltd., 1936.
64. Leontief, Wassily, "Interest on Capital and Distribution: A Problem in the Theory of Marginal Productivity," *Quarterly Journal of Economics*, vol. 49, 1935, pp. 147–161.
65. Weintraub, Sidney, *An Approach to the Theory of Income Distribution*, Philadelphia, Chilton Co., 1958.

E. Dynamic theories

a. Growth theories

66. Domar, Evsey, "Capital Expansion, Rate of Growth, and Employment," *Econometrica*, vol. 14, 1946, pp. 137–147.
67. Hahn, F. H., and R. C. O. Matthews, "The Theory of Economic Growth: A Survey," *Economic Journal*, vol. 74, 1964, pp. 779–902.
68. Harrod, Roy F., "An Essay in Dynamic Theory," *Economic Journal*, vol. 49, 1939, pp. 14–33.
69. Solow, Robert M., "A Contribution to the Theory of Economic Growth," *Quarterly Journal of Economics*, vol. 70, 1956, pp. 65–94.
70. Tinbergen, Jan, and Hendricus C. Bos, *Mathematical Models of Economic Growth*, New York, McGraw-Hill, Inc., 1962.

b. Business cycle theories

71. Haberler, Gottfried, *Prosperity and Depression; A Theoretical Analysis of Cyclical Movements*, Geneva, League of Nations, 1941.
72. Schumpeter, Joseph, *Business Cycles: A Theoretical, Historical, and Statistical Analysis of the Capitalist Process*, New York, McGraw-Hill, Inc., 1939.

c. Other dynamic theories

73. Baumol, William J., *Economic Dynamics, An Introduction*, New York, The Macmillan Co., 1957.

74. Hicks, John R., *A Contribution to the Theory of the Trade Cycle*, New York, Oxford University Press, 1950.
75. Metzler, Lloyd A., "The Nature and Stability of Inventory Cycles," *Review of Economic Statistics*, vol. 23, 1941, pp. 113–129.
76. Samuelson, Paul A., "Interactions between the Multiplier Analysis and the Principle of Acceleration," *Review of Economics and Statistics*, vol. 21, 1939, pp. 78–88.

III. Empirical studies

A. Econometric studies

77. Bronfenbrenner, Martin, and Thomas Mayer, "Liquidity Functions in the American Economy," *Econometrica*, vol. 28, 1960, pp. 810–834.
78. Duesenberry, James S., *Income, Saving, and the Theory of Consumer Behavior*, Oxford, Basil Blackwell & Mott, Ltd., 1956.
79. Evans, M. K., "A Study of Industry Investment Decisions," *Review of Economics and Statistics*, vol. 49, 1967, pp. 151–164.
80. Friedman, Milton, *A Theory of the Consumption Function*, National Bureau of Economic Research, Princeton, N.J., Princeton University Press, 1957.
81. Klein, L. R., "A Post-Mortem on Transition Predictions of National Product," *Journal of Political Economy*, vol, 54, 1946, pp. 289–308.
82. Phillips, A. W., "The Relation between Unemployment and the Rate of Change of Money Wage Rates in the United Kingdom, 1862–1957," *Economica*, vol. 25, 1958, pp. 283–299.
83. Teigen, Ronald L., "Demand and Supply Functions for Money in the U.S.: Some Structural Estimates," *Econometrica*, vol, 32, 1964, pp. 476–509.

B. Business cycles

84. Ames, Edward, "A Theoretical and Statistical Dilemma—The Contributions of Burns, Mitchell, and Frickey to Business Cycle Theory," *Econometrica*, vol, 16, 1948, pp. 347–369.
85. Burns, Arthur F., and W. C., Mitchell, *Measuring Business Cycles*, New York, National Bureau of Economic Research, 1946.
86. Frickey, Edwin, *Economic Fluctuations in the United States: A Systematic Analysis of Long-Run Trends and Business Cycles, 1866–1914*, Cambridge, Harvard University Press, 1942.
87. Friedman, Milton, and Anna J. Schwartz, "Money and Business Cycles," *Review of Economics and Statistics*, vol. 45, 1963, pp. 32–78.
88. Mitchell, Wesley, C., *Business Cycles and Their Causes*, Berkeley, University of California Press, 1959.
89. Mitchell, Wesley C., *What Happens During Business Cycles, A Progress Report*, New York, National Bureau of Economic Research, 1951.
90. Moore, Geoffrey H., ed., *Business Cycle Indicators*, 2 vol., Princeton, N.J., Princeton University Press, 1961.

IV. Mathematical background

A. Linear algebra, finite math, and calculus

91. Allen, R. G. D., *Mathematical Analysis for Economists*, London, Macmillan & Co., Ltd., 1956.
92. Goldberg, Samuel, *Introduction to Difference Equations*, New York, John Wiley & Sons, Inc., 1961.
93. Hadley, George, *Linear Algebra*, Reading, Mass., Addison-Wesley Publishing Co., Inc., 1964.
94. Kattsoff, Louis G., and Albert J. Simone, *Finite Mathematics, with Applications in the Social and Management Sciences*, New York, McGraw-Hill, Inc., 1965.
95. Samuelson, Paul A., "The Simple Mathematics of Income Determination," in *Income, Employment, and Public Policy, Essays in Honor of Alvin H. Hansen*, New York, W. W. Norton & Co., Inc., 1948.
96. Spivak, Michael, *Calculus on Manifolds, A Modern Approach to Classical Theorems of Advanced Calculus*, New York, W. A. Benjamin, Inc., 1965.

B. Programming

97. Chenery, H. B., and P. G. Clark, *Interindustry Economics*, New York, John Wiley & Sons, Inc., 1959.
98. Dorfman, R., P. A. Samuelson, and R. M. Solow, *Linear Programming and Economic Analysis*, New York, McGraw-Hill, Inc., 1958.
99. Gale, David, *The Theory of Linear Economic Models*, New York, McGraw-Hill, Inc., 1960.
100. Leontief, Wassily W., *The Structure of the American Economy, 1919–1939*, 2nd ed., New York, Oxford University Press, 1951.
101. Yan, C. S., *An Introduction to Input-Output Analysis*, New York, Holt, Rinehart, and Winston, Inc., 1968.

C. Statistics and econometrics

102. Ames, Edward, and Stanley Reiter, "Distributions of Correlation Coefficients in Economic Time Series," *Journal of the American Statistical Association*, vol. 56, 1961, pp. 637–656.
103. Christ, Carl F., *Econometric Models and Methods*, New York, John Wiley & Sons, Inc., 1966.
104. Kloek, T., "Convenient Matrix Notations in Multivariate Statistical Analysis," *International Economic Review*, vol. 2, 1961, p. 351.
105. Theil, Hans, *Economic Forecasts and Policy*, Amsterdam, North Holland, 1958, Chapter 6, Appendix.
106. Yamane, Taro, *Statistics, An Introductory Analysis*, New York, Harper & Row, 1964.

A Guide to the Bibliography and Suggested Reading List

Chapter	1 :	Items, 2, 9, 73, 99, 101.
Chapter	2 :	Section I. Also Items 88, 89.
Chapter	3 :	Items 93, 94, 95, 96, 99.
Chapter	4 :	Sections II A a, II A b, II B a, II B c, II C. Items 6, 9.
Appendix	:	Items 55, 57.
Chapter	5 :	Sections II A b, II A c.
Chapter	6 :	Items 6, 39, 40, 48, 51, 57, 60.
Chapter	7 :	Items 36, 38, 39, 45.
Chapter	8 :	Sections II E a, II E b. Also Item 73.
Chapter	9 :	Items 26, 29, 30, 31, 32, 33.
Chapter	10 :	Section II D. Also Items 38, 41, 45, 82.
Chapter	11 :	Section IV B. Also Items 93, 94.
Chapter	12 :	Sections IV C, III A, III B. Also Item 72.

Index